FROM THE
DANUBE
TO THE
YALU

FROM THE
DANUBE
TO THE
YALU

ENERAL MARK W. CLARK

MILITARY CLASSICS SERIES

FIRST TAB EDITION
FIRST TAB PRINTING

Published by arrangement with Harper & Row, Publishers, Inc. All rights reserved.

Copyright © 1988, 1954 by Mark W. Clark.
Printed in the United States of America

Reproduction or publication of the content in any manner, without express permission of the publisher, is prohibited. No liability is assumed with respect to the use of the information herein.

Library of Congress Cataloging in Publication Data

Clark, Mark W. (Mark Wayne). 1896-1984.
    From the Danube to the Yalu / by Mark Clark.
    p. cm.
    Reprint. Originally published: New York : Harper, c1954.
    Includes index.
    ISBN 0-8306-4001-0
    1. Korean War. 1950-1953. I. Title.
[DS918.C55 1988]
951.9'042—dc19   88-22743
                                         CIP

TAB BOOKS Inc. offers software for sale. For information and a catalog, please contact TAB Software Department, Blue Ridge Summit, PA 17294-0850.

Questions regarding the content of this book should be addressed to:

    Reader Inquiry Branch
    TAB BOOKS Inc.
    Blue Ridge Summit, PA 17294-0214

Military Classics Series

he U.S. military today is enjoying a renewed popularity with the American
ıblic. To help serve this burgeoning interest, TAB is proud to present the
ilitary Classics Series.

This series will bring back into print quality, hardcover editions of many
the most famous books by or about key figures in U.S. military history. When-
/er possible these will be firsthand accounts—the autobiographies of noted
ilitary figures or the memoirs of journalists who were at the front. Some will
: biographies written by knowledgeable friends and associates of the subject.
ll will provide the closest possible insight into the events that have shaped
ır military history.

The series will span the length of American military history—from the
evolution to Vietnam. Although the series will be limited to the wars and
ınflicts in which the United States participated, it occasionally will include an
ıtside perspective through the autobiographies of allies and enemies alike.

These books have long been unavailable in hardcover for both readers and
ıllectors. The *Military Classics Series* will present them in an affordable
:rsonal-library format that every military aficionado will want for their collection.

To Renie my five-star wife—who for thirty years has inspired me to do my utmost in the service of my country. To her love, courage, sacrifices, understanding and guidance I attribute whatever success I may have achieved.

For his valuable help in the writing of this book, I want to express to Howard Handleman my warmest thanks and appreciation.

Contents

1 Negotiating with the Russians 1

2 Two Years of Cold War 12

3 Stateside Post 21

4 The Koje Island Mutiny 33

5 How Our Communist POWs Ran Their Camps 50

6 Stalemate: 1952–53 68

7 The Face of the Enemy 83

8 The Armistice Talks Begin 102

9 The Job in Japan: Changing Our Status from
   Conquerors to Allies 118

10 Our Korean Ally 142

11 President Rhee and the Japanese 154

12 Building the ROK Army 168

13 Our Manpower Shortage 187

14 The War on the Propaganda Front 205

15 A United Nations Effort 220

16 The Eisenhower Visit 230

17 "Little Switch" 240

18 The Rocky Road to the Armistice   257
19 Inside the Communists' Prison Camps   298
20 The Over-all Picture in Asia   314
    Appendix: Documents Concerning the Armistice   331
    Index   365

FROM THE
DANUBE
TO THE
YALU

1

Negotiating with the Russians

In May, 1952, I was appointed Commander of the United Nations Forces, representing seventeen countries, fighting Communist aggression in Korea. Fifteen months later I signed a truce that suspended and—I devoutly hope—ended the fighting on that unhappy peninsula. For me it also marked the end of forty years of military service. It capped my career, but it was a cap without a feather in it. In carrying out the instructions of my government, I gained the unenviable distinction of being the first United States Army commander in history to sign an armistice without victory.

I suffered a sense of frustration that was shared, I imagine, by my two predecessors, Generals Douglas MacArthur and Matthew Ridgway. I was thankful the bloodshed had stopped, but like millions of other Americans I more than suspected that it all came under the heading of unfinished business.

Shortly after the truce was signed in July, 1953, I made a quick trip to the United States to attend my son's wedding and then to confer with the President and the Pentagon before announcing my retirement. I was shocked to discover at home widespread misconceptions regarding the conduct of the Korean War and the way it ended. I believe that now I can and should set the record straight as I saw it.

When the Eisenhower administration came into office in January, 1953, it appeared to me there were three courses of action open to it in Korea. It could "hold the line," continuing the stalemate that had characterized most of the thirty-one-months-old war. It could seek a decisive military victory. It could attempt to negotiate an armistice on terms it deemed honorable.

The first course was odious. No one in his right mind would advocate fighting indefinitely a war we were not permitted to win, but which cost us approximately thirty thousand casualties a year. The second course, a military decision, we could take only by massing additional ground, sea and air forces for offensive use *and* changing the "ground rules" to permit bombing of vital targets in China and Manchuria. Without lifting this restriction, a drive to the Yalu by any means would have incurred overwhelming losses.

That we signed a truce at all was in no way due to sweet reasonableness on the Communists' part or the unanswerable logic of our arguments at the Panmunjom conference table. We got an armistice because the United States Government wanted one and the Communists *needed* one. The Reds had been hurt on the battlefield. Moreover, I think they feared that a new administration, with the backing of an exasperated American people, *would* go all out for a military decision, whatever the cost, if a stalemate continued much longer.

I believe that the Armistice, by and large, was a fair one—considering that we lacked the determination to win the war.

History may prove that President Syngman Rhee of Korea was more right than we were in his desire to fight it out to a finish. But his deliberate attempts to block the Armistice and his threats to take unilateral action whenever it suited him might well have forced our government and the United Nations to continue a war it was not their policy to continue, and must be subject to severe criticism. More of this later.

I emphatically disagree with statements of so-called military experts that victory was ours for the taking at any time during my period of command with the limited forces at our disposal and without widening the scope of the conflict. Korea's mountainous terrain literally soaks up infantry. We never had enough men, whereas the enemy not only had sufficient manpower to block our offensives, but could make and hold small gains of his own.

The Air Force and the Navy carriers may have kept us from losing the war, but they were denied the opportunity of influencing the outcome decisively in our favor. They gained complete mastery of the skies, gave magnificent support to the infantry, destroyed every worthwhile target in North Korea and took a costly toll of enemy personnel and supplies.

But as in Italy, where we learned the same bitter lesson in the same kind of rugged country, our air power could not keep a steady stream of enemy supplies and reinforcements from reaching the battle line. Air could not "isolate" the front. This made it a footslogger's war. To have pushed that war to a conclusion in the mud and mountains of Korea would have required more trained divisions, more supporting air and naval forces, would have incurred staggering casualties and could not have been attempted with any hope of success unless we had lifted the self-imposed tactical restrictions which gave the enemy a sanctuary north of the Yalu.

I believe, however, that we could have obtained better truce terms quicker, shortened the war and saved lives, if we had got tougher faster.

About this, I made specific recommendations which I will discuss more fully elsewhere. These included a rapid build-up of South Korean forces, the use of Chinese Nationalist divisions from Formosa in Korea, and, in the event of a decision by my government really to win the war, the use of the atomic bomb. Some of these recommendations were not original with me. But I must point out that at the times I made them America was far better prepared to call the turn than in 1950. In the intervening two years we had pumped more than $100 billion into our military establishment, sharply reducing Russia's temptation to start World War III, or our danger of losing it.

Korea was my first experience of fighting a shooting war and a conference table war at the same time. But I had had two years of head-knocking with the Russians to teach me what it is that Communists respect: FORCE.

From mid-1945 to mid-1947, as American High Commissioner for Austria, and later in Moscow as deputy to the then Secretary of State, General George C. Marshall, on the negotiations for the Austrian peace treaty, I took a full course in Soviet duplicity. The Austrian peace treaty, incidentally, is as far away at this writing as it was when we met in Moscow six years ago.

The Soviet objective was first to loot Austria, and then by making it a satellite like Hungary, Bulgaria and Rumania, to turn the Blue Danube red from the Black Sea to Bavaria.

In the concluding paragraphs of my book *Calculated Risk*, I wrote: "Having seen the Red Army and Russian diplomacy in action, my own belief is that there is nothing the Soviets would not do to achieve world domination. But I am convinced also that they respect force; perhaps they respect nothing in the world except force."

If I were to rewrite that last sentence today, I would strike out the word "perhaps."

Whether it was the Soviet High Commissioner Konev in Vienna, Gusev in London at the Deputy Foreign Ministers' meeting, Vishinsky and Molotov at the 1947 Council of Foreign Ministers in Moscow or Nam Il at Panmunjom, I found the Communists to be the same breed of bandits. They are ruthless in their exploitation of weakness; they stop, look and listen only when confronted with force.

And certainly during and after World War II we gave them ample opportunities to exploit our political weakness.

One World was the idealistic objective of the second World War, an objective first put into words by Wendell Willkie and then seized upon by people everywhere as the slogan of a greater hope than they ever had known. The peoples of the free nations won a glorious victory over the Axis powers in that war but instead of gaining One World of Peace they were immediately threatened with One World of War more terrible than any before.

New tyrants parading under the banner of communism leaped forward to try to fill the vacuum of power left when the old tyrants of fascism were overthrown.

The free peoples, weary of war and yearning for the security and peace that should have come with their victory, temporized, hoped and appeased. More than all else they feared.

They feared in Austria in 1945, so they appeased. They feared in Korea, so they appeased. I executed the orders of my government in both places, as U.S. High Commissioner of Austria and as Commander in Chief, United Nations Command, in Korea. In each country I executed many of those orders with misgivings.

My doubts were based on my conviction that the Communist

enemy is a voracious beast. The more he is given, the hungrier he becomes. And as long as we of the free nations continue to lead from fear, to react from fright, he will be a well-fed enemy.

I began dealing with the Russians confident that I would be able to get along with them even though others failed. In this I was not alone. From Franklin D. Roosevelt on down, each American official who dealt with the Russians was confident at the outset that he was the one who could get along with them, that he was the one who finally could bring about the understanding that was necessary to realize the dream of One World of Peace.

There was some excuse for that in the beginning. The Russians were our allies. The Russians had fought valiantly against the German Nazis. The Russian people had suffered terribly in that fight. There even was a sentimental feeling that because the Russian people had suffered so much, we Americans should make concessions to them.

It was some time before we, as a people and government, realized that the concessions the Russians demanded were concessions designed to build Soviet power at our expense. The things the Russian leaders demanded were not necessarily good for the Russian people, with whom we had sympathy, and certainly were bad for us.

By the time we fully realized this fact it was getting mighty late. For by then we were fearful and all too prone to grant concessions, to placate, to appease, to ward off some real or imagined threat.

The threats came from everywhere. Soviet Russia had learned that the role of the bully boy was profitable. I was in Austria. There, as in Germany, the American, British and French forces had but a toehold in a capital city surrounded by the Russian Red Army. We had to go through Russian lines to get to our sector of Vienna. We even had to go through Russian lines to get from our sector of Vienna to our airport at Tulln.

The Russians often stopped our train, the Mozart Express, as it went through their zone between our headquarters in Vienna and our zone in Salzburg. Russian soldiers and officers, often drunk, boarded the train, waved guns, talked tough and sometimes robbed our men and women.

I protested repeatedly to the Soviet High Commissioner, Marshal

I. S. Konev, but failed to get any satisfaction. Finally I warned Konev formally and in writing that I had ordered our military police to keep Russian soldiers off our trains. I told him the effective date of the order. Nothing changed. The Russians ignored my warning, continued to harass our trains.

One day late in the winter of 1946 several Red Army officers and enlisted men forced their way aboard the Mozart Express. A captain named Klementiev threatened Technical Sergeant Shirley B. Dixon of our military police with a pistol. Dixon persuaded him to lower the pistol but the argument continued. At last Klementiev started to make a move with his pistol. Dixon shot him dead and wounded a Russian lieutenant who tried to draw his gun.

For six weeks Konev sent me protest after protest, each couched in the most vindictive language. Konev wanted Dixon's head. I wouldn't give it to him. Finally the protests ceased—and so had the interruptions in our train service between Vienna and Salzburg.

I had had my first demonstration of the fact that it pays to be firm with the Russians.

But it was not the last. The air corridor was narrow between Vienna and our sector of Austria. Russian warplanes began crowding us inside the corridor. Sometimes they fired on our planes and once a Russian warplane fired on the airplane in which I was flying.

I protested again to Konev and then, when protests were to no avail, was guided by the lesson I had learned through the incident of the Mozart Express. I ordered that every American airplane flying the corridor be armed, and ordered that American airmen were to fire on any Russian plane that made a menacing move inside the corridor. I so advised Konev, again formally and in writing.

The firm policy worked again. Never more did the Russians challenge us inside that corridor.

Unfortunately, to my way of thinking, the Russians knew that if they carried their threat to Washington they might win concessions. They did that twice on the issue of the Danube and succeeded both times.

Originally the American zone of Austria included both banks of the Danube from the vicinity of Linz to Passau. The Russians soon informed Washington, however, that an error had been made and that they intended to extend their zone along the entire north bank of the river, which otherwise was entirely in their control.

Over my protests from the scene, my government immediately ceded the north bank to the Russians.

The profit to the Russians was enormous. At a stroke they severed our land link between Czechoslovakia and the American-controlled zone of Austria. The Czechs were left ripe for Soviet plucking. At the same time the Austrian people were made fearful and uneasy. The quick American compliance with the Russian demand made the Austrians fear that we had little interest in their part of the world and would agree to anything to avoid unpleasantness with the Russians.

In the fall the Communists made another protest to Washington, this time over the important Danube River barges which the Germans had assembled in Linz during the closing days of the war. Linz was in the American zone and therefore the Austrian, Yugoslav, Hungarian and other barges so vital to river trade were denied to the Communists. When the north bank of the Danube was ceded to the Russians I moved the barges up river to Passau, in the American Zone of Germany. My purpose was to keep the barges as an ace up our sleeves for future bargaining with the Communists. Once Danube River traffic was resumed the barges would be essential.

In September, 1946, I flew to Washington. The barge fleet was high on the list of things I wanted to talk about because the way things were developing in Vienna I knew we would need every bit of bargaining power we could get. I talked to everyone I could about the barges, and every door was open to me.

Most important I talked at length about the barge fleet with President Harry S. Truman. He had a surprising amount of information about the barges and the Austrian problem. After I had presented my case the President said: "Mark, I heartily agree with you. You hang on to those barges."

I felt my mission had been a success. I could go back to Vienna and face the Russians with some trumps in my hand.

Back in Vienna, though, my staff officers were worried. They had heard disquieting rumors that the State Department wanted to return some of the barges to Yugoslavia, which had demanded them. I set my officers at ease. "I've seen the Commander in Chief himself about those barges," I told them, "and he said to hang on to them."

My staff was reassured. But within a week of my return to Vienna instructions came from the State Department to give the boats to Yugoslavia. I was dumbfounded. The President had told me personally to keep those barges. There must have been a mistake. I messaged Washington, told the State Department that President Truman had agreed that we keep them. There was a lull of about a week. It looked as though we had won our point.

But then the State Department sent me a stern order to carry out its instructions, return the barges or else. The Yugoslavs got the barges and we lost some more bargaining power.

At that time bargaining power did not appear to be the main objective of our policy planners. They seemed hell-bent on signing agreements to tidy up the world after the war.

The treaties signed with the Balkan satellites of Hitler Germany were the stark and tragic examples of this trend. The treaties with the Balkan countries were signed early. The formal objective was to insure that each country would be free, sovereign and democratic. In that era of good will and good fellowship, on our part, nobody could imagine that questions of reparations and disposition of foreign property could distort the whole purpose of the treaties.

But they did. The language the Russians insisted upon in the clauses on reparations and disposition of foreign property was so vague and open to such misinterpretation that the Russians, whose armies occupied the Balkans, were able to claim legal justification for manipulations that became irresistible economic weapons. Behind this facade of legality provided by the satellite treaties the Russians controlled the whole economies of Balkan nations. It was but a short step from economic to full political control and the Balkan countries slid behind the Iron Curtain.

On the local level, area commanders could use forceful policies to settle problems like the Mozart Express and the air corridor to Vienna. But at the governmental level such measures were not often employed. As a result the Russians used the postwar era to make tremendous strides toward their goal of world domination.

I use the terms "Washington" and "governmental level" to trace our course of action only because it was the government that was the agent of the people in formulating these policies which I considered to be weakness.

The American people as a whole certainly cannot escape their share of responsibility. In large measure the government was forced to follow Teddy Roosevelt's old political axiom that said, "Lead the people where they want to go."

Remember the political climate in America at the close of World War II. Remember the exhilaration, the riotous demonstrations in the streets of our cities. Remember the marching mothers demanding that their boys be returned to them from overseas. Remember the soldier demonstrations for demobilization.

It is my conviction that most of these demonstrations of a desire for demobilization were motivated honestly, but it also is my definite knowledge that at least some of them were deliberate Communist maneuvers. A strong American military establishment would have deterred Soviet Russia in her plans for postwar power grabs, so the orders went out to do everything possible to hasten demobilization of the greatest military force the world had known to that time.

My knowledge comes from intelligence data on the American soldiers who led the campaigns for demobilization in Germany and Austria. Some of these leaders were acting on orders of the Communist Party, and had been all through their army careers. Intelligence agencies in my headquarters in Austria uncovered this story of intrigue.

Our agents learned that some of the leaders in the ostensibly spontaneous "go home" movements of the soldiers received their Communist Party orders at the beginning of their service in the American Army. The orders were for these men to prepare themselves for postwar leadership among their buddies by striving to become outstanding combat soldiers. This would be evidence of patriotism as well as win them the admiration of their fellow soldiers. Their real work for the Party and for Russia would begin with the Armistice. The Party directed them to try to sap the strength of our military establishment by agitating for overhasty demobilization.

Apparently the Russians were trying to offset the advantage we gained through the early development of the atom bomb. They wanted their army big and ours small so that when their negotiators met ours in conferences around the world the Russian, too, would have a big stick, and a big stick that was more immediately useful than our atom bomb, for Russian soldiers were on the ground in many of the countries Russia wanted as satellites.

Here is a typical case of one of the soldier-agents of the Communist Party. In Vienna we had one who had been with me right through Italy and had an excellent combat record as a noncom. The technique in Austria was to smear the Army through letters to columnists and others at home. He was uncovered as the instigator of these letters. The letters charged, mainly, that many soldiers were being held in Austria on unimportant jobs.

This pressure from Communist and non-Communist sources was heavy on our government. The people apparently wanted relief from the burden of paying for a huge military establishment, and saw little need for one now that the Axis was defeated. They wanted their families reunited. They had had enough of war. Every indication was that they would elect only men who promised them the relief they wanted. In our system, quite properly, the government must be sensitive to such demonstrations of the will of the people. Whether our government in this instance did enough to make the people fully understand their jeopardy is questionable to me. There is even a question in my mind whether our government itself fully recognized the menace to our country at that time.

As a result of the public pressure for demobilization and the lack of governmental steps to counter it through full explanation to the people, our postwar negotiators had to think in terms of arranging agreements that would permit us to reduce overseas military commitments. We had to pull troops out of overseas bases to satisfy the clamor for demobilization, to permit the immediate and sharp reduction in the size and cost of our Army, Navy and Air Force.

To most Americans such a course seemed safe in 1945 and 1946.

After all, hadn't we had a twenty-year respite between World Wars I and II? And further, hadn't World War II exhausted the powers far more than the first war had?

It seemed to most Americans that it would be a long time before any nation would be ready to fight a big war again.

Gradually as I watched the Russians make important gains at our expense in Europe, an uneasy, frightening suspicion entered my mind. I could see that concessions favorable to the Russians had been made. I had the evidence that Communists had been planted in our Army to try to sap the power of the United States through well-conceived campaigns to demobilize too quickly. Two Secretaries of State, Byrnes and Marshall, had told me that their names were signed to some important messages to me without their knowledge. I realize that it is common practice to sign the name of the Secretary of State to all outgoing messages, but the ones I refer to were answers to important radios I had sent them personally. Byrnes said he never saw a message which told me not to take my own staff from Vienna to London for the Council of Foreign Ministers meeting in January of 1947. Marshall told me he never saw the message which gave me similar instructions about the staff to go to Moscow for the Council of Foreign Ministers meeting in March of the same year. Apparently someone in the State Department had taken action on these messages without the knowledge of the chiefs.

These were things I knew from my own experience when the Alger Hiss case broke.

The nagging fear was that perhaps Communists had wormed their way so deeply into our government on both the working and planning levels that they were able to exercise an inordinate degree of power in shaping the course of America in the dangerous postwar era.

I could not help wondering and worrying whether we were faced with open enemies across the conference table and hidden enemies who sat with us in our most secret councils.

Two Years of Cold War

A partial list of our concessions fills out the sorry picture of the mightiest and most benevolent power on earth yielding little by little for a short bit of tranquillity, a false dream of security.

Look what we did during and immediately after the war:

We halted our victorious armies short of Berlin and gave the Russians the honor, glory and profit of conquering the enemy capital. The result: disunity and civil strife for the Germans.

We agreed to wily Joseph Stalin's demand that we invade southern France rather than the Balkans after we had won the battle for Rome. The result: militarily, a German army badly mauled and in flight was let off the hook in Italy; politically, we turned over the Balkan States to the Soviet Army and communism.

We turned over the vital Danube River waterway to the Communists. The result: communism controlled the main communications line of Central and Eastern Europe.

We signed the Balkan satellite treaties agreeing to too much that the Russians wanted. The result: communism took over these countries lock, stock and barrel.

We agreed to permit the Russian Army to surround both Berlin and Vienna. The result: the American, British and French high commands were stuck out on the ends of two causeways, surrounded by hostile waters, dependent upon largesse of the enemy for transportation of all supplies, including food, for rail, air and signal communications and even for the travel of our own officials.

We agreed to permit Russian agents to enter our zone of Austria to seek out "war criminals" and "Red Army deserters" among the 750,000 White Russians, Balts, Poles, Yugoslavs, Ukrainians, Jews and others who fled from Russian-controlled lands in fear of their lives. The result: the Russian Repatriation Mission moved into our rear areas, agitated, propagandized, coerced and spied.

There were other decisions and policies which offset to some extent our weakness in our day-to-day patchwork negotiations with the Communists on these individual problems. The Marshall Plan and Point Four were instances of positive long-range policy which helped build economic bulwarks against communism in many countries.

But I was like an infantryman who sees things through the sights of his rifle. That was my perspective. I write of these things which affected my job.

The decisions of weakness I have listed directly affected my immediate postwar job in Austria. Other decisions, other concessions, were being made in the Far East which were to have a far greater effect on my life and on the lives of hundreds of thousands of Americans, some 142,000 of whom were killed, wounded or captured in Korea.

One of the most damaging of these decisions, and certainly the decision which has cost America more lives than any other single decision in the postwar era, was the one to divide Korea at the 38th Parallel when the Pacific War ended. The Russians took the industrial north, we took the agricultural south. But as in Germany and Austria, division was to have been temporary. That was the plan, another of the plans which the Russians made sure would never work.

At the same time that Marshal Konev in Vienna was laughing and telling me that, if I accepted all of his preposterous demands one day, he would have ten new ones to hit me with the next, General John R. Hodge, U.S. Army, was having similar troubles over in Korea. Korea seemed none of my business then, a tiny Asian country which didn't seem to be important enough to cause anyone any real trouble.

But it was causing Hodge real trouble. Hodge was a career soldier, and a good one, who fought his way from the Solomons through the Philippines and on to Okinawa, commanding the 43d Division on New Georgia and the Americal Division on Bougainville in the Solomons, and the hard-punching XXIV Corps on Leyte and Okinawa. Later he was to succeed me as chief of the Army Field Forces at home.

Hodge literally was cleaning his guns on Okinawa immediately after Japan surrendered when he was ordered to move his corps to Korea and take charge of the occupation there. He went with an open mind. While still en route to Korea he received a radio message from the Japanese general in command at Seoul. The Japanese said Russian soldiers had crossed the 38th Parallel illegally and were looting and raping and that Communist agents were fomenting strikes and riots in Seoul. Hodge called the few newsmen aboard up to his cabin and handed them the message. He explained that the message was from the enemy and in the clear, so it was public property. He also explained that he had no way of knowing whether the report was true. But he showed that he was keeping his mind open about the Russians by cautioning the newsmen that "if I were the Japanese commanding general in Seoul right now I would do everything in my power to create friction among the Allies and would send some such message as this."

It developed, of course, that the report was absolutely true. The Russians reached Korea weeks ahead of us and took every advantage possible of their early arrival. There were reports from Koreans and testimony of American Army officers to substantiate the charge of Russian looting south of the 38th Parallel. James Keller, a young West Pointer who later was a lieutenant colonel in my Plans and Operations Section in Tokyo, reported that he broke up one Russian looting party in Kaesong when he went into the city with the first American troops. Keller, with the 32nd Regiment of the 7th Division, said he found a truckload of Russian officers and enlisted men looting house by house in Kaesong, three miles inside the American zone. Sewing machines and yellow wine seemed to be the most prized booty, Keller reported.

Hodge in Seoul ran into the same kind of negotiating problems that I was having in Vienna. In December of 1945 the foreign ministers met in Moscow and formulated plans for the Joint U.S.–

U.S.S.R. Commission for the Unification of Korea to begin work. The record of the meetings of this commission is revealing. Almost all the meetings, spread over a two-year period, were held in Seoul. The Russians didn't want Americans in Pyongyang, the northern capital, if they could help it. And the discussions never got beyond Point One, which was the question of which Korean political parties would be considered democratic enough to be consulted about unification of the country. The terms of reference for the commission said only democratic parties would be consulted. The Russians refused to admit that any but Communist-line parties were democratic enough to be consulted, thus ruling out every anti-Communist and non-Communist group in Korea.

Hodge took such a beating from the Russians on the one hand and the South Koreans, headed by Dr. Syngman Rhee, on the other that he once confided to me that if he were a civilian, free of military or government orders, he wouldn't stay on his job for a million dollars a year. I later came to understand exactly how he felt.

While the Russians stalled the talks for unification, they worked feverishly to organize North Korea. They brought in Kim Il Sung, a young fighter with a good record in anti-Japanese guerrilla warfare and as a Soviet officer at Stalingrad, and made him the North Korean boss. They brought in hundreds of Koreans who had fled the Japanese occupation in the mid-thirties and been given refuge in Siberia. Most of these held dual Soviet-Korean citizenship. They became leaders. Financially and industrially the Russians organized joint Soviet-Korean stock companies which controlled the economic life of North Korea. Naturally, the Russian members controlled the companies.

The Russians had the same setup in Austria. There people used to describe these companies by telling a story about a special rabbit stew. The cook was asked if there was horse meat in the rabbit stew and he admitted it. He was asked how much horse meat and he said, "Fifty-fifty—one rabbit and one horse." The North Koreans, like the Austrians, were the "rabbits" in the "fifty-fifty" stew with the Soviet horse.

The Russians also developed a tough North Korean army, fully equipped with Russian tanks, warplanes and artillery, and strong enough by 1950 to overwhelm the weak and inadequately equipped South Korean forces and the outgunned and outmanned American units rushed from Japan to fill the breach.

The Russians had prepared the North Koreans for war. The objective was long range—the preparation of a satellite to fight to add more land and more people to the Soviet orbit. Our objective, on the other hand, was short range. It was to sit tight, hope for the best and avoid any action that might upset the status quo. In order to avoid provocation of the Communists we were careful to keep out of South Korean hands any weapons that would encourage them to make good their frequently voiced threat to attack north.

Here again, as in Europe, we settled for the short range approach and refused to recognize the realities of the Communist drive for domination of the world. We tried to make it impossible for the South Koreans to attack the Communists to the north, and hoped that the Communists would not attack our friends in the south.

These concessions to weakness and fear frustrated and bedeviled Americans who had to execute policy overseas after the war. These policies often were formulated by men who too often disregarded the knowledge, experience and recommendations of the man on the scene. Much later I was to hear a long and bitter discourse on this from General Douglas MacArthur in Tokyo.

And even later than that I was to sit by and watch "experts" from Washington explore their way through situations in Korea which I knew those on the spot could have handled with far more success for the United States. Most of these experts were men of good will, much ability and fine accomplishment. But many of them never had been in Korea or even the Far East, and they came with little but a theoretical knowledge of their task. This academic knowledge ill prepared them to deal with such shrewd bargainers as our friends, Syngman Rhee or Shigeru Yoshida, or our enemies, the tightly controlled, experienced Communist negotiators sent to Panmunjom to say "Nyet" to our plans for peace. Everywhere we went to negotiate with Communists we met professionals, men who had devoted a lifetime preparing to do their particular job for communism. Against them we sent men who had proven their brilliance in other fields. Rarely did we send a man who had made a career of fighting for his country across a conference table.

It takes long and intimate association with a situation abroad to give an American the feeling of a foreign problem, the ability to sense quickly the meaning and danger to his country of any situation. I know that when I arrived in Tokyo, and for a long time thereafter, I leaned heavily on the Americans who had arrived long before me. Our experts, armed with broad authority from Washington, were good Americans, able Americans, but too often they were Americans anxious to succeed in a given mission, to sign a paper, to get a job done and go home. In Korea these men anxious for quick results were pitted against the ageless patience of the Orient.

Beyond that was the overriding consideration that whenever we dealt with Communists we were faced with Red determination to dominate the world.

This drive for world domination masquerades under various names—liberty, liberation, freedom, independence, even nationalism. These Communist-used labels constitute a basic lie in the Red fabric of lies, a fabric made up of the claim of tyrants that they fight for freedom, the claim of oppressors that they struggle for liberation.

Most of the time the men who negotiate for the Communists are harsh, implacable men who spout their lies and show none of the niceties or even common courtesies of ordinary discourse. But sometimes they turn on the charm. For a long time Konev in Austria was a jovial companion. In the beginning we had good times together, including a few drinks. We talked often of hunting and I even gave him a hunting rifle the first Christmas. He never thanked me or even acknowledged the gift. But he talked of giving me a hunting dog because he knew I, too, enjoy hunting.

At first, like so many other Americans called on to deal with the Russians, I thought I could get on with such a friendly fellow. But I soon learned that Konev, the social companion, and Konev, the servant of world revolution, were two different beings. Konev at the dinner table was capable even of joking about Russian negotiating techniques, as he did when he said he would have ten new demands if I agreed to all his pending proposals. But Konev at the conference table was an enemy, tightly controlled by his masters. He was a mental robot saying only what had been written for him, as though his tongue moved only when wound by a key in the Kremlin. If instructions were late he feigned illness, or ignored the discussion of the day by repeating exactly what he had been authorized to say at a previous meeting.

I was to learn that no matter the color of the skin, the sound of the language or the place of the meeting, a Communist anywhere was just the same as every other Communist. That was why some visitors to Korea surprised me by being surprised that the North Korean and Chinese Communists acted like Communists.

The face might look different and the tongue might sound different, but the heart was the same and the goal was the same. Konev in Vienna and Nam Il at Panmunjom were like illegitimate brothers, raised by the same mother to serve the same function for communism. The function was to lie, cheat, kill if necessary, to eat away at the strength of the free world and add that much to the strength of the Communist world.

The function was to advance step-by-step toward the day when the free world no longer would have the strength to hold out against communism, the day when through fear, through exhaustion, through quarrels among the Allies or through war itself, the free world would fail and the Communists would inherit the earth.

In Austria, in Germany and in Korea I watched the Communists struggle to advance their campaigns by methods short of a war that would involve Russia, the seat of Communist power. In each country I felt that we of the free world tackled the problems individually, worked to tidy up one nasty situation at a time, without fully meeting the enormity of the master plan designed to destroy us. In each country our enemies used each conflict, big or little, as an incident to promote their campaign, to gain a little ground, to sow seeds of dissension among us, to frighten some more people on the edge of the Iron Curtain.

And everywhere we improvised. We counterpunched. We waited, anxiously, to see what the Russians would do next. They led and we followed. We tried reason and logic with people who scoffed at such old-fashioned devices and who reacted to nothing but the pressure of forceful action.

A case in point was the Moscow meeting of the Council of Foreign Ministers in 1947. I attended, reluctantly, as deputy to our new Secretary of State, General George C. Marshall. He had just taken the cabinet post and was off to Moscow before he had a chance to become grounded on the issues at hand.

I joined the Marshall party in Berlin on March 8. We had our top people in that mission—John Foster Dulles, Benjamin Cohen, Robert Murphy and General Lucius Clay. We were flying to Moscow the next day to begin discussions of the German and Austrian treaties. Time was very short but I figured the men with Marshall would give me a quick policy fill-in so I could formulate my thinking about Austria to fit in with their concepts.

Therefore, I was completely unprepared for the first meeting with Marshall in Berlin. I was amazed to discover that we didn't have a definite program of action. On the eve of the most important conference since Potsdam, everybody still was discussing what we should do in Moscow.

In addition, General Marshall was so new in the office of Secretary of State that he had had little opportunity to study up on various issues; hence we held daily briefings throughout the two months of the Moscow conference in order to keep ahead of the discussions.

He was briefed at the Embassy at ten o'clock in the morning. The first meeting of the foreign ministers was at eleven each day and the afternoon session usually began at 2:00 P.M.

Ben Cohen acted as Marshall's chief of staff. He was the top expert on the proposed treaties by virtue of his familiarity with the unhappy treaties for the Balkan satellite countries. But actually during the negotiations for a German treaty Murphy and Clay had to spend much time briefing Cohen so he would have all the right answers for Marshall.

When the ministers were ready to go to work on the Austrian treaty I had a small booklet prepared with a section to explain each clause of the proposed pact. It briefly stated the American, British,

Russian and French proposition on each clause and recommended how much we could compromise without sacrificing basic principles.

The vital clause was the one that defined German assets in Austria. It was obvious that through this definition and the arrangements for reparations, the Russians were trying to win full control of the Austrian economy.

I typed out my concept of what our minimum position should be and handed copies to Marshall, Dulles, Murphy and Cohen. Marshall asked Cohen what he thought of it and Cohen said, "The Russians won't accept it." Marshall asked Dulles, who said, "They won't accept it."

"Well," Marshall asked, "what do we do?"

"I recommend," Cohen said, "that we adopt the language used in the satellite treaties."

Without being asked, I broke in. I argued that the language of the satellite treaties on reparations and foreign assets, if used in the Austrian peace treaty, would sell Austria down the river to the Communists, just as it had the Balkan countries.

Quietly, Marshall asked me to write the statement that he would make at the afternoon meeting, and to incorporate my recommendations.

He read it. The Russians realized, through the force of his statement, that Marshall would not agree to the vague phraseology that would permit the Soviets to seize Austrian industry and commerce as they had seized the economies of the Balkan states. That was the last meeting of the conference. At this writing, seven years later, there still is no Austrian treaty.

There could have been if we had yielded to the impulse to "tidy things up," even at the expense of selling another whole people into communism.

3

Stateside Post

My personal respite from war, hot and cold, came in May, 1947. The previous autumn General Eisenhower had told me in Washington that I could have an assignment in the States, probably as Commanding General, Sixth Army, with headquarters at the Presidio, San Francisco.

The Cold War delayed things for a while, however. First there was the London meeting of the Council of Foreign Ministers where I served as deputy to Secretary of State Byrnes and then there was the March meeting of the Council, at which I served in the same capacity for the new Secretary of State, Marshall.

But finally, in May of 1947, my wife and I boarded the S.S. *America* for home and the first stateside post for me in five years. A time like that is a time for reminiscence. I looked back over the past five years of hot and cold war, the longest five years of my life. There had been the hot war in North Africa, Salerno, Anzio, Rome, the Gustav Line, names that recalled glory and misery for Americans and their allies. There had been that wonderful day of hope when General von Senger und Etterlin walked into my 15th Army Group Headquarters in Florence to accept surrender terms for all German and Italian forces fighting us in Italy. This warm feeling of hope was still with me when I first went to Vienna to work with our Russian, English and French allies on postwar problems. It seemed to me then that certainly we who had fought together to whip the Nazis could work together to create a decent world in which to live.

Disillusionment came fast in Vienna, however, and by the time my wife and I stepped aboard the S.S. *America* I had been through two years of what was just then beginning to be called the Cold War with the Russians. There was a double disillusionment. The first was that our wartime Russian allies now were our enemies. The second as it appeared to me was our soft approach to the new menace which threatened all we held dear.

My frustration got unexpected release even before we reached the United States. Two days out of New York I received a radiogram from the War Department requesting me to speak on a national radio program after I landed. I did this with pleasure. I spoke as I thought, said just what I believed and called a spade a spade.

The gist of my talk was that there is no fair play in the Russians. I said they were liars, murderers and cheaters and that they would stoop to anything to gain world domination. I said their solemn pledge meant nothing. Honesty, I said, was not part of their national character.

"When you play poker with a cheater," I broadcast, "somebody is going to lose his shirt. And it's not going to be the cheater."

I raised a hornet's nest around my ears. My good friend, Secretary of State Marshall, whom I admired greatly and who had been largely responsible for giving me opportunity for advancement in the Army, was disturbed. He suggested that I tone down my comment on the Soviets. People were fearful of antagonizing or provoking the Russians, and there still was a lingering hope that we could talk the Soviets into being friendly. Tensions had to be relaxed, not aggravated.

Marshall knew my views. I felt strongly that we had to resign ourselves to an eventual showdown with the Russians and that every concession we made to them strengthened them and weakened us for the eventual test.

This conviction was bolstered in the two years I spent in Austria, watching the Russians gird themselves for the final test with the free world. Every Russian action in Vienna, as elsewhere, was calculated to build Soviet power and weaken the free world. The Russians already were fighting the war, without shooting.

When I made trips to Washington from Vienna in 1946 and 1947, I gave my views to President Truman, as well as to Marshall and everyone else I could reach in high places. I recommended a strong, firm policy that would force the Russians to back down while we still had the military lead through the atom bomb and other technical advantages.

All this was in my mind when I made my radio report to America. I was still out of step, however. People in Washington still hoped to be able to straighten things out by talking reason with the Communists. So Marshall told me to calm down, not to rock the boat, not to provoke the Russians.

In speeches after that I pulled my punches.

I felt vindicated when almost two years later General Marshall, still Secretary of State, told me during a visit to the Presidio: "Clark, you can do a lot of good as a result of your experiences with the Communists if you tell the public of the real difficulties we are having with these people."

I now felt I could go ahead and lay it on the line about the Russians whenever I talked in public.

My two happy years at the Presidio ended one day in August, 1949, when General Omar Bradley telephoned to tell me I had been appointed Chief of Army Field Forces. This was still respite from cold war, however, and an assignment close to the heart of any soldier for it dealt solely and completely with military problems, the kind of problems a soldier spends his lifetime learning to meet. It was a challenging job because, quite simply, it was the job of planning and supervising the training of our whole army and recommending to Washington the kind of equipment with which we would fight.

I had some definite ideas about changes that should be made in our whole concept of Army training. I had brought those ideas out of the mud and snow and mountains of Italy, where I learned the hard way that our system of training had to be improved. We wasted manpower. There were too many noncombatants in our army. I wanted every man to be a fighting man, so he would be ready when needed.

My idea was that every recruit should have the full infantry training before he was put in the artillery, the engineers or the armored units for supporting front-line duty or to supply or desk jobs in the rear areas. Every soldier, I firmly believed, should be taught to fight on the ground, with his rifle, before he was assigned to specialized branches. Then when he had to, as many men have, he could fight like an infantryman and protect himself and his fellows like a doughboy.

Along with this training I wanted to make the rifle the symbol, the personal symbol, of each infantryman. Each rifle is individual and has its own characteristics which a man must learn. I wanted to institute a system in which each soldier would have a single rifle throughout his tour of duty, a rifle that would be given to him with ceremony, preferably by his general, when he earned the right to carry it.

When I was Chief of Army Field Forces I was able to give every man eight weeks of infantry training before he was transferred to other branches of service, but I still am convinced that every man should have the full sixteen weeks of infantry training before he is placed in another branch. Basically I want an army of trained foot soldiers. There is a fundamental reason for this, a reason that I believe is basic to the security of our nation. I will expand on that reason later, against the background of manpower disadvantage we faced in Korea when we fought the hordes the Communists had at their command. I also was interested in the spiritual training and welfare of the men and always sought ways of helping the Chaplain Corps work more effectively with the troops.

One day while observing a live ammunition training exercise, in which recruits crawled on their bellies under barbed wire while machine-gun bullets whined overhead, I noticed several chaplains standing nearby, also observing.

I approached one, a rather stout man, and asked whether he had been through the training. He said "No," so I asked him, "Don't you think it would be a good idea if you shared the hardships and the dangers of the men and went through these exercises?"

The chaplain thought it was a fine idea and I told him, "Of course, you'll have to take about six inches off your belly before you can get under that barbed wire."

Shortly thereafter I put out a training directive for the guidance of chaplains in which I said they should share as many of the trainees' hardships and dangers as they could. The plan worked. We found that the chaplains, by crawling through the mud with the soldiers and by making the long marches, won the respect and confidence of the troops. They became "regular fellows" to the men, not distant symbols of conscience.

As a result I was pleased to note that attendance at Sunday services rose markedly and to hear that the men went to the chaplains more often with their troubles.

Later in Korea I was impressed with the devoutness of the majority of our men, particularly those in dangerous spots. I was convinced that at least part of their devoutness was due to the fact that the individual chaplain had shared their hardships and their dangers. The relationship was so good that the men looked forward to the opportunity of attending Sunday services on the Korean hillsides.

Less than a year after I took over the training command, the Korean Communists crashed across the 38th Parallel and President Truman instructed MacArthur to send what troops he could spare from Japan to save the Republic of Korea. The training command job took on fire-alarm urgency that day. The ground forces swelled with men almost overnight and our job was to prepare these newcomers for the peculiar type of fighting they would encounter from an enemy who conformed to none of the accepted rules of land warfare.

No war is ever fought exactly like any other before it, and history is full of stories of commanders who came to grief trying to follow an old pattern of victory once too often. Whatever is new in tactics, equipment or method must be taught at the squad level *before* a soldier gets into combat. Together with a team of experts, I went to Korea in February, 1951, to get a firsthand view of the situation so I would know better what the recruits back home would have to learn in their squad training.

Stopping off in Tokyo, I renewed an old acquaintance with General Douglas MacArthur, then Supreme Commander of the UN Forces. Ours really was an old acquaintanceship dating back to 1910, when my father, Charles C. Clark, then a major of infantry, was attending the Command and General Staff School at Fort Leavenworth, Kansas. MacArthur, then a first lieutenant in the engineers, used to visit our house regularly, but at the time of our meeting in Tokyo I hadn't seen him for forty years.

As we shook hands, MacArthur asked, "How's your mother? Give her my love; I'm a great admirer of hers." I knew that the general's courtly inquiry would please my mother, who was then over eighty and who has had her husband or son in every big shoot from the Spanish-American War to Korea.

I talked a little about training problems, which was the purpose of my mission. But MacArthur was more intent on telling me about the big picture conduct of the Korean War, and his bitterness about what he considered policy errors of great magnitude and danger to the United States. He told me a story that reminded me of my old troubles back in Vienna. Washington, MacArthur said, had ignored many of his views and recommendations at critical times, had implemented a policy which he considered fraught with pitfalls for our country. Specifically he was most critical of the Joint Chiefs of Staff.

We discussed the current situation—the Communists had captured Seoul for the second time only weeks before—and General MacArthur went into considerable detail on how we had been catapulted into the ground warfare in Korea.

MacArthur could not understand why we had permitted the enemy, the Chinese Communists, to have the advantage of a sanctuary as their base of supply and air operations. He expressed the strong conviction that had we carried the war to the Chinese with air attacks across the Yalu River, or even with the threat of such attacks, the war in Korea would have taken a course far more favorable to the United States and the United Nations.

When the Chinese came into the war, masquerading their best armies as "volunteers," we should have hit them hard, MacArthur said. He said he couldn't conceive that our government would fail to retaliate when a nation came to war against us and crossed over the border into the country in which our troops were in battle.

MacArthur was particularly bitter that his government had failed to do everything in its power to protect the American and Allied troops under his command when those men were menaced by the Chinese armies that were hurled into the Korean War.

I fully agreed with MacArthur that we should not have allowed the enemy a sanctuary north of the Yalu. I never changed my opinion.

It was only two months later that President Truman relieved MacArthur of his command. I was at a camp in the Southern states on a field-training inspection tour at the time. Someone told me the news as I came out of my billet early in the morning. My first thought was, "I wonder if I'm going to get the job." The answer was yes—but not until about a year later.

MacArthur's dismissal was not exactly unexpected in view of his feud with the Joint Chiefs of Staff. However, like most other officers in the Army, I was shocked at the abrupt termination of such a distinguished career.

While in Korea I was asked whether there would be a rotation system to get the troops home after a specified length of service. I said there would have to be. That made headlines in America and Washington sent me a mild rebuke in which I was asked to say something to counteract the first statement. I couldn't do that, for it was a legitimate question in the minds of our men and one that had to be discussed.

While in Korea I stayed with General Matt Ridgway, a West Point classmate then commanding the Eighth Army. In addition to being classmates, Matt Ridgway and I had been closely associated throughout our Army careers. Ridgway's 82nd Airborne Division had supported me at Salerno and half way through the Italian campaign. Never was there a finer soldier.

In Korea we toured the front together, returning at night to Ridgway's advance headquarters, a tiny cluster of tents at Yoju, on the south bank of the Han River. As a result of talks with commanders at all levels, I determined to put more emphasis on training for night operations—a favorite tactic of the Chinese and North Koreans who preferred to attack at night or in heavy weather when our air and artillery observers were blind. I also stressed more work with some long-neglected close quarter weapons—the bayonet, grenades and the M-1 rifle.

And again it was impressed upon me that in a war in which we were chronically short of manpower, it was absolutely necessary to train every man in the ground forces—cooks, bakers, clerks and truck drivers—to be a combat infantryman. I had no idea at that time that I would be the UN Commander to reap whatever benefits there were from my own recommendations. In fifteen months Korea would be my baby.

There were benefits from that trip. As soon as I got back to the United States I changed our training program in several ways. I instituted a system whereby one third of each man's training was at night. Our lads grow up more or less afraid of darkness. I wanted them to get enough night training so they would realize that night-time was their best friend because it enabled them to move about without being observed, as the enemy did.

I also emphasized bayonet training and marksmanship and set up a program to glorify the infantryman, to raise his stature in the eyes of his countrymen and make him proud of his branch of the service.

Naturally when I was assigned to the Korean command I watched carefully to see whether the training had paid off and called for direct letters to me from subordinate commanders to get their ideas of the caliber of the men being turned out by the Army Field Forces. I was pleased that the reports indicated an increasing efficiency in the individual soldier trained in the States.

The sentimental highspot of my 1951 trip to Korea was meeting my son Bill. Captain Clark was aide to Major General Bryant Moore, Commanding General, IX Corps. Moore told me Bill had asked for a rifle company and probably was going to get it. A few days later Moore was killed in a helicopter crash. Soon afterwards Bill commanded George Company of the 9th Infantry, Second Division. The next time I saw him was as he arrived on a hospital plane at Andrews Air Force Base, Washington, D.C., en route to Walter Reed Hospital.

This was his third and most serious battle wound, received at

Heartbreak Ridge. During his year at the front he had earned the Distinguished Service Cross, two Silver Stars, three Purple Hearts, the Presidential Citation, the Combat Infantry Badge and battlefield promotion to major. I know you will forgive a proud father for referring to his only son, but I have another motive for mentioning Bill's record here. Shortly after the cease-fire, I received a most abusive letter from a Chicago woman who, among other things, demanded to know what influences I had used to keep my son out of Korea!

To the families of 142,000 Americans killed, missing or wounded in the Korean War, it is small comfort to hear of the misfortunes of others. But for anyone who thinks generals' sons as well as generals die in bed, it should be pointed out that during the Korean War there were in service a total of 142 men whose fathers were generals. Of these, thirty-five were casualties in Korea. Statistics can be tricky, but it would be difficult to discover any other category of young men with such a high casualty ratio. Included among the thirty-five casualties was the pilot son of General James A. Van Fleet, who was Commanding General of Eighth Army in Korea when his boy failed to return from a mission in a B-26 night bomber.

Despite the importance of training the Army Field Forces, it was during the autumn of 1951 that I came close to receiving my first nonmilitary assignment from the Commander in Chief. President Truman called me to the White House to ask if I would be the first official U.S. representative to the Vatican. "I need a Protestant, a 33rd degree Mason and a military man," the President said, grinning, "and someone who knows and is respected in Italy. You fill the bill."

I had misgivings about the whole proposal and inwardly thought of my six feet two in knee breeches. I said, however, that being a soldier I would carry out any assignment the President gave me. The issue raised such a controversy that I requested the President to withdraw my name from nomination.

I continued the satisfying job of training men for our army, a job which gives a soldier full opportunity to put into practice all the things he learned and thought during his career in uniform.

In the United States I followed the Far East developments with more than routine interest. It was well that I did. Although President Truman appointed Ridgway to succeed MacArthur, I was given the Far Eastern Command a year later on Ridgway's departure for Paris to take over Supreme Command of the Allied Forces in Europe from General Dwight D. Eisenhower.

I was visiting Camp Roberts, California, in April, 1952, when I got a 5:00 A.M. telephone call from General Omar N. Bradley telling me of the appointment. It did not come as a complete surprise because I had had some indication that the President was considering me for the Far East.

I had no illusions about the task. I had been in on much of the Korean planning in Washington and knew that this would be the toughest job of my career.

The Bradley call came at 5:00 A.M. because I was in California that day and he was in Washington, where it was three hours later. I was to be troubled by this time differential for a long time because people in Washington always put in these calls during their working hours and when I got to Tokyo their working day coincided with my sleeping night.

I flew to Washington for a rapid round of briefings by the Department of Army and the State Department on almost every subject imaginable. Generals Collins, Hull and Taylor briefed me. I spent a lunch hour with Secretary of Army Frank Pace, who talked at length of his desire to expand the Republic of Korea Army into a bigger fighting force. John Allison, then head of the State Department Far Eastern Desk and later Ambassador to Japan, gave me an over-all briefing on the State Department attitudes on various problems in Korea and Japan. Bedell Smith over at the Central Intelligence Agency filled me in on the general situation of the enemy.

The briefings for three or four days were so intensive that information was spilling out my ears. I was brought up to date on personnel matters, supply problems, the ammunition situation both in Korea and at the source of supply at home, the tactical situation in Korea, the problem of the defense of Japan, the rules that governed my relationship with the government of Japan, the highlights of the armistice negotiations at Panmunjom, our aims at Panmunjom, our military objective in Korea and our general objectives in Japan.

There was one major problem that nobody even mentioned, however, and lack of briefing on that set the stage for one of the greatest shocks of my career.

While all this briefing was under way I was being pressured to get on my way to Tokyo. They wanted me there by May 4 or 5. Therefore when Secretary-General Trygve Lie of United Nations asked me to come to see him in New York I had to tell him that I was obliged to decline because of lack of time. The wires must have burned for a while because within a few hours I was informed that I had better accept his invitation. I replied I would be glad to accept if Washington approved a delay in my takeoff for Tokyo. Washington approved and I traveled up to New York to see Lie.

Lie wanted to talk about the importance of the experiment in which so many nations were banded together to fight for a single cause. That always made me smile a little because I had so many more men of different nationalities under me in Italy than I did in Korea.

In Korea only the Americans, the Koreans, the British Commonwealth and the Turks put more than a battalion of infantry into the ground fighting, and altogether there were infantry detachments from sixteen nations.

But I did realize fully that the war in Korea was a step forward in human political concept, for in Korea for the first time an international organization established to maintain world peace had put an army into the field under its own international flag to fight for an international cause. Many of the nations that sent troops to fight and die in Korea were not immediately threatened by the North Koreans, the Chinese Communists or, in some instances, by communism itself.

But each, in varying degree, understood that the cause for which the United Nations fought in Korea was the cause of every free nation. We had a parallel in our own American history. The American revolutionary battle slogan of "United We Stand, Divided We Fall" was beginning to apply on a worldwide scale.

Finally my aide, Lieutenant Colonel Donald Bennett, and I took off for Tokyo. We landed at Haneda Airport on May 7. Japan had been independent and sovereign again for just nine days. The period of relative quiet and stability in Korea had less than one day to go.

4

The Koje Island Mutiny

The one thing that nobody in Washington briefed me about, or even mentioned, was the prisoner-of-war problem. And that was the one problem on which I needed briefing, quickly.

I hadn't bothered to ask anyone in Washington about the POWs because my experience had been with old-fashioned wars in which prisoners were people who had to be fed, housed, clothed and guarded, nothing more. Never had I experienced a situation in which prisoners remained combatants and carried out orders smuggled to them from the enemy high command. In North Africa and Italy we captured hundreds of thousands of Germans and Italians and they all conformed to the provisions of the Geneva Convention, which establishes the whole modern concept of a prisoner's rights and obligations in captivity. He may try to escape, but while under restraint he *must* obey his captors or suffer the consequences. He cannot be forced to reveal military information. He must be treated humanely, fed, housed and clothed as well as possible.

The Communists, making their own rules as they went along, didn't see it that way.

They did everything they could to make profitable use of prisoners on both sides of the line, in our camps and theirs. And unfortunately they profited. During the war they ordered prisoners to riot in our camps in South Korea so that we would lose prestige in the eyes of the world, lose bargaining power at the armistice talks and be forced to drain off combat troops from the front to guard the POWs. At the same time they gained great propaganda ammunition by forcing or inducing a handful of Americans they captured to "confess" to the absolutely false charges that we waged germ warfare in Korea.

In the longer range they will make propaganda use of the prisoner situation in Korea for years to come. That is the kind of fodder they seek to attack us and, if need be, to counterattack us to cover their own shortcomings. This tactic, common to Communists everywhere, is well illustrated by the old tale of the American engineers who visited Moscow. Their Russian hosts showed them the best the city had to offer in architectural and engineering accomplishments. But the very best was saved for last. That was the Metro, the Moscow subway. The Americans were astounded. They never had seen such a clean subway, so well appointed and so beautified with murals. Finally an American said:

"This is wonderful, beautiful, much better than anything we have at home. But we have been here thirty minutes now and haven't seen a single train, or a customer. Tell me, when do the trains run?"

"Ah, ah, ah," admonished the Russian host, "how about your lynchings in the South?"

I arrived at Tokyo's Haneda Airport on the morning of May 7, filled with anticipation of the new assignment. Before we landed I had received a radio message from my good friend Bob Murphy, the new Ambassador to Japan. The message said, "You're staying with me until you get settled—Bob." That little message did a lot to eliminate any feeling of strangeness I might have had as we moved toward Tokyo.

With two good friends, Bob Murphy and Matt Ridgway, waiting for me I felt I would be off to a good start.

Also my briefing had made me understand that although the job would be difficult, things had been quiet so long I would have time to get my feet on the ground. The last great military offensive in Korea had ended just short of a year before. The armistice talks had been brought to a head only nine days earlier when Vice-Admiral C. Turner Joy at Panmunjom gave the Communists our "final" offer on the exchange of prisoners of war. The prisoner exchange was the only unsettled problem of the Armistice and for the moment, at least, all I would have to do would be to wait for the Communist reaction to our offer.

The Japan situation looked like a more immediate problem. On May Day about eight thousand Japanese Communists had rioted along one block edging the Imperial Palace moat, only a short distance from the Dai Ichi Building which was headquarters for the Far East and United Nations Commands. They had overturned and burned a dozen American automobiles and fought with Japanese police.

In addition to that there were all the problems of changing the relationship between Americans and Japanese now that the peace treaty had made Japan free and sovereign. The peace treaty became effective just nine days before I arrived and thus I was the first American commander to arrive in Japan after the occupation ended.

Matt Ridgway and Bob Murphy met us at the airport. It was good to meet old friends and even better to meet them at a time when each of us was entering an exciting new job. That night I dined with Matt and his attractive wife, Penny, at Maeda House, the Far East Commander's home I was to occupy shortly. After dinner and a pleasant chat I drove back to the American Embassy for a nightcap with Murphy before turning in early. Ridgway and I were flying to Korea in the morning so that Matt could say good-by to his field commanders and at the same time introduce me to them. It was all routine.

I woke up next morning eager to get on the job. I drove to the airport and met Ridgway. After takeoff he said to me:

"Wayne, we've got a little situation over in Korea where it's reported some prisoners have taken in one of the camp commanders, General Dodd, and are holding him as a hostage. We'll have to get into that situation when we arrive at Eighth Army Headquarters and find out what the score is."

We found out. The score was exactly no hits, no runs and more errors than any scorekeeper would have the heart to tally.

It happened at 3:15 P.M. the previous day, just a few hours after I landed at Haneda. Communications from Koje Island were not good and there may have been some tendency to go slow with that kind of bad news. Everybody knew that once word reached Tokyo there would be the devil to pay.

Therefore when Ridgway and I said good night after dinner the night before Matt didn't know that some hours before the biggest flap of the whole war had started on Koje, the POW island thirty miles off the southeast tip of Korea. He didn't know when he said good night that Brigadier General Francis T. Dodd, the POW camp commander, had been manhandled and kidnaped by the very men he was charged with holding captive.

As Ridgway elaborated on the incident I got the feeling I was walking into something that felt remarkably like a swinging door. This was astounding news to me, something for which I had no preparation whatever. Although I had been briefed in Washington on every conceivable subject, this was the first time I had ever heard of Koje or the critical prisoner-of-war problem that existed behind our lines.

A nasty little temptation entered my mind. In Italy there were 25,000 Brazilians in my Fifth Army. The Brazilian Defense Minister, Eurico G. Dutra, visited my headquarters and insisted on getting into some kind of action. I organized a Brazilian force with Americans in support and put him in command. We called it "The Dutra Task Force." He did all right, too. After the war Dutra became President of Brazil and in August of 1950 he signed the legislative act which made me an honorary general of the Brazilian Army. As Matt explained what I was getting into in Korea. I couldn't help but think that it would be nice right then to write a letter to Dutra and arrange to exchange armies.

As Matt explained it, the aggressiveness of the Red POWs had increased in direct proportion to the delicacy of the prisoner exchange arguments at Panmunjom. The UN had taken the position that no prisoner should be forced to return to the Communists against his will. The Chinese and North Koreans charged this was "forcible retention" and demanded that every POW be returned, willing or not.

About 40 per cent of the Chinese and North Korean POWs we held at that time had indicated they preferred to fight to the death rather than to return to homes behind the Iron Curtain. I recalled the 750,000 displaced persons in our zone of Austria and the Soviet mission that came ostensibly to look for war criminals and Red Army deserters but actually to spy, coerce and agitate for the return of these unhappy souls to terror behind the Iron Curtain. Before I had been in the Far East twenty-four hours I ran head on into the same pattern of Communist conspiracy and action that I had known in Europe.

The revelation that about seventy thousand Chinese and North Korean POWs would fight to block any move to send them to Communist homelands was a serious propaganda blow to the Reds. In particular the Communists were hurt by the fact that fifteen thousand of the twenty thousand Chinese we held prisoner had declared they would rather die than return to communism. These were fifteen thousand of the Chinese the Reds claimed were "volunteers," who left their homeland of their own volition because they were filled with zeal to fight the "American aggressors" in Korea.

The Communist countermeasures were typical. Specially trained agents permitted themselves to be captured on the front in order to get the latest Communist instructions to the "loyal" prisoners. These instructions were brutally simple—raise hell, spill blood, make martyrs if necessary, but give the UN Command a black eye and prevent any more screening of prisoners to see who wished to return to China or North Korea and who didn't.

If, in trying to keep order, American or Allied soldiers shot rioting prisoners, this would "prove" to the world we were trying to force them to refuse repatriation, and thus "prove" the propaganda line already being blared by Communist press and radio.

After it was all over we learned through interrogation that there were specific orders from the Communist High Command to the prisoners to capture American officers and hold them in the compounds. But even the most optimistic of the Reds could not have anticipated such a prize as the one a "honey bucket" work detail of POWs captured on that tragic afternoon of May 7. They caught the highest prize on the island, the island commander himself, Brigadier General Francis T. Dodd.

At Eighth Army Headquarters in Seoul, General Ridgway got a firsthand picture of the Dodd snafu from General Van Fleet. Van was an aggressive combat soldier who had whipped the guerrillas in Greece and smashed an all-out Chinese offensive the previous spring, but his duties covered too much territory. He ran the war on a 155-mile front, the complicated liaison with the South Korean Government, and was finally responsible for the security of prisoners of war, supplies, communications and everything that happened from the battle line all the way back to Pusan, which meant the whole of South Korea. I later remedied the situation by setting up a Communications Zone in Van's rear which relieved him of all responsibilities except those pertaining to the battle.

From Van we learned for the first time the amazing *initial* demands the prisoners were making on Dodd as a condition for his release. They insisted they be allowed to form a vast prisoner-of-war association, complete with bylaws and an intercompound telephone, and be provided with additional tents, desks, chairs, reams and reams of paper, ink, fountain pens, mimeograph machines and even two three-quarter-ton trucks!

The physical circumstances of Dodd's capture were detailed later by Dodd himself in these words:

On the morning of May 7, I received a message that the spokesman of Compound 76 requested an interview with me. At 2 o'clock I proceeded to the compound gate where the interview was held. The outer gate was opened and the compound spokesman and leader were permitted to step just outside the gate for the conference. The interview consisted of the usual communist complaints concerning their needs for additional food, clothing, medical supplies etc., as well as a number of demands concerning forced repatriation, acceptance of Russia as a neutral nation, and other matters not appropriate for such an interview.

As the interview proceeded, additional members from the leaders group within the compound gathered around inside the gate to listen to the discussion. At about 3:15 I had decided that the interview was at an end, and turned to depart; whereupon I was rushed by some 20 leaders, dragged into the compound and quickly carried to a building where I was searched and my personal possessions removed.

Neither Dodd nor Lieutenant Colonel Wilbur Raven, who was with him at the interview, was armed. Raven saved himself from capture by clinging to a gatepost for dear life. The "leaders" who actually rushed Dodd and Raven were POWs returning to the compound after emptying buckets of latrine sewage. The whole operation had been planned carefully and the "honey bucket" detail arrived right on time.

Just why Dodd went to the prisoners instead of requiring them to send their representatives to him was and is beyond my understanding. The action was made even more incomprehensible to me when I learned during my study of the incident that the month before the Koje intelligence officer reported that prisoner interrogation revealed that the Communists had issued orders for the prisoners to capture Allied personnel, particularly officers.

Ridgway immediately directed the appointment of a successor to Dodd. After we visited I Corps Headquarters north of Seoul I learned Van Fleet had designated Brigadier General Charles F. Colson, I Corps Chief of Staff, to take command at Koje.

Ridgway and I visited some forward units and then flew to Munsan to call on Vice-Admiral C. Turner Joy, the chief UN truce negotiator who had distinguished himself throughout the negotiations by his dignified conduct and quick ability to sense Communist traps at the conference table.

Joy was absolutely flabbergasted by the Dodd incident. He felt it had pulled the rug out from under him in his negotiations with the Communists, and he said, "I'm certainly going to take a beating over this at the conference table." None of us yet knew how much worse it was going to get.

Ridgway had arranged for Eighth Army representatives to meet him at Munsan. From them he assembled data for a more comprehensive report on what was happening on Koje. The report was not reassuring. We didn't even know exactly how many prisoners were on the island, for the fanatical Communists hadn't permitted our authorities inside some compounds for many months. Therefore our camp officials had been unable to count their prisoners.

The best figure Eighth Army could give Ridgway was eighty thousand which was an approximation. At the time the report was compiled at Munsan these prisoners were at the height of their "victory demonstration." They were in open defiance of their guards.

They flew Communist flags, strung insulting English-language banners on the barbed wire of their enclosures, and mounted barracks rooftops to wigwag signals from one compound to another and to shout insults at our guards. They evidenced no disposition to release Dodd.

The Communist leaders inside the compounds had whipped up a spirit of fervent fanaticism among the prisoners. The capture of Dodd fed the POWs the kind of success and excitement needed to make them exultant and ready to do battle.

Matt got off his first report on the incident to Washington and included the instructions he gave Van Fleet to use whatever force necessary to obtain the *prompt* release of Dodd. Ridgway stressed to Van Fleet in the order that speed was urgent and that Dodd's release must be accomplished without delay.

There were eleven thousand troops on Koje, one third of whom were South Koreans. An American infantry battalion and a company of tanks were on the way. Ridgway told Washington all this and added that the intelligence officer on Koje reported that the prisoners were capable of capturing the island itself. I disagreed with that assessment, since we had a large contingent of combat veterans well armed on the island and I could not conceive of how they could be overcome by unarmed prisoners.

Next day, May 9, Ridgway and I flew to Pusan to pay our respects to President Syngman Rhee. This was my first meeting with the man who has been called the George Washington of Korea and a lot of other things.

The meeting was perfunctory. Matt said good-by and President Rhee welcomed me cordially, assuring me that as the new United Nations Commander I would receive the same support from his splendid forces as had my predecessor.

Ridgway and I then took off for Tokyo, first circling low over Koje to get a good look at the topography of the island. It looked peaceful enough from the air. There was no airfield on the island large enough to permit us to land in our big four-engined transport plane.

The next two days in Tokyo were devoted to more briefings and getting acquainted with members of the UN and Far East Command staffs. Ridgway was frantically busy with the Dodd affair, sending reports to Washington and getting ready for his departure on the twelfth. More reinforcements were sent to Koje, until by the afternoon of the tenth there were twelve thousand troops on the island, and a goodly number of tanks; all men were combat veterans, sufficient, in my opinion, to have effected Dodd's forcible release, dead or alive.

Van Fleet made two trips to Koje, the last on the ninth, to get firsthand information. The negotiations between Colson and the prisoners for Dodd's release appeared to be reaching a climax, but minor concessions by both sides postponed almost hour by hour the order to rescue Dodd forcibly. This was interpreted—and correctly—by the Communists as a sign of weakness on our part.

It was a rough situation. It was not made easier for Colson by frequent telephone conversations with Dodd inside the compound, which subjected Colson to added psychological pressure. In this way the prisoners used Dodd to argue their case. Among other things they told Dodd that if efforts were made to rescue him by force the prisoners would kill him.

I was on the sidelines at this juncture but was filled in on every move because in only a few hours the Dodd incident would be my baby. My feeling was that we should have gone in with force to release Dodd. Ridgway had given Eighth Army full authority to use force and had underlined the need for quick action. I am convinced that if there had been bloodshed it would have been mostly Communist blood.

Of one thing I was certain. You don't negotiate with prisoners of war, particularly fanatical Communist PWs who consider themselves combatants despite capture. At best, negotiation with prisoners is a losing game.

The price for Dodd's freedom had been fixed by the prisoners in an outrageous set of demands they wanted Colson to sign. These included a promise that there would be no more forcible screening (to which of course we had never resorted) nor any nominal screening to determine which prisoners were willing to return to communism and which ones were not. Such a commitment was tantamount to a field commander's changing the policy of his government, which in this case was to screen prisoners. The screening process had been established to implement our government's policy of refusing to force any prisoner back to communism. The demands also were so worded that if accepted they would have constituted tacit admission of a whole list of trumped up crimes the Communists alleged the UN Command had committed against the prisoners. They were questions of the "have you stopped beating your wife?" category.

The demands, signed by "PW Representative Group of North Korean Peoples Army and Chinese Peoples Volunteer Army" were written in the Korean language and hastily and poorly translated for Colson exactly as follows:

1. Immediate ceasing the barbarous behavior, insults, torture, forcible protest with blood writing, threatening, confine, mass murdering, gun and machine-gun shooting, using poison gas, germ weapons, experiment object of A-bomb, by your command. You should guarantee PW human rights and individual life with the base on the International Law.

2. Immediate stopping the so-called illegal and unreasonable voluntary repatriation of North Korean Peoples Army and Chinese Peoples Volunteer Army PW.

3. Immediate ceasing the forcible investigation (screening) which thousands of PW of North Korean Peoples Army and Chinese Peoples Volunteer be rearmed and falled in slavery, permanently and illegally.

4. Immediate recognition of the PW Representative Group (Commission) consisted of North Korean Peoples Army and Chinese Peoples Volunteer Army PW and close cooperation to it by your command.

This Representative Group will turn in Brig Gen Dodd, USA, on your hand after we receive the satisfactory written declaration to resolve the above items by your command. We will wait for your warm and sincere answer.

These demands were sent to Colson on the morning of May 10. Later, after his release, Dodd gave the following account of what happened inside the compound that day during the exchange of notes between the prisoners and Colson:

On the morning of May 10 Dodd said: their four-point agenda was delivered to General Colson. There was the normal delay of translation, and General Colson immediately gave them a written answer.

They studied this answer until noon. They then came to my tent and reported to me that the answer was entirely unsatisfactory. Actually, General Colson had agreed to their demands, but from their translation from English into Kwangji it was obvious that they did not understand this.

I then modified General Colson's letter to their liking, and asked them if such a modified statement would be satisfactory. They informed me that it would. General Colson signed this statement and returned it to them promptly. However they then found minor corrections necessary, to which they attached considerable importance. It was, therefore, necessary to prepare a third statement. Colonel Lee Hak Koo [leader of the prisoners' association] had sent a written statement to General Colson that as soon as they had received a satisfactory statement signed by him and had an opportunity to read and understand it they would release me unharmed.

The statement Colson finally signed to secure Dodd's release said:

1. With reference to your Item 1 of that message, I do admit that there have been instances of bloodshed where many prisoners of war have been killed and wounded by UN Forces. I can assure you that in the future the prisoners of war can expect humane treatment in this camp according to the principles of International Law. I will do all within my power to eliminate further violence and bloodshed. If such incidents happen in the future, I will be responsible.

2. Reference your Item 2 regarding voluntary repatriation of NKPA and CPVA prisoners of war, that is a matter which is being discussed at Panmunjom. I have no control or influence over the decisions at the Peace Conference.

3. Regarding your Item 3 pertaining to forcible investigation (screening), I can inform you that after Gen. Dodd's release, unharmed, there will be no more forcible screening or any rearming of prisoners of war in this camp, nor will any attempt be made at nominal screening.

4. Reference your Item 4, we approve the organization of a PW Representative Group or Commission consisting of NKPA and CPVA prisoners of war, according to the details agreed by Gen Dodd and approved by me.

I am furnishing this reply in writing over my signature as requested by you, through Gen Dodd with the understanding that upon the receipt of this reply you will release Gen Dodd, unharmed, as soon as possible, but under no circumstances later than 8 o'clock PM, this date. Signed Charlie F. Colson, Brig Gen USA, Commanding General.

Dodd was released at 9:30 that night, unharmed, but only after the Communist prisoners made one more effort to wring a final propaganda plum from the affair. Dodd declared that after the prisoners agreed that he would be released on the basis of the Colson note, they then said the weather was so bad that they would hold him until morning. He stated:

I then discovered that they had prepared another letter to General Colson informing him of the arrangements for the release ceremony. Apparently I was to be decorated in flowers and escorted to the gate between formed lines of PWs.

I was to be met at the gate by General Colson where I would be delivered into his custody. I informed them that we could call the whole matter off, that they had not lived up to their promises, that they had admitted that General Colson's statement was satisfactory and now they wished to place other unacceptable conditions upon my release.

I informed them that if they could not live up to their promises we would not live up to ours. By this time it was 9 o'clock. They immediately agreed that I was right and requested that I inform General Colson that I would be released at 9:30. There was some further discussion about the possibility of the removal of the troops in order that I might depart in a peaceful atmosphere. This I refused to discuss. They then agreed to arrange for my release at 9:30 and at this time I was delivered to the gate by the principal leaders and released.

The Dodd affair was far from over but it was not the only thing I had to think of to prepare myself to take over from Matt Ridgway. During the two days after Dodd's release I was briefed from morning to night on every aspect of the command, the battle and armistice talks in Korea, the political position of Japan, the defense of Japan, the disposition of troops, the enemy situation in Korea and all manner of broad subjects such as the political and economic situation in Korea.

The second morning after Dodd's release (the twelfth) I was sitting at Matt Ridgway's desk in the Dai Ichi Building in Tokyo prior to the actual assumption of command, scheduled to take place as his plane left Haneda that afternoon. The telephone rang. It was Matt. Would I, he asked, please formally take over at 10:00 A.M. instead of at the 3:00 P.M. take-off time? Earlier in the week Matt had asked me when I wanted to take command and I laughed that "in view of this POW situation maybe I'd better wait a couple of months." I still felt that way when Matt asked me to take over five hours early so he could handle all the last minute chores of moving. My honest preference was to catch a plane myself and get out fast, but I agreed that a few hours one way or the other wouldn't matter.

Dodd had been whisked to Eighth Army Headquarters in Seoul. He had not been permitted to see reporters and the Colson ransom note still had not been made public thirty-six hours after the bare announcement that Dodd was free. The press was clamoring to get the full story from him, from Eighth Army, from anybody.

I asked my aide to get me the Public Information Officer, for I realized something had to be put out to let off steam. I was told that the man who handled press affairs for Ridgway was Burrows Matthews, a civilian—and he was packing to leave on the same plane as Matt.

There was a Marine lieutenant colonel, however, who had been GHQ military PIO for a short time. I sent for him. My first reaction to Don Nugent was one of reassurance and my confidence in him increased during the next seventeen months. I found him to be a sound thinker, courageous and respected by the press. I dictated a statement on the Koje situation, for release after concurrence by General Ridgway.

I didn't see Ridgway until the actual time of his departure from Haneda at 3:10 P.M. The lid was still on the Dodd-Colson business and the press sniping had developed into a barrage. I might insert here the fact that it had always been my policy in North Africa and Italy to take the press into my confidence and that often I gave reporters information days or weeks before they could use it. Never once did a single newsman betray my confidence.

During the Honor Guard farewell ceremony, I whispered to Matt that I felt it essential a statement be released. I slipped a copy into his hand and told him to radio me his views on it right after takeoff.

Matt walked up the plane ramp with his wife, his two-year-old son and a broad smile on his face. As he waved good-by, I visualized him throwing me a blazing forward pass. Within minutes after takeoff I received a message from the plane that he concurred in my proposed press release and felt it was necessary. The press release reviewed the history of Dodd's capture and gave the text of the POW demands and of Colson's agreement. I denounced the agreement as follows:

The reply by General Colson to the communist prisoners was made under great duress at a time when the life of General Dodd was at stake. The communist demands were unadulterated blackmail and any commitments made by General Colson as a result of such demands should be interpreted accordingly.

That the allegations set forth in the first demand of the communist prisoners are wholly without foundation is indicated by the fact that the prisoners subsequently agreed to eliminate these allegations from their original message. The baseless charges concerning germ warfare already have been refuted by my predecessor, and I can state unequivocally that the United Nations has at no time engaged in any such illegal type of warfare.

Any violence that has occurred at Koje-do has been the result of the deliberate and planned machinations of unprincipled communist leaders whose avowed intent has been to disrupt the orderly operation of the camp and to embarrass the UNC in every way possible.

It is obvious that these demonstrations were motivated by attempts to influence the Armistice negotiations. It has been equally obvious from the very start that the riots we have had were carefully plotted and deliberately instigated by hard-core communist leaders.

The provisions of the Geneva Convention have been observed in the administration of UN POW Camp # 1 at Koje-do. The few incidents which have resulted in bloodshed were deliberately instigated by communist prisoners of war and the force employed by the UNC in connection with these incidents was for the purpose of restoring order and control.

Representatives of the International Committee of the Red Cross have had access to the camp at all times, have visited every compound on the island and have talked to numerous prisoners. Many correspondents have visited the island in the past and have reported to the world on all aspects of the prisoners' lives.

That evening at Van Fleet's headquarters in Seoul, Dodd read to the press an account of his capture and release which closed with the extraordinary statement that "the demands made by the PWs are inconsequential and the concessions granted by the camp authorities were of minor importance." Van Fleet expressed similar sentiments in a message to me.

I was amazed soon thereafter when a board of officers convened by Eighth Army to determine the responsibility for the affair found that General Colson displayed coolness and excellent judgment in handling the negotiations and recommended that no blame should fall on Dodd for being captured.

Van Fleet did not concur in this, but recommended administrative action against both officers. By this time there was a cross fire from another direction. Washington wanted a lot more—preferably someone's head on a pike.

Army Secretary Pace, General Bradley, the Joint Chiefs of Staff, everybody in Washington was frantically calling for action. It was bad enough to have the Koje incident thrown in my lap, but it was made doubly difficult by the way Washington put on the pressure for immediate action.

The people in Washington realized, as I did, that something was wrong with a setup in which the prisoners could seize control of their prison compounds and keep it, in which the island commander was captured and in which his successor made damaging concessions to obtain his release.

But the pressure they put on me slowed the work. I had no sleep the first seventy-two hours after assuming this hot command. I was either preparing messages to Washington or participating in telecon communications with the Pentagon. The telecon is a device which flashes incoming and outgoing teletype messages on a large screen for ready reading, and the radio teletype circuits were busy between Washington and Tokyo during the whole Koje incident and its cleanup.

General Bradley called one telecon for ten o'clock in the morning on May 12. That was midnight in Tokyo. My staff and I sat in the communications room all night answering Bradley's questions. When we finished it was 5:00 A.M. in Tokyo. Brad said, "Well, thanks so much, Wayne, and good night." I flashed back on the screen, "Good night, hell, it's morning here." I arranged to call the next telecon at two o'clock in the afternoon, Tokyo time, which was midnight in Washington. It didn't take long, after that demonstration, to establish reciprocity on minimizing midnight conversations.

I also persuaded Washington to ease the physical pressure upon me for immediate action. I explained that in my view they had to leave the Koje investigation to those of us on the spot and knew it would take some time to reach fair conclusions which I would get to Washington as soon as possible with my recommendations.

My attitude at that time was to forget the past and clean up the situation to take care of the future. That included the job of investigating Dodd and Colson. Dissatisfied with the report of the Eighth Army Board of Officers, I appointed a new board of investigation, headed by Major General Blackshear M. Bryan, Jr., then my Deputy Chief of Staff and later Senior Member of the United Nations Military Armistice Commission. He had served with distinction earlier in the Korean fighting as 24th Division Commander.

To take care of the future, I sent tough, capable Brigadier General Hayden L. Boatner, the stocky, cocky Assistant Commander of the Second Division, to replace Colson on Koje and gave him additional reinforcements, including the 187th Regimental Combat Team of crack paratroopers which was flown in from Japan.

On the findings of the new board, I recommended that Dodd and Colson be reduced in rank. These recommendations were approved in Washington.

I was aware that there was a suppressed background of violence and bloodshed on Koje and asked permission of the Department of the Army to release a full narrative account of past incidents. It was never granted, possibly because of the adverse effect it was believed this might have on the truce talks. But the skeletons tumbled out of the closet anyway. Members of the press had been barred from Koje during Dodd's capture, but were allowed on the island immediately thereafter. They soon uncovered an eight-month history of anti-UN riots and "civil war" between Communist and anti-Communist PW factions that had cost the lives of hundreds of prisoners, four South Korean guards and one American. Much of this information had never been made public.

Soon after assuming command, I gave instructions that all events at prisoner-of-war camps be announced officially and promptly. It had been my experience in Italy that news of incidents, good and bad, should be released to members of the press, in confidence if security required it. This is a practical, not an idealistic, approach; someone is going to get the story anyway, and a story always looks worse if it is broken despite official efforts to keep it under cover.

I am convinced that if newspapers had begun to carry stories of the trouble at Koje when it started, eight months before Dodd was captured, the unbelievable conditions which made possible the Dodd incident would have been cleaned up before they really became critical. But great care was taken to make sure the newspapers did not get the story. With the feeling running high that a truce was imminent, the PW problem had been soft pedaled in the hope that a quick armistice would resolve everything and the fear that revelation of the fights, murders and disturbances at Koje would give the Communists another excuse to delay the truce.

It is interesting to note that two days before Dodd was captured General Ridgway had called the attention of the Eighth Army Commander to the Koje situation and voiced concern "over the possibility of increasing boldness on the part of the Communist leaders."

5

How Our Communist POWs
Ran Their Camps

The story of the Communist High Command campaign to gain control of the prisoners of war in our compounds and use them as active combatants in our rear is in itself both a case study of the technique of Communist intrigue and a dire warning of the efficiency and imagination of the Communist conspiracy against us.

At my direction the UN and Far East Command Military Intelligence Section published in January of 1953 a detailed history of this Communist campaign which was as much a purely military operation as any other of the Korean War, even though it was a military operation unparalleled in the history of ground warfare. The foreword to this report said:

> From time to time during the past year, communists in the United Nations prisoner-of-war camps in Korea have demonstrated, rioted, refused to obey orders, held kangaroo courts, kidnaped and murdered. Many of these incidents have been of a nature or on a scale requiring suppression by force, with resultant deaths and injuries. These the communists everywhere assiduously propagandized. By no means accidental is the connection between the incidents and their exploitation by the communists. The United Nations Command offers the following information about that connection as a contribution to wider and fuller understanding of communism and its methods.

The detailed study was based on interrogation of POWs after the Koje and other incidents, on examination of documents captured inside the prison compounds and on intelligence data gathered from various other sources.

The findings were shocking because they showed the Communists spread the area of combat beyond that of any previous war, into the camps of the prisoners of war. Among the main findings were:

1. The Communist High Command regarded the prisoners in United Nations camps as still in combatant status, and used them in planned military operations.

2. Prisoners inside the camps were controlled by the same system of political commissars as were soldiers in the Red armies.

3. The Communist High Command maintained effective communication with the Communist leaders in the POW camps so that orders for specific action were received by the prisoners from the North Korean Army.

4. The prisoners were ordered to take various actions, without regard to casualties, to embarrass the United Nations Command in the eyes of the world, to strengthen the position of the Communists negotiating for armistice at Panmunjom and to force the UN Command to siphon off combat infantrymen from the front lines to guard the prisoners effectively.

5. The very men who negotiated the Armistice at Panmunjom formulated and directed the plans for prisoner mutinies and other operations so that incidents could be timed to help the negotiators during crucial periods of the armistice talks.

The prisoner problem became acute for the United Nations Command in late 1950 after the Chinese Communists were hurled across the Yalu and into the war in Korea. Victory over the North Korean army had left 100,000 Communist POWs in Allied hands. In the withdrawal before the great mass of Chinese troops the United Nations had to evacuate these prisoners from their well-dispersed prison camps and to concentrate them in the area of Pusan, on the southern tip of Korea. There the large number of prisoners, plus the far greater number of refugees, became a major barrier to the smooth movement of supplies for Allied troops.

It was decided to establish a POW installation on the island of Koje, large enough to accommodate the entire mass of Communist prisoners and close enough to the Korean coast for relatively easy transport.

Initial construction and first shipments of prisoners began early in 1951 and by the middle of the year there were 130,000 Koreans and 20,000 Chinese on the island. Heavy fighting in the spring of 1951 had swollen the ranks of the prisoners.

There was little or no trouble in the early days on Koje-do. But early in 1952, when the armistice talks began to boil down to the question of prisoner exchange, the POWs became restive and incidents began. The Communist armistice negotiators, in effect, requested the screening process to determine how many captured Communist soldiers would resist repatriation to their homes in North Korea and China. The Red negotiators said they could not discuss the issue of voluntary repatriation until they knew beforehand about how many of the prisoners would refuse to return home.

For a long time the screening went along without incident. And a surprisingly large number of North Koreans and Chinese swore they would rather die than go back to communism. Once the opportunity of choice seemed open to them they wrote letters in blood and tattooed anti-Communist slogans on their bodies.

But finally the screening teams reached the first of a group of compounds in which the prisoners were led and controlled by fanatical Communists who did everything in their power to block the program. Screening could have been accomplished at that time with force, but the trend of the armistice negotiations appeared favorable and it was decided to let well enough alone rather than risk trouble that would further delay a truce.

In the late winter and early spring of 1952 the spirit of rebellion mounted among the prisoners in the Communist-controlled compounds on Koje-do until finally, on May 7, the series of scattered incidents was climaxed by the capture of General Dodd.

General Boatner, an experienced and splendid combat leader who had a diversified background of service in the Orient, was able to gain complete control of all Communist compounds in short order after he moved in to clean up following the Dodd affair.

But regaining control of prisoners was only the immediate problem and one that we knew we could solve through the use of force.

More important for us was the need to learn all we could about how the Communist High Command had gained control of the prisoners and used it. That information was essential so that we could combat this form of military operation in Korea and in any future war with communism.

It was not until late in 1951 that our intelligence got conclusive proof that the Communists had organized a special unit to take the leadership in making the prisoners of war combatants in Korea. This unit, attached to the headquarters of the North Korean Army, had two specific missions. First, it was to train agents who would permit themselves to be captured so they could go into the camps as POWs and carry out specified leadership missions. The second was to furnish intelligence to the Communist negotiators at Panmunjom.

The chief Communist negotiator was General Nam Il, trained in Russia for his role as a top leader of the Communists in Korea. At the same time that he was negotiating the cease-fire in the talks at Panmunjom, this general was in command of the most powerful political machinery in the North Korean Army—the Political Control Organization. This was the familiar Communist commissar system. In Korea it had the broadest kind of powers. It did everything from dealing out physical punishment to traitors to censoring mail of North Korean foot soldiers. It published newspapers, organized service shows, handled troop indoctrination, spied for dissident elements in the army, trained and assigned agents and controlled a soldier's career by either admitting him to or suspending him from party membership.

To this all-powerful group was given the added task of fomenting trouble in the prison camps. Apparently the Communists were satisfied with the results. After the Armistice was signed, Nam Il, a comparatively young general, was made Foreign Minister of the Pyongyang Communist government.

Nam had early evidence of the success of his intrigue with the prisoners. In December of 1951, Allied intelligence captured a document signed by the chief of the Southern Section of the Korean Labor Party (Communist) which said, "According to information from the party in Kyongsang Namdo, South Korea, approximately thirty thousand to sixty thousand North Korean Army soldiers interned in the Koje-do prisoner-of-war camp have been organized and the Kyongsang Namdo Branch of the Korean Labor Communist Party will start activities in their behalf."

Subsequently many prisoners captured by the Allies admitted that they were deliberate plants, assigned the task of permitting themselves to be captured so they could carry plans and orders into the POW camps. Male agents were dispersed in front-line Communist units and, during small skirmishes with UN troops, either surrendered or were "captured." They then were put into the normal UN prisoner-of-war channels and transported to their goal by us, undetected. Women agents were sent south as refugees with instructions to find work in or near POW hospitals or camps so they could help the Red agents inside the barbed wire compounds.

The men and women picked for these jobs as agents in and around the POW camps were Communist Party members of good standing who had demonstrated that they were hard-core Communists. After they were picked for the job they were given an intensive two-month training course in the history of the USSR Communist Party and the Korean Labor Party, Communist theory, methods of organizing military and civilian party groups, Korean revolution and the world situation and the situation in South Korea. The agents were directed specifically to spread propaganda among the prisoners to the effect that unification of Korea under the North Korean Government was a certainty and that withdrawal of United Nations forces from Korea was imminent.

The agents also were instructed to emphasize to the POWs that modern equipment was being given to the North Korean Army by the Soviet Union and China, that the life of the North Korean soldier had vastly improved, that high North Korean Government officials were concerned about the welfare of the prisoners of war and that high respect and consideration would be shown them when they returned.

The Communist leaders had to work psychology on the agents, too. The agents were told that their period of voluntary imprisonment would be short because an armistice definitely would be signed and they soon could return home to North Korea. The Red leaders had to counteract their own propaganda which created fear that all Communist prisoners of the UN were killed. They told the agents about to become prisoners that the UN had stopped murdering prisoners because of the imminence of the Armistice.

Finally the Communist leaders told the agents that when they returned to North Korea they would be decorated and publicly praised as heroes of the North Korean people.

The assigned missions followed a definite pattern and plan. Each agent was instructed to establish "cell organization committees" in each POW camp. North Korean officers were to be assigned by the agents to responsible positions within the network of the Red cells so they could enforce rigid military discipline. As the cells grew strong, and their control of the prison compounds became trustworthy, they were to instigate and carry out strikes, protests and demonstrations.

Another function of the agent was to investigate the attitude and conduct of each prisoner. The specific instructions directed the agent to obtain the names of those who had deserted or surrendered voluntarily, those who were unsympathetic to the North Korean Government and those who were suspected informers because of the frequency with which they were questioned by Allied camp authorities. In addition the agents were to get the names of the Republic of Korea guards and all informers posing as prisoners. These names were to be used for future reference, when the Communists were able to prosecute "war criminals" in Korea.

The communications system set up by the prisoners was intricate and effective. Their problem was threefold. There had to be communications between different compounds. There had to be communications from the Communist High Command to the prisoners in addition to the link of the agents who permitted themselves to be captured. And there had to be communications *from* the prisoners to the High Command in North Korea.

The prisoners' "message center" was the 64th Field Hospital where we treated them when they were ill. Prisoners with a message to send feigned illness to get into the hospital. There communication was established between wards by word of mouth or by messages tied to rocks and tossed from one compound to another.

The officers' ward was the nerve center of the hospital communication system. All information and directives were centralized in this ward and then disseminated by patients released to different compounds.

Military organization was maintained throughout. Each ward was known as a "yuk" or company and each group of wards a "ku" or battalion.

Most of the prisoner workers in the hospital joined the Communist organization either voluntarily or involuntarily. Each was questioned carefully by his ward leader to ascertain whether or not he was already a good Communist. If acceptable, he was then made a member of the Korean Labor Party and became an integral part of the communication system.

Good military practice in any army dictates that a commander must provide alternate means of communication. The Communist prisoners on Koje were no exception. Although the hospital was the best channel for intercompound communications, there were alternate methods, including semaphore flags, hand signals, whistling, chanting and throwing messages tied to rocks. Messages also were hidden in rations, clothing and supplies being delivered to the compounds. No possible means of communication was overlooked, as evidenced by the effort of some prisoners to tie messages to large dragonflies.

The Communist High Command also had to arrange means of getting word to the prisoners quickly in order to better co-ordinate the war effort of Communist prisoners on Koje and Communist cease-fire negotiators at Panmunjom. Two agencies were utilized in this work, the Guerrilla Guidance Bureau and the elite Espionage Department of the North Korean Army Military Intelligence Section. The Guidance Bureau, under General Pae Chol, a Korean who was an officer in the Russian Army, provided couriers to run messages. The Espionage Department provided agent teams of ten to twelve officers and noncommissioned officers. Team commanders ranged in rank from senior lieutenant to full colonel. Each team had Russian-made portable receiving radio sets. There was no monitor pickup or other indication the agents were able to send radio signals.

The Guerrilla Guidance Bureau and the Espionage Department also served to channel messages from the prisoners to the High Command in the north. Much of the work of transmitting messages from the prisoners to the High Command was entrusted to the Espionage Department covert intelligence teams who operated the main Communist spy net in South Korea. Allied authorities confiscated many messages from prisoners inside the compounds, including some addressed to Mao Tse-tung in Peiping and Kim Il Sung in Pyongyang.

The method of passing messages in and out of the compounds was so simple as to be elementary. There were many civilians on the island, including a village in the general area of the prison camp. Agents lived in the village and mingled with the people. These agents dropped notes where prisoner work detail members could find them. Members of the work details got word out of the compounds and into the Communist communications network by the same method, dropping notes where agents could pick them up.

Effective liaison with the North Korean Army Headquarters was made possible by the tight political and then military organization of the Communists inside the compounds. It was the political organization which developed a section to make contact with Communists outside the compounds so that the note-drop grapevine could be established.

Political groups were organized as early as the spring of 1951. In May of that year the Communists in Compound 92 established the Koje-do branch of the Korean Labor Party (Communist) and similar groups were formed in most other compounds. A statement of aims and principles circulated among the political groups declared:

We are reborn members of the Party and will sacrifice our lives and display all our ability for the Party so that the North Korean People's Republic may win the final victory.

We are reborn members of the Party and will be faithful to the Party and carry out the Party's proclamation to educate all prisoners of war.

Our Party will implement the platform of the People's Republic to have all prisoners of war, indigenous refugees, or officers and soldiers of the Republic of Korea recognize the platform.

Our Party will foster internationalism, try to be friendly with the Chinese Communist forces, and infuse class consciousness into United Nations soldiers.

As directives and instructions began to flow in over the network of communications Nam Il devised the tone of the prisoners' slogans and declarations became sharper, less general.

We must consider the possible rupture of the cease-fire negotiations which are now underway [said one declaration of objectives] and be ready to liberate ourselves in accordance with orders from Kim Il Sung. The prisoners of war should educate themselves and surround themselves with Party members. All types of units must be organized to rise in revolt simultaneously in order to liberate all the prisoners of war and attack the ROK [Republic of Korea] and American forces that now occupy Koje-do. After we win autonomous rights we will keep in touch with the commanding officer of the North Korean People's Army by wireless and will land on Korea proper. After that we will join the NKPA [North Korean People's Army] together with the Chiri-san guerrilla units.

The Chiri-san guerrilla units were the strongest in South Korea. They were based in mountain fastnesses northwest of Pusan.

Nam Il's control grew stronger. Under his direction a political committee consisting of four sections—Political, Security, Organization, Military and Agitation—was established to control the prisoners in the various compounds.

Military administration committees were organized in all compounds under Communist control and they, in turn, organized so-called military units to enforce the plans and directives of the committees. The "reign of terror" was about to begin. People's Courts appeared to punish offenders who deviated from the Party's policies or refused to join its military organizations.

One of the real big shots in the Communist hierarchy of North Korea was boss of the Political Committee, or "General Leading

Headquarters," as the Communists called it. He was Pak Sang Hyon, one of the original group of thirty-six Soviet-Koreans brought into North Korea in 1945 by the Russians to organize the North Korean satellite regime. Kim Il Sung and Nam Il were others among the thirty-six.

Pak was listed as "Jeon Moon Il" on prison records and he was rated as a private in the North Korean Army. Fellow prisoners, however, identified him as a top-ranking Communist who came to Korea from Russia after the Japanese were defeated in World War II.

Prisoners stated that Pak controlled all the compounds and personally ordered the capture of General Dodd. He also was allegedly responsible for instigating the riots in Compound 77 against the United Nations screening program for voluntary repatriation. He issued instructions, directives and propaganda. And it was he who sentenced to death many of the prisoners who had dared to defy the Party directives.

After the Koje incident Pak was removed from the compounds and held separately.

After the Armistice Pak was repatriated to North Korea along with the other Communist ringleaders who had perpetrated crimes not only against other POWs but also against UN personnel on Koje and other islands.

Right after the Koje incident I had requested the authority to bring to trial all of these ringleaders responsible for crimes in the prison camps. Washington delayed acting on my request, presumably for fear that the trials might jeopardize the chances of an armistice.

However, as additional crimes were committed and Allied personnel were killed or wounded, I repeated my request for authority to bring these criminals to justice as the only means of enforcing discipline. I also pointed out that under the Geneva Convention we had the responsibility to safeguard the prisoners in our control and that we failed to fulfill this obligation when we failed to halt the kangaroo courts which ordered anti-Communist prisoners to be beaten to death.

Finally I was given authority to try these Communist criminals for postcapture offenses. I had prisoners who were known to have committed atrocities against American and other Allied troops before they were captured, but I was not given authority to try these men.

I was in the process of establishing a United Nations tribunal to try prison camp criminals when the armistice negotiations were about to be consummated. I asked Washington whether I was to hold the accused or send them back to the Communists in the "Big Switch" prisoner exchange. I was instructed to give these criminals back to the Communists. The decision, I was informed, was based on fear that if we held back some of these prominent Communist leaders, who had served their masters so well in the military campaign in the POW camps, then the enemy would retaliate by retaining Major General William F. Dean and other senior UN prisoners still in their hands.

The main Communist criminals that we held and then turned loose at Panmunjom were members of the "General Leading Headquarters" of the Communist political organization inside the prison compounds.

The four sections of the "General Leading Headquarters" had carefully defined functions and responsibilities.

The First Section, Political Security, policed Party members to eliminate those guilty of "factionalism, opportunism and cowardice," to select "superior experienced members" for key jobs, to recruit Party members and to "take precautionary measures against spies and agents to include agents of the Republic of Korea Army, civil interpreters, Christian ministers, Party members with bad qualities, religionists, former security chiefs, draft evaders, reactionary groups and those who associate with reactionary elements." All these were to be "blacklisted." The First Section placed trusted Communists in each company, platoon and squad. The agents kept their affiliation secret so they could spy on their fellows in the military-type units.

The Second Section, Organization and Planning, was to maintain external liaison and contact with guerrillas in order to keep the flow of messages moving both ways between the prison compounds and the Communist High Command in North Korea. It also prepared and submitted intelligence reports on camp guards and col-

lected and distributed news. One subsection, for External Liaison
and Reconnaissance, was charged with the duty of making contact
with guerrillas on the mainland and of preparing for a leading role
in a mass breakout. The specific directive to this subsection said in
part:

> Whenever the time is appropriate for an uprising or break, the mem-
> bers dispatched to the outside will assist the basic fighting units to get
> out of the compound by occupying stationary firing posts and guard
> posts by surprise attack, light signal fires on the hills, capture weapons
> and destroy United Nations ammunition and armory store houses. This
> sub-section will be organized from Party members experienced in guer-
> rilla fighting in China and South Korea, those who have a thorough
> knowledge of enemy weapons and those who served in the North
> Korean Army in engineering and reconnaissance.

Members of the group were given explicit instructions on procedures to be followed once they escaped the compounds.

> After extrication [the instructions said] construct a partisan base and
> set fire to the camp's headquarters petroleum dump, food storage and
> other supply areas and destroy the transportation route. After completion
> of this duty, they will get to the mainland and report to an officer higher
> than major and join the partisans. Extrication or escape will be accom-
> plished before dawn, while on work details or during foggy weather.

The External Intelligence Subsection of the Organization and
Planning group was ordered to gather straight military intelligence
on all Allied units and movements on the island, plus the nonmilitary
task of compiling the full name, age, birthplace, address and political ideas of all ROK soldiers, police, civilians and government
officials.

The Third Section, Guard Unit, was to safeguard staff members
of the "General Leading Headquarters" as well as documents and
communications, and also was given the job of punishing reactionaries and violators of Party law. The Guard Unit not only had to
protect staff members from attack, but was even admonished that
"constant care should be exercised regarding the staff's health conditions (securing their health, food and clothes)." That adds up to

a system in which the Communist bosses had prisoners assigned to them as orderlies.

The other group in the Guard Unit was the hangman's detachment, directed to "punish, beat and execute violators condemned by the 'people's courts.' "

There was ample work, for the executioners for the People's Courts were busy. Intelligence files of the United Nations Command are filled with accounts of executions in the compounds. Reports of a few will suffice to show the methods used by the Communist leaders to cow prisoners into obedience. Reports of these kangaroo court sentences include:

A 1,000-man "jury" [250 men from each battalion] on June 6, 1952, conducted a "self criticism" of prisoners and sentenced one to death. The prisoner who received the death sentence was a member of an anti-communist group which, it was alleged, had plotted to kill the communist leaders and take control of Compound 85.

In December, 1951, three prisoners were stoned to death on orders of the communist "people's court."

A prisoner accused of being anti-communist refused to speak before the Chief of the Political Committee in Compound 66 on November 11, 1951. All platoon members kicked or struck the prisoner. Two of them then took a section of a tent pole and beat him to death.

The Guard Unit also stationed sentries to prevent the escape of anti-Communists from the compounds.

The Fourth Section, Agitation and Propaganda, was organized to keep statistics and documents and to plan and prepare material for instruction and propaganda.

Once the political apparatus was organized, Military Administrative committees were created in various compounds. The committees established brigade or regimental headquarters to which the compound spokesman, interpreter, monitor and security chief were attached.

The battalion, immediately below brigade or regiment, was the basic "fighting" unit and was broken down, in good military order, into three or four companies, each of which was divided into platoons and squads.

The plans for military action were detailed and precise. Through prisoner interrogation we learned many of these.

In April of 1952 [prisoners told us], the leaders instructed the men to seize any US or ROK guards who entered Compound 77.

In the event of entry by UN troops, 1,500 Communist prisoners will lead the attack and be led by the compound commandant and vice-commandant. This first line will be backed by 3,500 other prisoners led by their platoon leaders. The estimated 2,500 anti-Communist prisoners will remain in their quarters and not join in the attack. The plan is to attack UN troops from the flanks, capturing weapons and troops, preferably officers. The weapons to be utilized in the attack are spears made from tent poles, a piece of pipe six inches long, knives, flails and clubs.

This amazing, unbelievable situation, in which the POWs controlled their compounds, did not end with the release of Dodd. On the contrary it was strengthened if anything by the demonstration of rebellious power and by the concessions signed by Colson. So when the big test came, and General Boatner moved in to assert UN Command control of the compounds, the Communists in some camps tried to put their military plans into effect. They failed because of the firm determination and action of Boatner and his men.

Staff planning for this operation was done as carefully as for any orthodox military campaign. We knew by this time that the Communist POWs were active combatants and had to be dealt with as soldiers, not prisoners in the traditional sense. The object was to reduce the density of the POW population in the Koje-do compounds and move the prisoners into small compounds in which they could be managed more easily.

Boatner began with the toughest of the compounds, Number 76, the "Dodd compound." He moved into the compound on June 10, exactly one month after the release of Dodd. There had been a month-long series of relatively minor incidents since Dodd was freed as the Communists celebrated their "victory" of Koje-do. The temper of the Communist prisoners still was high.

At 5:45 A.M. on the morning of June 10 messages were broadcast over public address loudspeakers to inform the prisoners of Compound 76 that they were to be moved to new areas that day and that they would not be harmed if they co-operated. They reacted badly, shouting and chanting their defiance as their leaders obviously tried to whip them up to fighting pitch. The prisoners pointedly ignored Boatner's order to form into groups for the movement and, instead, openly armed themselves with sharpened tent poles of spear length, knives and other weapons.

At 6:15 A.M., half an hour after the messages to the POWs had been started, the troops moved into the compound with a show of force. The objective was to segregate and then move the prisoners.

The UN troops fired tear gas grenades into the ranks of the prisoners and advanced to the middle of the compound. Most of the prisoners permitted themselves to be evacuated without difficulty, but the last fifteen hundred of the six thousand POWs of the compound formed ranks in a moblike group in one corner. They resisted with stubborn fanaticism as the UN soldiers tried to break them up into smaller groups.

Boatner well knew the propaganda use the Communist High Command made of Red "martyrs" in the POW camps, so he did everything he could to avoid casualties. He ordered his men to attack with tear gas and concussion grenades only. They followed his orders effectively and brought the mob under control without firing a single shot.

There were casualties, however. By 8:45 A.M., when the fight was over and the prisoners under control, one American enlisted man was dead and fourteen others wounded. Among the prisoners thirty-one were killed and 139 wounded.

It was significant that in the heat of the action prisoners were seen fighting among themselves as the Communist leaders inside the compound fought not only to hold off the American troops but to prevent defections of prisoners who wanted to surrender.

Search and examination of the compound after it was cleared by prisoners revealed shocking conditions. The prisoners had fashioned about 3,000 spears from tent poles, 1,000 gasoline grenades, 4,500 knives and an uncounted number of clubs, hatchets, hammers and barbed wire flails. A tunnel was under construction from Compound 76 to Compound 77. Trenches surrounded each hut and connected one building to another in a network that covered the compound.

The battle in Compound 76 yielded some of the top Communist leaders in the camp, including Colonel Lee Hak Koo, who had disregarded a direct order from Boatner to form his people into groups of 150 for easy movement to the new compounds. Lee and other compound leaders were segregated, but there were others to take their places later.

In addition to the weapons and entrenchments found in Compound 76, our troops discovered a document detailing a complete plan of battle for the resistance to the breakup operation. The well-disciplined prisoners had followed the plan almost to the letter in their fight against Boatner's troops.

The resolute, swift action in Compound 76 took the steam out of resistance in other compounds. Compound 77, where the POWs were just as hostile and tough as those in 76, submitted without resistance. In the compound, in addition to the anticipated weapons, our troops found the bodies of sixteen PWs who had been murdered by order of the People's Courts or the Red compound bosses.

The prisoners were moved into small compounds that housed five hundred to six hundred POWs, instead of ten times that many as the old compounds had. The month between the release of Dodd and the start of the breakup operation was necessitated, largely, by the time it took to plan and build these new compounds.

Boatner also removed another sore spot which had shocked me when I learned of it. He moved the village that served as a key center in the communications network Nam Il's men established with the prisoners far away from the prison area and tightened controls so that contact between villagers and prisoners was next to impossible.

He instituted other precautionary measures. Compound inspections by camp authorities, impossible in some of the enclosures in the past, were made daily in every compound. The POWs no longer were able to declare any part of the camps off limits to UN troops. There were regular searches for contraband to prevent any repetition of the astonishing build-up of an arsenal by the POWs. Anti-Communist prisoners were moved to separate camps, safe from the terror of the Communist organization, but not free completely, for Red agents posing as anti-Communists went with them to most of the new camps. The POW population of Koje was reduced by more than half by moving thousands of pro-Communists to new camps on other islands.

Intelligence systems were expanded to give more complete information about what was going on inside the compounds and especially to identify and segregate the men who were leaders in Nam Il's organization. The hospital setup was revised so that no longer did the prisoners have such a convenient message center for their communications network. And effective steps were taken to catch the Nam Il agents who permitted themselves to be captured so they could carry messages and directives into the prison compounds. The safeguards were simple. I directed that newly captured POWs be kept in new compounds, apart from old prisoners.

In ten days Boatner had moved more than seventy thousand POWs to the new compounds and segregated the anti-Communists from those who wanted to return to North Korea or China.

The first evidence that Communist agents may have infiltrated into the camps for the anti-Communists came from investigation of an incident at Nonsan UN POW Camp No. 16 on July 27, 1952. Anti-Communist prisoners charged that a group of North Koreans had been shipped from Koje-do posing as anti-Communists in order to penetrate mainland camps and create unrest and violence. The anti-Communist prisoners charged these alleged agents planned to assassinate anti-Communist leaders and take over control of entire compounds in much the same manner as their predecessors on Koje. The anti-Communists used the tactics of the Communists, seized the agitators, interrogated them and attempted to force confessions of planned resistance by beating them. One prisoner died from the beatings and seven others were hospitalized.

Three days later twenty-four more North Korean prisoners at Nonsan were injured in a similar disturbance. Investigation made it apparent that there were Communist agents in the camp and that they were struggling to seize power from the anti-Communists, who were organized.

More serious trouble broke out on December 14, 1952, at the camp for civilian pro-Communists at Pongam Island near Koje. There had been a series of small disturbances in the camp all month. On December 4 POWs in one compound refused to show their clothing and equipment for inspection. Two days later camp authorities at Koje said they had uncovered evidence which indicated that prisoners in the main camp and its branches, which included Pongam, might be planning a mass escape. Next day prisoners at Pongam defied camp authorities and conducted military drills in three compounds. Three days later, on the tenth, a small group of Pongam prisoners attacked an administrative soldier at a dispensary enclosure and next day two prisoners attacked an enclosure commander.

This gradual build-up of defiance and mutiny finally erupted on December 14 when POWs in six compounds joined in a mass demonstration which appeared to be in preparation for a breakout. UN troops moved in to break up the demonstration and in the resultant fighting 85 prisoners were killed and 113 hospitalized.

The Communists seized upon this incident immediately. A letter was circulated among Party members inside the compounds exhorting them to emulate the example of the "heroes" who died at Pongam. Object: force the Americans to kill more prisoners so that "throughout the world" the Yankee will be "known as the enemy of human beings."

That is a case history of our enemy wherever he may be found—resourceful, imaginative, fanatic, dangerous.

6

Stalemate: 1952-53

Both the Korean War and the armistice negotiations were in a complete deadlock at the time I was appointed UN Commander in May, 1952.

The 155-mile front had been stabilized six months before on a twisting line extending from the Han River estuary, ten miles south of the 38th Parallel on the West Coast, to Kosong, forty miles north of the parallel on the East Coast. And there it remained, except for minor gains by the Chinese in their final face-saving offensive a month before the truce.

This frozen front represented a true balance of power. The enemy had almost one and a half times more combat troops than we did inside Korea and a considerable reserve across the Manchurian border, two hundred miles north of the battle line. The best estimate was that 1,200,000 Chinese were in North Korea. They were lavishly supplied with artillery. They had some armor and approximately two thousand first-line warplanes, slightly more than half of which were Russian-built MIG-15 jets based on the untouchable side of the Yalu.

We had superiority in tanks, and our naval units gave us uncontested control of Korean waters. Our Air Force and Navy carrier planes ruled the skies as far as they were allowed to fly—up to the Yalu—although we actually had slightly less combat aircraft of all types than the Communists had MIGs alone!

Thus the enemy's greater manpower was equalized by our greater striking force, a balance that swung in the enemy's favor with every mile we pushed north. The shorter the enemy's supply lines to his Manchurian base, which we were not permitted to bomb, the less opportunity our airpower had to destroy these supplies moving down from the Yalu to the battle line. It was a simple matter of opportunity. The longer the supply line, the more time the enemy supply trucks and trains had to stay in the open where they were vulnerable to our air.

The tragedy of this frozen front was this: it cost the UN Command half as many dead, wounded and missing going nowhere as the defense of the Pusan perimeter, the Inchon landing, the 1950 advance to the Yalu and the grim winter retreat from North Korea combined.

Since it was not our government's policy to seek a military decision, the next best thing was to make the stalemate more expensive for the Communists than for us, to hit them where it hurt, to worry them, to convince them by force that the price tag on an armistice was going up, not down.

I determined to do this as best I could, always bearing in mind the fundamental military and political conditions under which we waged war in Korea, and which affected my planning.

Militarily, we were fighting communism's second team. Manpower was their long suit and superior technology was ours. I would not and could not afford to swap UN and Communist lives man for man. In fact I wouldn't, if I could help it, trade one American or Allied life for ten or more dead Communists with nothing to show for it but a few additional acres of Korean real estate.

Politically I was guided by the basic terms of my mission, which was defensive. I was given neither the authority nor the military resources to achieve victory. I was instructed, rather, to bend every effort toward realizing an armistice quickly.

Very early I submitted to Washington a broad plan through which I was convinced we could have won the war, the first we ever had with communism.

But at the same time I looked about for means of influencing the war by steps that were within both my power and authority. To do this, as soon as I had extricated myself from the Koje crisis, I began a survey to answer the fundamental questions of "What can I do, within existing directives and strength levels, to influence the action in Korea?" and the corollary, "What can I do militarily and otherwise to make the Communists realize that the price of peace is not as cheap as they are trying to make it?"

To answer these questions my staff and I had to go over every aspect of the ground, air and sea wars, seeking military targets. We had to make a detailed study of intelligence reports to determine how we might hurt the enemy psychologically as well as physically. We made an intensive review of the armistice negotiations, looking for weak spots in the enemy position at the conference table. And we made a thorough study of the general situation in the Far East to determine if any permissible military resources had been overlooked and were lying idle.

Out of these studies I found four military and four political courses which were either open to me under existing directives or borderline cases for which authority might be granted.

Militarily, within the limits of authority already granted, I found I could:

1. Bomb the untouched hydroelectric complexes, excluding the Suiho dam and generators, which provided much of the power to the Communist war machine in Manchuria and serviced what remained of North Korean industry. Washington reserved the authority to hit Suiho. These generators and dams had been spared, first because we had hopes of using them when we raced into North Korea after the Inchon landing, and later because a truce seemed imminent.

2. Bomb military targets in the North Korean capital of Pyongyang, untouched for a year. We learned the Communists had stocked it full of combat troops and war supplies and had made it a high command headquarters and communications center.

3. Bomb the main Communist supply line from Pyongyang down towards Kaesong, where the Communist armistice negotiators had their headquarters. We had agreed in the first days of the armistice negotiations to grant immunity from air attack to properly marked motor convoys carrying personnel and supplies to the Red armistice headquarters, but in effect we lifted the bombing of that highway almost completely.

4. Bomb innumerable small targets which, taken as a whole, turned out significant amounts of equipment of various kinds, repaired locomotives, trucks and tanks, sheltered small, well-dispersed stockpiles of military equipment and housed troops and officers' training schools.

There were four other provocative actions, none wholly military in character, which I believed I might be permitted to pursue. They were:

1. Release anti-Communist prisoners of war, particularly Koreans. We had precedent for this as the Communists earlier in the conflict had "released" fifty thousand captured South Koreans "at the front," and impressed them into military service.

2. If and when it became apparent that no progress was being made in the armistice negotiations and that the Communists were using the talks solely for a propaganda forum, I wanted the right to look the Communists in the eye and recess the conference.

3. Build the ROK Army into a bigger and more effective fighting force.

4. Show the Communists we really meant business by putting two divisions of Chiang Kai-shek's Nationalist Chinese troops in the line against the Communists in Korea.

Overall I was in favor of these eight measures because of my conviction that only through forceful action could the Communists be made to agree to an armistice the United States considered honorable. I had no real hope that these actions in themselves would be enough, but at least they would make the Communists realize we were ready to take forceful action, the only thing they understand.

My recommendation for the use of Chiang's troops was never answered by Washington. It died by pocket veto. My recommendation for the buildup of the ROK forces was not approved until it became a presidential campaign issue in October of 1952.

The resurvey of targets revealed that the choicest plum of all was the hydroelectric complexes which were in the general area of the Suiho. I discovered that I had the authority to bomb all but the biggest plant—the Suiho itself, thirty-six miles northeast of the Manchurian river town of Antung, site of the biggest base for MIGs used against us. The Suiho plant was just on the Korean side of the Yalu. This Japanese-built dam and six generators is the largest hydroelectric installation in the Far East and fourth largest in the world. It was designed to produce a maximum of 640,000 kilowatts. It was out of bounds because of its proximity to the border.

General O. P. Weyland's Far East Air Force prepared plans for the destruction of the smaller plants and I notified the Joint Chiefs of Staff in Washington of my intentions. To my surprise and pleasure they came right back authorizing me to bomb the Suiho as well.

While I was preparing this jolt for the enemy, I discovered another provocative but peaceful course of action open to me. Some 27,000 Korean prisoners of war had been reclassified according to the Geneva Convention as civilian internees. They were refugees from North and South Korea, persons once considered security risks, a whole miserable grab bag of men, women and some children swept up in the retreats and advances of the first eighteen months of the war. They had put themselves on record as not wanting to be delivered to the Communists in any prisoner exchange.

With Washington's approval and to the accompaniment of outraged howls from the Communists, the internees were released in Operation Homecoming during June, July and August of 1952. A month later we reclassified eleven thousand more and released them throughout October and November. All of these internees were among those persons the Communists claimed should be forced behind the Iron Curtain.

The Koje incident had broken before I took command. The first real headache that was all mine came toward the end of June. It was the Suiho attack. The command mounted the biggest combined Air Force-Navy air assault of the entire war against the Suiho complex on June 23, 1952, and repeated the attack the next day. Altogether thirteen vital hydroelectric installations were hit by the bombers that swarmed up to the Yalu itself with their bombs. We knew what we were hitting. The power from Suiho and the smaller plants was vital to war production in Manchuria and we knew it was used by power plants repairing military equipment and manufacturing both arms and explosives. These were attacks against legitimate military targets and were designed to deny the power plants to the enemy as a source of energy to support his operations in Korea.

The assaults were pressed against targets within sight of large Communist air bases in Manchuria, but not a single MIG rose to challenge the vast air armada we hurled to the Yalu that day.

The whole operation was so purely military in character, and so clearly within the limits of Korea, that I was astounded by the vehement outcries of protest that came immediately from the British Labor Party and a part of the British press.

My good friend from North Africa and Italy, Lord Alexander of Tunis, had visited me in Tokyo just before the Suiho operation. He was then the British Defense Minister, and we spent much time discussing means of strengthening the alliance between our two countries. When Alexander left I felt we had done much to bridge whatever misunderstandings existed on the conduct of the war and the truce negotiations. It was all the more disheartening, therefore, to get a blast of criticism from the British press almost before the Defense Minister got home.

The British press asked why I hadn't consulted Alexander, who had left Tokyo on the eighteenth, before making such a provocative move. It expressed fear that now the Communists would be so angry they would break off the truce talks.

Events proved these fears groundless. In fact, we hit the Suiho four more times, the last lick less than sixty days before the Armistice.

Although I would have informed Alexander of the Suiho bombing as a matter of courtesy, the authorization did not come from Washington until after he had gone. When Alexander was in Tokyo I did not know Washington was going to give me authority to bomb Suiho.

I felt it necessary to issue a statement to the press in which I said:

I note with astonishment the questions raised with regard to the bombing of the Suiho hydro-electric plant. Lest there be any misunderstanding, let me make it clear that this target and any other remunerative targets in North Korea are subject to attack by United Nations forces while hostilities continue and while the enemy continues his ground attacks against our lines.

The Suiho hydro-electric plant produces electric power which, transmitted to Manchuria, is used in war industries—industries whose end products are used against the men of our own forces who are fighting the battle of the free world against communist aggression.

As a commander, I would be remiss in my duty if I did not employ all means at my disposal to save lives and minimize casualties among the men serving under me. Until a just and honorable armistice definitely is assured, therefore, I will continue to authorize attacks on enemy targets in North Korea, the destruction of which will save the lives of our men and reduce the power of a vicious enemy to continue his treacherous aggression.

I am confident that the people of the free world would not have me do otherwise.

Even more provocative than bombing dams and power stations was my recommendation to Washington that two of Generalissimo Chiang Kai-shek's Nationalist Chinese divisions be made available to me in Korea. Admittedly this was political dynamite, but it had, in my view, solid advantages.

First, the United Nations would be tapping a manpower pool of close to half a million anti-Communist fighting men who were not getting any younger.

Second, by rotating Chiang's divisions two at a time on the Korean front, using the same equipment to save transport, we could give fresh battle experience under favorable conditions to men who had tasted defeat in 1948 and 1949. This would heighten their potential threat to the Chinese Communists in the south when they had finished their Korean tour of duty.

Third, although I had every confidence these divisions would give an excellent account of themselves, if they were going to fall apart fighting their old enemies, Korea was the best place to find that out.

If they were to fall apart it was better that it happen in Korea where we could handle it than in some future battle in which the Chinese Nationalists had to face the Communists on their own on the Chinese mainland or on Chiang's bastion of Formosa. It would help in our future planning to know just how good the Nationalists were in combat.

Fourth, the appearance of Chinese Nationalists on the front would give us and the world an opportunity to see who would defect to whom. My feeling was that it would give the Chinese Communists an opportunity to desert to the Nationalists. I had some solid evidence for this feeling. Of the twenty thousand Chinese Communist soldiers we had captured in Korea, fifteen thousand said they would rather die than return to communism.

When I visited Formosa ten months later, Chiang offered me three divisions, plus supporting air. But I never received authority from Washington on the proposal to use them.

In June I also sent the Pentagon the first of a series of recommendations to boost the size of the South Korean ground forces. These recommendations consisted of one of my own and one from General Van Fleet, which I strongly endorsed. As UN Ground Forces Commander, Van felt keenly the pinch of our chronic manpower shortage. By hoarding equipment and supplies, he had actually trained more ROK units than had been authorized by Washington, but official approval for their support was necessary before they could be used at the front.

Part of the Washington hesitance was due to economic problems in South Korea and another part was due to the difficulty of providing equipment from the United States. Inflation was a constant danger. We needed some resemblance of economic order in our rear in order best to prosecute the war. It was argued by some in Washington that there was a ceiling to the number of young Koreans who could be put in uniform. They explained that to increase the size of the Army would mean many young Koreans would be removed from productive work on farms, in factories and in the small shop and home industries that turned out much of Korea's consumer goods. Such production, they said, was essential to reduce inflation by sopping up Korean purchasing power. They feared the military gain achieved by increasing the ROK Army forces would be more than offset by the economic loss to South Korea and that the net result would be a loss for the UN war effort.

This was not the case. Before I ever sent the recommendation to build up the ROK Army I directed that a careful manpower study be made in Korea to determine just how much of an army the country could support. We found the Koreans could support, on an all-out war basis, an army of approximately twenty divisions in the field and still maintain their industrial and agricultural production at high enough levels to insure against inflation.

A more legitimate obstacle to the creation of additional ROK divisions was the equipment shortage in the United States. With our country providing arms to nations all over the world under MSA agreements, our equipment had to be allocated carefully.

President Syngman Rhee of Korea believed his country could support a larger army under the conditions of the war. He made that clear when he objected to proposals to move Chiang Kai-shek's troops into the Korean fighting. Rhee objected on two counts. First, he said, he did not want Korea turned into a battlefield of the Chinese Civil War. Secondly, he said, if the United States had enough equipment for two Chinese divisions to fight in Korea, why not give him the equipment so he could organize two more ROK divisions?

As a matter of record, the first authorization to expand ROK ground forces (by about 70 per cent) came on October 31, two days after the press published a letter by Van Fleet expressing pessimism and exasperation over the delay. The size of the ROK Army immediately became a presidential campaign issue.

I don't think any competent American military man seriously believed that ROK ground forces ever would have been able to take over the entire front against the Chinese and North Koreans. Brave as they are, the ROKs lack trained senior officers, numbers and logistical support units. But I do believe Washington dragged its feet in getting more of them in the field.

Lacking such transfusions of manpower, I confined our aggressive tactics to the air war and the Panmunjom conference table.

Throughout the summer of 1952 armistice teams met in executive sessions without budging from their positions. Major General William K. Harrison, my senior delegate, frequently called short recesses and finally, in September, we got around to doing what we had wanted to do in May.

After summing up our position and offering four alternate ways of disposing of prisoners unwilling to be repatriated through the offices of neutral nations, Harrison gave the Reds ten days to accept. When they didn't, he recessed the meetings indefinitely on October 8, with the announcement that the UN truce team would not come back to Panmunjom unless the Communists agreed to one of our solutions or offered an acceptable written counterproposal.

This action put an official stamp on what everyone had known for months—that the truce was stalled, perhaps indefinitely.

It also raised a morale problem among our troops, who knew they were not going anywhere except home—if they lived. They had two things to look forward to: a five-day leave in Japan for R&R (rest and recreation) and the "Big R"—rotation to the States after ten or twelve months on the line, or longer in rear areas. From September 1950 to the truce, 700,000 men were airlifted to and from Japan on R&R. A total of 565,000 men were rotated through Korea in three years.

When a man's rotation time drew near, everybody felt a responsibility to see that he made it. I like the story about Corporal Charles H. Gordon, of Liberty, Mississippi, a squad leader on a night patrol in enemy territory. The radio man scrambled up to him when the patrol was halfway to its objective. "I just talked to the CO," the radio man whispered. "He says for you to lay down right where you are and wait for the patrol to come back. That's orders. You're going home tomorrow." Every man, of course, hoped that he would get similar consideration when his time came.

On the front and behind the front, troops had been so long in fixed positions that they came to have a proprietary regard for their particular sector. Unit pride manifested itself in a kind of billboard war. You crossed a bridge "by courtesy of B Company, 1st Battalion, 8th Engineers," who built it. You entered what remained of a Korean town by "courtesy of the 9th Infantry Regiment," which held it. On the road to Panmunjom you passed a sentry box surrounded by sandbags and barbed wire and decorated with a huge, well-painted black and white sign that said, "You are now passing the main line of resistance."

The ultimate in pride of ownership was displayed on the inside of a latrine, notifying users they were afforded this privilege by "courtesy of Machine Gun Platoon, Co. M, 14th Inf."

The 24th Division, the first into Korea in 1950, considered building a sign to end all signs. It was to be erected at the port of Pusan, announcing to all new units and replacements: "You are entering Korea through the courtesy of the 24th U.S. Infantry Division." The project was dropped, however.

In a much grimmer vein was the sign, in the Marine sector, over a battered helmet full of holes and mounted on a cross: "Here lies the body of Corporal Joe Blow. He walked on the skyline. Hava no."

The 25th Infantry Division was strong on these educational signs. On a main supply line across the Imjin River the 25th erected a large billboard, tacked a torn bulletproof vest to it and painted the sign: "This vest saved a man's life. Wear yours."

Van Fleet and his subordinate commanders chafed under the conditions of this defensive war, as did I, and he occasionally submitted plans for limited offensives in narrow sectors. Except in rare instances I rejected them. There was no point in losing men if we weren't going the whole hog. One exception was the Sniper's Ridge-Triangle Hill operation that began on October 14, 1952, just six days after Harrison had recessed the armistice talks for what proved to be the whole winter.

As originally conceived, two battalions—one from the U.S. 7th Division and one from the ROK 2nd Division—were to seize two separate but well-defended terrain objectives about a mile and a quarter apart. These objectives, Triangle Hill on the left and Sniper's Ridge on the right, gave the enemy excellent observation to our rear in the Kumhwa Valley and permitted him to pepper our main supply route with artillery, with resultant UN casualties.

Backing up our infantry were sixteen battalions of artillery—approximately 280 guns ranging from 105's to 8-inchers. Several hundred fighter bomber sorties were allocated to insure maximum close support. The field commanders concerned estimated the operation would take five days and cost us approximately two hundred casualties.

On the jump-off day the infantry committed was doubled to four battalions—two on each objective—for a total of approximately four thousand men.

What ensued was the stiffest UN-initiated fight since Heartbreak Ridge the preceding year. The Chinese were dug in deep, had as much if not more artillery than we did, and fought stubbornly and well. The enemy had the advantage of perfect observation from 3,500-foot Papa-san, a dominating mountain two and a half miles to the rear.

What began as a limited objective attack developed into a grim, face-saving slugging match with each side upping the ante when the other gained a temporary advantage. Heavy fighting raged for fourteen days and spasmodically thereafter for another month. We won Jane Russell Hill, one corner of Triangle and about half of Sniper's Ridge. We suffered more than eight thousand casualties, mostly ROKs, a loss out of all proportion to our gains. The enemy lost at least half again as many men, but I considered the operation unsuccessful.

The authority I had to mount limited objective attacks was a constant temptation, but I couldn't see the wisdom of paying lives for pieces of ground in Korea unless we were going all out to win the war. Just as in Italy, where we faced the same kind of determined enemy and mountainous terrain, there always was the lure of the next highest hill just ahead of you. The enemy had it for observation which permited him to hurt your troops. You wanted it so you could look down his throat. But you never really did, for always there was just one more hill, a little higher, up ahead of you. Each hill soaked up doughboys, cost lives.

And in Korea the enemy could and would mass several times as many men as we could put into a single battle. If necessary, he would be willing to lose his men in order to give us a local black eye and thus increase the resentment and frustration that the people of the free world felt about this war. Always the enemy banked on the conviction that the resentment of the free world toward the Korean War would more likely result in further concessions than in an all-out fight. Twice he had seen a UN commander under fire from influential UN quarters. The first time was when MacArthur crossed the 38th Parallel. The second was when I bombed Suiho. These outbursts from our allies must have strengthened the Communist feeling of security against an all-out UN effort to win the war.

The Communist couldn't be completely certain, of course, and he did expend a lot of effort, almost frantically, to prepare for a possible major UN offensive inside Korea. But in the enemy negotiations at Panmunjom and propaganda from Peiping and Pyongyang radios there never was any hint that the Communists feared provoking us, as the UN feared provoking them.

Under the circumstances, with the Communists ever willing to expend any number of men to try to win a local battle for a single hill or other terrain feature, I was in complete agreement with Matt Ridgway's order which prevented Van Fleet from making any attacks involving more than a battalion, approximately one thousand men, without first obtaining the approval of the UN Commander in Chief.

I was in favor, however, after carefully studying the situation and discussing it with all my senior commanders, who concurred, of an all-out offensive to win the war, providing Washington could furnish me both the authority and the additional infantry divisions and air and naval support required.

I decided to be prepared in case our government decided to go for victory in Korea.

I set up a joint planning group from the three services to develop carefully the broad outline of plans for a military victory. This planning was done secretly and discussed with my top commanders on a "need to know" basis. That meant the project was so top secret that nobody was told anything about it except those officers who needed to know. There were very few.

Therefore I discussed the plan first with my Air Force Commander, General O. P. Weyland, and Vice-Admiral Robert Briscoe, Commander in Chief Navy, Far East. From there the work was expanded by the formation of an ultrasecret planning group comprising men of each of the three services. The entire work was confined to my headquarters in Tokyo.

One purpose of the planning was to determine the additional strength we needed from the Army, Navy and Air Force to enable us to launch an all-out offensive to win the war.

The whole concept of the plan was an offensive in which we removed the self-imposed ground rule that denied us the right to bomb targets beyond the Yalu. We could not hope to succeed in such an undertaking if we permitted the enemy a free home base from which to mount air attacks against us. Control of the skies begins with the destruction of enemy air bases. I wouldn't advocate an offensive nor care to be the commander in chief of one that did not remove the self-imposed tactical restriction which prevented us from giving full support to our ground forces hurling the full weight of American bombers on the enemy's home targets.

Shortly after our planning had started, I went to Korea and discussed it with Van Fleet, who heartily endorsed an all-out offensive.

The plans were developed carefully so that I could inform the Joint Chiefs of my requirements if the decision to win the war were made. In final form, the plans were sent in to the Joint Chiefs.

Every commander I conferred with in the Far East, whether Army, Navy or Air Force, heartily endorsed this course of action and expressed hope that our government would approve the plans, give us what we needed and let us go after the Communist enemy in Korea.

For my part, I shared the hope. But apart from the hope, I also felt strongly that any commander would be remiss if he failed to have a detailed plan for any eventuality. And even though I realized Washington might not adopt the course of action that would put it into operation, I knew we had to be ready with the plan if the turn of events called for a more vigorous prosecution of the war.

This was the first time that we had been pitted against the unscrupulous Communist foe in a shooting war anywhere in the world. In my mind it was essential for the security of our nation and the free world that we defeat him decisively in this first test of arms.

I knew that victory would entail heavy losses, but I also was convinced, and still am, that the losses we suffered gaining victory in Korea would be far less than losses we would have to take eventually if we failed to win militarily in Korea and waited until the Communists were ready to fight on their own terms.

Even without the attack, in my opinion we could have gained merely by massing greater strength in the Far East, and letting the enemy know it. The threat of an all-out assault and of air attacks against the hitherto proctected sanctuary in Manchuria in themselves probably would have produced a more favorable, and more rapid, armistice.

In my opinion this would not have dragged the Russians into the war or started World War III. They will go to war only at places and on a time schedule of their own choosing.

7

The Face of the Enemy

The failure of the free world to win victory in Korea strengthened the Communist enemy by giving him increased confidence in his second-team armies and at the same time casting doubts in the minds of the smaller and weaker non-Communist nations about the ability and determination of the free world to protect them against Red aggression.

The Japanese, now dependent upon the United States for protection against Russian or Communist overt aggression, took a hard-headed view of our record in Korea. There is no doubt in my mind that the Japanese fear and hate the Russians more than any nation on earth and that they hope they can afford to remain on our side in the global struggle between freedom and totalitarianism.

But some of the best minds in Japan made a most careful evaluation of our actions and accomplishments in Korea, and found us wanting. They translated our fight in Korea into terms of a hypothetical Russian invasion of Japan. In this hypothetical war the Japanese compared their northernmost shore, at the top of Hokkaido, to the 38th Parallel in Korea. Then they pointed out that in Korea we merely held the line at the 38th Parallel, or thereabouts. The end result, they said, was that war destroyed much of South Korea physically and spiritually and that at the conclusion of the fighting little had been accomplished positively to safeguard South Korea in the military or political sense.

The Japanese pointed out that the Communist armies still threatened South Korea, from the same lines they used as the jump-off platform in June of 1950. They were concerned because we had failed to eliminate that threat despite all the sacrifice made by America, the United Nations and South Korea.

To these Japanese, whose job it was to think in terms of security for Japan, our record in Korea was not reassuring. If Japan had to fight, these Japanese wanted something more than a purely defensive war. They wanted the positive objective of security for their country as the goal of any war they fought. If war had to come to their homes they wanted it fought for something more than the Koreans got from their war.

This basic yearning for security from the Communist threat was a major reason for the popularity of President Syngman Rhee among non-Communist Asians everywhere. Also impressive to the Asian was Rhee's courageous stand against the Communists and the fact that Rhee stood up against the United Nations and the United States in his struggle for policies he believed would assure security for his country. He symbolized the deep-seated desire for security of every non-Communist Asian. He was well aware of that, of course.

Militarily the warning that the Korean War gave to the free world was much more clear and understandable. It was a warning written in the blood of the fighting men of the free nations.

It was the warning that the Russian system had devised a way of harnessing the surging manpower of Asia into effective fighting forces.

The great mass of Chinese, one fifth of the people of the earth, had been whipped into shape almost overnight, in the historic sense, to fight a modern war. They were still well behind us in technical skills, individual firepower and individual know-how, but they made up for these disadvantages by sheer numbers of men. And they were improving all the time right up to the end of the fighting in Korea. What they hadn't known at the beginning of the war they were learning from us in combat.

Communist leadership in Korea was a skillful blend of military and political sagacity. It was able not only to maintain what had been considered "a peasant army of unorganized mass" in the field against a modern military power, but it also was able to forge a trained, equipped and cohesive fighting machine in the face of reversal and retreat.

There was a complete lack of morality and an utter ruthlessness of method in the North Korean military command, qualities that were assets to the Communists in the kind of war they chose to wage, a war in which they used the "big lie" to confuse their enemies and in part, at least, take the sting out of world condemnation of their methods. This technique had been tried before, but never so successfully. For one thing, decades of Communist proselyting in every country in the world had prepared many people in all nations to either accept the big lie or to be confused and hesitant because of it.

The Soviet influence on the Korean operation was made apparent almost as soon as the Communists struck across the 38th Parallel to begin the war. The well-co-ordinated tank-infantry-artillery teams of North Koreans were patterned after the Soviet military practice.

And clearest evidence of all, of course, was the fact that initially the North Korean Communist Army was equipped with tanks and weapons and warplanes of Russian make. We were facing the Russian burp gun, the Russian T/34 light tank, the Russian Yak propellor-driven fighter plane the day the war started.

This North Korean Army was destroyed by our superior firepower and techniques. It never recovered from the rout that followed our landing at Inchon in September of 1950. After that we were at war with the Chinese.

The initial success of the North Koreans, however, can be attributed to the able leadership of Marshal Kim Il Sung as well as to Soviet training and supply. Marshal Kim, born Kim Sung Chu, served under the legendary Kim Il Sung in the guerrilla war that Koreans waged against the Japanese for years before the Japanese were defeated in World War II. The younger Kim had a good record as a guerrilla leader and later took the name of his commander. It was good politics, for the name Kim Il Sung was revered by every Korean and symbolized the best in Korean patriotic action. These anti-Japanese guerrillas were the finest expression of Korean resentment to the forty-year rule of the Japanese on the peninsula. The Japanese admitted officially that in a single year in the 'thirties these Korean guerrillas, based in the mountains of Manchuria, averaged several forays a day across the Yalu to strike at Japanese troops. Some of the forays were made by a handful of men but others were big operations involving up to two thousand guerrillas.

Trained in this hard school, Kim Sung Chu became a clever fighting man and an effective leader. He and many of his fellows in the guerrilla ranks finally were driven out of Manchuria by the Japanese. They took refuge in Soviet Siberia. There Kim rose rapidly. He had been a Communist Party member since 1929 and the Russians had their eye on him. He became an officer in the Soviet Red Army and served with distinction as a captain in the battle at Stalingrad.

In 1945 he was one of the key men shipped back to North Korea by the Russians to solidify Communist power there and make North Korea a satellite state. Very early, before the end of 1945, he became head of the Communist Party in Korea and began the task of converting the civilian masses to Marxian doctrine. His power and prestige climbed until he was made Commander in Chief of the North Korean military forces and Premier of the North Korean state, the People's Republic of Korea.

Although lacking in formal education, Marshal Kim demonstrated early those qualities of leadership and ruthlessness the Russians look for in men they want to take foremost roles in their conspiracy for world domination. And Kim also had the necessary qualification of being amenable to Russian direction.

Hand in glove with Marshal Kim was one of his oldest and closest friends, Lieutenant General Nam Il, the man who negotiated the Armistice at Panmunjom and at the same time planned and directed the sixth column organization of Communists in our PW camps. As Chief of Staff of the North Korean Army, General Nam not only trained the North Korean troops to fight but breathed communism into their spirit. Nam is considered the most completely Russianized of all North Korean Communist leaders. Most of his life he was an exile from his native Korea. And in contrast to Marshal Kim, General Nam is well educated and is fluent in English, Russian and Chinese as well as the Korean language. Nam, like his friend Marshal Kim, returned to Korea from exile in 1945 as a captain in the Soviet Army.

Nam was entrusted with the most important kind of jobs in North Korea. He was Vice-Minister of Education before the war, a post which carried with it the control of all military education. He was Chief of Staff of the Army, chairman of the Communist armistice negotiating team and, after the Armistice, was made Foreign Minister of North Korea.

The Chinese counterparts of Kim and Nam in Korea were equally well prepared for their roles in the Communist world conspiracy. The Chinese Communist Command at the outset was faced with major challenges in Korea. The Chinese Communist Army that made the initial intervention in Korea was a composite force consisting of sizeable formations from each of the major field armies in China. Its combat effectiveness was limited to the tactic of the "human sea" because all it had initially was overwhelming superiority in numbers of men. Troop quality was poor and the Chinese were weak in artillery and air support and in supply, maintenance and repair services.

General Peng Teh-huai brought order out of this comparative chaos. He was a real old-timer in the service of the Communists, and he served them well in Korea. Peng joined the Chinese Nationalist Army at the age of twelve. He was graduated from a Chinese military academy and rose to the rank of regimental commander in Chiang Kai-shek's army. After Chiang split with the Communists, Peng joined the Communist Party in 1928 and became Commander of the Fifth Red Army.

He had signal success in operations against the Nationalists in the Civil War and won successive promotions until, at the time he moved into Korea, he was Vice-Chairman of the People's Revolutionary Military Council, the highest military planning body in China.

Peng is an expert tactician. Very early in Korea he recognized that reorganization and realignment of the structure of his field force was necessary if it was to exist in Korea against first-class troops with superior firepower and air support. Therefore he undertook the monumental task of revamping the Chinese Communist armies organizationally in the field, or shuffling personnel to get the most effective leaders, of improving the system of supply and of correcting tactical doctrine which had failed in the first seven months of the Chinese campaign in Korea.

As Commander in Chief, United Nations Forces, I had to recognize Peng Teh-huai as a foe of high merit. We were not in the field against a pushover.

Beneath this top-level command the Communists drew leaders from both China and Korea. Many of their most effective commanders were Chinese or Koreans who held Soviet citizenship. The military background of most of these Chinese and Koreans was based on guerrilla fighting against the Japanese and the Chinese Nationalists. In addition there was the common background of indoctrination in Communist ideology and complete loyalty to the Communist Party and the international conspiracy for world domination.

The political officer system patterned exactly along Russian lines to guide troops at all levels was an effective means of making the political ideology a motivating force in military operations.

Orders given to the leaders of the Communist armies in Korea and passed down to subordinate commanders never were questioned. They were fulfilled to the letter without regard to their meaning in terms of local victory or defeat. This cohesion of the troops was achieved through political indoctrination and control, together with relatively good treatment of the men, by Oriental standards.

In the Chinese armies the counterpart of Nam Il was General Teng Hua, a deputy commander to General Peng Teh-huai and chief of the Chinese delegation to the armistice talks at Panmunjom for some time. Political indoctrination of the Chinese troops was Teng's responsibility. Teng had a long career of service as a political officer and as a combat commander of Chinese Communist forces in the Chinese Civil War before he was assigned to Korea. Immediately before moving to Korea, General Teng had commanded the successful invasion of Hainan Island against the Chinese Nationalists in the south. He was ranked among the best of the Communist propagandists and was outstanding in the political field.

At the corps and division level the Chinese and North Korean commanders in the main polished up their military proficiency after they arrived in Korea, after they got into battle.

They were selected originally for their unquestioned loyalty to the Communist cause first, and for their military knowledge and ability second. They rose to positions of command in Korea as they demonstrated qualities of leadership in combat. Unlike our system of training and promotion, the Communist armies require strict adherence to political doctrine as a qualification for command.

This system had both advantages and disadvantages for the Communists in a country like China, which historically always had difficulty welding together an army evidencing patriotism on a national scale. The role of the political officer was all-important because through this system the Communists were able to control the minds of their troops sufficiently to hold them together as a fighting force.

At the same time, however, the system resulted in a weakness in military leadership at lower levels and forced the Chinese to sacrifice flexibility in their operations. Individual initiative during action was rare in the Chinese army. Communist operations were almost always planned and rehearsed well in advance so that each subordinate commander could do his job by the book. This gave us an advantage while we were fighting a war of movement, for our subordinate commanders are trained to deviate from plan when necessary during an action in order to take advantage of enemy weakness or to counteract unexpected enemy strength.

Once the war settled down to old-fashioned trench warfare of World War I style, however, the inflexibility of command was not so damaging to the Communists, for they were able to take the time to prepare for each operation. After the war of movement was over in Korea the Communists frequently rehearsed operations of regimental strength or larger for six weeks or more before they went into action. The Communist planners selected terrain carefully for the rehearsals so that the maneuvers would be held under conditions as similar as possible to the real target area.

This, then, was the picture of the Communist High Command that was pitted against us in Korea. At the top level were men who were solid both in their devotion to the Communist cause and in their ability to train and command large armies in a large-scale war. It was no mean task to command an army of 1,200,000 Chinese in Korea, as Peng Teh-huai did. And he kept them fed, clothed and armed despite our complete control of the air over Korea and the seas around it. At the next level were men devoted to the Communist cause and making swift progress in their efforts to learn military science under combat conditions. At the bottom were the Chinese foot soldiers, welded into an effective striking force by a combination of political teaching and threat. The importance of the chain of political officers that runs through any Communist army cannot be overestimated.

When I arrived in the Far East to take over the United Nations Command I found that I had a top-notch team which more than matched this Communist High Command.

General James A. Van Fleet, a friend of long standing, was Commanding General, Eighth Army, which meant he was commanding general of all United Nations and ROK ground forces in Korea. Van was in the Class of 1915 at West Point, two classes ahead of mine, and we had known each other through our careers in the Army. I had watched Van's rapid rise in World War II, in which he started as a regimental commander and through brilliant and courageous leadership in the field won successive and rapid promotions to corps commander by the war's end. He was a typical soldier's man who knew the problems of his men, and met them. After the war he was selected to help the Greeks fight their Communist guerrillas and there he did a splendid job. After Greece Van returned home and commanded the Second Army while I was Chief of Army Field Forces. It was at this time that he was tabbed to succeed Matt Ridgway as Eighth Army Commanding General if any command change had to be made. It is Army practice always to have a replacement ready for any man with a high command post so that if the fortunes of war necessitate a replacement it can be made quickly.

Thus, when Ridgway moved up from Eighth Army to take over the United Nations Command, Van Fleet was on his way to Korea without delay.

I was happy to know as I arrived in the Far East that my ground commander was an old friend with whom I was glad to work and one who had demonstrated in combat at Normandy, in Greece and in Korea that he was a splendid battlefield commander. I knew of the fine fighting spirit he had put into the Eighth Army. And I knew that he knew I recognized that my most important job as United Nations Commander was to support him, to give him the backing and physical facilities he needed to do his task. That is exactly what I did.

General O. P. Weyland as Commanding General, Far East Air Forces, was my air commander. He already had achieved so much success in the Korean War that just about the time I arrived he was promoted to four-star rank. I had known Weyland slightly in Europe and knew that he had won the reputation of a man who would co-operate well and effectively while he was air support commander with Georgie Patton's Third Army in France.

My contact with Weyland had been in training matters while I was Chief of Army Field Forces. He then was Deputy Commanding General, Tactical Air Command, and one of his principal jobs was to give close air support to Army troops.

In the Far East I soon learned that Weyland was a "can do" operator, highly efficient and willing to play on the team. This was important to me as UN Commander for at that time a burning issue in Washington was the control and adequacy of close air support for the infantryman. As Commanding General of the Fifth Army and 15th Army Group in Italy and later with the Army Field Forces at home, I always had felt that a ground army, to be successful, must be adequately supported by aviation which was trained to work on this mission. I always had felt that the ground forces should have the right to a voice in determining the types of aircraft that would be developed for close support missions.

I hadn't come out to the Far East to aggravate this basic difference of opinion between the Air Force and the Army. It was my job to work around the fringes of this unsolved problem. With a specific job to do, I had to maintain an air-ground team working as efficiently as possible. O. P. Weyland supported me completely in this effort, as did Lieutenant General Glenn Barcus, who commanded the 5th Air Force in Korea when I arrived, and his successor, Lieutenant General Samuel Anderson.

During the entire time I was in command in the Far East the front-line infantry units and tactical air support units worked closely together in Korea, and understood and respected each other's problems. When the foot soldier needed close air support, he got it.

Another man willing to co-operate for the good of the team was Vice-Admiral Bob Briscoe, affable, capable and more intent on working for the good of the three-service combined effort than in bothering about the differences of opinion that had prevailed in Washington in the past with regard to carrier-based versus land-based aviation. Briscoe, as Commander in Chief, US Navy, Far East, had the over-all responsibility for directing our complicated naval support of the ground war in Korea. His forces lived up to the finest traditions of the Navy, gave us every kind of support we asked for and maintained the undisputed control of the seas so vital to our ground effort on the Korean peninsula.

He had a fine assistant in Vice-Admiral Jocko Clarke, who commanded the U.S. Seventh Fleet. This fleet had two task forces working all the time, one off each coast of Korea, to keep the sea lanes clear, to blockade the enemy ports and coastlines, and to bombard with surface and air assaults anything that moved on either enemy coastline. The Seventh Fleet did a magnificent job for us.

The Navy fighter airplanes operating from Clarke's carriers gave wonderful support to our front-line units with tree-top level attacks in co-ordination with Air Force support missions. I always felt that if I had told Jocko Clarke to take his flagship, the Mighty *Mo*, up the Yalu River his reply would have been, "Aye, aye, sir."

At headquarters in Tokyo I had a tower of strength in Lieutenant General Doyle Hickey, Chief of Staff successively for MacArthur, Ridgway and me. Doyle had a world of background information on the problems and issues in both Korea and Japan and I leaned heavily upon him, particularly in the early days when I was familiarizing myself with the detailed problems involved in my job.

All told this was a fine team. I could not have asked for a better one. I have always found that the farther you get from Washington, the closer the harmony and understanding between the three services. It was that way in Japan and Korea.

I would be remiss if I failed to go into the political side of the picture, for in the peculiar kind of a war we were fighting in the Far East there were more political than military ramifications. The enemy high command was filled with generals of great political experience, such as Kim Il Sung, Peng Teh-huai, Nam Il and Teng Hua. Every military decision had its political implications. So you can imagine my satisfaction to find myself teamed once more with my old friend Bob Murphy.

I first saw Bob in 1942 when my government sent him from North Africa to London to report to General Eisenhower and brief us on the military and political situation on the Dark Continent. At that time Murphy was Consul General in Algiers. His mission to London was top secret, so he posed as a Lieutenant Colonel McGowan. Ike and I went out to a house secretly to meet this fellow. We hid smiles when we were introduced for Bob was wearing a military uniform for the first time in his life and this was more than evident. He was most uneasy in the clothes that were so strange to him.

For several days Bob provided us with valuable information on the situation in North Africa, and then he went back to his post. The next time I saw him was when I came ashore in North Africa in 1942 in the middle of the night in a rubber boat from a submarine. I was on a secret mission to negotiate and confer with French generals and admirals prior to our North African invasion.

Bob was with me all through the North African and Italian campaigns and after the war was political advisor to Ike in Berlin while I was in Austria. We each had the rank of Deputy Secretary of State at the London and Moscow meetings of the Council of Foreign Ministers in 1947. Once again in 1952 we were working together, this time in the Far East. We arrived within a few days of each other for our new jobs so we were to be initiated into the intricacies of the Far Eastern issues together.

I cannot write about Bob Murphy without praising him. His country's interests are always first in his mind. He is an honest, two-fisted, square-shooting American who has a keen grasp of military as well as political problems. He learned to appreciate the military problems during his long association with soldiers during World War II.

Bob and I saw eye to eye on the issues in Korea and Japan. We were in complete agreement that the best way to do business with the Communists was with a big club. I leaned heavily on him for guidance in all political problems that arose during my tour in the Far East.

I would like to note further that this intimate, smooth-working relationship Bob Murphy and I had from North Africa to Korea demonstrates what I believe is the ever-growing necessity to correlate military and political thinking and action.

It is no secret that there has been friction between the military and diplomatic arms of our government overseas from time to time. There is an elementary conflict in viewpoint between military and diplomatic men because of the differences in their training and the nature of the problems they meet during their careers. Only through close association, such as I had with Bob Murphy, can a team be created to weld the two viewpoints into a single course of action in the interests of America.

I was and am convinced that steps can be taken by our government to strengthen the ties between the military and diplomatic branches and thus strengthen the unity of the front America presents to the world in this era of peril. An important step in this direction was taken when the National War College instituted the policy of taking in promising young State Department officials along with Army, Navy and Air Force officers. These men, tabbed to rise to the top as diplomats or military officers, can thus get to know each other during their formative years. The firm friendships formed during this period could be noted by the separate services and the State Department, so that during ensuing years, when the men who were together in the National War College rise in rank and responsibility, they can be assigned to jobs which would enable them to maintain their association and develop their friendship in a kind of high level buddy system. In the Army we try to team friends because we have learned men work and fight better when they are alongside their friends. Both the men and our country would benefit once the men rose to position of high responsibility.

The Communists had a built-in military-political co-ordination in their system. The political faction was dominant but the Communists made certain that neither the military nor the political sides were slighted by the simple device of making politicians of their generals and generals of their politicians. Kim Il Sung had to build an army and convert a nation to communism at the same time. Nam Il was chief of staff of an army and had to teach it Communist dogma at the same time.

Such concentration of power is anathema to us, who have developed a system to block any such regimentation of our people. But to meet the threat of the Communist worldwide conspiracy we must develop better co-ordination within our traditional pattern of freedom. We must minimize the small jealousies, the petty competition between branches of government for prestige or little privileges.

On a larger scale the Communists never missed a bet in their military-political co-ordination. In June of 1951, after the Eighth Army had smashed the last of the great Chinese offensives of the war, Jacob Malik of Russia made almost certain there would be no United Nations counteroffensive when he proposed armistice talks.

Eleven months later, when the Communists suffered a propaganda jolt by the revelation that ninety thousand captured soldiers and civilians had refused repatriation to Communist homelands, the Reds stalled politically at the Panmunjom truce talks and planned militarily for the prison camp coup at Koje.

The armistice talks themselves constituted the finest example of the Communist ability to co-ordinate military and political warfare.

In May of 1951 the second of the two great Chinese spring offensives was smashed. Twice in two months the Chinese had thrown their Sunday punch, and each time they had been beaten decisively. The second offensive was the last either side launched in a serious effort to win the war militarily.

Unable to win the war with his best effort, the Communist enemy took another tack. Malik, speaking on the radio from New York, "suggested" almost as an afterthought that the time might be ripe for talk of cease-fire. His afterthought was so phrased that the UN had to follow it up, ask questions. Ridgway asked the questions and Kim and Peng replied that they thought armistice talks should begin.

That ended the year of shooting war. What followed were two years of talking war. American casualties alone were thirty thousand men during each of the two years of the talking war, but they were casualties suffered in skirmishes and minor battles of a war nobody was trying to win.

There were ample signs that the UN had no intention of really trying to fight to military victory, but the Communists never could be completely certain. So they used their two-year respite to build defense lines that probably were as strong as any the world has known anywhere. I did not fight against the German West Wall and Siegfried Line on Europe in World War II, but General Maxwell D. Taylor, who did, said after he took over command of the Eighth Army that the defense belt the Chinese dug along the 155-mile front of Korea was more formidable than the German defenses.

The Communist side of the battle line was an underground defense works as much as twenty-five miles deep in some places. It stretched from one coast of Korea to the other and was so well entrenched that most of it was impervious to air and even artillery attack.

In essence the Communists had gone back to trench warfare—and glorified it. They had a set system of development which they used on every hill they captured from us. As soon as the hill was secured by Red ground forces the soldiers pulled out their shovels and dug a protective trench near the top of the hill facing us. This trench they later extended until it circled the hill. With the encircling trench completed, the Communists got to work on the key to their defenses—the tunnel. They dug the tunnel from the back, the protected, side of the hill towards the side that faced our lines. The whole hill itself was top cover for the tunnel, protection against air assault.

Gradually, inside each hill, the tunnel was expanded to provide a honeycomb network of passages and gun positions. The Red artillery pieces in these cave-tunnels were rolled into the mouth of the tunnel to fire and then pulled back out of harm's way.

There were underground hill fortresses of this pattern for every Communist unit on the front and in close reserve. Our air had taught them the folly of leaving troops in the open, and they had learned the lesson well.

This massive defense works was built largely during the first year of the armistice talks, during the respite that the Communists won by diplomatic maneuver.

At the same time the enemy had an overwhelming preoccupation with the defense of his coastline. He had tasted the whip of our amphibious techniques at Inchon and was afraid of it. He did everything he could, particularly on the beaches around Wonsan on the East Coast, to prepare for a possible new assault from the sea by our amphibious infantry units. And he knew that every one of our American divisions had been or could be trained easily to wage amphibious warfare.

Hundreds of thousands of North Koreans built and manned the beach defenses along every stretch of coastline that conceivably could be used for an amphibious invasion. Behind them were Chinese Communist forces in reserve positions from which they could move quickly to bolster the defenses at any beach under attack.

The defense system along the beaches, like the defense system at the front, was very deep and depended in large measure on underground installations for its effectiveness. But in addition to the underground works there were lines of open trenches spreading back from the beaches so that any troops attacking from the sea would be forced to attack one line of trenches after another once they attained their foothold on dry land. Barbed wire was strung along the water's edge. Minefields were plentiful. Large areas of rice paddy land were flooded to make them giant tank traps which would mire our equipment in mud. Preparations were made to flood other areas during an invasion so that flood waters themselves could be used as a defensive weapon.

My headquarters was well aware of this evidence of fear among the Communists, and I directed that everything possible be done to keep the fear of amphibious invasion alive among them. We gave the enemy no rest or any comfort in this aspect of psychological warfare. We worked hard on amphibious training exercises in Japan and Korea, and did little or nothing to hide this work from the enemy. I knew that their efficient spy system couldn't miss our large maneuvers.

In Korea the First Marine Division was in the line at the front most of the time but they maintained their skill in amphibious warfare by detaching units in turn for landing exercises on the coasts of Korea. The Communists had observation posts so they could see the work the Marines were doing. Our purpose was twofold. Basically it was to maintain the fine edge the Marines had achieved in amphibious techniques. But also the maneuvers served the purpose of keeping the enemy worried. The more he worried, the more troop strength and effort would have to be diverted to building defenses behind the lines.

My campaign to worry and harass the enemy with the threat of amphibious assault reached its climax late in October of 1952. The First Cavalry Division was in northern Japan with the XVI Corps on Japan defense duty. I decided to move part of the cavalry to Korea for duty in the Communications Zone. Troops were needed there and I didn't want to weaken the Eighth Army by transferring units out of the line.

I combined the routine movement of the cavalrymen with the twin objective of training men for amphibious assault and worrying the enemy. In Japan the cavalry units were put through intensive amphibious training, capped by a full-scale landing rehearsal. Then they were put aboard attack transports, battle loaded and ready to fight. In fact for security purposes when the troops went aboard the ships they thought they were on their way to a real landing.

As the amphibious assault fleet moved from Japan toward Wonsan our air and navy went into a regular preinvasion bombardment of the "target" beaches. The Air and Navy worked in the pattern that became well known to the intelligence services of every army in the world during World War II, in which we made so many amphibious landings in both Europe and the Pacific. The whole maneuver was realistic, right down to the last minute when some of the men of the First Cavalry Division left their transports in the open sea off Wonsan and climbed into tiny assault boats which circled in regular preattack formations.

The single deviation from the tactics of a real landing was that the transport area, where the big ships unloaded troops and cargo, was further from shore than it would have been in an actual attack. I didn't want the ships in range of enemy shore batteries during this feint and exercise.

Our intelligence reported that the enemy was in a tailspin on the beach near Wonsan. The movement of enemy units and equipment in last minute efforts to strengthen the defenses was terrific despite the continuing bombardment from our aircraft and surface naval vessels. That Wonsan demonstration alone was enough to prove that the enemy was genuinely afraid of our amphibious threat.

It also was enough to prove that any assault on that beach would have been most difficult. The Communists were organized right from the water line into positions deep in the coastal mountains. They had a great number of artillery positions in well-planned sites. The enemy had put guns in some of these positions and left others empty so that he could move guns quickly into places where they would do the most good.

Artillery was becoming an ever more important part of the enemy defenses. For a long time the enemy was deficient in artillery but suddenly, in the late fall of 1951, the front blossomed out with massive Communist artillery barrages. The British Commonwealth Division in the mountains of the western front ran into heavy Communist artillery in November of 1951 and a new factor was injected into the Korean War. The Communists used their artillery in the Russian way, the saturation tactic. And there were Russians with them. We knew that there at least were Russian advisors because in that first heavy bombardment of the British artillery firing instructions in the Russian language were intercepted by British radio operators and translated by Russian-speaking men in the British forces. In addition we had strong evidence to indicate that not only Russian advisors but entire Russian antiaircraft units were in the war against the United Nations in Korea.

As the war progressed both the artillery and antiaircraft of the Communists improved in volume and quantity. The antiaircraft units had radar-controlled aiming devices of high quality. These units of crack antiaircraft batteries kept growing in number right down to the time of the Armistice and covered an ever-increasing portion of North Korea.

Defensively the Communists were very strong during the last two years of the war, the "talking" years. Offensively they were not as strong. They couldn't sustain an attack for very long because of their difficulty with supply. The Communists had to run the gantlet of our air and sea assaults to move battle supplies down to the front-line troops. This worked a particular hardship when he tried to move heavy stuff, such as artillery, tanks and ammunition. Our air force was able to make it so difficult to move big shipments that the enemy never was able to stock up enough artillery ammunition to support a full offensive for more than a couple of weeks.

The enemy was willing to expend his manpower ruthlessly. He had plenty, and, in addition, the enemy command could take the cynical attitude that if the men didn't die on the field of battle many would starve or freeze to death back home in China.

At no time while I was in the Far East could I have launched successfully a large offensive.

The enemy was aware of this, although he did not know when or if a decision would be made to give me that capability, so that we could make a sudden and unexpected assault amphibiously with infantry divisions and air and naval units sent directly from America.

Therefore the enemy was able to plan his ground operations, along the front line, with relative certainty that our forces inside Korea were inadequate to mount a decisive offensive against him. No commander could ask for a more comforting assurance.

With this assurance the enemy was able at any time to mass enough men to dent our line wherever and whenever he desired. No defense line can be so strong that it cannot be dented by an enemy who is ready to expend the lives necessary to make the dent.

When the enemy made these pushes we rolled with the punch rather than stand our ground stubbornly and be overrun. Then, if the Communists had taken terrain features important to our defense line we had to counterattack to recapture them.

That is where we suffered our heaviest casualties. The enemy knew that he was able to provoke us into these local counterattacks whenever he wished. Therefore he was able at any time to spill our blood. On his exchange, the blood of Chinese and North Korean soldiers was a cheap commodity. The blood of United Nations soldiers was very dear to me. Throughout the period of the stalemated war the enemy had the advantage of the power to force us to trade lives that were dear to us for lives that were cheap to him.

Every time we attacked a hill the Communist reaction was violent. The enemy hurled overwhelming numbers of men at us, apparently heedless of how many he lost as long as he also killed UN and ROK troops.

With the forces we had at hand and with the ban on bombing the enemy's home bases, we could not have reached the Yalu through the Chinese defense system without sustaining totally unacceptable casualties. And as I have already pointed out, the enemy would have become stronger with every mile of our advance because he would have been that much closer to his base of supply and man-power—the sanctuary in Manchuria.

I didn't want to start something over there unless we were prepared to finish it.

We weren't, so I didn't. We let the enemy do the attacking and suffer the casualties.

8

The Armistice Talks Begin

The outlook for an armistice in Korea was bleak when I arrived in the Far East. Only nine days before my arrival the United Nations Command had made its "final" offer and the Communists rejected it.

One issue alone blocked an armistice, but it was a big issue of fundamental importance to both the UN and the Communists. Some ninety thousand enemy prisoners indicated they would never return to their Communist masters in war or peace. The Reds said that they must. The United States Government declared that they need not, that no prisoner would be forced against his will to return to communism. All other major disagreements had been ironed out in nine months of acrimonious negotiations.

More was at stake than the custody of ninety thousand human beings. In this or any future war the principle of granting a combatant permanent asylum in the free world would give millions in the robot armies and Russia and her satellites something to hope for besides death or a return to Communist slavery. The Reds recognized our stand for what it was—a bonus to defect—and fought it with propaganda and a shooting war.

We pointed out that by their own admission they had released fifty thousand South Korean prisoners "at the front," early in the war, which meant, of course, that these prisoners had been impressed into the North Korean Army in violation of every principle of the treatment of POWs in land warfare. And we embarrassed, but failed to sway, the Communist negotiators at Panmunjom by pointing out that toward the end of World War II Soviet Russia recognized the principle of voluntary repatriation by offering Axis PWs the choice of a new homeland.

Consistency in argument never was a characteristic of the Communist negotiator. Nam Il was no exception. We might be able to embarrass him occasionally, but we never could budge him by argument or logic.

The manner in which the armistice talks were conducted gave free rein to this Communist tactic of negotiation. There was no moderator to decide whether a point had been proven satisfactorily. There was no chairman to decide whether a speaker was in order. There were no rules to require either side to answer questions.

Under these conditions the Communists could, and did, ignore questions, make statements and later deny them. Once very early in the talks Nam Il sat silent for two hours and eleven minutes after he was asked a direct question by Admiral Joy. There was no one to call the meeting to order so the conference room was absolutely silent for 131 minutes. Joy would not give Nam the satisfaction of cracking first under this nerve-racking technique.

The Communists later worked variations of this theme, extending meetings through the lunch hour and late into the afternoon to try to wear down Allied patience through sheer physical fatigue and hunger. The UN negotiators quickly got the answer to that. They had sandwiches sent up to a tent adjoining the conference hut and one by one they would excuse themselves from the conference and walk out for a sandwich. The Communists sat right through and by day's end realized their plan had backfired.

On the issue of the prisoner exchange the Communists stuck to their guns for fourteen months. So did we, and the guns, not the arguments, bought the truce with our PW provisions. For the Communists finally bowed to our plan for prisoner exchange, which provided a way for an anti-Communist to win refuge in the free world, only because the military pressure on them was so great they had to yield.

Whether this moral victory—and it was a victory—was worth the fourteen extra months of stalemate and 130,000 UN and South Korean casualties, only future events can demonstrate.

Formally there were three issues blocking the Armistice when I arrived in the Far East, but two of them already had been settled for all practical purposes. Besides the prisoner exchange problem there was our opposition to the construction of airfields in North Korea during the Armistice and the enemy's demand that Soviet Russia be a member of the Neutral Nations Supervisory Commission which was to serve as policeman to insure compliance with armistice terms.

On April 28, 1952, the UN Command presented a package proposal which Admiral Joy told the Communists was our "final" offer. The proposal, presented in the form of a completed draft of an armistice agreement, provided assurance of political asylum for anti-Communists we held as POWs, but also offered to give the Communists the right to build airfields in North Korea during an armistice if the Reds would drop their demand to put Russia on the Neutral Nations Supervisory Commission. We knew we were offering something for nothing, as the issue of Russian membership on the commission was clearly a straw man, but Washington was willing to let them build the airfields.

The Communists rejected this final offer and on May 2 came back with a "firm and final" offer of their own which narrowed disagreement to the prisoner exchange issue. The Communist offer agreed to exclude Russia from the armistice policing organization in trade for the right to build airfields in North Korea during the Armistice. To some of us this right to build airfields appeared to be a clear violation of the agreement already made to forbid either side from increasing its military power in Korea during the Armistice, but for the sake of reaching a cease-fire the United States agreed to it. As a face-saver for us the agreement specified that the airfields were to be for civil air traffic only, not military.

The Communists held firm on their demand that all ninety thousand anti-Communists we held in prison camps be sent back to them, by force if necessary. The UN Command rejected the Red offer.

That was the situation I found when I arrived in Tokyo five days later. From my experience with the Communists in Europe I knew that it would be taken as an indication of weakness if we returned to Panmunjom day after day to sit and listen to their propaganda, their lies, their distortion of facts. Such submission to a daily fare of insult, arrogance and vituperation could only strengthen the Communists in their belief that we were so anxious for a cease-fire in Korea that eventually we would knuckle under and give them every prisoner they demanded, just as we had conceded on the airfield issue.

Return of all prisoners was an objective worth struggling for from the Communist viewpoint. Defensively, they had to try to prevent a show of anti-communism by ninety thousand people who had lived under the Reds and rejected them. Positively, we had made such a strong stand for freedom for the prisoners that if we were forced to back down at this late date the Reds would be able to make propaganda hay with a campaign to tell the people of the world that we did not have the backbone to stand up against the Communists long enough or strongly enough to beat them on a vital issue.

Our government, supported with varying degrees of enthusiasm by our UN allies, was determined that we would not yield on the prisoner issue and that those prisoners who wanted asylum could have it. But the instructions when I took over command were to send my representatives to the Panmunjom meeting any time the Communists wanted to talk. Remembering Europe, I had no liking for arrangements which forced us to be a party to Red propaganda maneuvers.

Therefore, on May 12, the day I took command, I strongly endorsed the recommendation of Admiral Joy that we unilaterally suspend further meetings until the Communists accepted the UN Command package proposal of April 28. The Joy recommendation was one of the first communications I sent to the Joint Chiefs of Staff on the armistice talks.

A few days later the Joint Chiefs transmitted a State-Defense view that the proposal was considered premature in view of the confused attitudes at home and among our Allies as a result of the Koje affair and the other troubles we had had with the prisoners. The Joint Chiefs instructed me to keep the meetings going and said that our efforts should be intensified by daily statements that stressed three main themes. These were:

1. Scrupulously fair UNC screening of POWs was tacitly approved by the Communists when they requested data on the number of prisoners who would be returned if anti-Communists were given asylum.

2. The UNC offer to permit the Reds to witness a new screening of the prisoners refuted the Communist charge that the UN was guilty of "forceful retention" of prisoners.

3. The Communists, by insisting on the use of force if necessary to repatriate unwilling POWs, sought to jeopardize the lives of anti-Communist prisoners.

Two days later I informed the Joint Chiefs of Staff that I would that day announce that Major General William K. Harrison would succeed Admiral Joy as our senior representative on the truce team. Joy, who had done an outstanding job against the terrible odds of Communist recalcitrance, long had been scheduled for transfer to Annapolis to become Superintendent of the Naval Academy. And Joy, quite correctly, felt there was little he could do after submitting the "final" UNC offer to the Communists on April 28.

For the rest of the month of May we carried out the instructions from Washington. Every day the Communists called us to Panmunjom and every day Harrison and the others on the truce team were obliged to sit and listen to a constant flood of abusive and irrelevant Communist propaganda.

I liked it less and less each day. Finally on May 31 I sent new recommendations to the Joint Chiefs, based on a thorough analysis of the negotiations. The gist of the new recommendations was:

1. We would continue to meet at Panmunjom, as infrequently as possible, until the screening process was completed and a new, firm figure of the number of prisoners who wanted to be repatriated could be given to the Reds. We were then in the process of screening thousands we had been unable to question while they were in compounds controlled by the Communist POWs.

2. When the new figures were ready, we would give them to the Reds at Panmunjom with a clear indication that if the Communists still refused to accept our proposal we would unilaterally recess negotiations until they did.

3. If the Communists failed to accept our plan within a week, the UN Command would recess the meetings unilaterally with the declaration that the Communists must either accept our proposal or break off negotiations.

4. If these moves failed to bring an armistice, the idea of a neutral nation commission to handle repatriation should be broached through circuitous channels so that if the Communists wanted to save face they could propose the idea as their own at Panmunjom. As a last resort, if the Communists could not be induced to submit such a proposal, the United Nations or some of the member nations should use diplomatic channels to make the proposal for a neutral nations agency to handle prisoners.

The Joint Chiefs informed me that my government did not accept this proposal, but neither did they reject it out of hand. And they did go part way toward accepting the plan to break off meetings for short periods. In a message on June 6 they told me again that it would be all right to recess the meetings for three or four days at a time if the Communists agreed. And in the same message they came a little closer to our way of thinking by suggesting that even if Communist agreement was lacking the UNC delegation occasionally could indicate without explanation that it would be unable to meet for two or three days. It had been fairly common practice through the negotiations for one side or the other to call such brief recesses, which usually indicated time was necessary to work on new proposals or new answers to old proposals.

I wasted no time in acting on this new authority. I passed the instructions on to General Harrison at his camp in Munsan immediately and the very next day he did what he and Joy before him had been yearning to do for months. At the end of the fruitless session at Panmunjom, after the Communists had completed their daily propaganda harangue, Nam Il went through his usual procedure by saying, "I move we adjourn until 11:00 A.M. tomorrow."

Always in the past, Harrison had been obliged to agree to this proposal, had been obliged to come back the next day to sit and listen to the Communist blather. As time went on, Harrison and the UNC looked weaker and weaker, for all Harrison could do was to repeat constantly our old position without offering anything new. Our "final" offer had been made over a month before.

What I wanted, and what Harrison and Joy wanted, was authority to look Nam Il in the eye and say, "We've listened to your false allegations repeatedly and until you have something constructive to offer I propose that we adjourn." Such a suggestion would be without teeth, of course, unless Harrison had the authority to back it up with a unilateral declaration that the talks were recessed.

Harrison still did not have that authority on June 7 but he did have authority to tell Nam Il, "We are not coming back tomorrow," and to add, "We are coming back on June 11."

The effect was startling. Nam Il, usually an unruffled, deadly calm operator, came very close to losing control. Harrison, obviously pleased, reported the scene to me in detail. Nam Il was so shocked and upset that he pleaded with Harrison to sit down and talk the thing over a little. Harrison said he never saw such a change in a man, a change wrought by a single, simple sentence. He was flabbergasted. Obviously his instructions were to keep the talks going so that he could put Communist propaganda on the record for the world press every day. The Communists at this stage were emphasizing the war of words and Panmunjom was the main battleground. And now Harrison had made it impossible for him to carry out his instructions to the letter. Harrison had taken away the propaganda platform, even though for only three short days.

But that was enough to throw Nam Il into a spin. The initiative had been taken away from him and the Communists. The Red plan was not working according to letter. He was so overwhelmed that he lost the face-saving, cold dignity which was his customary protective mask at the meetings.

He was overwhelmed because here was determined action, here was the kind of firm attitude which had worked over and over again with the Communists everywhere whenever we used it.

Harrison reported in formal language to me that the Communist reaction to this first UNC walkout at Panmunjom was one of "chagrin, alarm and annoyance."

I had another annoyance ready for the Communists at this time.

On June 5 I proposed to the Joint Chiefs that I be authorized to release 27,000 civilian internees who were opposed to repatriation.

These were civilians rounded up at various times during the first eighteen months of the war. They included many arrested in the very early days in the dragnet spread to catch the guerrillas who harassed our lines, hampered our train movements and took pot shots at our soldiers. In the frantic effort to clear our rear of this obstacle many non-Communists were interned along with the pro-Communists. They included refugees interned during the first eighteen months on suspicion. The UN Command had to be alert constantly to control dissident elements or spies in the rear.

On June 11 the Joint Chiefs transmitted an approval of the release in principle and four days later I was given authority to go ahead and release all 27,000 civilian internees who said they would resist repatriation to communism. Washington suggested that I accomplish the release with as little publicity as possible. This was hard to do. The South Koreans made it a holiday affair, while the enemy denounced it over their radios.

At long last we were more on the offensive in the armistice talks. Three and four day UNC walkouts became the rule. We dug into history to find arguments that might embarrass the Communist negotiators, and found a good one. On June 21 Harrison read the historical record of Soviet disposition of prisoners of war in the closing days of World War II. The Soviets had demanded the right of asylum for many captured Axis soldiers. Harrison declared this precedent by the leading Communist nation was full justification for the UNC principle of voluntary repatriation. After reading the record of the Soviet stand Harrison pressed the attack home with a series of searching and embarrassing questions. He reported to me that Nam Il was confused and disconcerted by this new line of attack and appeared to be at a loss for any pertinent reply.

But it was no debating society at Panmunjom. Nobody won points by a telling argument. We all recognized fully that the only way we would get an armistice was to fight for it with guns and planes and warships. And in the end we got the cease-fire only because the enemy had been hurt so badly on the field of battle.

The Communists did not want to give up the propaganda platform at Panmunjom unless they had to. There were too many things they could say and do there to help their cause everywhere.

Their propaganda tirades were of the vicious kind the world has come to expect from the Communist, tirades that ran roughshod over fact and logic.

From the Panmunjom propaganda platform Nam Il charged repeatedly that the United States of America goaded the South Koreans into starting the war in Korea. That was one of the basic big lies in the Communist repertoire. The story the Communist leaders told their people was that a mighty South Korean army, equipped with many terrible weapons by the Americans, stormed across the 38th Parallel in a treacherous surprise attack before dawn on June 25, 1950, but that despite the strength and surprise of the assault the valiant People's Army of North Korea halted the offensive before it had gone half a mile and hurled the South Koreans back along the whole line. Of such whole cloth are the legends of the Communist world made.

Vituperative lies and distortions flowed in great abundance from the nimble tongue of Nam Il who had the ability to voice the most blatant falsehoods while keeping a straight face. Among the propaganda charges he hurled across the conference table were the flat declarations that America had "press ganged" Great Britain, France and other nations into fighting against communism in Korea, and that the United States wanted all Korea as a colony from which to invade China and start World War III. The mere fact that America, Britain and France sent troops thousands of miles to fight in Korea, he said, proved that America and the United Nations were the aggressor.

Time and again Nam Il warned that the United Nations was taking dangerous steps toward World War III. These warnings, often timed immediately after some speech in the House of Commons in London, indicated there was a hope of driving a wedge between England and America.

The Koje incident gave Nam a great new field for propaganda. He charged the UN used force to screen the prisoners and made it impossible for them to exercise their right to return home. The United States, Nam said, prompted agents of Generalissimo Chiang Kai-shek and President Syngman Rhee to coerce prisoners into tattooing anti-Communist slogans on their bodies and signing anti-Communist petitions with their own blood. These agents, Nam Il charged, mauled and beat prisoners until they were unconscious and then dipped the prisoners' hands in their own blood and put their fingerprints on the antirepatriation petitions. The American objective was to retain the prisoners by force so they could be used as cannon fodder in war against the Communists.

He made use of the Colson ransom note on Koje, as Joy had anticipated. "Is it a sign of your good faith," he asked, "to continue to slaughter war prisoners in open repudiation of the pledge of no further maltreatment or murder of war prisoners made by Colson before the whole world as well as before all the war prisoners?"

Another field for Nam's propaganda was the alleged violations of the neutralized conference zone by our air and artillery. The one-thousand-yard neutralized Panmunjom circle was just about at the battle line, although during the course of negotiations the Communists took advantage of the rules almost to encircle it. From positions just outside the neutralized zone they were able to fire at our forward positions and then cry foul if return fire was long and landed inside the untouchable circle. We had a Marine outpost on a height overlooking the flat Panmunjom area. This Marine outpost was most important because the men who manned it were under standing instructions to be ready at all times to rush into the neutralized circle and rescue our delegation if the Communists broke off the negotiations suddenly and tried to capture our people. The Communists moved into positions between the Marines and the neutralized zone and fired at the Americans. The Marines fired back, and, as is usual in all fighting, some of their shots ricocheted into the attack-free area. Each time this happened we got a formal protest from the Communists. Finally I told them through staff officers that as long as they fired at us from such a position we were going to shoot back and further that we would ignore any protest they made about fragments falling in the Panmunjom area from our return fire. It seemed to me the Chinese were trying to set up a miniature sanctuary along the lines of their Manchurian attackproof base. As soon as the Communists received our firm declaration of intention to keep on shooting at the Chinese in front of the neutralized circle their attacks on our Marine outpost diminished considerably.

Repeatedly Nam Il charged at Panmunjom that our planes attacked camps in which the Communists held captured American, ROK and United Nation troops. We were constantly concerned about the possibility of a mistake bombing of such POW camps because the Communists refused to give us complete information on the camp locations and because they violated the basic concept of security for prisoners by deliberately locating many camps close to important military targets.

Our big attack on Pyongyang, for instance, had to be planned and executed with extreme caution because there were prison camps in the area. The enemy, cleverly and contrary to the Geneva Convention, had located POW camps in close proximity to the targets we wanted to hit. As a result some of these targets had to go untouched and others were hit only with the utmost care to pinpoint bombs on certain portions of the objective.

Despite our extreme precautions to avoid unintentional attacks on the prison camps, including instructions to pilots to be on the lookout always for POW signs over areas not listed by the Communists as prison sectors, the Peiping and Pyongyang radio propagandists invariably screamed after attacks that we had killed many of our own people in the camps. Nam Il at Panmunjom picked up these accusations and threw them at us.

In addition to the attack precautions, we always took full photographic reconnaissance of our raids and were able to prove with pictures that each of the Communist accusations was false. That failed to deter them, of course, but we were able to get our answers on the record each time they accused us of killing our own people.

The Communists at Panmunjom weren't really talking to us. They were using us. The talks were simply a channel for their propaganda. Their purpose was to make us appear as latter-day barbarians, bloodthirsty conquerors willing to kill our own people if necessary to serve our money-mad masters on Wall Street. Yes, even at Panmunjom Nam Il dragged out the old canard that America was pushed into wars by the profit-hungry speculators on Wall Street.

It was more effective for the Peiping *People's Daily* to publish propaganda as voiced by Nam Il at an international conference than it was to publish a straight editorial. The fact that Nam Il made his charges at a meeting with the capitalistic enemy gave them an official tone and also made them appear more factual to the Chinese people who had been conditioned so long to acceptance of Communist propaganda.

Their propaganda was so effective, in fact, that poor, bedraggled people in North Korea were made to believe we Americans were so much worse off that they actually pitied us.

This was a trick of psychology as old as time. Make a beggar feel superior to a rich man and he'll be happy. It worked well for the Communists.

Bill Harrison, who had to fight this propaganda campaign after Admiral Joy was transferred to Annapolis, was an old friend and classmate of mine at West Point. He was quiet and dignified, brilliant and courageous. In addition he was a deeply religious man. During World War II, in which he won the Distinguished Service Cross while commanding an infantry division, Bill Harrison conducted regular Sunday services for the men in his command. At Munsan, the base camp for the armistice negotiating team, he did the same thing.

Another old friend became involved with me in a tangle about the armistice talks right at that time. That was Lord Alexander of Tunis, Defense Minister of Great Britain. The Suiho bombing and the armistice talks were two issues in which we were caught up together.

Soon after being assigned the Far East Command, I got a letter of congratulations from Lord Alexander and in my reply I included the hope he might find time to visit his Commonwealth forces in Korea. I had served under Alexander in Italy and had a tremendous personal regard for him—as a soldier, a friend and one who understood the American point of view.

We were first name friends and corresponded regularly. The last time I had seen him was in Ottawa in 1951 when he was Governor General of Canada and I was Chief of Army Field Forces. Alex violated a long-standing rule during this visit and permitted a photographer to enter the Governor General's residence to take our picture together. Photographers ordinarily were barred from the residence. We stood rather stifflly under a portrait of King George VI and the photographer tried to loosen us up by saying, "Please gentlemen, say something."

A very proper and sedate individual, Alexander turned to me and said, "You're looking fine, Wayne." I looked at him and replied, "Oh, come on, Alex, we're just a couple of old Roman ruins."

Next day a picture appeared in the papers over the caption, "Just a Couple of Roman Ruins." I doubt that any more photographers were welcomed during Alexander's term as Governor General.

I was pleased to learn early in June that Alexander had announced that he was coming to see me at my invitation. As he passed through Hong Kong, accompanied by Selwyn Lloyd, the British Minister of State for Foreign Affairs, he was quoted in news dispatches as saying that if General Clark "asked him to name a British representative to the Korean armistice team, he would name him."

I knew the British were impatient for a truce and upset over the POW situation and the measures we were taking to get matters under control. I welcomed the chance for two of their leaders to see first-hand what we were up against, but I was dead set against changing the composition of our truce team. A change such as that during the critical stage of negotiations would only be an indication of weakness and indecision to the Communists. It would give them hope that differences of opinion between America and Britain had become more acute. They certainly would try to make capital of any division of opinion at the conference table. And at the very least the appointment of a Briton to the armistice team at that late date would give

them a good reason to stand pat and wait for us to make new concessions.

Alexander and Lloyd arrived in Tokyo shortly after Washington
had given me the authority to recess the talks for three- or four-day
periods.

I am sure our government would never have agreed to British
representation at Panmunjom. If nothing else, it would have raised
the question of other United Nations participating in the talks. But
I convinced Alex of the inadvisability of such a move, and invited
him instead to assign a British general officer to my UN staff in
Tokyo. As Commander of the Fifteenth Army Group in Italy, which
comprised the American Fifth Army and the British Eighth Army,
I had intermingled American and British staff officers with excellent
results.

Alexander welcomed the idea and later nominated Major General Stephen N. Shoosmith, a comrade-in-arms in the Italian campaign. Shoosmith served with me until the end of my tour in the Far
East, and proved a sound and capable deputy.

Alexander was satisfied with the composition of our team at Panmunjom. He told me that in a letter he wrote to me from the British
Embassy in Tokyo on June 16, 1952. He listed several points that
covered our discussions. In one paragraph he wrote:

"As regards the armistice talks at Panmunjom, I do not feel that
having British representation would help. I have complete confidence in General Harrison and the way in which he and his team
are tackling this job and I don't see any object in altering the present
arrangement."

I was not free to make this letter public at the time, even though
I felt it would help calm waters that were being disturbed by demands of some British leaders for more voice at Panmunjom. But
it was good to know there was a meeting of the minds with Alexander and that back in London he would try to explain the situation
and remove this one point of friction.

Relations with the British on the Korean problem always were
delicate. Because of her greater contributions to the fight Britain
quite naturally thought that she had a greater stake in the Far East

generally and the Korean War in particular than the other countries in the United Nations, and that therefore she should have a greater voice in the Korean affair.

Yet these nations quite understandably considered themselves as important as Britain to the Korean war effort and would have resented as discrimination any system that would give the British Government access to information denied them.

There was one change in the truce team that I did feel had to be made, however. The South Koreans, who suffered more and sacrificed more than any other nation, including ours, in the Korean fighting, had been represented on the truce team since the beginning, but it was perfunctory representation. The four Americans on the team ran things and the South Korean general was more of an observer than anything else.

I issued instructions that the South Korean delegate was to be treated as a full working member of the team. I also told the ROK member personally that he was authorized to report directly to President Rhee on the truce talks, an authorization he had not previously had.

My personal feeling at this time was that there was but dim hope for an armistice at all. The briefings given me in Washington, my conversations with Joy and Harrison, and an intensive study of the records of the meetings led me to believe that we had reached an impasse, a roadblock established by two diametrically opposed points of view.

Having gone through the cleanup of World War II in Austria I knew full well how badly the Communists wanted back those people who had fled from communism and thereby stood in the free world as living proof of the tyranny of the Reds. I knew from that experience that at the very best we would have a long, hard struggle before we achieved an armistice in Korea.

We had made it crystal clear to the Communists that we would not compromise on the basic issue of political asylum for those prisoners who wanted it. The Communists gave no indication that they ever would give up their demand that we force every prisoner back, at gunpoint if necessary.

This impasse was one of the things that led me to look around to determine what we could do militarily to exert more pressure on the Communists and thus increase the chances of an armistice. To my mind an armistice was an objective that had to be won by military means. Others before me, including Admiral Joy, had reached the same conclusions.

The deadlock was one of the factors that led me to prepare plans for an all-out offensive for military victory, in case it came to that.

But I was not optimistic about the truce. I had but slight hope that the military measures within my power and authority would be enough to force the Communists to sign an armistice that gave the men we captured the right of choice between communism and freedom. But at least the prosecution of the war to the utmost of my ability and authority would be a show of determination that might have an effect on the Reds.

For months I lay awake at night, trying to think of alternate solutions which might be acceptable to the Communists without sacrificing our principle of no forced repatriation. Time and again we proposed in different forms the plan of turning the POWs over to a group of neutral nations jointly selected by the opposing negotiators at Panmunjom.

But none of these efforts worked. The Communists just wouldn't believe that we would hold out indefinitely, taking thirty thousand American casualties a year in the stalemated war, for the right to freedom for ninety thousand Asians. Historically no non-Asian nation ever had shown any particular concern about the fate of the Asian masses.

I, too, had to worry about that. I knew we couldn't go on indefinitely taking those casualties. A solution had to be reached. That's why we kept throwing new proposals onto the table at Panmunjom.

We either had to get an armistice, win the war or get out of Korea.

9

The Job in Japan: Changing Our Status from Conquerors to Allies

The shooting war and the talking war in Korea held the spotlight during the whole of my tour of command in the Far East but there was another aspect of my assignment that also was of great importance to the United States.

That was the defense of Japan and related problems, such as measures to improve relations between the ordinary Japanese on the street and the American soldier. These relations had to be good to provide a healthy foundation for friendly relations between our two countries. The problem became acute just as I arrived in Japan, for the Japanese achieved sovereignty and independence from military occupation only nine days before I landed at Tokyo. Through all history the armies of occupation of all countries have been resented and hated by the occupied. MacArthur, Ridgway and I, in turn, had to do what we could to prevent that from happening to us.

There was a good practical reason for our efforts to make friends of our former enemies. There was and is no question in my mind that Japan is a vital link in our system of defense in the Far East and in the free world's system of security against the Communist drive for world domination.

There are no illusions in the minds of the Japanese about the kinds of devils these Communists are.

Several times in the first half of the twentieth century the Russians and Japanese waged war. Several times the Japanese have been the victims of the voracious Russian hunger for land in the Far East. After their war with the Chinese in 1895 the Japanese exacted title to the Liaotung Peninsula, which includes strategic Dairen and

Port Arthur. The Russians, who had no part in the Sino-Japanese War, organized a diplomatic front against Japan to force the Japanese to relinquish rights to the peninsula at the top of the Yellow Sea. The Russian slogan then was that the territorial integrity of China could not be violated without endangering the peace. The Japanese withdrew from the Liaotung Peninsula under this diplomatic pressure from Russia, Germany and France, only to see the Russian fleet move into Port Arthur in less than two years and Russian soldiers seize the port city and nearby Dairen. The weak Chinese Empire three months later "leased" the territory to Czarist Russia. Japanese to this day resent this incident in which they feel they were cheated.

After World War II, in which the Russians waged a one-week war against the Japanese, the Russians were given the entire Kurile Island chain stretching north from Hokkaido and the half of Sakhalin Island that had been Japanese. All these islands have both economic and strategic importance.

The great point of friction between Soviet Russia and Japan after World War II, however, was the question of the fate of more than 370,000 Japanese men, women and children taken captive by the Russians in Manchuria and North Korea in August and September of 1945.

A relative handful of these people was repatriated in 1949 and 1950, but the great mass of them just disappeared without trace or word. The few who came back brought stories of slave labor and misery. They said thousands had died that first winter after the war for want of adequate food, clothing and shelter to withstand the terrible cold in their Siberian prison camps. But they said thousands more remained in the slave labor camps and that their work was an important part of the Soviet effort to develop Siberia and Soviet Central Asia industrially. Some said they worked for years to build factories and even whole new cities in hitherto undeveloped sectors of the Soviet interior. They said the slave labor included Frenchmen, Germans, Poles, Czechs, Ukrainians and many others, including Russians sentenced to exile for big and little crimes.

The Japanese feeling about the Russians was well illustrated in the summer of 1949 when the Soviets sent back a batch of Japanese who had been well indoctrinated in Marxian thought. The repatriates marched off the ships in Maizuru with their clenched fists upraised and the Communist "Internationale" on their lips. They gave every sign of being dedicated Communists.

The Japanese Government handled things in a purely Japanese way. There were no reindoctrination camps for these repatriates. There were no lecture courses. There was food and drink at the dock, medical care and a ticket home for each man.

Japanese police and American intelligence officers, of course, maintained surveillance to find out what happened after the repatriates got to their homes. Almost without exception the Japanese plan, the most simple plan possible, worked well. It was simply to let the age-old Oriental family system of the Japanese people go to work on the converted Communists.

One story is illustrative. One of the men from the Russian camps went home to the farm village of his family. For centuries the Japanese have had village meetings similar in many ways to the town meetings of our New England. At the first village meeting the repatriate stood before his father's neighbors and extolled communism, charged the Americans were despoiling Japan and making it a colony, called for resistance to the Americans.

By that time, 1949, it had become clear to every Japanese that America had no territorial ambitions in their country and that America, in fact, was spending billions of dollars to make Japan economically healthy so that later she could be politically independent.

The village elders heard out the young repatriate. When he sat down his father rose. He bowed low until his hands were crossed at his knees. Then with the great sadness of a brokenhearted father, he apologized to his neighbours for his responsibility for inflicting on them the kind of speech they had just heard from his son.

The brothers of the repatriate rose in turn after their father and they, too, expressed shame that their family had brought this thing upon the village.

The scene was almost Biblical in nature, the father and sons begging forgiveness from the village for the disgrace of the family.

The impact was not lost upon the converted Communist. Japanese fashion, he went away from the village, alone, to meditate. Several days he was gone. Then he returned to the home of his father, got down on his knees before his family, touched his forehead to the straw mat floor, and begged forgiveness.

The ancient family system of Japan, and much of the Orient, had won a victory over the modern experts in the Communist brainwashing technique.

Few, if any, of the converted repatriates of 1949 remained Communists. Japanese police working on the subversive problem said they feared that 1 per cent of the repatriates would remain Communist in thought and action.

Another aspect of Japanese thinking was reflected by the oft-repeated statement that we Americans could never know how tragic an experience it was for a great country to be defeated as decisively as Japan was by the United States. A Japanese friend once told me, "You never can appreciate the humiliation of such a defeat."

I replied: "I can imagine your emotions and feelings. But you should be on your knees every night thanking whoever you thank that if you had to be defeated it was by the benevolent United States rather than by the murderous Soviet Union."

My friend agreed emphatically and expressed surprise that I had thought it necessary even to mention the point.

I knew when I arrived to begin my work in Japan and Korea that it was absolutely essential for Japan to rearm, not for offensive conquest but for the defense of the country. I felt the United States would not undertake for any really extended period the task of guaranteeing the security of Japan with a ground garrison.

There are many problems connected with the maintenance of a large army within the borders of a friendly nation. Not the least of these is the problem of relations between the troops and the people of the country. It is next to impossible to avoid friction and most difficult to minimize it.

In Japan, of course, the Communists were looking for every incident to help them in their campaign to create anti-American feeling. But non-Communist Japanese also had reason to be concerned.

When I first went to Japan I was confronted with a number of incidents, brawls and other trouble between Japanese on the one hand and American and other UN personnel on the other. In addition to these incidents there were social problems of a grave nature to the Japanese. We were moving our headquarters and other installations out of the big cities and into rural areas as part of the process of reducing the number of acquisitions of real estate and restoring sovereignty to the Japanese.

That caused unexpected troubles. As in every defeated nation, prostitution had become a problem in Japan after the war. The old licensed quarters, through which the Japanese had controlled prostitition from time immemorial, were off limits to our troops, so Japan, for the first time in its history according to the Japanese, had streetwalkers. Cabarets with well-dressed hostesses flourished in every city in which large numbers of Americans were stationed. In the big cities, like Tokyo and Osaka, these conditions did not concern the Japanese too much. They were not too noticeable.

But when we moved some of our activities out of the cities the situation changed. The girls who worked in cabarets or walked the streets in Tokyo were forced by economic necessity to move with the troops, like camp followers down through history. In the little farm villages that surrounded our new installations these city girls became a real social problem. A farmer could make a great deal of money by taking in the girls as boarders, and some farmers took the opportunity to earn some extra cash.

We had no control over the girls, of course. They were citizens of a free and independent Japan. However, through military-civilian committees of Americans and Japanese we tackled the problem with some success. We also went to work on our soldiers so that they would realize the dangers that beset them.

Rapidly we cut down the number of incidents that created rough spots in our relations with the Japanese. The chief measure we took was a gigantic educational program to make our soldiers realize that it was a patriotic duty for them to get along with the Japanese people, to avoid fights.

Through our Information and Education Section we stressed the idea that each soldier was a kind of ambassador of good will to Japan and that it was his duty to his country to help foster friendship with the Japanese. We made our men realize that by their appearance and conduct and friendliness and understanding of Japanese history, culture and traditions they could make a positive contribution to amicable relations with Japan and, therefore, the security of the United States.

We used well-established American advertising methods on our Armed Forces radio stations, the Far East Network, to sell these concepts. Overall, the program paid off in big dividends.

I would be guilty of a disservice to the American soldier if I left the impression that many of the men we sent to Japan were brawling, unruly troublemakers. The fact is a very small percentage of them were troublesome. The ratio was less than it is in the States among the young men of our population. Our soldiers, for the most part, reflected the creditable moral training they received in their American homes.

An aggravating factor in our relations was that Japan was the playground for hundreds of thousands of UN soldiers flown from the battle lines for five days Rest and Recreation leaves in this country free from war. These men, who knew that after five days they would go right back into the grueling battle in Korea, played every minute they could stay awake while they were in Japan. Nobody has the right to ask a soldier just out of battle to do anything else. I wouldn't.

Throughout the Occupation and the Korean War, however, our soldiers had built a big backlog of good will by many acts of kindness which the Japanese appreciated.

American contributions of money, goods and services to orphanages, hospitals and other charities were enormous. One regiment or one division would "adopt" an orphanage, as the U.S. 25th Division did in the Osaka area, and make regular contributions to keep it going. In the case of the 25th Division, the soldiers continued their contributions even after they were moved to Korea to fight the Communists.

Individually thousands of homesick American lads sought out

good Japanese families in the hopes that they could develop friendships that would give them the flavor of the home life they missed.
Japanese families, on their part, were more than happy to offer their
hospitality to the soldier who was a stranger in their country.

We also made an effort to formalize co-operation between the
American military and the Japanese communities in which they
lived. We organized Japanese-American co-ordinating committees
in which American military and Japanese civilian leaders met regularly to work out mutual problems and to develop projects that
would increase the understanding and sympathy between the two
groups. Baseball games, tennis and golf tournaments were among
these projects, the Japanese liking these sports as much as
we do.

Japan is a land of disaster. Flood, fire and earthquake are common
enemies. The warm sympathy of the American soldier was demonstrated to the Japanese each time disaster struck. In the summer of
1953 a typhoon lashed the southern island, Kyushu, and it was
followed by devastating floods. We had troops of the Southwestern
Command on the island, plus air and naval units. They went to work
on relief for the stricken civilian population, side by side with the
Japanese and American relief agencies, such as the Red Cross, of
both countries.

The troops worked full time on disaster relief and rehabilitation.
Blankets, food, medical care, transportation, clothing and other
material aid were given to the destitute Japanese by our men. In
addition millions upon millions of yen were donated by the three
services for the relief of these people.

The relief work of the Americans was outstanding not only because of the physical measures taken to relieve the stricken people,
but also because of the sympathetic way in which the soldiers took
the initiative to do what they could to help.

Japanese gratitude was heartfelt. Prime Minister Yoshida sent me
an official letter of thanks. So did Foreign Minister Okazaki and the
provincial governors and mayors of the disaster area. More than
that, business and civic leaders and the common people, the farmers
and shopkeepers who had lost their homes and their means of liveli-

hood, wrote to me to express their thanks for the work of the American service men who in many instances had saved their lives and the lives of their loved ones.

Newspapers picked up the feeling and many carried front-page editorials extolling our United States forces for their magnificent mission of mercy.

I was very pleased. This was the climax of a record that already had filled me with pride about the conduct of our American men and women in Japan.

Sometimes the record appeared clouded. Religious and charitable leaders among the Japanese raised a big issue about the number of illegitimate children fathered by American men in Japan. On the basis of unsupported charges some people in America issued statements which made it appear that Japan was filled with homeless waifs fathered by American soldiers who abandoned them. The popular figure in these unsupported charges was 200,000 Japanese-American orphans.

The Japanese government investigated thoroughly. In Japan that is not difficult because every man, woman and child must be registered in order to receive rations of rice, vegetables and other food. The investigation showed that instead of 200,000 of these Occupation babies there were about four thousand. The investigation also showed that although it was true, as the critics charged, that there were few orphanages for these children, the reason wasn't neglect but rather the fact that in all but a handful of instances the mother and her family took the child into the home and raised it as an ordinary Japanese.

Another controversial issue blown up far beyond its actual importance came from reports that the "dope" problem was acute in the Far East Command. It was serious, as is any narcotics problem, particularly in that part of the world. But it was not "acute" or even of dangerous proportions.

A special investigation was made into the use of narcotics by service men and women. The report concluded that addiction was lower in the Far East Command than in many American cities of comparable population.

During the Occupation, Generals MacArthur and Ridgway had held power over the Japanese Government through their position as Supreme Commander for the Allied Powers (SCAP). That relationship ended with the effective date of the peace treaty. By the time I arrived the position of SCAP had been discontinued and my relations with the Japanese Government were primarily of a military nature. The Japanese Government was sovereign and any political or diplomatic problem it had with our government was handled through the Ambassador, initially Bob Murphy. This division of functions was outlined in a Presidential directive which restored normal relations between the United States and Japan.

This was a difficult transition period. In seven years of Occupation the Japanese and the Americans had become accustomed to looking toward the military as the highest representative of the American government in Japan. If it had not been for the close friendship between Bob Murphy and me and his fine understanding of the transition problems the changeover might have created frictions between the Embassy and the military.

But Bob and I tackled the job as friends with a common goal and mutual understanding. Very early we decided to set up joint working groups of military and State Department officials so that he was thoroughly familiar with the military problems I faced and I was conversant with the political problems he had to solve.

The Presidential directive which outlined my mission in Japan was explicit in delegating to me direct contact with the Japanese Government on matters pertaining to the defense of the country.

My basic responsibility was to defend Japan against any possible external attack. At the time that meant Soviet Russia, which had bases within a few miles of the Japanese northern coastline. Defense of Japan was one of my most serious missions in the Far East, a mission that was vital to the security of the United States.

It was my responsibility, too, to encourage the Japanese to build up a defense force and train it to be an effective anti-invasion army. This force, originally called the Japanese National Police Reserve and nicknamed the "Junipers," later was renamed the National Safety Force.

My headquarters was in charge of the system through which we procured Japanese-made supplies for our army in Korea and for the maintenance of our own troops in Japan. This was close to a million-dollar-a-day project. It was important to us because it saved us millions in the cost of supplying our troops for the Korean War. It also was far and away the most important market for the rapidly expanding Japanese industry.

Finally I was responsible for the conduct and care not only of American troops in Japan but also those United Nations troops stationed in and about Japan in connection with the Korean War. The fact that these troops were in Japan by invitation rather than as the result of victory and occupation complicated this part of the job, for I had to revise a whole system of rules governing the conduct of our troops in Japan. One of the first things I did was to authorize our troops to wear civilian clothes during off-duty hours. Besides the comfort of the men, one of the objectives in this, and many other steps taken during the time of transition, was to change the face of Japan, and particularly Tokyo, so that the Japanese would have visual evidence that the peace treaty had brought some relief from military occupation.

The proximity of Russian forces made the preparations for the defense of Japan urgent. Russian warplanes and ships based in Siberia, Sakhalin and the Kuriles were in close range of the Japanese coast and all Japan was vulnerable to attack.

Under the provisions of the Japanese Constitution written in 1946 the Japanese Government was forbidden to create and maintain military forces of any kind. Inasmuch as the "no war" Article Six of the Constitution was one that was approved by my government and by General MacArthur it made it doubly difficult for me to impress upon the Japanese Government that it must provide forces for the defense of the country.

Rearmament became a hot political issue in Japan and Japanese leaders were quick to realize the advantage this gave them in dealing with the United States. The Japanese knew full well we could not risk the chance of losing the Japanese islands, with the best industrial plant in all Asia; therefore until the Japanese appropriated the funds and enlisted the men to defend themselves they were counting on Uncle Sam to keep troops on the islands.

This was smart politically and economically from the Japanese viewpoint. As long as we provided for the defense of Japan we paid the bill. Japanese industry and commerce profited by millions of dollars that we spent to maintain our armed forces in the country and by the untold amounts of money our troops spent for entertainment, food and souvenirs.

As a matter of fact, this great outpouring of American defense money, coupled with the gigantic procurement program, spelled the difference between a balanced and unbalanced Japanese national budget.

Therefore it paid the Japanese to drag their feet on rearmament for a while at least.

When I assumed command there were seventy thousand men in the National Police Reserve. When I left there were 110,000 men in the National Safety Force which succeeded the police reserve. This was a much smaller figure than I had hoped for, but it appeared that the Japanese Government finally was in a mood to go to work on creating a defensive ground force big enough to help materially in combatting an invasion attempt from the sea or by airborne troops.

There was no question about the combat quality of the Japanese foot soldier individually. Every American who fought in the Pacific War knows just how good a soldier the Japanese can be. The Japanese enlisting in the National Safety Force during the period of its creation was a good fighting man. But there were difficulties to be overcome before the force as a whole was an effective fighting army.

Most of the battle-trained leaders of the old Japanese Imperial Army that was defeated in World War II had been purged from public life during the Occupation. Under existing law they were barred from the defense force. It was only with great difficulty that the Japanese Government was able to depurge some of the younger officers who had seen service against the Allies in World War II.

Our purge, ordered when the Pacific War had been over but four and a half months, had stripped all Japanese career soldiers of the right to any government or military position in Japan. Many of the men thus barred from public life had been military academy students at the end of the war, had never fought in battle.

The depurge of some of these younger men gave the National Safety Force a corps of men with military training to serve as company and field grade officers.

But the Japanese faced a far more difficult task in their efforts to find men capable of moving into commands that require men of the caliber and experience of general officers. They needed men to command divisions and corps, not just companies and battalions.

Our government helped as much as it could in this effort to develop men to move into the top defense jobs in Japan. The Japanese requested help in training officers and Washington approved. Before I left the Japanese already had selected a number of National Safety Force officers and sent them to America for intensive training.

The National Safety Force was equipped with American war materiel, including tanks and artillery pieces, and as I left Japan negotiations were under way for a new MSA agreement under which Japan would agree to a certain rate of development of the defense force over a period of a few years in return for commitments of money and equipment from the United States.

There was no question in Japanese minds about the need for a defense force. Everyday their newspapers carried stories about an incident with the Russians. Japanese fishing boats were being seized regularly in northern waters by Soviet patrol boats. The fishermen were taken to the Kuriles or Sakhalin and questioned intensively about defense preparations along the northern coast of Hokkaido. Some fishermen came back, others didn't.

The Russians seized the Habomai Islands as part of the Kuriles immediately after World War II. The islands lie south of the northern tip of Hokkaido and the Japanese always considered them to be part of Hokkaido, rather than the Kuriles. These islands, within sight of the Hokkaido coast, have been a constant sore point to the Japanese.

The island bases and the seizure of fishing boats were more potential threats, but an active invasion of Japanese territory began midway during the Korean War. Soviet Russian jet fighter planes began flying over Hokkaido. They were MIG-15s and they came from Sakhalin and the Kuriles to buzz Japan on obvious reconnaissance missions to get photographic intelligence of our troop dispositions and defense preparations.

The invasion of Japanese territorial air posed a most difficult problem for us. The Japanese had a legal right under international law to shoot down such invaders. But the Japanese had neither an air force nor antiaircraft batteries that could touch the MIGs. We had undertaken the defense of Japan, but did that mean we had the right to shoot down invading reconnaissance warplanes? If we shot one down what would that mean to sovereign Japan?

Bob Murphy and I threshed out the problem and then together discussed it with the Japanese.

Japan issued the invitation to us to protect Japanese air from invading Russian warplanes. On January 13, 1953, the Japanese Foreign Office issued the following statement:

> Violations of our territorial air over Hokkaido by foreign military planes have of late become increasingly frequent. Such trespasses are not only forbidden under international law but they constitute also a grave menace to the security of Japan.
>
> The Government has therefore decided to take the necessary measures, with the cooperation of the United States Security Forces stationed in Japan, to prevent such violations of Japanese aerial domains in the future.
>
> The Japanese Government takes this opportunity to caution the foreign power concerned against repetition of such violations, and to declare that hereafter, for any consequences of the measures to be taken in order to repel intruding aircraft, the entire responsibility will rest with the country to which the aircraft belongs.

Simultaneously I issued a warning that I had ordered American jet fighter warplanes to shoot down any foreign warplane that intruded into Japanese territorial air without authorization.

Arrangements were made for a joint Japanese-American investigation in the event a Soviet warplane was shot down on Japanese soil.

I ordered F-86 Sabrejets manned by combat veterans from Korea to make the anti-Soviet patrol over Hokkaido, and to shoot if and when they contacted the Communist MIGs. Then we waited for the Soviet pilots to come back.

We know of one MIG flight that did come over Hokkaido after the warning had been published. Our Sabrejets intercepted the MIGs and fired on them. There was a trail of smoke but the American jet was close to the end of its fuel and the pilot was unable to pursue the MIG to evaluate damage.

We got plenty of circumstantial evidence, however, that a MIG had gone down. There was a great deal of activity off the southernmost Kuriles that night. Boats with searchlights that could be seen clearly from the Japanese shore swept a wide area. We suspected that a MIG had gone down in the sea and that the Russians were seeking the pilot.

That was the last we saw of Russian warplanes over Hokkaido, except for an occasional MIG which obviously was flown by a pilot who had misjudged his instruments and had crossed the invisible line dividing Russian and Japanese waters. Obviously the Russians themselves were not ready to become involved in a shooting war.

When I first arrived in Japan I was displeased with the large number of headquarters establishments that were in operation. It looked to me as though we had another situation where too few were commanded by too many. Certainly we needed more combat troops in Korea and I felt we could do with fewer desk soldiers in Japan.

I found that I was able to eliminate whole headquarters. We had three separate commands for the defense forces—Northern, Central and Southwest. We also had the XVI Corps Headquarters operating in the Northern Command Sector. I merged the corps and Northern Command headquarters. In Tokyo we had a huge Headquarters and Service Command that housed and fed troops in and around Tokyo, included the Provost Marshal setup, and requisitioned and kept in repair all buildings used by the American forces.

I merged this giant organization with the Central Command and eliminated a good deal of overlapping in command and administrative functions. In Yokohama the Japan Logistical Command was headquarters for the supply and maintenance of troops in the Far East. I did away with that organization entirely. Finally I cut down the personnel working behind desks in my own headquarters.

Overall we saved over seven thousand men, not a vast number but enough to form some of the combat units needed at the front in Korea.

I was happy to have this opportunity to put into practice my long-standing idea that we could do with fewer men in the rear and thus get more to the front.

Matt Ridgway had already begun to return to the Japanese the buildings that we had requisitioned at the beginning of the Occupation and used for seven years. I wanted to hurry it along as part of the process of demonstrating to the Japanese that the Occupation was over.

In particular I wanted to get out of the Dai Ichi Building where my office was located. That was a bad news building to me. It was there I had to wrestle with the Koje problem. But of much more importance was the location of the building. It was a magnificent modern structure that once was headquarters for the Dai Ichi Insurance Company. It possibly was the most imposing building in all Tokyo.

It was located directly across the street from the moated palace of the Emperor of Japan and within a block of one of the busiest intersections in the capital. In the beginning, when it was a good idea to impress the Japanese with the power of our Occupation, the Dai Ichi was fine for the American headquarters. But by the time I arrived a new era was just starting and we no longer wanted that kind of visual demonstration of power in Japan. We were allies, not conquerors, by this time.

Another important objection to the location of the Dai Ichi Building was that it was right in the area of every kind of demonstration the Japanese held, and they held many. Within sight of the building, and only a few hundred yards away, was the Imperial Palace Plaza which everyone from emperor-worshippers to Communists used for demonstrations. In sovereign Japan the American Military

Headquarters was out of place in the middle of Japanese demonstrations.

I therefore expedited the move to the outskirts of town, to the huge, hilly compound that had once been Hideki Tojo's headquarters and later was the site of the tribunal which tried and sentenced him to death. Often as I sat at my desk I thought that I had better not make the mistake of losing a war, as he did.

Organizationally I felt my headquarters should be a joint, tri-service operation, rather than an army project. When I arrived I found that the Army was providing nearly all of the personnel for this Supreme Headquarters of a combined operation. Inasmuch as it was a unified command it seemed to me the Navy and Air Force should be better represented. I felt that if the other two services shared the personnel burden, it would increase the effectiveness of the team play that was so needed in Korea.

Starting at the top, my old friend Doyle Hickey was designated as the chief of the joint staff. I named one man from each of the three services as a deputy chief of staff and gave each a regular staff job, rather than assigning them to work necessarily connected with their own branch of service.

A soldier and later an airman headed my operations section, planning air and sea, as well as ground, activities. An admiral ran the logistics section that handled all supply and equipment problems. An Army general was my intelligence officer and another was head of the personnel section. An admiral was in charge of civil affairs and relations with the Korean and Japanese governments.

Each man was carefuly selected. I knew and had served intimately with most of them. They all had outstanding records, were a fine bunch and most important pulled together on the tri-service team. I felt lucky to have such a splendid group of advisors. Here was the lineup:

Chief of Staff—Lieutenant General Doyle Hickey (Army).
Deputy Chiefs of Staff—
    Major General William S. Lawton (Army).
    Major General Mickey Moore (Air Force).
    Rear Admiral Thomas C. Ragan (Navy).

J-1 (Personnel)—Major General Bryan L. Milburn (Army).

J-2 (Intelligence)—Major General Riley F. Ennis (Army).

J-3 (Operations)—Major General Gilman C. Mudgett (Army).

J-4 (Supply)—Rear Admiral Lorenzo S. Sabin (Navy).

J-5 (Civil Affairs)—Rear Admiral Byron H. Hanlon (Navy).

Certainly where joint operations were envisaged as they were in Korea it was a matter of common sense to get good men from each of the three services to work on your staff. Had we carried the war to a victorious conclusion it would have required the closest kind of integration of ground, naval, air and amphibious operations. A truly integrated staff of the three services, in which men were picked for their ability rather than the color of their uniforms, is the answer to combined operations.

I was the beneficiary of this plan in an unexpected way. I hadn't realized how anxious the Navy and Air Force had been to get their people into this supreme headquarters nor how determined they were to make certain that the admirals and air generals who were named to the staff be top-notch men who would look good in competition with those of other services and would represent their points of view.

Each morning at eight o'clock in the War Room I would be briefed on the conduct of operations in Korea during the previous twenty-four hours. There the specialists took over. An airman would report on air operations, a sailor on the war at sea and a soldier on ground operations and intelligence.

Other subjects covered in these morning briefings included the POW camp situation, the armistice talks at Panmunjom, ground, sea and air casualties, and the strength of the command, including projected shipments of replacements from America.

The strength of the command discussion was of importance each day. I had to know how many troops I had ready to fight. In addition I had to follow the trend of troop strength which for a considerable time dropped alarmingly. Casualties and rotation dug deep into troop strength and the number of replacements from the States was declining. We were getting less replacements than we needed to make up for the losses in casualties and rotation. Our strength dipped below authorized levels and at one time I was twenty thousand men short—the equivalent of a full combat division.

The war in Korea was far from my only headache. There were so many others that the top-notch young officers who briefed me had to hew close to a schedule which would give perhaps ten minutes for consideration of one problem, and three minutes for another. Each of these briefing officers brought with him a paper requiring my action, and after he explained it I had to make my decision and go to the next problem. The young men from the three services lined up to await their turn to get at me.

It was S.O.P.—standard operating procedure—in my headquarters for my staff to break any bad news to me first and there was a regular flow of it which came my way in the Far East. I knew the good news could wait. When they broke the bad news to me the first question I asked was "Is this B.C. or A.D.?" Translated that meant, "Before Clark or After Douglas?"

There was always the problem in Japan of the Communist minority led by the members of the illegal Russian legation and by Japanese Communist big shots who went underground during the first month of the Korean War.

Direction of the well-organized Communist minority came straight from the big Russian Embassy building just on the outskirts of the downtown district in Tokyo. The Russians shouldn't have been there. They came as part of the Allied Council on Japan, an advisory body of four World War II Allied nations. When the peace treaty became effective the Allied Council went out of existence automatically. The missions that had represented the United States, the British Commonwealth and Nationalist China on the Council were converted into regular embassies. But the Russians had refused to sign the peace treaty with Japan. That left their envoys in Japan without legal status. The Japanese never cared to make enough of an issue about it to kick them out, although the Soviet mission leaders later left Japan by request of the Japanese Government.

When I left Japan there still were about fifteen or twenty subordinate Russian government officials in the Embassy building. The hammer and sickle flag flew over the compound. The Russians who were left led a secluded life, banned from normal diplomatic contacts, their names stricken from official guest lists of every embassy and legation. The Russians went no place openly but did move about the city like conspirators, furtively, secretly.

From the mansion that was the Soviet Embassy the handful of Russians remaining after the peace treaty directed Soviet espionage in Japan and handed down orders to the Japanese Communists.

The Russians made an interesting maneuver after Joseph Stalin died in 1953. They sent out invitations to some members of the diplomatic corps and leaders of the Japanese Government to attend memorial services. This was a trap, possibly an entering wedge back into diplomatic society and recognition. Therefore most embassies stayed away from the services, although out of courtesy they sent a card through some fifth or sixth ranking official. I, of course, was not invited.

There was a lighter, happier side to my stay in Japan. The friendship with Miss Yoshiye Ikuoka I shall remember with warm pleasure all my life. Yoshiye was four years old when we arrived in Japan. She lived with her parents and her grandfather in a house not far from Maeda House, which was our residence. Yoshiye and her grandfather stood at the same place on my route to the office every day of my seventeen month stay in Japan to smile and wave to me. This pleasant custom began right at the beginning even though I was going to the office night and day to work on the Koje incident.

Finally, after seeing this same little girl smiling and waving every day for several days, I stopped to say hello. We became fast friends. At various times we exchanged little gifts. The wave and smile from Yoshiye was one pleasant moment I could look forward to every day, no matter how black everything else was. We had her out to our house a few times, and once Mrs. Clark gave a party for all the Japanese and American kids in our neighborhood.

On the day we left Japan, Yoshiye, her mother, grandfather and whole family were at our gate, waving American and Japanese flags. I stopped the car, got out and had a picture taken of me hold-

ing her in my arms. Next day Japanese newspapers, which were
sent on to me in America, said that as our automobile pulled away
from the little group Yoshiye called, "Dear Uncle Clark, sayonara
(farewell)."

We received a parting gift from Yoshiye and her grandfather,
Rokunosuke Ikuoka, an old man who had captured the essence of
the democratic spirit we were trying to bring to Japan and who
seemed to appreciate fully our objectives.

The gift was an album, and with it was a letter signed by
Yoshiye and her grandfather which said:

Dear General and Mrs. Clark:
    We respectfully extend our greetings to General and Mrs. Clark who
will shortly return to their homeland. We pray for your good health
and happiness. We are ever so grateful for the many acts of courtesies
and kindness extended us. On the eve of your departure, we would very
much like you to accept this as a token of our high esteem for you.

That letter, and the English translation of the Japanese charac-
ters Mr. Ikuoka penned, are among the most prized of our memen-
toes from Japan.

Such a pleasant relationship as this was a welcome relief from
the cares and irritations of the job in Japan. As soon as Japan
became independent some individuals and groups in the country,
understandably, began to give voice to their grievances, real and
imagined. One of these concerned the conduct of American troops.
There was a regular flood of complaints about our soldiers. I recognized the campaign for what it was—an effort to hurry the day
when Japanese police would be given the right to arrest my troops
and Japanese criminal courts the right to try them. That right had
been promised during the negotiations for the peace treaty, long
before I even thought of going to Japan. In those negotiations our
government had promised that after the peace treaty had been in
effect for one year discussions on criminal jurisdiction would be
held with the Japanese.

The Japanese wanted to make certain they secured that jurisdiction, so there was a campaign to get it. One of the highlights of

this campaign came in August of 1952 when the President of the Federation of Bar Associations of Japan, Mr. Kunisuke Nagano, sent a petition to my office and at the same time released it to the newspapers. I was unhappy that he publicized it before I had read it and told Nagano bluntly that such a procedure might imply that his primary motive was publicity rather than a sincere desire to achieve a satisfactory solution to the situation he alleged existed.

Then I wrote him:

You speak of the frequency of serious and vicious crimes against Japanese by members of the United Nations forces. As I personally make it my business to keep informed about the behavior of my men, I can assert with authority that we are not in the midst of a growing crime wave. On the contrary, there has been a steady drop in crimes and incidents.

The official statistics for the United States Forces, for example, show 64 offenses against persons, including such minor incidents as pushing and shoving, in May, 62 in June and 41 in July. Offenses against property, again including such minor crimes as the breaking of a window, numbered 55 in May, 44 in June and 30 last month.

Though even a single misdemeanor is to be regretted, anyone familiar with the behavior of mankind in the mass will recognize that these figures are remarkably low. I am proud that they have declined during the three months I have been in command in Japan. I am proud, too, of the men of the United Nations Command who served under me, the overall excellence of their conduct, the sacrifices they and their families are making in the defense of the free world, and the many instances which have come to my attention of their friendly helpfulness to the Japanese people.

I told Nagano of the educational and disciplinary action we were taking to reduce even further incidents involving American and UN soldiers. In conclusion I tried to show that one of the main complaints of the Japanese was based on error. I wrote:

Unfortunately the belief has been allowed to spread without contradiction that men of the United Nations forces, if not tried in Japanese courts, go unpunished when found to have broken the law. Not only are they punished by their own courts-martial, but their punishment is likely to be all the more severe because their crimes have been committed in a foreign land which we have undertaken to befriend and defend.

Naturally, I, as commander of our troops, was reluctant to pass over to the Japanese the right to arrest and try my soldiers on criminal charges. No commander willingly permits such outside control over his troops.

In the negotiations handled by Ambassador John Allison, the Japanese Government promised that in all but the most flagrant cases of violation of Japanese law it would permit our military to court martial our own people.

Just before I left Japan Washington asked me to concur in the plan to relinquish criminal jurisdiction of our troops. I replied that I had no other recourse than to comply because my government had committed itself to this course of action before I assumed command. I said that naturally I would prefer, as commander, to handle the misconduct of my men in our own American way, rather than in Japanese courts, but added that in view of the prior commitment I felt we had made the best arrangement possible.

The Japanese assumed the criminal jurisdiction of our American troops everywhere except on our military posts.

The efforts to avert friction between Americans and Japanese were carried to extremes in some instances. We even established a "Condition Green" which prohibited American soldiers from entering areas in which large gatherings were scheduled, particularly gatherings of radical or potentially uncivil nature.

The system of education and discipline paid off. The Japanese reported that in the first year after the peace treaty was signed the number of crimes committed by foreign troops in Japan fell 46 per cent below the number committed in the last year of the Occupation.

Sometimes I found escape from the Korean War, crime in Japan and other problems by rising at 3:00 A.M. on a Sunday morning and driving an hour and a half out of Tokyo to a lake where the duck hunting was good. Captain Hank Emerson, who became my aide after making a magnificent record in combat in Korea, accompanied me on these occasional trips.

Hank was an excellent shot. I was mediocre. We had a standing joke between us. Every time he saw me aim he would aim, too. We usually fired together, and when only one duck fell, Hank would say, "Nice shot, General," and was always courteous enough to wait until I laughed at his little joke before he loosened his face with a broad grin.

One Sunday after returning from one of these trips with Hank I was out in the garden of my home at dusk and heard a great flutter of wings overhead. A formation of about fifteen ducks was circling the garden at tree-top level. The Maeda House had a huge yard, so there was room to shoot without endangering anyone. I got my gun and dropped one of the ducks right in the middle of the lawn.

I sent the duck to the kitchen. After some delay the cook himself came out, bowed low and said: "This Emperor's sacred mandarin duck. We no shoot in Japan."

Furthermore the cook made it clear to me that he wouldn't eat it or prepare it for anyone else to eat. "Nobody eat Emperor's duck in Japan," he explained. I felt like a little boy caught in the jam when I told him very quietly that he should get rid of the duck somehow and not tell anyone about the incident.

The Maeda House had been used by American commanders since the first days of the Occupation. The Air Force had it first for the Commanding General of the Far East Air Forces. It was given to Matt Ridgway when he moved out of the American Embassy to make way for the Ambassador, Bob Murphy. I took it when Matt left. The Japanese offered it as the official residence for the Commander in Chief, United Nations Forces, so that it could be kept when all other private residences were being turned back to their Japanese owners.

The Japanese Government insisted on providing guards and being responsible for the protection of my residence. Manpower was not one of the commodities in short supply for the Japanese and therefore there were more than enough police and security guards around my house. They were making certain that nothing untoward happened to me, my family or any of the high-ranking visitors who stayed there from time to time.

The Japanese did one thing, however, which had little relation to the security of my family, myself or my visitors.

They tapped my telephone.

How long it was tapped I do not know. An Army Signal Corps technician discovered it a month or two before we left Japan. Our Signal Corps personnel had to do a lot of work in the Japanese telephone exchanges because our lines in Tokyo passed through their switchboards.

We also found that my telephone conversations were being monitored at a Japanese police station nearby, and that a full record of everything said on the telephone was kept by the police.

I had my J-2, Major General Riley Ennis, make a protest which, as far as I know, ended the wire tapping at the Clark house.

Despite the petty annoyances like the wire tapping and the big annoyances like the campaign of misrepresentation about soldier crime in Japan, I left Tokyo convinced that the Japanese Government wanted our Army, Navy and Air Force to stay in their country for the time being.

I knew that most Japanese would have dearly loved to be rid of the sight of American soldiers which reminded them daily of their humiliating defeat, but I also was convinced that the Japanese, a hardheaded people, realized that it was best for them to bear with us.

There were two main reasons they wanted us to stay.

First, our forces spelled security from Soviet attack.

Second, the money our military forces and our individual servicemen spent in Japan was essential to the quick economic rehabilitation of their war-devastated country.

Japan, after all, had to be an exporting country to exist.

In effect we brought the customers to them by stationing our troops and their families in Japan.

10

Our Korean Ally

By the time the Korean War reached the cease-fire stage, tough old Syngman Rhee had been fighting for over a half century without letup to achieve freedom and independence for all Korea. He had been jailed in Seoul before the turn of the century, and had stayed in jail seven years. After that he went into exile and except for one brief return to Korea stayed out of the country until after Japan was defeated in 1945.

After struggling that long for a single goal Rhee was ready to take on anyone, friend or foe, who stood in the way of his strategic concept. I had to admire him for the steadfastness of purpose that had run through his entire life, and shaped his career. It impressed me to realize that the same objective motivated Rhee when he visited Theodore Roosevelt at Oyster Bay in 1904 as motivated him when he negotiated shrewdly with Walter Robertson in Seoul in 1953. Each time Rhee fought for the course that he thought would free and unify Korea.

By the time of the Korean War Rhee had been working for independence and unity so long that he had come to identify himself as the living embodiment of Korean patriotism, the sole prophet who could show the way to unity and freedom for Koreans. Opposition to Rhee's ideas seemed to him to be anti-Korean, not anti-Rhee. I first sensed this feeling when I met him for the second time. The issue then was his fight with the Korean National Assembly over the presidential election that was coming up in 1952. His advanced age made him humanly impatient to achieve his lifetime ambition to become the first president of a unified, free Korea. Anything that helped him attain that goal was good;

anything that impeded or postponed it—such as an armistice—was bad.

Therefore, although I respected Syngman Rhee for his indomitable determination to free his country and for his long fight against Japanese or Russian totalitarianism, and although personally I liked the man, I still found him as exasperating an ally as anyone could have.

The Korean Government, by Western standards, was not well organized administratively. It suffered keenly from a shortage of trained bureaucrats. It was plagued by party politics. Finally, the government machinery was dominated by Rhee personally. The President took a hand in most of the decisions of the many governmental agencies.

The lack of training of ROK governmental officials enormously increased the problems of waging military operations and extending our economic aid in a businesslike fashion.

Governmental weakness resulted from inexperience. During the long Japanese rule of Korea, which covered two generations, Koreans were denied responsible posts in the government. The inevitable confusion of war posed monumental tasks for the inexperienced Korean officials.

Government salaries were completely out of line with the inflated cost of living. Beyond that there was little job security for the top-level governmental workers. Rhee was quick to sense any indication of disaffection among his subordinates. This was evidenced by the frequent changes in his cabinet and in other responsible government positions.

I wore several hats in the Far East. As Commander in Chief, United Nations Forces, I was in command of a multination army, navy and air force fighting the Communists. I also was responsible for the conduct of armistice negotiations at Panmunjom. Further complications were created for the command in 1951 when, because an armistice appeared at hand, the United Nations hastily threw together several organizations which were to help rehabilitate South Korea economically and politically *after* a cease-fire. Thus we had in Korea organizations called the UN Commission for the Unification and Reconstruction of Korea, the UN Civil Assistance Command, Korea, and the UN Korean Reconstruction Agency. Two of these commissions, UNCURK and UNKRA, operated through the last two years of the war without clear-cut functions, as in effect they tried to justify their existence until such time as an armistice gave them the opportunity to do the work for which they were created.

As Commander in Chief, Far East Command, I also directed all American Army, Navy and Air Force activities in Japan and the Ryukyu Islands. That job included preparations for the defense of all these areas. I was proud of the fact that those in my command, whether Army, Navy or Air Force, fully comprehended the meaning of interservice unity and our command was truly integrated, with every subordinate commander from each service eager to carry his share of the load.

A third hat made me Governor of the Ryukyus, which meant I had the responsibility of insuring a healthy civil condition among the people so that our mighty air base at Okinawa would be free from the threat of civil disturbance.

Then there was a job without a hat, and that was where I was in trouble so often with Syngman Rhee. This job was an essential corollary of my job as UN Commander. In order to prosecute the war effectively, it was necessary to make certain that unrest, disease and starvation were eliminated or at least minimized in South Korea. It was a simple matter of military expediency, quite apart from the political and humane considerations that made it natural for us to want to create the best life possible for the South Korean civil population. I had to do everything I could to make it safe for UN troops to move over South Korean highways, to keep the railroads operating so that supplies could be moved on schedule, to maintain public utilities for use of both Korean civilians and UN personnel, and to keep the ports in condition to receive our big ships loaded with heavy cargoes of ammunition and other supplies. All this meant I had to have the final word on how rehabilitation funds from America and United Nations were used in Korea. I couldn't afford to let a group of UN economists decide to rehabilitate textile factories, for instance, with money we sorely needed to dredge a harbor or a channel to make way for our supply ships. I had to have the authority to make decisions which would funnel relief and reconstruction aid money into projects that would be beneficial to the war effort at the same time that they helped the Korean economy.

These economic and financial affairs of South Korea were a continuous headache to me. I would have been delighted to turn them over to almost anyone, with the proviso that his first concern would be to use relief money in a way to help, not hurt, the prosecution of the war. We got such a system, finally, in the last weeks of the war when C. Tyler Wood was sent out from Washington and became my economic co-ordinator in Korea. Agreements with the ROK Government and United Nations made it possible by then for me to have such a co-ordinator, but even then Wood was responsible to me and did a magnificent job of dovetailing reconstruction and rehabilitation work with military necessity.

Actually my work to co-ordinate rehabilitation projects with military problems was the job normally handled by an ambassador. The question may arise as to why we had an ambassador in Korea if the UN Military Commander assumed most of his duties. The answer simply is that we wanted to do everything we could to build the prestige of our ROK ally and one way to do that was to send an ambassador to Seoul. I do not mean to imply that our ambassador, Ellis O. Briggs, was a figurehead. Far from it. He served America well and worked closely and effectively with me in our many joint and complicated problems. But his position was made difficult, for I, as Commander in Chief of the United Nations Forces, had considerable authority in what normally would have been his area of responsibility.

Within the limits of my authority I did what I could to button up the loose ends so that we would have the maximum co-ordination. In July of 1952 I created the Communication Zone in order to free Van Fleet of all responsibility save that of fighting the war. To straddle him with all the prisoner-of-war problems and the economic job of rehabilitating Korea was to load him with more work than any one man could handle properly and fight a ground war at the same time. He needed to be able to fight the war without having to look over his shoulder to keep tabs on what was happening in the rear areas. I had done the same thing in Italy. As soon as the Port of Naples was secured by Fifth Army I asked that a separate command be created to take over the task of operating the port and moving supplies forward. I wanted to be able to forget about the rear and devote my full attention to the battle with the Germans in front of us.

The new command, under Major General Thomas W. Herren, took over all the problems of the rear areas in Korea, including prisoner-of-war camps, supply movements and stockpiling, maintenance of ports and railroads and co-ordination of relief and reconstruction work as much as was possible under the divided authority between my command and UN agencies.

Many of our problems with the ROK Government were handled directly with my headquarters. The big disagreement, of course, was the Armistice, which Rhee opposed right down to the last minute. But there were plenty of less fundamental issues earlier that gave an insight into the kind of intransigence we could expect from our ROK allies when the big issue was reached. A list of some of these points of difference is interesting as it shows the diversified and controversial issues involved in co-ordinating the financial, economic and political aspects of war with the military objectives.

Well before I arrived in the Far East there were a few. In May of 1951 some ROK forces did not perform well in battle. To focus attention elsewhere, reports were issued to the press that American troops could be withdrawn from Korea if America would equip the ROK Army adequately. This created embarrassment for the UN Command and our government.

Two months later, after Matt Ridgway made the decision to permit Japanese newspapermen to cover the Panmunjom armistice talks, Rhee demanded that they be withdrawn. Some of them actually were advised to leave Korea. President Rhee later made the same demand upon me.

Rhee was inaugurated for his second term in August of 1952. He agitated continuously to move his capital from Pusan, far in the south, to Seoul, only forty miles from the battle lines. I opposed such a move which would have meant a troublesome situation close to the front and would interfere with the conduct of military operations. Denied authority to make a formal move back to Seoul, Rhee shifted much of the government back to the old capital without declaration. He made his personal headquarters in Seoul, thus obliging other government officials to move to the city with their ministries and agencies. Thousands of civilians also returned, complicating the difficult situation further. The pressure from Rhee was so strong that finally in February of 1953 I had to intervene personally to emphasize the UN Command position that it was premature to return the government to Seoul. Despite this the government conducted a piecemeal movement to the old capital and most of the ministries were established in Seoul by the time the Armistice was signed.

There was the issue of the Liancourt Rocks, also known as Takeshima Islands to the Japanese and Dokdo Islands to the Koreans. These rocks are about midway between Japan and Korea. Since 1905 they have been part of Japan and there was no evidence that Korea ever had claimed them. My command used the rocks as a bombing range. South Korea protested in September of 1952 against this bombing of "Korean" territory and in June of 1953 ROK police fired on a Japanese patrol boat in the water near the islands.

We had trouble with the ROK Government over money matters. In two separate agreements the ROK had approved a plan by which their currency would be provided for use by our troops in Korea. Because of the strain thereby imposed upon the limited South Korean resources we decided to settle such ROK "won" drawings in dollars.

After we had made our decision the ROK Government first demanded that we settle three months before the agreed time, and then threatened to cut off our supply of "won" currency until we paid in full for past advances. New currency, the "hwan," was established and in February of 1953 a new financial agreement with the ROK Government provided that hwan would be advanced for our troops and that our government would settle the account with dollar payments monthly. The agreement was that the rate of exchange would be based on the Pusan wholesale price index and that the rate would be adjusted every three months. Inflationary conditions were such in Korea that we had to protect ourselves from being pegged to a rate that would perhaps force us some day to pay ten to a hundred times the price the hwan was worth. The ROK Government violated this agreement in less than three months and the whole thing was thrown back into negotiation. A compromise rate of 180 hwan to the dollar was agreed upon, but very shortly the ROK Government came back with a new demand, again running counter to solemn agreement, that the 180 to one rate be made permanent or that we drop the rate to a long obsolete sixty to one.

We had written agreements with the ROK Government which regulated our use of conscript Korean labor, the Korean Service Corps, to help prosecute the war. In July of 1953 the Government unilaterally wiped out these agreements by declaring that the new Wartime Labor Service Act applied to the KSC. My headquarters had figured we stood to lose 105 million dollars a year through increased costs for the KSC, and that in addition we would lose efficiency because the new law cut the term of service from a minimum of six months to a minimum of three. General Taylor was negotiating this problem as I left the Far East.

We argued with the ROKs about a 1952 crop survey made to determine how much grain had to be sent to Korea. There were significant differences in ROK and UNC findings. The ROK went to the newspapers to denounce the UNC survey result. The ROK wanted more grain than our survey showed they needed.

Each of these issues was a big one when it was under negotiation, but each was a minor annoyance compared to the issues on which we really tangled with Rhee.

One of the great points of friction was based on Rhee's intense antipathy to anything Japanese. At the outset of the war it was necessary to employ some Japanese technicians and their equipment to do certain war work in Korea. The Japanese had developed virtually all of the modern industry of Korea, the railroads, ports, refrigerating plants and public utilities. During the forty years of Japanese rule in Korea the Koreans were not permitted to become expert technicians or administrators in any of these fields. Most of the machinery and equipment was Japanese-made. The whole idea at that time was to Japanize Korea, to make Korea so dependent upon Japan for the necessities of life that, willing or not, Koreans would have to stay in the Japanese Empire.

When the war came the UN Command found that Koreans and Korean equipment were not available to do the necessary work in support of the armies at the front. Japanese had to be brought back to Korea to operate dredges and lighters in the harbors, to run power plants and other essential industries. They had to take their equipment with them to Korea.

The command could have imported American or other foreign technicians and equipment but the Japanese were more quickly available, could be transported and maintained at far less cost, and were better suited to do the job because they would be working with their own equipment, which they understood.

Soon after I took command in the Far East, President Rhee protested against the employment of these Japanese. I investigated and found there were three to four thousand of them employed in or around Korea on various essential war industry jobs. I also found there were few Koreans available to take their places. And finally I found that the Japanese were doing a fine job.

To comply with the Rhee demand that every Japanese be ousted from Korea would have meant staggering increased costs to our government and a probable drop in efficiency.

I was in sympathy with Rhee's desire to employ more of his own people, however, and had a study made to determine whether he had any manpower resources that had not been discovered in the first quick survey. A chart was made of all the services and facilities in which Japanese were employed in Korea. The chart showed what the Japanese technicians did, and what Japanese equipment was involved in the war work. Finally I had this chart furnished to the ROK Government and personally told President Rhee that "I'll take the Japanese and their equipment off these jobs as fast as you can provide the people and things to take their places." As a matter of fact, there were some Japanese working on barges and lighters who were replaced very shortly.

The offer and the fact that I replaced a few Japanese harbor workers showed Rhee that at least my heart was with him in this instance and that I was trying to do something. As a result the issue died down, but not before the ROKs had embarrassed us by arresting and bringing to trial some Japanese who set foot on Korean soil. We had to take makeshift measures to counteract these arrests. All the Japanese working on barges and lighters slept aboard their vessels but occasionally some of them would have to come ashore in connection with their work. We made certain that when they did it was inside American installations, where ROK police could not get them.

A corollary of the Japanese labor problem was that of procurement of supplies and services in the billion-dollar reconstruction and relief program contemplated for South Korea.

The ROKs wanted the power to tell us where we could buy supplies and services for the rehabilitation of their country with our money. Our government promised the billion-dollar program as part of the deal that won Rhee's reluctant agreement to refrain from disrupting the Armistice.

What they wanted was the power to refuse to permit us to buy anything in Japan for their country. The basic issue was the dislike of Rhee and the ROK Government for anything Japanese and their determination that none of the money we appropriated for the reconstruction of Korea should benefit Japan in any way. Right from the end of the Pacific War the Koreans had been unhappy because they thought American aid was helping Japan faster than Korea.

Washington, of course, was dead set against such restriction on our procurement. For one thing Japan offered the cheapest market for many commodities needed in Korea, both because of initial cost and the short cargo haul. Purchasing in Japan would make our billion dollars go further toward the reconstruction of Korea. Also, it was the policy of the United States to provide and sustain a high degree of economic well-being in Japan. We had spent two billion dollars in relief and reconstruction aid to Japan during the six post-war years and in addition had poured millions of dollars into Japanese industry to procure war material to support the fighting in Korea.

Specifically the ROKs demanded the right to approve all procurement purchases, right down to the last nut and bolt. They also wanted the right to sign the actual procurement contracts. We could not legally grant another government the power to validate purchases made by America, but even if it had been possible legally to give them the right to sign contracts the process would have been so tedious it would have bogged down the whole Korean rehabilitation effort.

The labor and procurement difficulties demonstrated graphically that these old hatreds between enemies such as Korea and Japan, no matter how justified they might have been at one time, are a luxury that no nation can now afford in the face of the common danger threatening all free nations.

It became clear that the United States would have to do whatever it could to persuade Rhee and his countrymen to forget the old threat and concentrate on meeting the new. Our government and our people did not attempt to keep alive our World War II hatreds against Japan and Germany. We concentrated on banding together all peoples of good will who were determined in their desire to stem the Communist effort to win world domination.

The Japanese labor and procurement issues and the issue of the ROK election of 1952 were the biggest we had to face with Rhee short of the controversy on the Armistice itself and the running battle on Japanese fishing rights.

The wartime election in 1952 approached while the constitution of the Republic of Korea still provided that the National Assembly would elect the president. Rhee, it seemed to me, considered that he was the chief prophet of patriotism in Korea and therefore the nation's indispensable man. But he could not be quite certain that the politicians in the Assembly would re-elect him. He insisted upon a constitutional amendment to provide election of the president by popular vote of the people.

There was a good deal of Korean resistance to this move within a few short weeks of the election. Strong methods were used to quell the opposition. Martial law was declared and maintained despite opposition by the Assembly and the UN Command.

The martial law commander was Lieutenant General Won Yon Duk, who later did such yeoman service for Rhee by turning loose 27,000 anti-Communist prisoners of war from UN prison camps.

Several opposition assemblymen were jailed on charges of Communist affiliation, none of which were ever sustained in court as far as I know. Popular demonstrations were stirred up to demand the recall of anti-Rhee assemblymen. Rhee threatened to dissolve the Assembly, even though he had no such constitutional power.

Protests poured in from around the world and I protested. So did the American Ambassador and other UN nation envoys. The same concern motivated us all. We feared the Rhee drive for re-election was being conducted along undemocratic lines that threatened to develop civil unrest and thus hamper our war effort.

Some assemblymen fled to our American military installations for refuge, were held in jail, or were beaten up in little restaurants or other meeting places in Pusan. Finally Rhee won his goal, the constitutional amendment that provided for the popular vote election of the president. The rest was easy. He was swept back into office by a landslide. There was no serious challenge to his power.

I learned a lot about Rhee during the talks we had alone in this period. It did little good for me to try to talk on the basis of American history. He was an expert. He could, and would, in these talks, spout our American Constitution word for word to prove a point.

This was his field of study. A sketch of Rhee's career is useful in judging the man and the methods he used which irked us at times. Officially his birth date is set at April 26, 1875, but there are some who claim he was born four or five years earlier. As a boy he was educated in the Chinese classics, and studied English at a missionary school in Korea. He founded and edited the first Korean daily newspaper and at the same time was the leader in starting youth and student patriotic groups. He was jailed in 1897 at Seoul and on his release, in 1904, he fled to the United States.

There he continued his agitation for a free and independent Korea, carrying his plea to the highest quarters. At the end of the Russo-Japanese War he went right to President Theodore Roosevelt at Oyster Bay to demand a place for Korea at the peace conference, arranged for Portsmouth, N.H. He failed, but this was only the start of his long career as a leader of the Korean exiles.

He studied at George Washington University, Harvard and Princeton, where he earned his Ph.D. in 1910 with a thesis on the neutrality policies of the United States. Woodrow Wilson, then president of Princeton, handed Rhee his degree. Rhee spent fifteen months back in Korea in YMCA and Methodist mission work and then fled when he was warned the Japanese planned to arrest him. From 1912 to 1939 he ran a school in Hawaii, with the exception of some time in Shanghai and two years during the depression when he was in Washington. Finally in 1939 he went to Washington as head of the Korean Mission which had been appealing for U.S. recognition of Korea since 1919. He stayed in Washington until the surrender of Japan permitted him to fly back to Korea and begin his struggle for unity and independence.

Never once during this long career did Rhee deviate from his purpose. YMCA and school work were merely a means of supporting him in his struggle to free his country.

His goal was unchanged from the days of his youth.

It was more than just the patriotic effort to free the country.

In the words of his countryman, his dream was to become "the nation's father."

11

President Rhee and the Japanese

Syngman Rhee's hatred of anything Japanese brought on the knockdown, drag-out battle of the Sea Defense Zone of Korea, a battle still undecided when I left the Far East. Reduced to its essentials, the issue was Rhee's insistence that territorial waters of Korea extended as far as sixty miles off shore and that neither Japanese nor anyone else had the right to fish in those waters.

The basis for the boundary line Rhee tried to draw was the Korean Sea Defense Zone I proclaimed in September of 1952 after consultation with the ROK and the American governments. The Sea Defense Zone to my mind was strictly a wartime measure designed to safeguard the Korean coastline and our lines of communication and to bar the Korean coast to enemy agents and contraband.

Before the Sea Defense Zone was proclaimed there was continuing trouble in our rear, a battle between ROK Navy and police patrol boats and the Japanese fishing vessels that crossed over what was then called the "MacArthur Line" that divided Korean and Japanese waters. The Japanese vessels were unarmed and the Korean naval and patrol ships were shooting up the fishing boats and seizing both fishermen and boats.

I felt that this was an added burden I could not tolerate, particularly since the presence of so many small boats in the area gave enemy agents and spies opportunity to infiltrate into Korea generally and into the island prison camp areas specifically.

Man smuggling is a fine and well-practiced art in that corner of Asia. During the occupation of Japan American and Japanese agents *caught* many thousands of Koreans trying to smuggle themselves into Japan. How many made it undetected nobody ever knew. During

154

the war the Koreans told stories of regular man-smuggling brokers who were established in communities close to the battle lines to sell a regular all-expense trip to Japan. The story was that a single broker, for a single over-all payment, would sell a Korean a ticket that would provide rail passage to Pusan, food, lodging and a 120-mile ride on a smuggler's boat to Japan.

The traffic worked both ways, of course, and the Communists were well organized among the 600,000 Koreans we knew were living in Japan when the war started.

This man-smuggling trade was one of the weaknesses in our setup that I wanted to eliminate through a closer guard of the Korean coast by the establishment of the Sea Defense Zone.

One of the first reactions came from the Russians. On November 4, 1952, the USSR protested formally to our State Department.

The Soviet Government [said the protest note], does not recognize as lawful the establishment by the government of the USA of a so-called Sea Defense Zone around Korea and places upon the government of the USA the entire responsibility for the consequences of this new act of aggression and for the damage which may be caused to the interests of the Soviet Union.

Our government was in agreement with me and sent the Soviet Embassy in Washington a reply that called attention to the fact that I established the Sea Defense Zone on behalf of the UN Command and not for the U.S. Government. The State Department reminded the Soviet Government that sea defense zones were established often by nations or groups of nations exercising belligerent rights and that such safeguards are not inconsistent with international law. Our government assured the Soviets that neutral vessels in transit in the zone would be protected and would be subject only to those restrictions necessary for military security. It further pointed out that the Korean Sea Defense Zone was established in keeping with the UN Security Council and General Assembly resolutions as a matter of military necessity in the furtherance of UN action in repelling Communist aggression against the Republic of Korea.

The State Department told the Russian Embassy the U.S. Government considered the Soviet note to be unfounded and that the protest was rejected.

The Russians, of course, cared little about the waters included in the Sea Defense Zone. Their ships did not sail those waters. Their sea supply route to North Korea and Manchuria was the long way around, running through the Kuriles and out into the Pacific for the long path around the Islands of Japan and into the Yellow Sea for the last lap up to Port Arthur and Dairen, on the Liaotung Peninsula of Manchuria. The Russians used this roundabout course before the Sea Defense Zone ever was proclaimed and did not use the Tsushima Straits between Japan and Korea while hostilities were under way.

The Russians, in their protest, obviously were playing to a Japanese gallery. The Sea Defense Zone definitely barred Japanese fishing vessels. The Soviets, following their well-established pattern, saw an opportunity of embarrassing us by championing a cause they knew would be popular with one of our allies. The Japanese is a fairly clearheaded fellow, however, and he remembered all the time that the Russians in the north were seizing Japanese fishermen and fishing boats just as the Koreans were in the south.

The Korean Sea Defense Zone existed for eleven months. In August of 1953 I was obliged to suspend the zone because of the armistice document prohibition of coastal blockade. The initiative for the suspension was taken by the State Department and relayed to me through the Embassy in Tokyo. The ROK Government reaction was violent. The official government spokesman in Seoul declared, "We are shocked over General Clark's precipitate and unwise action in lifting the Korean Sea Defense Zone, at a time when such a protective measure is needed more than ever before."

He said in his public statement that "We have always regarded General Clark as highly competent and a responsible commander," and then added, "It is, therefore, ironical and regrettable that now, near the conclusion of his major mission against communism, he should be unaware of what a valuable present large areas of unguarded seas can be to the enemy."

In conclusion the spokesman said:

Are the good friends of Korea so naive as to suppose that merely because there is something known as a truce that the Reds will relax their efforts to destroy us—and will fail to try to slip agents into our country, into our ports, harbors and remote places on our coastline?

The Sea Defense Zone should be restored immediately, for protection of Free Korea and the UN. The Republic of Korea will, of course, for protection of itself and its friends, continue to enforce the peace line proclaimed by President Rhee.

That was the pay-off line. Once again Rhee was going his own way. Once again he took the righteous attitude that he hoped America and the UN would see the problem as he did and go all the way with him, but if we couldn't or wouldn't then he would go on alone. Rhee was, of course, supremely confident that the United States, at least, would have to support him in any crisis. It is inconceivable to the Koreans that the United States would fail to back Korea in any trouble with the Communists. Their feeling is that Korea, by its resistance to communism, has become a showpiece for the world. Other small nations, the Koreans are convinced, will judge the profit in resistance to communism through the fate of the Republic of Korea. If the Koreans fare well, then they too will be encouraged to resist Communist aggression.

Many Americans shared this view, and many came from Washington as governmental experts to make quick surveys to determine what economic and financial aid was necessary to rebuild South Korea.

Most of these men were rushed out from Washington to make their studies and fix things up. I always felt, and still do, that in Tokyo, just as in Vienna before that, my headquarters included American civilian economists and financial experts who were just as capable as these specialists hurried from home as trouble shooters. In addition to being equal in ability, these "resident" economists had the advantage of familiarity with the people, the issues and the problems. They did not have to make a preliminary study to find out what resources Korea had in manpower, electric power, textile mills, rice paddy acreage, railroads, shipping and all the other things that go in to making up the national wealth and productive power of a nation. They already knew and furnished the data to our visitors.

Rhee was adept in playing the Washington experts off against us in the Command, or in trying to play our Embassy off against the military. He was quick to sense the most sympathetic ear, and he filled it. And he was on the lookout constantly for Americans who believed the United States had to bend over backwards on every issue to make certain Korea became a shining example of the profit that could be won by standing against communism.

President Rhee was always encouraged by the number of Americans he found to agree with him that come what may, America must stand by Korea. So he really didn't feel that he was taking much of a gamble when he went it alone in opposition to our announced policies.

In the case of the Sea Defense Zone the ROKs kept their naval and police vessels seizing Japanese fishing boats and sometimes the Korean seizures were made even outside the broad expanse of the old zone itself. This created a ticklish problem for me with the Japanese.

I thought perhaps a face-to-face informal discussion between Rhee and Prime Minister Shigeru Yoshida of Japan might help pave the way for a fishing agreement that would be beneficial to each country, and therefore to my country.

Rhee, always most cordial in personal relationships with me, frequently invited me to make social visits to him in Korea to go fishing. He knew how much I liked to fish and often extolled the fine fishing of Korea. Several times we had plans worked out so that I could relax with him for a short time but on each occasion a new crisis or bad weather forced us to cancel the plans. I took advantage of these repeated invitations, however, to suggest to the President that he might like to pay us a visit in Japan. I told him Mrs. Clark and I would be pleased to have him and Madame Rhee as our house guests in Tokyo. I repeated this invitation during several of my official visits to Seoul, but each time I was left with the feeling that the President had no desire to accept because of his antipathy for the Japanese.

It was with some surprise, therefore, that on December 20, 1952, I received a letter from the President in which he said he would like to visit me in Tokyo during the holiday season. I told him I was delighted and re-emphasized that he would be the personal guest of Mrs. Clark and me.

In addition I told him: "I think your coming would give you and some of the Japanese governmental officials an opportunity to discuss informally mutual problems. Such a get-together would result in advantage to all concerned."

Rhee knew exactly what I meant, of course, and made it clear in his reply that he had no intention of walking into any kind of trap.

It is all of a social nature [he wrote] and it can be arranged to meet with some of the Japanese officials if they do desire but not included in the program as a part of the purpose of my visit. I would like it announced as only a friendly visit with you and Mrs. Clark with no political significance attached to it.

Ostensibly there would be no politicking. It was agreed Rhee would visit me in Tokyo from the fifth to the seventh of January, 1953.

His trip posed something of a political and diplomatic problem because of the protocol involved in the visit of the chief of state of one free nation to the capital city of another. The host nation had to be aware of the visit, and had to concur in it. I got in touch with Bob Murphy and he in turn explained the situation to Prime Minister Yoshida, who welcomed the opportunity to talk with Rhee. He said he hoped that Rhee's visit would give him the opportunity the Japanese had long sought to sit down informally with Rhee to discuss the knotty problems in the relations of the two countries.

In addition to protocol, there was the problem of security. There were grave dangers in Japan from Communist and North Korean dissident elements. Assassinations were not uncommon in Korean history and there was definite fear that an attempt might be made on the life of the ROK president during his visit.

The Japanese were most concerned because they wanted no such incident to further complicate their relations with the Koreans. So the Japanese Government, quite properly, requested that they be responsible for the security of the President and his party during their stay in Japan. The Koreans had other ideas. The ROK minister in Tokyo wrote me that "my government realizes that since the visit will be a personal call upon you, all security matters will be in your hands."

I replied immediately that such was not the case and explained:

When the head of your Government visits the sovereign and independent country of Japan, that country is responsible for his safety at times when he is not located at my personal residence. This has been discussed with the Japanese police officials, who accept this responsibility and, I assure you, are taking the maximum measures necessary to provide safety for your President.

The plans were truly on a grand scale. As an example, hundreds of Japanese policemen lined the road between Haneda Airport, where President Rhee landed, and my home. The policemen stood on either side of the road, facing away from the entourage. They were there to watch the crowd, not the parade.

Security precautions even at my residence were elaborate and I was given to understand later that several thousand Japanese uniformed and plain-clothes police officers were used in the three-day security arrangements.

The first step toward security of the President was a bit of hide-and-seek with the airplane that flew him from Korea to Tokyo. His takeoff from Seoul was common knowledge, so our job was to protect him as he landed.

While the crowd was gathered at the main terminal the airplane was taxied far down to the end of a runway close to an exit road. The official greeting party arrived with clocklike precision. The automobiles carrying the welcoming group were out of sight until the airplane touched the runway. Then they were wheeled quickly to a rendezvous with the airplane, which came to a stop just as the automobiles arrived.

Among the welcomers were Foreign Minister and Mrs. Okazaki of Japan, Ambassador and Mrs. Murphy and their daughter Mildred, Korean Minister and Mrs. Kim and Major General Kim, Chief of the Korean Liaison Mission in my headquarters.

In the visiting party were President and Mrs. Rhee, Lieutenant General Sun Yup Paik, Chief of Staff, ROK Army, Vice Admiral Sohn Won Il, Chief of Naval Operations for the ROK, three officials from the Korean Office of Public Information, three secretaries and two bodyguards.

The Rhees were in a gay mood as they stepped from the airplane. The President shook hands all around, even with the Japanese, and posed for an official photographer who took pictures of Rhee being friendly with Okazaki.

Japanese security officers wanted to hurry us into the automobiles and get us moving through their protective gauntlet. Feeling was high between Communist and anti-Communist Koreans in Japan and the Japanese wanted no trouble with them. Mrs. Clark and I got into an automobile with the President and Mrs. Rhee and we were underway in good, quick order, just as the Japanese wanted.

But with a volatile character like Rhee there rarely is a time without incident. We had just started on the fifteen-mile drive to my home when the President insisted on stopping the motorcade. The Japanese guards were in a whirl. This was just the kind of opportunity they were determined to deny any would-be assassins. Rhee asked me to stop the car because he wanted to see one of his officials in a car somewhere behind us. "I want to talk to him," Rhee said. "I've got to see him about a press statement I want to make."

Fortunately for our security plans the official didn't have the statement readily available and Rhee agreed to wait until we got to our house before he went over it. I pricked up my ears as soon as I heard the term "press statement" because relations between Korea and Japan were so delicate at that juncture.

After we arrived home the paper was produced and Rhee was kind enough to show it to me and ask for my comment before it was published. I read it and was shocked. I considered parts of it provocative. It rehashed old controversies between Korea and Japan. It would have served no useful purpose and would have been most embarrassing if it had been released just as Rhee arrived in Japan to be my guest. The Japanese would have been antagonized, and some of their feeling would have spilled over onto us. Of course it would have made Rhee look like a hero back in Korea if he walked in to the lair of the old enemy and threw the hooks into him.

Rhee asked my frank opinion of the statement and I gave it to him. Much to my relief the President accepted my suggestions and modified the statement so much that it actually left open a door to possible solution of the fisheries controversy with Japan.

I had told Rhee that our guest house would accommodate himself, his wife and three others in his party and that arrangements would be made for the others to stay with his resident minister in Japan or in our military hotels. That isn't the way it worked out. He was the kind of boss who always had to be able to reach the people working for him so that whenever he got an idea or wanted something done, day or night, he could reach the man qualified to go to work. Therefore, our little guest house was overflowing most of the time.

Prime Minister Yoshida put his right foot forward. He invited the Rhees to a dinner in their honor at his home. I also had arranged to have a dinner at my house for the Rhees at which Yoshida and Okazaki would be guests. Rhee put thumbs down on both dinners. He said he would have no social contact with the Japanese. My hopes for amicable settlement dimmed. But he revived them a little by saying he would be glad to confer informally with the Japanese to discuss mutual problems.

The problem of security continued to haunt us. Rhee blandly announced a proposed itinerary which would have had him traveling all over the Tokyo area to speak at Korean rallies. The Japanese were aghast. They knew there were so many Communists among the Koreans in Japan that there was little chance that Rhee could go through with his plans without being shot at. They didn't want to tell the visiting president what he should do, but neither did they want riots or attempted assassinations. Everything was explained to the President in detail and with considerable disappointment he canceled some of the meetings he had planned. The itinerary upon which we settled included a visit to my headquarters for conferences and a review of the Guard of Honor, luncheon at Bob Murphy's home at the Embassy, a visit to the Korean Ministry and some free time when Yoshida and Okazaki could sit down with Rhee at my house.

Although Rhee agreed to abandon his plans to attend Korean meetings in Tokyo, he still wanted to confer with leaders in the Korean community. We set up a small apartment in a building at my headquarters as his reception room for these meetings. In that way we were able to determine the legitimacy of his visitors from a list provided to us earlier by the Korean Ministry.

The second afternoon of his visit we got down to the real business. Rhee, Yoshida and Okazaki gathered with Murphy and me in the study of my home for tea and talk. Rhee astounded me. He had never seemed so conciliatory. He spoke most frankly of the poor relations between Korea and Japan and said that he hoped ways and means could be found to improve them. He went right to the point of the fishing controversy. Korea, he stressed, was poverty stricken and was deeply dependent upon fishing for a livelihood. Then he picked up a suggestion I had made to him earlier and said he thought it would be a good idea if representatives of the Japanese fishery associations met with him in Korea so that he could explain to them in detail the problem as he saw it. Several times, Rhee stressed that Japan, as the bigger and richer nation, could afford to be more generous in its attitude toward little Korea. This type of appeal is not at all uncommon in the Orient.

Rhee admitted that at times he was outspoken in his views in regard to Japan but that in actuality he was motivated by a friendly spirit.

Bob Murphy and I, after making it clear that our country was most sympathetic to friendly relations between Japan and Korea, kept pretty much out of it. We avoided any word that could be interpreted as an effort by us to influence the talks.

Strangely, Yoshida said very little. But at the end of the conversation which was almost a Rhee monologue Yoshida said enigmatically that the virtue of patience was essential to the solution of any problem. Yoshida took the Rhee presentation for what it was, the opening move in a hard bargain.

Despite the reluctance of Yoshida to get excited about the apparently conciliatory tone of Rhee, the situation looked hopeful by the time the Rhee visit was over, not only for solution of the fishing issue but also for the procurement and Japanese labor problems. Newspapers in both Japan and Korea published editorials that were favorable and it seemed to me it augured well for improved relations.

The evening of the second day, a few hours after the talk with Yoshida and Okazaki, I had a large reception at our home for Rhee. During the evening I presented Rhee with a plaque bearing the flags of all the United Nations countries contributing to the war in Korea and inscribed to him personally. It was the same plaque we gave to all UN commanders who served on our UN team in Korea. Rhee, being Commander in Chief of the valiant ROK Army seemed to me to merit well this recognition. He appeared most grateful and made a fine speech of acceptance.

When Rhee, his wife and their party left for Korea next day I watched the airplane lift into the sky and wondered whether our efforts toward smoothing relations between Japan and Korea would bear fruit. The atmosphere seemed clearer and I was hopeful.

Rhee didn't let the matter drop, either. Five days after he left Japan he wrote me that "it was pleasant to sit together in a friendly atmosphere with the Prime Minister and Foreign Minister of Japan and to have a quiet talk with them."

Rhee noted that "although they refrained from expressing their views, they now have heard something of our story, and I believe they will have something to think about."

Shortly thereafter, I obtained the impression from a reliable source that the Japanese would like to return the visit and I was asked to raise the question with Rhee at an opportune time.

In a case like that I would not invite a representative of Japan to Korea even as the guest of my command without first clearing with the Korean head of state.

I broached the subject to Rhee during one of our many informal chats. I asked him if he would like to have a high-ranking Japanese official visit Seoul. Rhee was very cagey in his reply. He asked me who might make the trip. I told him I had indications that Foreign Minister Okazaki might think of visiting Seoul.

Rhee just looked at me, without answering.

I knew him well enough by then to get the point. So I took the direct approach.

"Do I get the impression, Mr. President," I asked, "that you would like someone to come but perhaps the Foreign Minister is not high-ranking enough?"

Rhee answered most indirectly, but there was no question left in my mind that Rhee felt strongly that if any official came from Japan it should be at least the Prime Minister. In many ways Rhee has great patience. It would have fulfilled a lifelong dream, I believe, if the Prime Minister of Japan had come to Seoul to pay a call on him.

Nothing ever came of the proposed Okazaki visit, and no other Japanese official visited Seoul.

Some Japanese fishermen did go to Korea and did talk with the ROK Government about the fishing problem, but that was as far as it went. When I left the Far East the two countries remained at loggerheads on the fisheries.

The revealing thing about Rhee's refusal to accept Okazaki as a representative of Japan to visit his country is this: it showed clearly how high Rhee ranked himself among the leaders of Asia.

Through the Korean War Rhee had attained a stature in Asia that ranked him with Chiang Kai-shek and Nehru. He had developed into the leader of anti-Communist and many non-Communist Asians. He became a leader not only through the fight against communism, but also through the fact that he was not afraid to stand up against even the United States of America on occasion.

Rhee was no puppet. Rhee was an Asian. Rhee was a strong leader. Rhee had a good army and it was growing. Rhee was anti-Communist and anticolonialist at the same time. To many Asians Rhee brought dignity and pride to the Far East by the struggles, right or wrong, that he made to shape the war in his country to his will rather than to the will of the more powerful nations that were his allies.

Acutely aware of all these factors, I felt that Rhee did not want to tarnish his reputation by dealing with other Asians below the rank of head of state.

His eyes were beyond Korea to the day when he might be the man or one of a handful of men to lead the free Asians against the Communist Asians in a tremendous struggle for survival.

The idea of a Pacific alliance of Asian nations has been a lure to Syngman Rhee for many years. In 1949 Chiang Kai-shek talked about such an alliance when he visited Rhee in the South of Korea, at Chinhae. In 1953, after the Armistice was signed, Rhee flew to Formosa to talk with Chiang again.

Rhee wanted a positive anti-Communist program of all Asians, and he wanted to be a top leader this time, not a slighted man such as he felt he was at times during the war in his own country.

This ambition and vision made him at times difficult to work with. After I suspended the Sea Defense Zone the ROKs took action to clear it of Japanese fishermen. On September 7, 1953, two or three Japanese fishing vessels were seized by ROK patrol boats forty miles east of the Korean island of Cheju and a warning was transmitted from a ROK patrol boat to the Japanese vessel, the *Seiyu Maru*, that said in effect that "all Japanese fishing vessels within the Rhee line must leave the area before midnight."

This caused a sensation in Japan. It was estimated as many as four hundred Japanese fishing vessels were within the "Rhee Line" that day and thus were subject to seizure at midnight.

Officials of the Foreign Ministry, the National Safety Force, the Fishery Board and the Coastal Security Force held an emergency meeting in Tokyo late in the afternoon. It was agreed that if ROK patrol boats violated Japanese territorial waters in seizing Japanese fishing boats the Cabinet itself should decide what to do. In the Diet (Japanese parliament) it was suggested that international mediation be sought if difficulties continued.

And on the high seas there was a mad race of Japanese fishing boats to get back across the Rhee Line.

I was deeply disturbed. Finally, on September 22, 1953, I sent a message to the Joint Chiefs of Staff in which I said that the problem was becoming more acute and that there was no indication of any more conciliatory attitude by Rhee. I said the time was at hand for positive action on our part.

We could not have an effective alliance of free nations in the Orient if each felt free to run a private little war with his neighbor that could disrupt the whole system of security the free world was striving to create.

Shortly after I sent my recommendations to Washington I left the Far East for home and retirement. As far as I know, months after the Armistice was signed there still was no solution to this knotty problem.

12

Building the ROK Army

Whatever criticism we Americans may have had of President Rhee and the ROK Government for their campaign to sabotage our efforts to achieve an armistice in Korea, we must have deep respect for Rhee for his steadfast hatred of the Communist evil, the leadership he displayed in sparking his people to fight even to the death against the aggressor, and for the willingness of Rhee and his people to make any sacrifice in their struggle to keep their precious bit of earth, their homeland, free of the Red tyranny.

And I must repeat that I was never completely at ease in my own mind about the rights and wrongs of the controversy over our anti-Communist strategy in Korea. History well may prove that Rhee was more right than we were when he opposed the Armistice and declared that for the good of the free world as well as for Korea the Communists had to be defeated militarily in Korea.

The relationship of the ROK Government and Army to the United Nations Command was based solely upon an almost informal letter President Rhee sent to General MacArthur on July 15, 1950. In twenty days the North Korean Communist Army, given heavy equipment, tanks and war planes by the Russians, had crushed the South Korean Army, which had little more than police riot weapons. MacArthur had rushed the understrength 24th U.S. Infantry Division over to Korea from Kyushu, Japan, to stem the Red tide long enough to permit him to move stronger forces over to the peninsula. The 24th, under Major General William F. Dean, fought a valiant rearguard action and was successful in slowing down the Reds long enough to permit MacArthur to move the 25th U.S. Infantry Division and the 1st U.S. Cavalry Division to Korea with heavy equipment.

On July 15th, just six days before the epic stand of the 24th was broken at Taejon, where General Dean was cut off from his troops, President Rhee wrote to General MacArthur:

In view of the joint military effort of the United Nations on behalf of the Republic of Korea, in which all military forces, land, sea and air, of all the United Nations fighting in or near Korea have been placed under your operational command, and in which you have been designated Supreme Commander of United Nations Forces, I am happy to assign to you command authority over all land, sea and air forces of the Republic of Korea during the period of the continuation of the present state of hostilities; such command to be exercised either by you personally or by such military commander or commanders to whom you may delegate the exercise of this authority within Korea or in adjacent seas.

The Korean army will be proud to serve under your command, and the Korean people and Government will be equally proud and encouraged to have the over-all direction of our combined combat effort in the hands of so famous and distinguished a soldier, who also in his person possesses the delegated military authority of all the United Nations who have joined together to resist the infamous Communist assault on the independence and integrity of our beloved land.

With continued highest and warmest of personal regard,

Syngman Rhee.

MacArthur replied through channels as follows:

Please express to President Rhee my thanks and deepest appreciation for the action taken in his letter of 15 July. It cannot fail to increase the coordinated power of the United Nations forces operating in Korea. I am proud indeed to have the gallant Republic of Korea forces under my command. Tell him I am grateful for his generous references to me personally and how sincerely I reciprocate his sentiments of regard. Tell him also not to lose heart, that the way may be long and hard but the ultimate result cannot fail to be victory.

MacArthur.

This letter from Rhee and message from MacArthur constituted the entire basis for the legal relationships between the United Nations Command and the Republic of Korea through the war in Korea. The Rhee letter to MacArthur was the sole legal basis of my command control over the ROK Army two years later when I took over in the Far East.

It was binding, however, and Rhee only deviated from it once. That was when he issued orders unilaterally to certain elements of his army to release anti-Communist prisoners of war. The elements involved in the release were part of Lieutenant General Won Yon Duk's special Provost Marshal Command, which the Koreans insisted was a special arm of the ROK Government and therefore not under my control. This, of course, was a legalism which would have been difficult to support and which, in any event, was a clear violation of the spirit of the agreement Rhee made with MacArthur.

In the early days the ROK Army was long on courage but short on everything else needed to fight a war successfully. The ROK units were overrun. Some broke and failed to carry out assigned missions. They were criticized by fighting men of other nations who, on the basis of the early months of the struggle, said the ROKs were unable to stand before the enemy.

With hindsight it could be said that nothing else could have been expected. The South Koreans went into battle pretty much with their bare hands against the mechanized legions the Communists hurled across the 38th Parallel before dawn on June 25, 1950. The North Koreans had World War II equipment, it was true, but the T/34 Russian medium tank and the propellor-driven Russian YAK fighter planes that fought the Germans in 1945 were still effective weapons in 1950, particularly against an enemy that had neither tanks nor warplanes nor antitank guns. Shells from the light bazookas carried by both South Koreans and Americans during the first weeks of the war bounced off the Russian tanks, which for a while were considered invincible machines with a new type of armor impervious to any antitank shells America had. Arrival of the heavier 3.5 bazookas dispelled this old wives' tale.

As the war progressed and developed into a pattern the ROKs still were a weak link in the UN lines because of a number of factors. They were the last to receive adequate artillery support. Their commanders, new to the art of battle, were reluctant at times to call for close air support, not because they were unfamiliar or fearful of the technique but because they considered it a loss of face to call for help. But good combat divisions were developing in the ROK Army and our American officers in the Korean Military Advisory Group (KMAG) began sending back glowing reports of men like General Sun Yup Paik and outfits like the ROK Capitol Division. The ROK units began to live up to these reports with valor in combat. In addition that essential for a good army, pride in the unit, was developing among the ROK troops and there was a keen and healthy competition among the divisions.

At the very first briefing conference I was given in Washington after my appointment to the command in the Far East, I got the feeling that we should build up the ROK Army to its maximum capability. I favored a military establishment in which the ground forces were predominant, but also believed we should do everything possible to create the nucleus of a navy and air force and expand them as technical skills of the Koreans permitted and as equipment became available.

As my familiarity with the ROK forces grew in the Far East I became an even stronger advocate of beefing up the ROK military establishment as a necessary arm of the worldwide system of free forces opposing the Communist drive for power.

As a base, the ROK Army had splendid manpower resources on which to build, though the physical condition of the South Koreans by and large did not measure up to that of the men we recruit into the American Army at home, chiefly because of a high incidence of tuberculosis. It wasn't until late in the development of the ROK Army that proper safeguards were taken to weed out the physically unqualified men before they were inducted into the Army.

All of us in the American Army were pleasantly surprised by the development of the South Korean as an individual fighting man. We went into the job of building a ROK army with the idea that the South Korean would make a good footslogger but that when it came to technical skills, such as radio and radar, artillery fire control, engineering, communications and other specialized and mechanical aspects of the art of war, he would be found wanting. The mere language difficulty, we felt, would make it next to impossible to train any large number of Koreans to operate our complicated war machinery.

We overlooked the astounding ingenuity of the Oriental, who has been forced to learn to improvise because he lacks so much. The Korean could make things out of nothing or find the needle in the haystack when he had to. There was an elderly Korean who mended GI clothing with an old creaky sewing machine at an American showerpoint near the front. One day the bobbin broke on the old machine to the dismay of the old tailor and the annoyance of the GIs. The young officer in charge hurried out a requisition for a new bobbin necessary to put the sewing machine back in operation. The entire organization of the Far East Command Quartermaster Corps was set in motion. There were telephone calls and requisitions galore.

But there was no bobbin.

The Quartermaster Corps couldn't find one.

All seemed lost until one night the old tailor appeared at the young officer's tent and timidly extended a hand in which lay a gleaming new bobbin.

Where it came from, whom it came from, how the old man had found it, were questions that remained unanswered mysteries of the East.

This native ingenuity paid off in the development of the ROK Army. The average ROK soldier, we found, was capable of assimilating all of the technical instruction we offered him. There was no skill in the American Army in which the South Korean, with proper training, failed to measure up to the high standards set by our own soldiers. There was a fierce determination among the South Koreans which helped to compensate for the language difficulty and the lack of educational opportunities.

I have been to artillery units in which American and ROK batteries fired side by side, under a single American command. I have seen the ROK batteries execute fire missions against the Communist enemy. And I was more than happy to see that their performance, according to our American standards, was as good as the splendid performance of our own American batteries. The American commanders, time after time, told me that the work of the ROK artillery-men measured up in every respect to the work of our own gunners.

Before I left the Far East each ROK division had its full comple-ment of divisional artillery, as combatworthy and as proficient as any commander could ask.

Similar progress was being made by ROK airmen, although lack of equipment from the United States was a deterring factor. When I left the Far East, the ROK airmen, who had been flying conven-tional-type fighter planes, were just in the stage of transition to jets. American Air Force commanders working with the ROKs reported to me that the South Koreans performed splendidly in difficult close support missions, not only for their own ROK infantrymen but also for American and other UN troops. Close support work in Korea was extremely difficult and dangerous. To be effective the airmen had to dive low into rugged valleys and even at the comparatively slow speeds of the F-51 Mustang which the ROKs flew each pilot had to keep one eye on his target and the other on the next hill ahead every time he went down to attack.

But the foundation of ROK military power was the South Korean infantryman, courageous, tireless, hungry for the knowledge that would give him more power as a fighting man, disciplined and will-ing to die in the service of the cause for which his country fought and bled. You didn't have to tell a South Korean that communism was evil. It was an evil that had blighted his beloved country and he saw it all around him, wherever he went.

I don't know what other characteristics you could want in a sol-dier, as an individual, but what South Korea lacked was trained leadership from the noncom ranks on up. As the war grew older he got the noncoms and junior grade officers he needed. They were forged in combat. They were the men who demonstrated on the battlefield that they were worthy of leadership. For these men there was rapid battlefield promotion.

Korea had a great historic military tradition. In Elizabethan times, when the Spanish Armada was being destroyed in the English Channel, the Koreans were winning a sea victory over Japan that was as important in the shaping of Oriental history as was Sir Francis Drake's victory over the Spaniard in shaping European history. Japanese legions, fighting to invade China through Korea, were all the way up to Pyongyang and driving hard for Manchuria when Korean Admiral Yi Sun Sin destroyed the Japanese supply and transport fleet and forced the Japanese to withdraw from all Korea. In Korean military history the significant thing about Admiral Yi's victory was that he employed ironclad ships in the sea battle, the first time any nation anywhere in the world used ironclads.

So there was a warrior's tradition in Korea. But Korea lacked men trained to command large numbers of soldiers, trained to maneuver in open warfare. There was no unbroken military tradition such as other countries have to develop regular classes of officers trained to command.

This deficiency had to be made up as quickly as possible. Younger officers who appeared the most likely to succeed were pushed into high command positions quickly. General Sun Yup Paik was a regimental commander when the war began. He was in his early thirties then. In combat he rose quickly to become a division and then corps commander and finally, still in his middle thirties, he was made a full general and chief of staff of the ROK Army. Other officers Paik's age or younger were division and corps commanders. These men had to learn the hard way, through trial and error. They had not been permitted high rank or first-rate training in the Japanese Army for the Japanese military men, like Japanese civilians, did not want to permit Koreans to learn enough to run their country without Japanese help.

Some of the younger officers who gave initial promise failed to meet the mark, as might have been expected. And had the ROK Army found itself in a fluid war of rapid maneuver and movement of whole divisions and corps this lack of leadership training and experience would have been costly, for few if any of the ROK generals yet knew enough or were sufficiently confident of themselves to command divisions of men in quick-breaking, open modern warfare.

One thing we did while I was Chief of Army Field Forces was

to make room in our already overcrowded schools at home for goodly numbers of Korean officers who had shown signs of high command potential. These officers were sent to the Infantry School, the Artillery School and our Command and General Staff College.

Invariably, despite linguistic difficulties, these Korean officers made fine records that compared well with the records of our own officers. Their eagerness to learn and succeed was astounding. They knew two things that spurred them on. One was that their country was in a death struggle right then and that they had to hurry to prepare themselves to take their part in the battle. The other was that they were at a disadvantage in language so they had to work harder than the American officers to complete the courses. These Korean officers worked all the time. They studied every night, all day on week ends, fighting all the time to learn despite handicaps.

I remember an incident when, as Chief of Army Field Forces, I went to Fort Benning, Georgia, to watch the instruction of the first class of Korean officers sent to America. I have seen a lot of training in my years of experience in the Army, but never had I seen more attentive concentration on the instructor. Not a Korean shifted his eyes from the instructor once during the session. It appeared to me that each Korean officer felt that in some way the mere physical process of unbroken sight of the instructor would speed the process by which he learned from the American teacher.

After I went to the Far East I witnessed this same concentration time after time in the schools the Koreans established for their officers and noncoms. The students would squat on their haunches for hours listening to an instructor explain something like the care and use of a light machine gun. They would focus their eyes on the instructor almost without blinking. Never once did a single student that I saw let his gaze wander. I even tested them. They knew who I was, and in addition the short-statured Oriental has a compulsion to look at a tall man. During class sessions I witnessed I deliberately strolled behind the instructor, looking at the students. I thought certainly some of the Korean students would break their concentration on the instructor and sneak a glance at me. I didn't catch a one.

I made it a practice to make this test often during visits to ROK training schools. Never once did I catch an eye looking my way.

I have never in my life been so impressed with the intensity of military students.

I was impressed, too, with the pride and care the ROK infantryman gave to his rifle. When the rifle was first issued to a South Korean soldier he fondled it, treated it like a baby and sometimes even slept with it. The result was a care of weapons that would make any army proud. In addition to holding his rifle as a mark of pride, the ROK soldier learned what made it work, learned how to take care of it so it always would work, and learned how to shoot it straight. He had the kind of pride in the rifle that I would like to see instilled in our American infantrymen.

The ROK Army military school system was patterned exactly after ours, as was their naval training system. The ROKs during the war developed a Korean West Point and a Korean Annapolis. They created their own war college to give their officers more education as they showed capacity for higher command.

All the senior instructors and most of the junior instructors have been through our schools as well as their own. They taught by our American methods, with our American weapons and from translated versions of our American military texts and manuals.

The ROK Army replacement training centers, where inductees were converted from civilians to soldiers, were exact replicas of ours. The basic infantry training course was sixteen weeks, like ours, and the drills and exercises were patterned after those our Army used to train so many millions of American soldiers during the troubled years of World War II and the Korean struggle.

There were differences in the ROK training program. It was more dangerous and they worked longer hours. More trainees were killed and hurt in their training camps than in ours. The ROK Army was more willing to kill men in training than we were at home. Naturally, I am not an advocate of unwarranted danger in training, but we in the American Army learned long ago that we fail in our duty to the new soldier unless we make his basic training conform as nearly as possible to the combat situation that he will confront.

That was why our Army decided it was important to use live ammunition in training. The new soldier had to become accustomed to the whine of rifle and machine-gun bullets zinging close to his head, and he had to learn the sound of artillery shells booming above him with the roar of a freight train to support his advances.

Live ammunition training is the only way a man can be prepared for the first shock of combat. When millions of men are trained with live ammunition some accidents are inevitable. But the few losses sustained in training accidents pay big dividends in that for every man killed or injured in training accidents many times as many are saved when they first go into battle because they have been prepared for the real thing.

The ROKs carried their live ammunition training program even further than we did and went further, perhaps, toward making their men veterans before they ever got into combat.

The ROKs often employed harsh methods to get things done. I was startled one day when a ton and a half ROK truck careened past our jeep at breakneck speed. I directed the ROK military police officer escorting us to catch the driver and warn him against such reckless driving on those dangerous dirt roads in Korea.

The MPs almost had to run the truck off the road to stop it. By the time we caught up, the MP officer had the story. He and the truck driver came to my jeep and explained the reason for the haste. The truck was loaded with ammunition direly needed at the front. The ROK officer back at the ammunition dump made certain the driver would not tarry along the way by telling him that the "time fuses" on the artillery shells were set to detonate in twenty minutes and that if the driver hadn't unloaded the shells at the front by then he would be blown to Kingdom Come.

It was difficult to keep a straight face, but we did, and I explained as well as I could through an interpreter that the driver had nothing to fear from the shells but that he had plenty to fear from reckless driving.

My assurance carried far less effect than the ammo dump commander's horrible warning, however. The truck driver hurried into his truck and sped off. We caught up with him a few miles further on, about nineteen minutes after we had talked with him. The truck was there, with ammunition intact. I later learned that they found the driver several hundred yards away, awaiting the explosion.

The joint effort of America and South Korea to create a first-rate fighting force of Asian farmers and laborers without technical and educational training for modern war was an outstanding success. The ROK Army was a fine fighting force by the time the Armistice was signed. This success provided a lesson for America and the free world, a lesson which, as I left the Far East, I hoped the free nations would heed.

That lesson was: We must, when necessary, develop Asian armies to fight shoulder-to-shoulder with our own men in the battles against Communist aggression.

As I saw it then, and see it now, each of the free nations must contribute its utmost to the struggle against the power drive of the Communists. Planning on a global scale would require such utilization of resources, and the struggle with the Communists is global.

The Communists are long on manpower, the free world comparatively short. Red China alone has within her borders approximately one fifth of the people in the world today. It would be folly to match American and Western manpower against the combined population resources the Communists now control. Our American men would have to fight in any big test between communism and freedom, and would have to fight in the foxholes and on the hillsides as they did in Korea. But, as in Korea, their ranks would have to be bolstered with the men of other nations so that the manpower advantage the Communists have would be greatly reduced.

There also is the cost factor. In Korea we had the chance to build a new army without all the frills and luxuries that our American army has. Therefore we were able to streamline their divisions. A ROK division did not have all the transportation and elaborate engineering equipment that our American divisions have. ROK soldiers lived on more meager rations, the kind of fish and rice diet they were accustomed to, and which required far less handling and transport than our American rations.

The pay of the ROK soldier, an obligation of the ROK Government, was but a fraction of the pay our men received.

Pay was so low in the ROK Army that it was not only a morale factor but forced whole ROK units to take time for extracurricular activities to make a living for families of their troops. Two divisions stationed on the fairly active East Coast, for instance, operated their own fishing fleets. These divisions were renowned in the ROK Army as wealthy divisions. They sold their fish to their own division mess halls and also to the civilian population. The divisions had an edge over their civilian competitors in the fishing business, of course, for the ROK troops had American Army trucks and gasoline to help them transport their catch.

But overall the low pay meant that a ROK division was on an austerity basis, as compared with ours. The cost of equipment for a ROK division was considerably less, too, than for an American division because the ROKs used far fewer vehicles, bulldozers and other heavy, costly equipment.

In addition the ROK Government did not have to finance the cost of a GI Bill of Rights or National Insurance that gave ten thousand dollars to the family of every American killed in action.

I am not advocating one way against the other, or even comparing the benefits and disadvantages of these two systems. I merely am pointing out that there are available vast numbers of men in free nations who can fight, are willing to fight and who fight at much less cost than do our American soldiers. These men must be prepared in great numbers by the free world to take their places in the war of the two worlds which threatens. There is every reason in the world for us to use these kinds of divisions, supported by our technical equipment and knowledge, rather than for us to try to slug it out alone with the numerically overwhelming Communists.

The same principle applies to Indo-China, Formosa and the other free nations of Asia where manpower is in longer supply than technical skills and abilities. It is not a question of one nation or group of nations using another. It is, rather, a problem in which each nation that wants to remain free must contribute to the common security to the best of its ability.

I do not mean that we Americans will not fight when it is to our interests. We have demonstrated in the past that we will. But I do mean that whenever possible we must find and utilize this untapped reserve of manpower of nations willing to fight to be free.

Our American air and naval support for these armies would be essential, along with tasks for which we are peculiarly suited. The concept must be that the best possible over-all use will be made of the power of the free world.

As of the time of the Korean Armistice, the best possible way to use American military power in such a concept would be air and naval support missions, airborne assaults, amphibious assaults and all the other new techniques of war we learned during and after World War II.

The peace-loving nations must so co-ordinate their military planning that if and when the great struggle begins each of them will be called upon to throw its best punch, its Sunday punch, so that the maximum striking power that can be mustered will crash against the Communists.

Without such planning and co-ordination the dissipation of the strength of the truly democratic world could be disastrous.

The cost of training and equipping an Asian army is not insignificant. It merely is less by comparison than the cost of creating an American army. Austere as the ROK division was, it cost the United tates about 150 million dollars to equip a single South Korean division and fight it for a year. And when our government undertakes, as it has, to maintain a ROK army of approximately twenty-one divisions, with proportionate increases in the strength of the navy and air arms, then it has undertaken a sizeable investment.

But in my opinion it is a good investment providing that we require a considerable degree of understanding and co-operation from the nations who are given this support.

We need them, yes, but they also need us.

This is the basis for any criticism I had of President Syngman Rhee. No matter what history may prove about his differences with our government on the wisdom of the Armistice in Korea, Rhee and the ROK Government were part of the free world, an important

In June 1942 General Clark went to Great Britain as the Commander of the Army Ground Forces in Europe and in October of that year was promoted to Major General. (U.S. Signal Corps Photograph)

Mrs. Maurine Clark, living in Washington, D.C., reminisces before a photograph of the general with his pet dog, Pal. (Photograph is from the Washington Star collection. Copyright Washington Post. Reprinted by permission of the D.C. Public Library.)

In North Africa General Clark maintained close diplomatic relations with the Sultan of Morocco. They are shown here having dinner in June of 1943. (U.S. Army photograph)

In the fall of 1943 General Clark arrives in Naples, Italy, to commend Major General Matthew B. Ridgway, Commander of the 82nd Airborne Division (seated to the left in the Jeep), for his military successes in Italy. (U.S. Signal Corps photograph)

General Clark, Commander of the U.S. Fifth Army, receives the Distinguished Service Cross from President Franklin D. Roosevelt during an unprecedented visit to the combat zone in December, 1943. (U.S. Signal Corps photograph)

General Clark gives the surrender orders to General Fridolin von Senger (left) in May 1945. General von Senger was the Commander of the German 14th Panzer Corps. Major General Benjamin W. Chidlaw (second from right), Commanding General of the 12th Air Force, is at the center of the photograph. (U.S. Army photograph)

General Clark on his return to Washington, D.C., in June 1945, with his wife, Maurine, and daughter, Ann at National Airport. (Photograph is from the Washington Star collection. Copyright Washington Post . Reprinted by permission of the D.C. Public Library.)

Shortly after returning to the United States following the end of World War II, General Clark had a chance meeting with former President Herbert Hoover at Union Railroad Station in Washington, D.C. (Photograph is from the Washington Star collection. Copyright Washington Post. Reprinted by permission of the D.C. Public Library.)

French General Charles E. Mast presents the Grand Cross of the Legion of Honor to Gener⟨al⟩ Clark, Commanding General of the 6th Army, at the Presidio in San Francisco, California, ⟨o⟩ December 18, 1947. (U.S. Signal Corps photograph)

*neral Clark in his favorite pose in a Jeep. In Korea he toured the battlefields in his Jeep, and
s photograph became his trademark there among the troops. (U.S. Army photograph)*

General Mark Clark, president of The Citadel, receives the colors in front of the Padgett-Thomas Barracks at The Citadel in a traditional ceremony. (Photograph is from The Mark W. Clark Collection, The Citadel Archives, Charleston, South Carolina.)

General and Mrs. Clark made many emissary visits back to Asia and to Europe after the general retired from The Citadel. They are seen here arriving in Japan where the general was serving as a U.S. Army Special Consultant. (U.S. Army photograph)

part, and for the good of the whole I considered it Rhee's place to go along with the majority decision after his own concepts were deliberated and rejected. This was particularly true in view of the fact that he did not have the capability to go it alone, and his plans and desires to continue the fight involved sacrifices which had to be made by America. Compromise is an essential ingredient in any alliance.

The whole subject of an "austere" Asian army is one of flux. The fact that the ROKs were accustomed to austerity in their army did not mean they would remain that way. The ROK soldiers became familiar during the Korean War with the abundance of the American Army. The ROK saw the wonderful equipment our industry produces for our American Army. He saw mechanical hole diggers for telephone poles. He saw bulldozers. He saw helicopters carry supplies to men atop mountains that ROK bearers would take many hours to climb. He saw hot food and ice cream delivered in giant tins to Americans in the front-line bunkers. He soon wanted all these things.

There were thousands of Katusas (Korean Army Troops with the U.S. Army) integrated with the men in our divisions, right down to squad level. These Korean soldiers saw a new way of life, and lived part of it through the generosity of our American soldiers. They learned how much our soldiers were paid, how much they were saving or sending home. They saw how many packages of cigarettes the American soldier could buy a week, saw how much money he spent in post exchanges for luxury foods, cameras, souvenirs for the home folks. The Katusas were impressed by the donations the American soldiers made to orphanages and other charities in Korea, how much candy they bought to give to Korean kids.

But most of all the Katusas were impressed with the food the Army provided its soldiers. At first we thought the oriental stomach could not adapt itself to the high caloric American ration.

The case of the powdered coffee sandwiches illustrated some of the difficulties that had to be overcome really to integrate Koreans into our American units.

The Katusas arrived at American units well trained in tactics, care of weapons and other necessary attributes of the soldier. But they didn't know how to eat our American rations.

The first Katusas assigned to the 27th "Wolfhound" Regiment of the 25th Division, for instance, made themselves good and sick very quickly by wolfing down all the sugar they could get hold of.

On the line the Katusas were given their first "C" ration, a can of meat or beans, a can of biscuits, sugar, cookies, powdered coffee and jam, and a plastic spoon. The Koreans were bewildered. They sat in a little group jabbering among themselves, obviously trying to figure out what to do with these cans. The interpreters, wise to the American ways, thought all this a big joke and made no effort to help. Finally a GI took pity on the Koreans and showed them how to open the cans. The Koreans went through the meat and bean cans quickly, right down to the last bit.

Then they came to the more intricate part of the operation. They opened cans that had foods such as they had never seen. Finally they solved their problem: crackers were put on the ground in pairs. Powdered coffee was poured equally on each of the two crackers. Then sugar was poured on the dry coffee and dry powdered milk was put on top of all. The remaining two crackers from the four in the can were used to cap the sandwich, which the Koreans ate with great grimaces of disgust.

It wasn't long, of course, before the ROK soldiers knew just as much about how to eat the rations as did any American GI. They learned all the tricks about which "C" ration cans had the best meal and how a soldier should gulp his first ration down fast so he could get in line in time for seconds.

Our concern about whether the Oriental stomach could take our high caloric rations was needless. The Korean soldier integrated with American units had no trouble learning to eat, enjoy and digest our American chow.

In fact, the desire for American food became a political issue. The ROKs set up a clamor that if their men were good enough to fight beside American troops they were good enough to eat the same as American troops. The ROKs wanted us to feed their whole army, an obligation that always had been that of the ROK Government.

This problem was put in my lap shortly after I arrived to take command. It boiled over in early February of 1953. The ROK Army complained to Eighth Army that the Communist prisoners of war in our camps were fed better than the ROK soldiers who guarded them. The ROKs publicized the charge, of course, and quite a commotion was raised, naturally, because here we were charged with treating captured enemy soldiers better than our allies.

New complaints followed and were publicized. There was the charge that malnutrition was so bad among ROK soldiers that the equivalent of two infantry regiments was hospitalized each month because of diet deficiencies. These charges, of course, were gross exaggerations.

General Harrison and General Herren, at a conference I called in Pusan to investigate this subject, told me on January 16 that the POWs were receiving in some cases more food than the average ROK soldier who was guarding them. The explanation was that the Department of Army set the caloric level of the POW ration and that the ration was issued from U.S. Army food stocks in conformity with procedures established by the Geneva Convention. The ROK Army ration, on the other hand, came from ROK sources directly and was not the responsibility of the UN Command. Some ROK units isolated at distant POW camps were not getting their share.

It was a problem to the command, however, for trouble like that could destroy the morale of ROK troops on whom we depended to hold large sections of the battle line. I directed that immediate action be taken to insure that supplemental rations be issued to all ROK units on guard duty so that they would eat better than Communist prisoners in their custody. This supplemental ration began the next day.

I pointed out to the Department of Army at the same time that the complaint about short rations for the ROKs in general could be a political maneuver to straddle us with the job of feeding the whole ROK Army. Other financial problems between our government and the ROK were simmering at the time and it was a common tactic for the ROK to pile on a number of complaints in hopes they could win concessions on at least some.

We went into the ration problem thoroughly. We found there were no large numbers of malnutrition cases attributable to the ROK Army ration. Some men already suffering malnutrition had been admitted into the Army through loose screening procedures.

The ROK Army then was giving front-line troops a ration of 3,800 calories a day. Men in rear areas, including inductees undergoing the rigorous sixteen-week training program, were given 3,300 calories a day. My experts told me this was not sufficient for men training as hard as these South Koreans were. We arranged that the trainees be given the same ration as front-line troops.

We had been aware for some time that the ROK supply system did not work too well. In the rear areas each soldier was given rice with a caloric value of 2,900 calories a day and his commanding officer was given money with which he was to go out and buy the rest of the ration.

This cash allowance was a jealously guarded command prerogative and, with no central procurement system working to purchase supplemental rations, the food each soldier ate depended upon the ability—or desire—of his commanding officer to go out and find vegetables, fish and meat to go with the rice.

There was no central storage system, no stockpiling of foodstuffs other than rice, so the ROK soldier ate better during harvest season than at other times of the year.

We even found that there was keen competition between ROK Army units for food on the open market, and sometimes there even was competitive bidding for available foods.

We decided that the ROK Army must be urged aggressively to establish a central ration delivery system like ours and to abolish the cash allotments to individual commanding officers.

My advisors believed that there were enough raw foodstuffs within Korea to feed the whole ROK Army if effective procurement and distribution systems were devised. And I felt that the sovereign ROK Government should do all in its power to feed its own troops before the American Government provided supplemental rations.

There was a working precedent for the ROK Government. We fed our tens of thousands of Korean Service Corps troops through a centrally directed procurement and distribution system. It worked.

When I left Korea and Japan the food situation for the ROK Army was improving rapidly.

The ROK Army did not just grow. It had to be nursed and trained and helped before it was old enough and big enough to stand alone.

To do this job we assigned some of our finest officers. Major General Cornelius E. Ryan was head of our Korean Military Advisory Group (KMAG) for a long tour and was succeeded by Major General Gordon B. Rogers. Each started his work with KMAG as a one-star general and was promoted for his record with KMAG.

It was Ryan who supervised the work of translation of our texts and manuals for use in ROK Army schools and training centers. With the help of our KMAG people, the ROKs selected and translated our texts as they went along until they had a fine supply with which to operate military schools in the Korean language.

To General James A. Van Fleet, of course, must go much of the credit for the development of the ROK Army. Van was the most active in promoting the growth of the ROK military forces and was intelligent in the manner in which he utilized the same courses and training methods that we had back home. In addition Van infused the ROK Army with some of his own great spirit.

The greatest boosters of the ROK Army were the American officers and noncoms assigned to work with them. These Americans lived and fought with the ROK front-line units. In combat they came to have tremendous mutual admiration for each other. I knew well how the ROK officers felt, for each time we suggested that perhaps they didn't need the KMAG people any more they protested vehemently.

Credit must be given, finally, to General Sun Yup Paik, the youngster who commanded an army of sixteen combat divisions by the time the Armistice was signed. It was a privilege for me to be associated with Paik. I found him to be a man of high integrity, great courage and fine professional ability, and also a man who was

a team player all the way. Throughout the tortuous course of the
war General Paik always supported the command without reserva-
tion. And always he worked in close co-ordination with Generals
Ryan and Rogers, the KMAG commanders.

Personally I will always remember one little incident with the
ROK soldiers. On sentry duty, the ROK guards always shout at the
top of their lungs when a visiting dignitary passes. I was a little
startled when I first heard these men shouting up towards the next
sentry, but it seemed to be a regular thing. I asked for a translation
of their call and was told that they shouted:

"Everything's all right."

"I only wish everything was all right," I muttered.

13

Our Manpower Shortage

During two terrible wars I, as a commander of American ground troops in action, was obliged to face up to the manpower problem which is an ever-increasing threat to the security of our nation. In Italy and again in Korea I was obliged to scrimp and save, to "cannibalize" rear area outfits in order to beef up our front-line combat units so as to make them more effective.

In Italy the situation was bad but in Korea it was worse. There we ran into the armies of the most populous nation on earth, Red China, and for the first time in our history had to fight an enemy who drew upon the masses of the Asian mainland for his military power.

In Italy and again in Korea I was tempted to speak out and warn Americans of this great danger, but such action, of course, would have violated security, for it would have revealed to our enemies the reduced strength of our armies. I did decide, however, that once it was militarily safe I would lay the facts on the table for Americans to read because I knew that only through this knowledge would my countrymen be prepared to make the sacrifices and psychological changes that I am convinced are necessary for our security as a nation.

Should the ultimate struggle between communism and freedom flare out in open, shooting war tomorrow the Communists would outman us numerically everywhere we fought. The arithmetic is simple. The Union of Soviet Socialist Republics and its satellites at the time of the Armistice in Korea controlled the minds and bodies of 750 million people, by far the greatest population any aggressive force in history has had at its command.

Against this host the United States and its allies would have to draw its armies from a combined population of about 300 million people.

The harsh police rule and the tight thought control of the Communists would, at least in the beginning of any war between the two worlds, weld the 750 million into a cohesive fighting force. That is the evidence of Korea, where the Communists were able to keep an army of 1,200,000 Chinese fighting hard for almost three years despite evidence that many of the Chinese hated communism. The evidence of this was the fact that of twenty thousand Chinese soldiers captured, fifteen thousand declared they would rather die than return to communism.

At the beginning of a war between the two worlds the long years of Communist conspiracy, intrigue and propaganda could be expected to pay dividends through internal troubles in the nations of the free world, troubles that would tend to dissipate the power of the free world by creating friction among allies.

The free world alliance is made up of nations politically equal. Each nation has the right to walk out of the alliance at any time. Not so the Communist "alliance." The masters of this aggressive bloc are in the Kremlin in Moscow and exercise tight control of each of the satellites, welding the whole group of Communist nations into a single force, sensitive to the direction of a single high command, politically as well as militarily.

With such control over so many millions, the Communist masters were able to be profligate with the expenditure of their manpower in Korea, where sometimes Chinese kept moving forward in a human sea over the bodies of their fallen comrades, stacked high like cordwood.

Throughout the Korean War, with the exception of the brief period after the Inchon landing when superior American techniques and firepower destroyed the North Korean Communist Army, the Red enemy was able to throw into battle several times the number of men we had in a given sector. Always the Communist commanders were willing to lose relatively large numbers of Chinese or North Koreans in order to kill relatively few of our men.

This manpower disadvantage may increase depending upon the attitude of India.

The reason goes back twenty years, to our great depression. Birth rates in America dropped alarmingly during those years and at the time of the Korean War we began to feel the manpower shortage that resulted. During the Korean fighting our country entered a period of seven lean years in the harvest of males. Draft calls and enlistments revealed the figures. In the year ending June of 1953 approximately 800,000 able-bodied young American men reached military age. Yet our armed forces called up 1,120,000 men, which forced the use of older men. Population forecasts for the next few years are no better. And in the face of this dearth of men to fight we increased our military commitments to the point where in 1953 we had American troops stationed in forty-nine countries around the world, as compared to troops in only three countries twenty years before. In 1953, American military commitments required the deployment of a million men abroad, not counting those in Korea. Just to meet present peacetime standards would require the draft of one million new soldiers every year for the next decade.

Population forecasts fall far short of this quota. The number of American youths between the ages of eighteen and a half and twenty-six available for induction was forecast as follows:

For the year ending:
>   June 30, 1953—800,000
>   June 30, 1954—840,000
>   June 30, 1955—825,000

In other words, the growing world threat found our normal population handicap vis-a-vis the Sino-Russian combine further aggravated by the fact that a generation ago during our big depression when many men were jobless and had to sell apples to live the birth rate in America dropped alarmingly. Not until 1959, said the population experts, would America begin harvesting as many as a million able-bodied youths a year.

This period of seven lean years coincides with the period of greatest danger to our nation, the years when the very existence of our country as a free democracy has been threatened by the vastest assemblage of manpower in history.

Yet we did not take all the steps possible to make certain that each American in uniform was the match for ten Communists. During the Korean War, when manpower shortage was acute, it was painful for me to land at an airfield in the Far East or in America and have a ramp wheeled out to the airplane by strapping college men, big smart fellows who could have been more profitably employed. I used to think, "A one-armed man could wheel out that ladder and that lad could be at the front with a gun."

I felt the same way when I saw so many soldiers, sailors and airmen driving automobiles in rear areas or even in the big cities of America. The same applied to many thousands of able-bodied men employed in administrative and supply work in the rear, work that well could have been done by women. I will speak more of this later.

Time and again the lesson was pounded home to me in Korea, the lesson that the enemy we faced had too many millions to permit us to waste any of the men we had in our outnumbered manpower pool. Time and again I was forced to realize that in the larger struggle, which was a constant threat, the old luxuries would have to be sacrificed.

I felt strongly that we would have to pull in our belts, cut off some fat. We have always wanted the best of everything for our men—the best medical care, the best equipment, the best-stocked post exchanges, the best service clubs, the best entertainment, the best in food and clothing. In Korea that search for the best went so far as to make ice cream an item of regular distribution to front-line units.

Our rotation system in Korea sent hundreds of thousands of our men home after nine to twelve months service in the front line. That was the Big R. The Little R was five days of Rest and Recreation leave in Japan for war-weary GIs who were given air travel to Japan and back.

Rotation is a subject always in the minds of men in combat. There is a danger that because American fighting men enjoyed the privilege of rotation in Korea they may in future wars consider it their inherent right.

Unfortunate as it may be, rotation cannot be the right of combat men in all-out war. There can be no time limit set on the duty an American citizen owes his nation during time of great danger.

The problem was with me in Italy. During the hard winter of 1943–44 there arose a great deal of discussion during the early winter about whether men should be shipped home after so many months of combat service. I was disturbed by this talk because I considered that it represented a lack of effective leadership in the units involved.

I instructed all my subordinate commanders to "give particularly careful attention" to the welfare of the troops and to keep the men informed of the progress of our operations in Italy and operations in other theaters so as to improve morale and spike unfounded rumors.

The *Mediterranean Stars and Stripes*, published for the soldiers and sympathetic to their point of view, tried to be as objective as possible about the rotation problem. It published many letters from men who thought there should be some system of rotation. This kept the controversy going. Again I wrote to my subordinate commanders, and said:

Unfortunately, our *Stars and Stripes* has stirred up this subject. An editorial in that paper has provoked letters from enlisted men urging that veteran troops be returned to their homes and that new divisions from the United States be brought into overseas theaters to replace them. It is natural for many soldiers to wish to return home, without realizing the problems involved in such a program.

I want you to take immediate steps to see that this subject is thoroughly explained to all individuals. Shipping is the most important factor. It will not permit exchange of divisions between the United States and the various theaters, even if they were available. Even now, we are struggling to build this theater up to the strength required. We can give no thought to troops going home at the present time.

During an all-out war, such as World War II, there could be no thought of rotation. Men had to be put into uniform for the duration, and the combat infantryman had to fight for the duration. Our enemy in Korea fought like that. There was no rotation for a Chinese or North Korean except in a wooden box or without a leg.

But rotation for us in Korea meant that we no sooner got a team working effectively than key men were through with their part of the war and were sent home, to be replaced by recruits from the United States or, at times, by Koreans from the Katusas.

Rotation was necessary for the kind of limited war we fought in Korea. It was necessary because it would have been unthinkable to call on a tiny percentage of young American manhood to carry the entire burden of the Korean War. The rotation system made it possible for us to achieve some degree of equalization of sacrifice.

I would be the last commander to be miserly with medical care, food, clothing and equipment for our fighting men. Certainly the men who fight to safeguard our nation should have the best that our people can produce to help them win as quickly, as efficiently and with as little sacrifice in lives as possible.

I always insisted that my men in battle have the finest care that our medical profession can provide. The same goes for fighting equipment, clothing and food.

But the amenities in the American Army will have to be the first casualty in any big war with communism.

The Communists have tough men on their side. The Russian or the Chinese lives in a rough, hard community from infancy. He has to learn to fight for what he gets, and he has to learn early. The hard life of war is not as great a break from normalcy for him as it is for our men.

For our high standard of living and our glorious system of political freedom permits us the luxury of spoiling our children, of protecting them from hard knocks which children in other countries accept as inevitable. We, in our homes, try to give our kids every advantage of the freedoms which we enjoy, and by giving them full advantage of these freedoms, by devoting our every effort to making things comfortable and easy for them, we make it that much tougher when they have to fight these Communists who are inured to hardship and privation from birth.

I know I spoiled my children in this way and that most Americans spoil theirs the same way. We give them security of the home, freedom from fear, freedom from worry about where their next meal is coming from. Those things our children take for granted. And the whole point of our effort for defense is to make certain that they keep on taking them for granted.

The Army has to take youngsters out of these protected homes and make them tough in a short time, tough in the sense that the Communist soldier is tough. I remember a woman once wrote me that she hoped I would make a man of her son, who had just entered the Army, that I would develop his character. I replied to her that I would do my best, that I was sure his military service would help him, but that she should realize that we would have him for eighteen months and she had had him for eighteen years. I added that the job of developing character in our youth was primarily the responsibility of the home, the churches and the schools.

I will say, though, that when these American lads did get into a fight, against the Germans, the Japanese, the North Koreans or the Chinese Communists, they were fighting men as smart and as tough as any commander could desire. Training was part of the answer. The fine combat leadership with which we were blessed in the field in Korea was another part of the answer. The American tradition of struggle for liberty and freedom from Concord, Lexington and Bunker Hill right down to Heartbreak Ridge was a greater part of the answer. The tradition we have, and I sincerely believe we will have always. The training and utilization of the men can be improved, always.

As I said earlier, I am dedicated to the concept that every man taken into the Army must be made a competent infantryman before he is transferred to any one of our specialized branches. When I was Chief of the Army Field Forces, we were able to give every soldier eight weeks basic infantry training before he was switched to the artillery or the tanks or signal corps or any of the other special branches. Eight weeks is only half enough. Each man should get the full sixteen-week course.

Then a commanding general would know that the great majority of the men in his division, corps or army were qualified infantrymen, trained to fight with a rifle, to work in a squad. Each division then would be able to spread the burden of war more equitably among its soldiers and would be able to relieve to a degree the nervous and physical strain of combat on most of its men.

With almost every soldier in a division a qualified doughboy, the commanding general would be able on a given day to issue a change-post order which would automatically relieve, say, 10 per cent of the front-line infantrymen and replace them with an equal number of artillerymen, engineers, clerks, cooks and other soldiers who had been in posts more protected than those of the infantrymen. By spreading the burden in this way each division commander would have the means to conserve his men and give his division more staying power. He also would have a powerful morale builder because his men would know that through this intradivision rotation system there was some promise of relief from combat.

Once during the Korean War I decided to set up a test in which some artillerymen and others would relieve an equal number of infantrymen on the line for a short time, just to see whether it would work. The test never was made, however, because the artillerymen had had only six weeks of basic infantry training and it would not have been fair to the men or their families to put them in the front line with rifles in their hands. I dropped the matter.

In Korea everybody wanted the Combat Infantry Badge. It is considered one of the highest awards of the American Army. Everybody in Korea also wanted full point credits toward rotation. The combat infantryman earns more points than anyone else, and should get them. We gave the Combat Infantry Badge to infantrymen and a similar one to the medics who served alongside them, and to nobody else. The others, serving in support roles for the fighting infantryman, were not awarded the Combat Infantry Badge and they got points for rotation at a slower rate than did the front-line doughboys.

Under a system of equal training and equal service through rotation of men in the line companies, most soldiers in a division could win the Combat Infantry Badge and rotation points would be distributed equally.

Pride in infantry service and in individual outfits is an essential element in making an army effective. The American Marines have it, and benefit from it. They are tough, cocky, sure of themselves and their buddies. They can fight and they know it. Our Army infantry divisions did get this same kind of pride in combat in World War II and in Korea. Success on the battlefield gave them a cocksure attitude which sometimes became a little hard to take. I can remember men of veteran Army divisions in World War II who would clear the sidewalks of soldiers wearing the shoulder patch of newly arrived, untried outfits.

Fighting is an ugly business at best, so if you must fight it is good to have men on your side who are in a fighting mood.

I strongly believe that the rifle must be made the basic symbol of pride for the infantryman. The award of the rifle must be made to mean something to each recruit. There should be ceremony attached to the award of this weapon. The recruit must be made to look forward to the day of this award as the goal of his training period. Then, when he earns it, the recruit should be handed his rifle by his general before his fellows, not by a supply sergeant behind a counter.

Once he gets that rifle he should keep it throughout his military service. It should not be taken away from him when he completes his training, just at the time that he has full confidence in it, knows its characteristics and how to hit the target.

Under our present system it is precisely at this time that the gun is taken away from the soldier. As a result, a man who went to fight in Korea would get another weapon just before he went into combat. Time and ammunition were required to familiarize him with the characteristics of this different weapon.

I recommended to Washington on more than one occasion that each new man coming from a training center to Korea bring with him his own tried and tested rifle. The logistical experts in Washington did not look favorably upon this plan, saying that it would cost more and require more rifles in service. I still think it's worth a try.

The backbone of our Army is the nine-man infantry squad. That is the basic fighting unit of our ground forces. It is the accumulated successes of a lot of these little teams that brings victory to an army. A general executing a plan of battle may find all of a sudden that he has had a victory. The reason is that these little squad teams have done their stuff.

The importance of good team spirit on the squad is this: an infantryman will go forward valorously, take the extra chance necessary for an heroic deed, only if he can be certain that Tom on his right and Dick on his left will do their part. In Korea it wasn't Tom and Dick; it was Gonzales and Kim because men of so many nationalities were teamed together in our squads. When a rifleman creeps forward alone toward the enemy he must be confident that his buddies on the squad will stand their ground and cover him if he runs into trouble. An American soldier is not a suicidal fighter. He wants an even chance. Given that chance by the help of his squad mates he is the equal of any soldier on earth in valor.

There is much talk these days about push-button warfare and the fact that the technical experts have developed such weapons of mass destruction that the role of the infantryman is now secondary. There has been great technical development in weapons and I hope our experts in research and development will continue to make improvements. However, in my opinion, and without in any way disparaging the vital roles of the Air Force and the Navy, the infantryman remains an indispensable element in any future war. Certainly he must be supported by the Air and the Navy and every kind of technical weapons, but he never will be relegated to an unimportant role. He is the fellow with the stout heart and a bellyful of guts, who, with his rifle and bayonet, is willing to advance another foot, fire another shot and die if need be in defense of his country.

Don't misunderstand me. By emphasizing the continuing importance of the role of the infantryman, I do not for a minute intend to detract from the importance of air power. Our ability to deliver the atomic bomb great distances and to deny the enemy the parallel ability to drop it on us is essential and certainly a deterrent to all-out war.

But air power cannot do the job alone. Infantrymen must protect the bases from which Air operates and must be prepared to fight to secure and protect more advanced bases.

I was always concerned with the squad, and always tried to form squads with men who could work and live and fight as a unit. This became an acute problem in Korea because of our manpower situation. We had men of many backgrounds and languages in our American divisions in Korea—whites, Negroes, Koreans, Hawaiians, Mexicans, American Indians and Puerto Ricans. The Negro infantrymen were spread through the regular Army divisions after their own regiment in the 25th Division and Negro battalions in other divisions were disbanded early in the war. Washington granted me approval to put up to 2,500 Koreans in each American division and to use them as regular infantrymen. It had been my idea that these Korean soldiers would be used to augment the strength of our divisions so as to increase their fighting power. It never was my intention to use Katusas to replace Americans in our divisions. But that is the way it worked out at times. Instead of being permitted to achieve an overstrength of 2,500 men in each division, I found that the number of replacements from the United States declined and the Katusas were used to keep the divisions up to regular strength. At one time I was 20,000 men short in the Far East Command.

By Armistice time in Korea our basic infantry squads were a hodgepodge of tongues and people. The Puerto Rican soldiers were American citizens but many spoke nothing but Spanish. The same was true of the Mexicans. This language difficulty diluted the fighting effectiveness of the all-American squad team. I investigated the composition of the average nine-man squad in Korea and was astonished to learn it was made up roughly as follows: four white Americans, one Negro American, two and a half Koreans and the remainder Puerto Ricans, Mexicans, Hawaiians and American Indians.

The Koreans, Puerto Ricans and Mexicans often had to get along with their squad mates without benefit of spoken language. The men quickly picked up enough words to talk of simple things, but it was difficult in a pinch when the squad leader had to control his men with one-word shouted orders.

In addition the Negro, the Korean, the Puerto Rican and the Mexican each presented an individual problem. The Negro, particularly, knew he had a lot to prove before he would be accepted as a full partner by the whites alongside him. Most Negro infantry units had spotty records in World War II and in the early fighting in Korea. Because of the way the Negro fought in an integrated army in Korea it would be worthwhile to review the judgment I made of him after World War II, when he fought in segregated units. In the book *Calculated Risk* I wrote:

Leadership was one of the biggest problems. There were many illiterates among the Negro troops; hence it took longer to train them, and there was, in general, a reluctance to accept responsibility for the hard, routine discipline that is essential in wartime. This failure I view not as a reflection on the Negro soldier or officer, but as a reflection on our handling of minority problems at home. The Negro had not had the opportunity to develop qualities of leadership. Most of all, perhaps, the Negro soldier needed greater incentive; a feeling that he was fighting for his home and country and that he was fighting as an equal. Only the proper environment in his own country can provide such an incentive.

It would be a grave error, however, to assume that no suitable officers can be found for Negro combat troops. In fact, they were found in Italy. When it became necessary to reorganize the 92nd in the following weeks, we were able to select certain battle-proven officers and men who responded to special training, and to build up battalion combat teams that participated much more effectively than before. I have decorated for bravery Negro officers and men of the 92nd Division and have known of others who were killed in extremely valorous actions on the field of battle.

Let me make it clear that I am opposed to discrimination. I believe there is a way to work toward a solution of the problems that handicap the Negro soldier, although I do not feel that at this stage of the game there should be an indiscriminate mixing of Negro and white soldiers in our Army. On the basis of performance in the last war, it would not produce the best fighting team and it would not be fair to anyone. I do believe, however, that there can be sound integration of Negro and white troops at the battalion and lower levels, that regiments could include one effective Negro battalion in any branch of the service, and that it could be provided with sound, responsible leadership.

I added at that time that "I do not think that this system should be practiced in units larger than the battalion," and said, "Our experience in Italy did not indicate that a Negro division could perform as effectively as a smaller unit under the severe test of modern warfare."

I always was reluctant to put a man on the basic infantry squad unless he qualified for the team. Necessity was the mother of invention in Korea, however, and we found complete integration the best solution to the problem. The Negro proved to be a better soldier when fighting alongside the whites than in an all-Negro unit. Besides, it helped break down many of the prejudices which existed at home. The Negro was winning a place he never before held among his fellow Americans.

A morale hardship in Korea developed from economy in Washington. Budgetary limitations made it difficult to promote men who had earned more stripes or higher rank through outstanding leadership in battle. Many corporals were holding down the job of squad sergeant, and doing fine work as a combat leader, but we were unable to promote them. Scores of lieutenants were commanding companies in combat. They were made company commanders because they had demonstrated their stuff in combat. But I could not give them their captain's bars. Each of these men must have wondered why the money to give him the rank commensurate with his job and responsibilities could not be provided.

Such doubts add to the morale problems in any army.

The American soldier, of course, does a great deal to take care of his own morale. He makes the best of some pretty bad situations, laughs his way out of many troubles, and one way or another, manages to get relief from the tedium of his task.

In any organization as big as our Army there is an overlapping of functions, duplication, unnecessary work, "fat" that can be eliminated and used for better purposes. I found this to be true when I arrived in the Far East in 1952. Very early I directed that a manpower-saving project be instituted. The results were surprising. In the nine months from the end of July of 1952 to the end of April, 1953, in the Far East Command alone we eliminated jobs for 7,106 enlisted men, 600 officers, 24 warrant officers, 22 American civilians and 3,716 Japanese. This was accomplished chiefly by consolidating headquarters, but we also went through all installations closely to reduce unnecessary or overlapping work. The elimination of jobs for 7,630 American officers and men in Japan meant that our over-all combat strength in the Far East gained by 7,630 men, the better part of two combat infantry regiments.

As the shooting ended in Korea I felt our nation would have to institute a four-point program to offset the formidable manpower advantage the Communists held over us and the free world. The four points interlocked, and each was part of a program aimed at making each American count for several Communists in any test of arms.

First and foremost we had to maintain and increase our technical advantages over the Communists with a speed-up in research to develop even better weapons of all types, from the mass destruction missiles that could circle the globe to the machine gun and rifle that must be carried by the footslogger in the man-to-man combat that remained the basis of warfare.

Next, we had to institute a program of tough infantry training for the full sixteen weeks for every able-bodied man entering the army. During the Italian campaign I knew what it was to have to dip into antiaircraft, tank and engineer units for replacements for the infantry. Heavy fighting so riddled our infantry units I had to pull men out of supporting units and order them forward to fill vacancies in the rifle companies. About that time an irate American mother wrote me a stinging rebuke. She threatened to sue me for transferring her son from an antiaircraft battalion, for which he had been trained, into an assault infantry company. In my answer

I told the mother I was as sorry as she was that our American army was in a position in which it had to "cannibalize" rear area units to maintain effective strength at the front. But I told her the bald, frightening fact that unless we pulled men out of their special fields and threw them forward into foxholes with rifles we might lose the war. The incident helped clarify my conviction that we had to train every man to fight with a rifle.

My third point was that luxuries had to go.

These three points I feel certain Americans will accept without too much fuss. The fourth point could become tremendously controversial for it would necessitate a radical change in the psychology of the average American. Personally, I did not like it when I first began to turn it over in my mind. But as time went on, when I realized more fully the manpower disadvantage we must overcome, the idea became less and less repugnant to me. By the time the Korean Armistice was signed I was ready to propose flatly:

AMERICAN WOMEN MUST BE DRAFTED FOR MILITARY SERVICE IF WE EVER ARE FORCED TO FIGHT WORLD COMMUNISM.

These women would not be called on to lead combat assaults like latter-day Joans of Arc, nor would they be forced to follow their men into battle carrying ammunition, food and other supplies and wielding bayonets on occasion, as the women of Russia have been forced to do.

But single women of draft age would have to be sent by the hundreds of thousands into every battle area in which our men must fight. Front-line duty would be the job of the men, but behind the lines there are thousands upon thousands of jobs which women can do and have done, jobs which when filled by women would free these men for duty at the front.

These women should be trained in the use of the pistol and carbine so that when necessary, in case of an enemy break-through, they could help to defend themselves. They also should be trained in some heavier weapons, such as antiaircraft guns, so they could take over men's work at home or in rear areas abroad. British women manned antiaircraft batteries in England during the last war when their country faced a dangerous shortage of manpower for combat duty. And in case of atomic attack, the women working the antiaircraft batteries would not be exposed to greater danger than the civilian population around them.

I would be the first to decry such a departure from the ideals fostered by a civilized democracy if it were not essential. I am aware that democracy has always aspired to protect and cushion the shock of war for its womenfolk. But I also am aware that in our national history there are countless stories of the heroism of women who picked up the rifles of their husbands to fight on in defense of their log cabin homes or their covered wagons against the onslaught of the Indian. And I also hold to the conviction that a democracy battling for survival cannot afford to grant immunity from the obligations of citizenship to anyone, man or woman.

In the past we have made the Woman's Army Corps completely volunteer. That proved inadequate during the Korean War. At the height of that war we were able to recruit only 48,000 WACs, WAVEs, WAFs and women Marines. In a big war we would have to have far more than that, and a draft appears the best answer.

Peacetime regulations prescribe strict limits to the use of women soldiers. They are that (a) the physical demands of the job must not exceed the capacities of the average enlisted woman; (b) the job is not performed in an undesirable or isolated field location; (c) the job does not involve factors psychologically unacceptable to an enlisted woman or to the persons she is in contact with on her job; (d) the job is of a type culturally acceptable to the American people as suitable employment for women. Obviously in a third world war some of these regulations would have to be modified.

But even with these strict peacetime regulations there exists a wide variety of jobs open to women, jobs now held largely by men. All told there are 145 different specialty jobs open to women in the peacetime army. There have been few women volunteers for these jobs, which include radio communication and Morse code interceptor, teletypewriter operator, gas mask repairman, fiscal specialist, cook, key punch operator, cartographer, nurse, medical corpsman, military policeman, counterintelligence agent, heavy vehicle driver, administrative NCO, photographer, pharmacy technician, shoe repairman, bandsman, QM supply specialist, ammunition supply specialist, small arms repairman, electrical instrument repairman, baker, interpreter and barber.

The first women soldiers to go into active operation in a combat theater with our American Army were the two hundred sent to my Fifth Army in North Africa. They arrived at a critical time, when we were having trouble mustering enough troops for the front lines. We needed clerks, stenographers and typists badly. The women did a magnificent job. They followed closely behind our invasion forces at Salerno and Anzio. Their deportment in the hard days that followed was admirable. As in most cases of women in the Army, they became efficiency experts, practically revolutionizing men's standards of speed for a given task. They bounced over bomb-cratered roads in jeeps in the snow and under the prostrating sun. They kept the typewriters clattering and the men's morale high. They did a whale of a job.

Some day we may need a million of their sisters.

It may be a hard thing for the American people to accept the draft of women into military service. But the alternative could be something far worse. Military men must think in terms of alternatives. I recall a story from World War II. Japanese on a mountaintop were firing down on American troops in a valley. The commanding officer ordered the men in the valley to climb to the mountaintop and destroy the enemy. "It may be cold up there," the commander said, "but it's a damn sight colder dead."

Our people in America have demonstrated time and again they have the courage to perform any service required for the security of our country. The magnificent infantryman fighting the frustrating, unhappy war in Korea demonstrated that.

His kinfolk and parents behind him demonstrated it, too. I wrote a letter to the parents of every lad killed in Korea. Only a small percentage of the parents replied, but in all the letters I got there was not one that was bitter. In my letter of condolence I always used the statement that the soldier "died manfully." Almost invariably, those people who answered made reference to that phrase with an expression of sad pride. To me the fact that a bereaved American father and mother could take consolation in the statement that their son died manfully in Korea was a sad but heartening thing.

To me it meant that the spirit of pride remains strong in America and will make itself felt against any threat.

14

The War on the Propaganda Front

Psychological warfare took many forms in Korea. It ranged from the virulent and completely false Communist charges that the United Nations Command used germ warfare to the unplanned, spontaneous generosity of American and Allied soldiers who contributed their spare time and money to help orphanages, schools and hospitals.

In essence psychological warfare means winning friends or influencing people. We won friends through the great generous heart of our soldiers in Korea. We influenced people with such devices as the leaflets that warned the people of the Communist capital of Pyongyang when military targets in their city would be bombed. The practical effect of these warnings was that people fled for cover and Communist war work was disrupted.

In large measure the Communist POW camp uprisings served the Red psychological warfare campaign, for they weakened the UN Command in the eyes of friend and foe and obscured the arguments at Panmunjom where the Communists had taken a terrible psychological warfare beating when so many thousands of their people in our prison camps vowed they would rather die than return to communism.

Our most spectacular psychological warfare exploit was our successful offer of a one hundred thousand dollars reward for the first MIG pilot to fly a combat MIG to us undamaged. I broadcast the offer in April of 1953 but I cannot claim credit for the plan which was hailed in some quarters as a master stroke of psychological warfare and denounced in others as a cheap and even unethical stunt. Personally, I never could comprehend what was unethical about the offer. It was made in good faith and the bargain was kept when a North Korean finally did fly a MIG into our lines. As far as I was concerned, the only people who would complain about such a tactic on any grounds were people who were less interested in the welfare of the United Nations than they were in avoiding anything that might hurt the Communists.

For my part, I think the idea hit the jackpot.

It originated early in 1952 in the fertile mind of a war correspondent who shall remain nameless at his own request. While communing with a bottle of brandy in the Seoul correspondents' billet, he got to thinking about the effect of "silver bullets" on the Chinese. He then dreamed up and wrote the MIG reward suggestion in an imaginary interview with an "anonymous" and nonexistent Air Force general.

Far from being upset, the Air Force in Tokyo decided the idea had merit, dressed it up and bucked it to the Department of the Air Force in Washington. From there it made the rounds of nearly every agency in the Pentagon and the State Department. The first I heard of it was in a Department of the Army message of November, 1952, suggesting that we obtain a Communist aircraft by psychological warfare. I thought it was a good idea and we got busy.

It wasn't until late April, however, that I made the offer of $100,-000 reward and political asylum to the first Communist pilot in Korea to deliver us an undamaged MIG and $50,000 and asylum for each succeeding MIG pilot who flew us a Communist jet airplane.

The offer was broadcast shortwave in Korean, Chinese and Russian and printed in the three languages on leaflets dropped as far north as the Yalu. We used the Russian language for the good reason that Russian pilots were flying some of these MIGs. Ever since the Russian-built jets made their first appearance in North Korean skies in November, 1950, the question of whether there were Russians at the controls had been a "hot" topic. Our pilots reported Russian spoken on the MIGs' radio intercom. A few returned UN POWs said they had talked to Russian pilots while in North Korean prison camps. From these and more positive sources it may be said categorically that the UN Command had in its possession adequate information that Soviet pilots—sometimes in considerable numbers and often the Russian first team—engaged our jets in combat.

I issued the reward offer the day after armistice talks resumed in April, toward the end of the exchange of sick and wounded POW's in Operation Little Switch. The timing was deliberate. We were having trouble with Syngman Rhee about the Armistice and I wanted the Communists to have some extracurricular worries of their own.

After the Armistice was signed we forgot all about the offer until a day two months later when a North Korean pilot zoomed his MIG out of nowhere, landed at Kimpo Airfield near Seoul and asked asylum. He claimed he never had heard of the $100,000 reward offer but was more than happy to accept the money. On orders from Washington, we withdrew the offer of fifty thousand dollars for each subsequent MIG and even offered to return the one we had if the "rightful owner" stepped up to claim it. Nobody made a claim. It might have been embarrassing right then for the Communists to have to present proof to the United Nations of the rightful ownership of that airplane for the Reds were even then preparing their big arguments to try to win a vote for Russia as a "neutral" at the political conference to consider Korean political problems.

Despite statements made at home that we were not particularly interested in *that* MIG because it was an old model, the Air Force got its $100,000 worth—and more. It was the first combat MIG we ever laid hands on long enough to test. The two MIGs flown to Denmark by Polish pilots were trainers and were returned to the Communists unflown. The North Korean pilot gave us invaluable information, including corroboration that the Communists were violating the Armistice terms by moving MIGs from Manchuria into the so-called non-military airfields in North Korea.

I also believe the reward offer bagged us at least a dozen other MIGs—shot down.

The Reds' first reaction to it was to ground all MIGs for eight days. It might have been because of the weather, or because they wanted time to screen out the politically unreliable pilots. Most likely it was the latter. An eight-day break in MIG operations in Korea was most unusual.

Significantly, an unlocated radio transmitter began jamming our *Russian* language broadcasts of the offer, but did not interfere with the Korean or Chinese language versions.

For whatever reason, the Communist MIG pilots who were permitted to fly after the offer was made were the worst—on their record—of the whole Korean War. They flew far fewer missions in those last ninety days than in the preceding three months, but American Sabrejet pilots shot down twice as many. In fact, the Sabres destroyed 165 MIGs against three friendly combat losses— a record ratio of 55 to one.

Which lends point to the cartoon in *Punch*, the British weekly, showing two Communist officers standing by a row of bunks. Over three bunks are pictures of Mao Tse-tung, while over a fourth is a picture of Marilyn Monroe. Lying in the fourth bunk is a relaxed and smiling airman whose footlocker is marked MIG PILOT. Near it is a leaflet, which says, "UN offers $100,000 for MIG." One inspecting officer says to the other, "It's okay, Tovarisch, he's been grounded." Perhaps the grounded MIG pilots with the secret yen for freedom, $100,000 and Marilyn Monroe were the best the Commies had.

Not as spectacular as the MIG offer, but perhaps even more profitable to us, was the Plan Strike tactic of dropping warning leaflets on areas scheduled for bombing attack. We could not have done this without complete mastery of the air, of course, so it is not a tactic which could be utilized in every stage of any war. General Curtis LeMay, who commanded the B-29 wings that smashed Japan during the last seven months of the Pacific War, used an earlier version of the same basic technique in the final weeks before Japan surrendered. With the Japanese air force unable to offer effective resistance to the B-29s, LeMay began calling his punches. He dropped leaflets advising the Japanese the names of ten Japanese cities that were possible targets.

We went further. We dropped leaflets on Pyongyang to tell the people specifically that we would hit their city. The objective was in part humanitarian and in part practical. We had to hit Pyongyang because the Communists had made it a major military headquarters and stockpile area. We wanted to warn the people away from danger areas. By warning them away we disrupted their daily lives and made it difficult for the Communists to maintain any kind of schedules of war work in the city.

By the end of September of 1952 the plan already had borne fruit. My Intelligence Section in Tokyo rated the effect of the tactic high. G-2 made its assessment on the basis of varied evidence. Enemy propagandists were vehement in denouncing both the bombing of Pyongyang military targets and the leaflet dropping to warn the people. Enemy propaganda reaction was almost invariably an excellent barometer by which to judge the effect of anything we did against the Communists.

The warning leaflets, coupled with the bombing, hurt North Korean civilian morale badly. The very audacity of the United Nations in warning the Communists where their bombers would strike hurt morale because it emphasized to the North Koreans just how complete was UN mastery of the air. Contrarily, it made them see even more clearly that the Communists were ineffectual in their efforts to ward off our air blows. There were indications immediately after Plan Strike began that the North Korean civilians evacuated some residential areas but the Communist authorities moved in quickly with controls to force the civilians to remain in the target areas. The Communists would not permit civilian movements to create congestion or hamper military movements.

As a result of the warnings, the bombings, the failure of the Communists to provide protection and the refusal of the Communists to permit evacuation of the clearly defined target areas, civilian resentment was channeled away from the UNC bombers and towards the Communist rulers.

Plan Strike forced the North Korean regime to work its security and control agents much longer and harder than ever. The agents had to be alert constantly to keep the leaflets from the peoples. Threats were broadcast that anyone caught picking up or reading one of the leaflets would be punished. And a continuous stream of propaganda flowed forth from the North Korean regime to try to counteract the UN warnings.

The broad term "psychological warfare" includes any action that forces the enemy to divert men and equipment from the active front, to tie down men and arms in preparation for defense against an attack that never comes. Our amphibious feint off Wonsan was just such a maneuver. We forced the enemy to expend a great deal of effort, move a large number of men and much equipment to bolster the defenses of a beach we had no intention of attacking.

We pinned down sizeable numbers of Chinese and North Korean Communist troops in Korea with our partisans, although that was but one of the objectives and achievements of these daring Koreans who warred incessantly against the Reds in the mountains of North Korea. Through a "pirate" fleet of more than two hundred small vessels, the guerrillas in North Korea had regular contact with the UN Forces in the South. American officers and enlisted men frequently went into North Korea to stay varying lengths of time with our friendly guerrillas. Overnight trips were common, and one American Army major went into enemy territory more than twenty-five different times to make contact with the guerrillas.

Full details of our guerrilla war against the Communists in North Korea must remain secret, for in North Korea many of the partisan tactics that will have to be used in any future war with the Communists were developed and refined. Partisan warfare, important in the war against the Axis powers, probably will be even more important in any future war with the Communists because the Reds have demonstrated an ability to harness whole populations to their war effort. The free world will have to combat this by developing guerrilla elements which, in case of war, can sap the strength of the populations used by the Communists.

The scope of this underground warfare can be judged from the fact that leaders of large numbers of anti-Communist guerrillas in North Korea were in contact with us and responsive to our direction. An unknown number of other guerrilla bands operated independently to harass the Reds, motivated solely by hatred of the forces that had despoiled their native land. The organized and

directed guerrillas were most effective in harassing the Reds and
helping the United Nations. They also were effective in bringing
the independent guerrilla bands into the organized underground
army.

One of the most useful functions of the guerrillas was the rescue
of our airmen shot down over enemy territory. The guerrilla system
was so well organized that every fighter and bomber pilot operating
over North Korea was well briefed on safe areas into which he
could parachute if he got into trouble. Each pilot was told where
he could go and whom he could ask for help after he got on the
ground behind enemy lines. Once contact was made the downed
pilot was put into a regular underground network that moved him
safely out to the coast. There he made his getaway by any one of a
number of methods. He might board one of the anti-Communist
pirate fleet boats that plied North Korean waters at night. He might
be picked up by an Air Force or Navy flying boat. Rescue helicopters from islands we held off the North Korean West Coast might
fly over to the mainland for the pickup. The system worked because it combined our American technical equipment, such as the
helicopter, with the determination and daring of both the American
airmen and the North Korean guerrillas. There were many rescues,
each of which did much to help the morale of our pilots. The whole
air war was fought over enemy territory. The MIGs never flew
close to the battle lines, rarely came as far south as Pyongyang.
That meant our pilots had to land in enemy territory if they were
shot down or ran into mechanical trouble. The remarkably high percentage of rescues from enemy territory was a big morale builder
throughout the war among the pilots. I will mention just one. Colonel Albert W. Schinz of Ottawa, Illinois, Deputy Commander of
the 51st Fighter-Interceptor Wing, failed to return from a Sabrejet
sweep over the far northwest corner of Korea on May 1, 1952.

He was listed as missing for more than a month and then was
delivered safely into Allied hands south of the battle line. Details
of the rescue still cannot be revealed. But it was obvious that
Schinz had been helped to freedom by North Korean dissident
elements who were sufficiently dedicated to the cause of freedom

and sufficiently well organized to carry out such a delicate and hazardous rescue operation.

The islands we held off the North Korean coast were of high importance to us for both rescue and intelligence operations. So were the warships of many United Nations that plied North Korean waters all the way up to the Yalu. From these island and ship bases contact was maintained with the guerrillas. The Albatross flying boats sometimes landed in open sea and taxied up to the North Korean beaches for a rendezvous with guerrilla leaders or messengers. Low-flying bomber and transport planes dropped communications, equipment and other supplies to the underground units.

The Chinese Communists were well aware of the guerrilla activity in their midst, of course, and in the winter of 1951–52 began a great counterguerrilla campaign against the underground. A promise of amnesty was made via wall posters and newspapers, and with the promise went the threat of extermination for holdouts. For a time this counterguerrilla campaign worried us in headquarters but it soon became apparent that the guerrillas were not going to break before promise or threat and that the Communists, numerically powerful as they were, had little real chance of crushing the movement as long as the bigger war continued on the front and in the air and sea. As soon as armistice became imminent, however, we had real concern for the safety of the partisans who had helped us so much. With cease-fire the Communists would be in a position to devote far more attention to the guerrilla problem and our people behind the lines would be in real danger. Therefore shortly before the Armistice was signed we mounted a full-scale amphibious evacuation of several tens of thousands of these valiant fighters for freedom and moved them safely out of North Korea. It is my belief that this operation was unprecedented in the annals of warfare. Many armies have had large partisan detachments fighting behind enemy lines, but none to my knowledge was able to remove large masses of the partisans to safety from behind enemy lines during a period of full hostilities.

Our formal psychological warfare against the Communists and the civilian population they controlled was conducted through radio broadcasts and leaflet drops. The few certain indications of effect, such as the use of safe-conduct surrender passes by enemy soldiers, convinced me that this formal campaign was worthwhile. Surrendering Communist soldiers did carry the safe-conduct passes our airplanes dropped to them. Intelligence reports also supported the conviction that our propaganda was effective.

Enemy propagandists in the Korean War reached a new low in the use of the "big lie" technique. Their high command ordered riots and uprisings in the prisoner-of-war camps and then shouted "atrocity" when we moved in to regain control and restore order. They refused to reveal precise locations of all the camps in which they held captured American and UN Allied soldiers and screamed "barbarian" if our bombers came close to any of these secret sites. We believed during the war that our bombers had avoided these camps and were gratified to learn from prisoners who returned to us in the spring and summer of 1953 that our air had been successful in keeping the bombs away from the POW camps. The Communists forced fifty thousand captured South Korean soldiers into their Red army and charged us with the intention of using captured Chinese and North Koreans as "cannon fodder."

But most dastardly of all, they mounted their campaign to charge us with waging germ warfare. This was the Communist "big lie" in its classic form. It was fabricated of whole cloth, without the slightest substance. Historically it will rank with such other Communist "big lie" campaigns as the ones that first sold much of the world on the idea that Mao Tse-tung was a Chinese agrarian reformer and not a Communist, and then made many people in every country believe that Generalissimo Chiang Kai-shek was thoroughly bad and a tyrant over the Chinese people.

Peiping radio began thundering the germ war charges in early 1952. A germ war "exhibit" was held in Peiping. Demonstrations and even riots were staged by Communists in many countries to protest the "germ war." Civilians in North Korea and in Manchuria were organized into "germ hunting parties" and pictures were published showing them picking up black specks from the snow with chopsticks. Captions under the pictures identified the specks as "germ-laden flies" dropped from American airplanes. Germ war charges were hurled in the United Nations. The whole machinery of Communist propaganda and lie was set in motion.

The purpose? It had but little to do with Korea. Korea was but the setting for the play. The Communist purpose was far more comprehensive than this little war on this little peninsula. The Communist purpose was to create an issue which would strengthen world communism and weaken the forces of freedom globally in preparation for a far greater test of strength than Korea. The lie, the smear, had worked before for the Reds and they were trying it again. A basic objective of all their propaganda in Korea as elsewhere was to plant the idea in men's minds that Americans were the new Nazis. American airmen were "butchers." American bombardiers aimed at hospitals and schools and reveled in a blood bath. Cartoons of our generals in Korea, from MacArthur on, showed us in caps shaped like the exaggerated military caps the Nazi generals used to wear. The term "new Nazis" was a cliché in the Communist doggerel. Talking with Communist agents at Panmunjom our people heard this doggerel and became familiar with it. The FBI was the "Gestapo." Senator McCarthy was a "Himmler." America was ruled by "Chicago gangsters" in the service of "Wall Street." America, like Hitler Germany, could not exist economically without war.

Fascist! Fascist! Fascist! That was the theme, the constant, pounding refrain of the Communists as they battled to turn men's minds against America.

And the charge of germ warfare, with all its revolting implications, was the climax to this operation. America was still the land of promise and hope to millions around the world. There was evidence of that almost daily with the reports of escapes from behind the Iron Curtain. This beacon of freedom in the world had to be destroyed by the Communists before they ever could be fully confident that they controlled the people in their own world well enough to risk a big war which would give the captive people opportunities to escape or strike back.

What the symbol of a Free Formosa is to the oppressed people of China, the symbol of a Free America is to the oppressed people around the world. That symbol is a major enemy of the Soviet Union and of world communism.

The germ warfare charge was a big gun the Communists used to fire on that symbol.

The germ warfare charges became most serious in May of 1952. Peiping radio declared that two American airmen had "confessed" that they participated in germ warfare. The campaign, which had been under way for several months, became so virulent that I warned the Department of the Army on June 7, 1952, that I feared it might be the prelude to Communist use of germ or chemical warfare in Korea. Such propaganda campaigns had been used in the past to justify the use of outlawed or extreme war measures.

On June 21, 1952, the Joint Chiefs recommended that I issue an aggressive statement to the Communist military leaders denying the germ war charges. Three days later I publicized a statement in which I said:

Communist leaders for the past three months have issued a series of insidious and false statements charging that UN forces are employing bacteriological warfare weapons in Korea and China. Recently the communists have attempted to substantiate these charges by claiming that UN personnel have "confessed" to participation in bacteriological warfare activities.

These charges are utterly false as are the alleged "confessions" of UN captured personnel. UN Forces in the Korean hostilities are not now employing, nor have they ever employed biological or germ warfare in any form whatsoever.

In reply to communist threats of trial of UN personnel, let it be made unmistakably clear that the UNC holds the communists responsible for the fair and humane treatment of all captured UNC personnel. The prosecution of UN personnel on the basis of obviously fallacious evidence and trumped up charges would constitute an open and unmitigated violation of universally recognized command responsibilities.

The Communists continued their fabrications unabated. In February of 1953 they declared that Colonel Frank H. Schwable, Chief of Staff of the 1st Marine Air Wing who was shot down and captured by the Reds, had made a lengthy statement in which it was charged that the United Nations Command, on order from the Joint

Chiefs of Staff, was using germ warfare in Korea. I publicly labeled this a falsehood, as it was.

The Communists reached new flights of fancy in their germ war propaganda. Some of their "documentary" still photographs of "evidence" purported to show common houseflies. The Communists claimed that since ordinary houseflies could not live in the frigid Korean winter, American science had created a new species of housefly that could live in subfreezing temperatures so that germ war could be carried to the coldest parts of the earth.

The Communists were capable of uttering any falsehood, any fantasy, for their purpose was not to prove anything but to sow seeds of doubt and fear that would deter their own people from thinking of freedom and would even create uneasiness in the minds of some liberals in the free world, particularly in the United States and Great Britain.

At the time of the Korean Armistice all signs indicated the Communists were far from their objective of destroying the symbol of American freedom in the minds and hearts of men around the world. Every sign, in Korea and elsewhere, showed that the symbol of American freedom remained a beacon light beckoning oppressed peoples everywhere.

In Korea between two and three million people fled the Communist north to seek refuge in the free south, running away from communism even when the Red Armies were on the march and appeared likely to be victorious. Thousands of Korean civilians in the far northeast pushed and crowded aboard our American Navy ships at Christmastime of 1950 to flee from their homes around Hungnam to the refugee camps of Pusan. They fled from the side that was winning that part of the war, and cast their lot with an army that was being chased into the sea. The X Corps, with its 1st Marine Division, the 7th Infantry Division and the 3rd Infantry Division, was making its "big bugout." The Chinese had crashed into the war with more men than the Americans could withstand. Yet this American army, in retreat, looked better to the Koreans than the victorious forces of communism.

This sort of thing happened too often to be ignored.

Whenever and wherever people in Korea had a chance to make a choice, they chose freedom. The most sensational example of this, of course, was the choice made by the Chinese and North Korean captives who vowed they would struggle to the death against anyone who tried to force them to return to their homes in Communist territory. But the free choice of the Koreans who fled Hungnam with our retreating army, and who fled many other areas of North Korea when our armies pulled back, was of great significance.

These expressions of preference for the free way of life, even at the cost of great sacrifice, are an opportunity and a challenge to the United States. The evidence that the people behind the Iron Curtain have a fear of, and revulsion toward, communism gives us proof of a weakness in the Communist armor which we have the opportunity to exploit. At the same time we must face the challenge of providing leadership around which these freedom-hungry people can rally. Upwards of three million Koreans chose freedom even at times when the Communists appeared to be the winning side.

The Communists are well aware of the dangers to them from this possibility and work diligently to create the impression that Communist victory is inevitable, that the inexorable march of history has ordained that communism must succeed capitalistic-democracy in the development of man. That is basic dogma to the Communist. Marx taught that a century before the Korean War.

An important center for Communist propaganda activity in Korea was within the neutralized zone at Panmunjom. There—in addition to the formal meetings of armistice negotiators—Red agents who called themselves "news correspondents" mingled freely with the newsmen of the free world and daily spread their poison. The most vicious of these agents, an Englishman named Alan Winnington, archly told American newsmen, "You are on the losing side, you know, old boys." This theme was voiced in many ways. It was the proud boast of the Communist agents at Panmunjom that America, "the most highly mechanized nation on earth," was fought to a standstill by the "poorly armed and poorly equipped" little people of China. The spirit of communism and the common man, said the agents, had risen above mere mechanical power.

Cleverly these agents played upon the very virtues of our system of freedom. They knew well the fierce competition among American newsmen. The Australian, Wilfred Burchett, had worked with the Americans as a war correspondent in the Pacific for a London newspaper during World War II. Some of the newsmen on our side at Panmunjom had known him well. Winnington and Burchett spoon-fed news to American correspondents at Panmunjom. The Americans were perfectly aware of what was happening. Winnington and Burchett were smart enough to avoid outright distortion and most of the news they ladled out was accurate. Distorted news would have destroyed their usefulness to their Communist masters. They made their propaganda points by handing out bits of news with careful timing. When the prisoner-of-war issue became vital in the armistice talks they were ready with photographs of groups of prisoners, complete with names and home-town addresses. They knew these pictures would be published in the papers in the United States and knew further that publication would increase the emotional pressure on our government to settle the problem any way at all to get the boys home quickly. The Communists were playing cleverly upon the heartstrings of America.

The Communist agents outside the conference tent were fully briefed on the line of argument their delegates planned to follow at the conference table, and thus were always prepared to plant stories that would create a favorable public reception of proposals that Nam Il planned to make.

They always were alert, too, for ways of discrediting the UN Command. Frequently they would ask whether the UN Command spokesman had revealed a specific point in the negotiations. Often for one reason or another, usually because of an agreement of secrecy with the Communist negotiators, the spokesman had not told United Nations newsmen of the specific point. The Red agents used these incidents in an effort to shake the confidence of the United Nations newsmen in their own sources, to make the newsmen fear they were being used by the UN Command. This Communist tactic lost much of its effect after Winnington was crossed up by his own people one day. Winnington demanded to know one morning whether the UN Command spokesman, Air Force Brigadier General William P. Nuckols, had revealed the nature of a Communist proposal which Winnington said had been made the previous afternoon. Nuckols had not mentioned it. At that time he did not attend the negotiating sessions, so Allied newsmen were able to question him right away. He said he had never heard of the proposal but would check. At the noon session Nuckols rushed into the correspondents' work tent with the transcript of the talks of that morning. The proposal had been made during the morning, not during the previous afternoon. Winnington, in his eagerness to discredit the UNC, had overshot the mark and exposed his technique nakedly.

The Red agents used every trick of the trade to influence or try to influence United Nations writers. They used flattery and ridicule, threat and promise. The Communists had an excellent monitoring service which gave the Red agents at Panmunjom copies of much that had been dispatched by Allied newsmen from Panmunjom and the base at Munsan. Copy transmitted at midnight from the Allied camp at Munsan was read back to Allied newsmen by the Communists at ten o'clock next morning. Often the Red agents would read this copy aloud to a large group of Allied newsmen and ridicule it and the writer. Other times the Reds would praise a writer for his "honesty" because he wrote something that happened to be pleasing or helpful to the Communists.

Winnington and Burchett carefully impressed on every Allied newsman that the Communists were keeping a dossier on him, noting every bit of his writing. The way the Red agents stressed this point made it clear that they were threatening a future trial in an effort to frighten Allied writers into letting a bit of softness toward the Communists creep into their dispatches. In fairness to the Allied writers I must say that this tactic failed miserably.

15

A United Nations Effort

The blue and white flag of United Nations was carried into battle for the first time in Korea.

The immediate objective was to stop aggression in Korea, but the larger objective was to deter future aggressors by demonstrating that the nations of the free world finally were ready to stand shoulder-to-shoulder and fight in defense of peace.

I doubt that the great aggressor of our time, the Soviet Union, was impressed very much by the contributions made in Korea by United Nations members other than the United States.

The United Nations did achieve its immediate objective. Aggression was stopped where it started in Korea. Whether the larger, more permanent objective of deterring aggression was achieved is a question which only the events of history can answer.

For we left the enemy stronger, better trained than he was at the beginning and still poised, ready to strike again from his jump-off line of 1950. He was still arrogant, still throwing insults at the time of the Armistice and afterwards, and through his propaganda had convinced the Communist world that he won a victory in Korea.

In blunt language the United Nations numerical contribution to the war in Korea was piddling in light of the strength of the free world. Of the fifty-three nations who endorsed the decision for United Nations action against the aggressor in Korea, only fifteen other than the United States provided ground, air or sea combat forces. The Republic of Korea, not a member of United Nations, made the greatest single contribution of ground troops. Five other United Nations members provided medical units.

During the three years of the Korean War the maximum contribution at one time from the United Nations Allies was 33,000 combat ground troops and 11,000 more air, sea and service personnel. America maintained a force of several hundred thousand combat ground troops plus tremendous numbers of men in air and sea combat and also a vast service organization. The South Koreans finally maintained sixteen combat infantry divisions with a numerical combat strength greater than all the others put together.

At the outset, let me make it clear that neither I nor any other responsible American commander had anything but praise for the valiant fighting men of our Allies in Korea. In addition, faced with the terrible manpower disadvantage of this Asian war, I was grateful for every contribution of fighting power. If nothing else, each contribution from each country strengthened the evidence of free-world solidarity against the Communist aggressor.

I was fully aware that some of our Allies made great sacrifices to contribute just enough to demonstrate their adherence to the free-world ideal. France, for instance, could ill afford to maintain a battalion in Korea. Her young manhood was being bled white in the frightful war in Indo-China against another arm of the same Communist aggressor. Yet France did maintain her battalion in Korea and that battalion became legendary for its valor in such bloody battles as Chipyong-ni and in the fighting to stem the last two great Chinese offensives in 1951.

But over-all to me there were bleak aspects to the picture. I could not help thinking in comparative terms. The great United Nations Organization was made up of so many peoples. It occupied such magnificent quarters in New York City. It held so many meetings on so many subjects. And it assumed such a pose of world leadership not only in the diplomatic field but in the world problems of economics, of social progress, of health, of population problems, of food distribution and of all the other ills that bedeviled mankind. Against this picture of grandeur I saw the tiny contribution made by these people to the first test of free world determination to stop aggression.

And I feared this small effort would impress the Soviets but little.

The picture was not all bleak, by any means. The men of our Allies, as I have said, fought with valor and great effect. Many other advantages accrued, high among which was the understanding, admiration and friendly rivalry that developed between the fighting men of the many nations. Healthy competition was common. The Belgian Battalion, as an example, was attached to the American 15th Infantry Regiment, which proudly called itself the "Can Do" outfit. Very shortly a Belgian jeep flaunted six-inch stenciled letters saying "Belgians Can Do Too."

In Italy I had far more men from as many nations fighting as part of my Fifth Army. These Allied troops in Italy fought just as well as our Allied troops in Korea, but they fought under their own national flags. Certainly the fact that the men of many tongues fought under one flag in Korea will be adjudged one day a most important benefit of the Korean War.

Here was our fighting Allied team in Korea:

Australia—two infantry battalions, which were part of the British Commonwealth Division, naval forces, a fighter squadron.

Belgium—one infantry battalion.

Canada—a reinforced infantry brigade including artillery and tank forces, all part of the British Commonwealth Division, naval forces and a squadron of transport aircraft.

Colombia—an infantry battalion and a naval frigate.

Ethiopia—one infantry battalion.

France—one reinforced infantry battalion.

Greece—one infantry battalion and transport aircraft.

Luxembourg—one infantry company.

Netherlands—one infantry battalion and naval forces.

New Zealand—a regiment of artillery, part of the British Commonwealth Division.

Philippines—one infantry battalion and one company of tanks.

Thailand—one infantry battalion, combat naval forces, air and naval transports.

Turkey—one infantry brigade.

Union of South Africa—one fighter squadron.

United Kingdom—three infantry brigades, one tank brigade, one and a half artillery regiments, one and a half combat engineer regiments and supporting ground forces, all part of the British Commonwealth Division, and the Far Eastern Fleet and units of the Royal Air Force.

In addition there were medical units from five nations—Denmark, India, Italy, Norway and Sweden.

As I have said, the mass of men who fought in Korea were provided by the ROK and by America. Next in line came the British Commonwealth with its First British Commonwealth Division. The fact that the Commonwealth had the only non-Korean or non-American division in the field in Korea was impressive.

The Commonwealth division was made up of Britons, Canadians and contingents of Australians and New Zealanders. It was a fine division, worthy of the best tradition of British arms, but in the total picture it was not a large contribution from this most powerful of our Allies.

The fighting forces the British Commonwealth sent to Korea cannot be praised too highly. Their navy, including cruisers and aircraft carriers, was most effective in the Yellow Sea operations off the Korean West Coast. British flying boats flew important and dangerous long-range patrol missions. British, Canadian and Australian infantrymen fought like tigers when the going was roughest on the Naktong River in the south and near the Imjin during the awful retreat of the winter of 1950–51. Their foot soldiers earned the respect and admiration of every fighting man in Korea. We just never had enough of them.

The Turks sent a five-thousand-man brigade to Korea, rough, tough bayonet-wielding Turks who looked fierce in their flowing mustachios and who fought fiercely and without quarter whenever they clashed with the Chinese. Turkish ferocity and valor became another of the Korean legends. A story that made the rounds illustrated the respect with which the Turks were held by their Allies. The story was that a badly wounded Turkish soldier was asked by the surgeon at an American hospital whether the treatment hurt. The answer was a simple "Me Turk!"

The hard-fighting Turks provided several examples of the problems a commander faces when he has to use men of different nationalities, problems of custom and habit that must be overcome. For quite a while the Turks, attached to the 25th Division, were reluctant to bathe. To an American commander, such as Major General Sam Williams, that is a real problem, for it threatens the health of his troops.

Sam had fine shower units but the Turks wouldn't use them. A shower unit in Korea consisted of two tents, one for bathing and the other for dressing. Korean workers kept the water hot and Korean boys gathered around to do a GI's laundry, for a price, while he showered.

Sam made efforts to learn why the Turks didn't use the showers. He learned that Turkish men do not disrobe in public and the shower units were pretty public, with a dozen men or more showering in the same tent at the same time. Sometimes, under orders, the Turks did go to the shower units but they bathed in their underwear. The Americans kidded them unmercifully about this. Sam finally solved the problem by setting up separate showers for the Turks. After that they were as clean as all the others.

Williams had other problems with the Turks. He had trouble getting them to begin fighting on time in operations in which co-ordination between units was essential. Each time he complained about the Turks lagging he was told by the Turkish commander, "Allah wasn't willing, or they wouldn't have been late." Finally Sam put his foot down and told the Turkish commander, "There are two men now; one is Allah and the other is Sam Williams, and Sam has to be satisfied and Allah wants Sam satisfied." The Turks ever after hit their objectives on time.

In Tokyo the Turkish commander, Lieutenant General Erdelhun, came to me with a problem that opened the way for one of the better opportunities to cement friendly relations with an ally. The commander said that he had received reports from Turkey that there was adverse public reaction to the fact that some Turkish veterans of Korea were walking the streets on wooden peg legs.

Turkish people were asking if that was the way Turks were treated. The General said to me:

My country would like awfully well if our amputees could be sent to America and processed through Walter Reed Hospital the same as your amputees so they could have the same artificial limbs that your men get. My country, of course, would pay all the expenses.

I thought this a fine idea, a fine gesture America could make to these wounded foreign lads. Our government approved my recommendation and, before I left, wounded Turks were being processed through America. The Commonwealth Nations and France had their own facilities for treating their wounded but I am sure that the same courtesy would have been extended to any country that desired it. I was told that the reaction in Turkey was most favorable.

Most of the nations contributing troops to Korea sent one battalion. These included France, Belgium, the Netherlands, Greece, the Philippines, Thailand, Colombia and Ethiopia, and little Luxembourg sent one company.

Each battalion ran about eight hundred men. I was happy to have every one of them. They all fought courageously. But there were problems of supply, which involved the different food habits of the various nations, of different religions, different customs and different languages. That meant a number of men had to be used on administrative tasks to take care of the relatively small contingent from each nation.

Except for the Canadians, whose army has adopted standard American arms to permit greater unity of effort, the Commonwealth Nations used different guns and different caliber ammunition than the other United Nations forces. This meant the establishment of separate stockpiles for the British Commonwealth Division, bad in that it increased administrative and supply work but worse in that it cut down the flexibility of the Eighth Army. As an example, when the Third U.S. Division relieved the British on the Western Front we had to leave the British artillery in the sector to support the Americans. The Americans didn't object because the British are good gunners. To have taken the British artillerymen off the line would have required the movement of a whole stockpile of American artillery ammunition into their area. The Third Division artillerymen were assigned to another sector, away from their own division. Under ordinary circumstances, with every outfit on the line using the same caliber guns and ammunition, the commander has much more leeway in shifting men because he does not have to move heavy stockpiles with them each time they are transferred to a new place in the line. The new men merely take over the stockpiles left by the men they relieve.

The lesson was clear. Increased standardization of military equipment must be an objective of the Allies in the United Nations, the Allies who have fought together as comrades in the past and are going to have to join forces to fight the common fight against aggressors in the future. This applies particularly to the British Commonwealth forces whose future is tied so intimately to our own. When a big test comes, differences of equipment should not stand in the way of the closest possible integration of our armed might.

Another important lesson of the united effort in Korea was that in any future United Nations military campaign, nations contributing ground forces to the joint operation must be persuaded to provide at least a proportionate share of their warmaking potential. The administrative and supply work required makes a small force uneconomic.

I was very proud to have been the United Nations Commander in Chief in this first free-world war against the Communists, but I always felt that much fighting efficiency and moral force was lost because of the limited contribution from the United Nations.

The Greeks recognized this aspect of the UN effort in Korea and despite their many other problems were preparing to boost their force from a battalion to a reduced-size regimental combat team at the end of the war.

To my mind it was essential that each of the United Nations share as fully as possible not only in the contributions of men and weapons, but also in the varied responsibilities, many of which were onerous.

Therefore I was surprised at the criticism from Canada when I sent a Canadian company, among others, to Koje in May of 1952 to help win control over the rebellious Communist prisoners of war.

In reinforcing the garrison on Koje I kept the Joint Chiefs of Staff fully informed of my plans because they involved movements that weakened the already inadequate defenses of Japan. The shift of the 187th Airborne Regiment from Japan to Koje, for instance, seriously reduced the defense force we had on duty in Japan. The Joint Chiefs suggested that for political as well as military reasons it might be well to have a showing of UN troops on Koje. I agreed and personally discussed the plan with the representatives of the various nations whose troops were immediately available.

After these discussions, in which each foreign liaison officer agreed with the plan, I asked General Van Fleet what troops of Allied nations could be assembled promptly. He listed, among others, one Canadian company.

I reported to Washington that the representatives of the Allied nations had been informed and that none had raised any objection to the movement of their troops to Koje.

Consequently, as I have said, I was surprised by the objections of the Canadian Government, voiced by Lester Pearson, the External Affairs Minister and a leader in the United Nations. After all, it was a United Nations command and one of its important responsibilities was to control and guard the recalcitrant POWs, all of whom were UN POWs, and many of whom had been captured by the Canadians themselves.

Later I learned why they had objected. The local Canadian commander on the spot agreed to the movement of Canadian troops to Koje, but apparently his government did not adequately understand our plan. Therefore the assignment of Canadians to Koje hit Canada with a surprise impact.

The UN reinforcements moved to Koje-do during this crisis were the First Company of the Royal Canadian Regiment, one company of the King's Shropshire Light Infantry (British), the First Company of the Greek Expeditionary Forces and the 187th Airborne Regiment (U.S.). These troops of four nations were integrated quickly into the over-all camp garrison force.

The same problem arose when the Armistice became imminent. My command was to be saddled with an overwhelming and difficult task in moving thousands of anti-Communist prisoners to the demilitarized zone of Korea where they would be turned over to the Indian forces. In addition, some eighty thousand die-hard Communists had to be moved to the Panmunjom and other exchange points. I was aware of the dangers inherent in this task and felt again that the POW Command should have a United Nations complexion.

Therefore the problem was discussed with the senior Allied representatives and officers were designated from some of the nations participating in the war for duty with the POW Command during this delicate period. One prerequisite was that the designated officer speak English. This plan worked well. It helped to have officers from the United Nations fighting in Korea take a hand in the movement of the prisoners.

The language problem was always with us in our united effort. It became necessary very early to establish a UN Liaison Section in the headquarters at Tokyo, partly to overcome language difficulties and partly to make certain that each nation with troops in the UN Command was kept aware of the plans involving its forces.

Hospitalization of troops of many tongues became a problem early in the war, as soon as foreign wounded began arriving at the Tokyo Army Hospital. The first temporary expedient was to hire English-speaking civilians from among the foreign colonies of Tokyo. These men and women served as interpreters in the hospital, but few had either military or medical training, so their usefulness was limited.

In the fall of 1950 the first foreign liaison officers arrived and they took over the work of interpretation in the hospital.

The normal work of the liaison officers became progressively heavier, however, and new answers had to be found for the problem. Each nation participating in the Korean War was requested to assign English-speaking nurses to the hospital. This system was the most efficient of all. The various foreign nurses assigned to the hospital erased the purely American atmosphere and made the Tokyo Army Hospital a truly international establishment.

All foreign wounded eventually were shifted to the Tokyo Army

Hospital so that they could be tended by nurses of their own country, an important factor in the psychological recovery of many of the men. All foreign dignitaries visiting Tokyo were able to spend time with their wounded countrymen, another important morale factor for the troops.

American officers, and particularly their wives, also helped as much as they could with visits to the hospital to talk with the American and other wounded soldiers. Mrs. Clark, as well as the wives of many other American senior officers, made frequent visits to the wounded.

The extent of American sympathy for wounded Allied soldiers was made apparent early in the war. In the first winter General MacArthur sent his personal airplane to southern Japan to pick up some wounded Turkish soldiers. They were flown back to Tokyo Army Hospital where they could be helped by men and women who spoke their language.

The hospital work was another of the fine examples of Allied co-operation in the Far East.

16

The Eisenhower Visit

During the presidential campaign of 1952 the Korean War was a major issue. It was the most unpopular war in United States history and the American people made it apparent they wanted an end to it, one way or another. General Eisenhower, as Republican candidate, promised that if elected he would visit Korea before his inauguration to try to find a way to end the fighting.

On November 21 I got word that Eisenhower, as the President-elect, was coming over. My reaction was one of pleasure. Obviously, a man with his military background would size up the problems confronting us quickly, if he did not already have a thorough grasp of the situation, which I was certain he did.

As soon as the news was out, President Rhee announced that a rousing reception would be given the President-elect in Seoul— parades, dinners and mass rallies. That brought me head on with the biggest security problem of my whole seventeen months in the Far East. I sent a number of messages back to Washington to make certain there was full understanding of just how far Rhee was going in preparing mass receptions for Eisenhower. I also wanted Washington to realize fully just how much of a shock it would be to Rhee when he learned that because of security considerations the President-elect would be unable to appear at these public demonstrations. I knew that there would be repercussions and that Rhee's feelings would be hurt. Therefore I was careful to get the story across to the Joint Chiefs of Staff so they could make their decision early and let me inform Rhee before he had gone too far with his plans. The decision was to eliminate all public functions, as I had known it would have to be.

I passed the word along to President Rhee that there would be
no public receptions or appearances. I advised him to cancel his
plans. The situation was far too risky. In any Korean crowd there
might be a secret Communist ready to sacrifice himself for the
chance to assassinate the President-elect of the United States. In
addition, we had intelligence reports that the enemy was infiltrating
agents into the Seoul area with the assignment to assassinate Eisenhower.

Secret Service men arrived in Tokyo a few days before the President-elect was scheduled to land in Korea. The exact time, date
and place were classified top secret. The Secret Service men and I
went over a proposed itinerary which included briefings at Eighth
Army Headquarters, visits to American, UN and ROK forward
units, a stop at a fighter-bomber squadron and a visit to a field
hospital. I was particularly anxious for Ike to see at least one of our
medical establishments so he could witness firsthand the magnificent care our Medical Corps gave to our sick and wounded. The
itinerary had to be planned so that the President-elect would never
come within range of enemy guns.

Time precluded a visit to naval units at sea, but I did arrange to
have all senior naval, air and ground commanders gather at Eighth
Army Headquarters to discuss their problems with Ike.

Not the least of my headaches was press coverage. Washington
had arranged for six top-flight correspondents to accompany Ike on
the round trip, but in Seoul the forty to fifty war correspondent
"regulars," who felt justifiably that this was their story, were being
joined by plane loads of others who flew from Tokyo just to cover
this event. The Seoul Press Billets, an old apartment house near the
Capitol, bulged with 130 newspaper, radio, television and maga-
zine writers and photographers from a dozen nations.

We found ourselves preparing one elaborate plan to safeguard
the President-elect through secrecy and another to help the press
corps tell the world about every phase of his visit. We resolved the
problem, with our fingers crossed, by requesting that no factual or
speculative stories be written that established Ike's arrival date. In
addition, the press was asked to observe a news blackout on Ike's

visit from the time we said the blackout was on until we lifted it following his departure. Then all stories would be released.

The number of correspondents covering Ike's actual movements had to be limited, but using almost every available light plane in Korea, we leapfrogged two complete press and photography pools ahead of Ike's party so that one was always on hand when he arrived at a unit in Korea.

I might as well say here, ahead of the story, that the correspondents co-operated magnificently—and they were certainly under as much pressure as the military. Hundreds of thousands of words were written, thousands of pictures taken, and nothing went out until Ike was on his way home.

Many other precautions had to be taken. We had to exercise the strictest censorship and control of all communications. We had to request the ROK Government to maintain secrecy on its radio circuits, and were happy at the complete co-operation it gave us.

One problem that worried me was our rotation system, the Rest and Recreation program that sent thousands of soldiers back to Japan each month for their five days of play. Ike would be landing on airfields at which these men were gathered awaiting transport to Japan. The men would see him and no power on earth could prevent them from talking about it to people in Japan, where we had no control over communications, and where we knew spies operated in some places frequented by our men.

After a good deal of consideration I decided to cancel the R&R program for the few days while Ike was in Korea. That was rough on the men in Korea awaiting their turn to fly to Japan, but it was wonderful for the soldiers caught in Japan. It doubled the R&R for many of them.

Ike was not going to stop in Japan. I was to meet him in Korea. This was hardly a secret. Therefore I had to plan my movements like a cloak-and-dagger conspirator. I left my airplane parked in its usual spot at Haneda Airport and took off in another plane from a military field outside Tokyo. I made my landing as secret as possible, too, by putting down at Suwon, about twenty miles south of Seoul, and driving to Eighth Army Headquarters after dark. I arrived an hour before Ike and his party.

It probably was the heaviest collection of military and civilian brass ever to travel so far together. Ike was accompanied by Charles E. Wilson, Secretary of Defense Designate; General Omar Bradley, Chairman of the Joint Chiefs of Staff; Herbert Brownell, Jr., Attorney General Designate; Admiral Arthur W. Radford, Commander in Chief of the Pacific; Major General Roger Ramey, U.S. Air Force; Major General Wilton B. Persons, Retired, Special Assistant to the President-elect; Press Secretary James Hagerty; Colonel Paul Carroll, aide, and Lieutenant John Davies, personal secretary.

The first thing Ike asked was, "Where's John?" That was his son, Major John Eisenhower, then Assistant Division Plans and Operations Officer of the Third Infantry Division. I had thought of John when working on the security problem. "John will be here first thing in the morning," I assured Ike. I explained that John's movements were being watched by the press and had we moved him down to Seoul in advance it would have given away the show.

The next morning was devoted to briefings. That evening President Rhee called on Ike. They had a brief social talk not touching on any of the knottier problems that confronted us. Ike explained that time did not permit his attending any social functions.

I had received no instructions from Washington on what Ike wanted to discuss, but I had prepared a list of subjects I knew would be of interest to him. These included a detailed estimate of the forces and plans required to obtain a military victory in Korea should the new administration decide to take such a course.

To me the most significant thing about the visit of the President-elect was that I never had the opportunity to present this estimate for his consideration. The question of how much it would take to win the war was never raised. It soon became apparent, in our many conversations, that he would seek an honorable truce.

I reported personally to Ike on the sadly depleted ammunition stocks in the theater. The subsequent Senate investigation gave rise to many erroneous statements in the press by persons not entirely acquainted with the facts.

The facts are these. There were shortages in ammunition of certain categories in the Far East theater at various times during my period of command. Those shortages existed mainly in the rear area stockpiles, not in forward combat zones, and when the situation demanded it, local commanders were authorized to and did shoot ammunition above the quotas set for them.

Going into a hypothetical situation, if the enemy had launched an all-out offensive at the time our ammunition reserve was at its lowest, we would have had a critical shortage and increased UN casualties as a result. The enemy did not launch such an offensive, however, and we had enough ammunition to meet the attacks he did make.

The quotas I did impose on artillery fire were necessary when the enemy *threatened* an all-out attack, when our reserve stocks were low and when inadequate shipments were forecast from the United States. But local commanders always were authorized to expend whatever was considered necessary in a tight situation. As early as July of 1952 I told Van Fleet in a letter that "however I wish to reaffirm my previous instructions to the effect that, should the immediate tactical situation require, you are authorized to exceed the published rates to the extent deemed necessary by your good judgment."

My concern over the ammunition shortage dated back to May of 1952 and was explained in numerous messages to the Department of the Army.

The public furor about the ammunition situation was but one of the occasional commotions caused by incidents in the Korean War. Another particularly regrettable one came some weeks after Eisenhower left Korea, and only a few days after his inauguration.

That was the famed Operation Smack which became a *cause célèbre* because it failed, because it was witnessed by a group of air and ground generals and some newspapermen, because a zealous individual in a division Public Information Office put a tricolored cover on the operations plan and because a newly arrived reporter wrote a sensational story.

The thing grew in the public mind, and the newspapers, until it became a major issue. Newspaper headlines in America screamed that American soldiers had been slaughtered in an operation conducted purely for the amusement of some visiting high brass. Some newspaper stories went so far as to compare the operation with the death orgies held for the pleasure of Roman nobles and ladies in the Coliseum.

I was understandably concerned and directed Van Fleet to investigate and give me complete details. Van's report was that the operation was part of a joint air-ground experiment then under way. This particular phase of the experiment provided for the corps commander to conduct an air-ground test and to have a maximum number of troops and key staff officers on hand to observe the techniques of employing tactical air support for ground troops.

The U.S. 7th Infantry Division was assigned to the operation and the Division Commander, Major General Wayne C. Smith, proposed a daylight raid on T-Bone Hill by two infantry platoons supported by tanks and tactical air. Eighth Army approved the plan which was put into operation after a complete briefing, orientation and reconnaissance, followed by a rehearsal of the troops involved.

On January 25, 1953, the day of Operation Smack, the invited observers gathered at division headquarters. In view of the nature of the experiment of which Operation Smack was a part the observers hardly could have been termed "touring brass." Lieutenant General Glenn O. Barcus, commanding the Fifth Air Force whose planes were to provide close support, was there. So was Lieutenant General Paul Kendall, Commanding General, I Corps, which provided the troops for the experiment. Others were the Director of Operations, Far East Air Forces, the Chief of Staff, I Corps, and a number of staff officers.

At headquarters the observers and the fifteen newsmen were briefed and given a mimeographed time-scheduled and data sheet which described exactly what had been planned, right down to the number of artillery shells and aerial bombs that would be thrown at the enemy. Such details are planned before any battle in which our troops take the offensive because the application of fire power in terms of quantity, timing and target cannot be left to chance but must be made to dovetail with the movement of troops in order to give them the greatest possible measure of protection.

All this was done in Operation Smack. The one deviation, if it can be called that, was that someone in the Public Information Office pasted the division insignia on the cover of the mimeographed plan, in three colors.

The objective of Operation Smack was to capture prisoners. In that, it failed. No prisoners were taken. The results of the fight were thirteen enemy counted dead, twenty-five enemy estimated killed in action and three enemy known wounded. Our losses were three killed in action and sixty-one wounded. The infantrymen destroyed eighteen enemy bunkers and damaged fifty-seven more.

The furor lasted but a short time as reporters who had witnessed the operation, among them the veteran Forrest Edwards of the Associated Press, straightened the record and reported that "both the briefing and the seven page mimeographed operational plan gave evidence of the weeks of intense, careful planning which had preceded the coordinated air-artillery-tank-infantry raid."

President-elect Eisenhower's tour of forward areas went off smoothly, as we had hoped. Each night we returned to Eighth Army Headquarters where we usually had a highball before a late supper. The President-elect seemed to me a much more preoccupied man than he was during the days when soldiering was his only profession. He was preparing himself for the biggest job on earth, so he had plenty to preoccupy him.

During his visit to Korea Eisenhower's hope and belief was that an honorable truce *must* be forthcoming—an optimism that I admit I did not share at the time.

It was not yet common knowledge that General Van Fleet was about to retire. Ike asked me, in view of this, who was my choice of a successor. I said my first choice was Lieutenant General Maxwell D. Taylor, then Deputy Chief of Staff for Operations and Administration, Department of the Army. Taylor had distinguished himself as the Assistant Division Commander of the 82nd Airborne Division in Italy and later as Commanding General of the 101st Airborne Division in France. Max took over Eighth Army on February 11, 1953.

The big military conference Eisenhower held during his Korean

trip was at Eighth Army Headquarters. I had every senior commander there to talk with him. There were Van Fleet from the
ground forces, Weyland and Barcus from the air forces, Admirals
Briscoe and Jocko Clarke from the Navy and Herren from the
Communications Zone and POW Command.

We even brought Major General William C. Chase up from
Formosa, where he was chief of the American Military Advisory
and Assistance Group. The question of the availability of rice for
Japan and Korea was broached. Chase pointed out that the Chinese
Nationalists were itching to dispose of 100,000 tons of rice they had
on Formosa.

The President-elect turned to me and said, "Wayne, I thought
you were short of rice. Why don't you buy it from Formosa?"

"Good idea," I said, and left the room to call my headquarters in
Tokyo. I got Doyle Hickey, my Chief of Staff, on the telephone and
told him about the Formosan rice. And I added, "I want to button
this thing up and want an answer by this afternoon."

A few hours later Doyle called back. He said the figure of
100,000 tons was based on a new crop estimate, but that thirty-
thousand tons were available and a deal could be closed right away.

A few minutes later I saw Ike and said, "Well, you've just bought
yourself thirty thousand tons of rice from Formosa."

"Gosh, Wayne," he said, looking at his watch, "it was only five
hours ago that we discussed this business."

As an added attraction I had Jocko Clarke bring three of his star
Pantherjet pilots, Lieutenant I. B. Williams and Lieutenants (jg)
J. D. Middleton and D. M. Rawlings. On November 18, 1952,
Williams and Middleton each shot down a MIG-15 that probably
was flown by a Russian and Rawlings damaged a third.

The three Navy pilots were operating in the far northeast of
Korea, in the Chongjin area, when they encountered seven MIGs
flying down from the direction of Vladivostok, which is less than
one hundred miles across the Korean border in Siberia. Four MIGs
attacked. The evidence was strong that the MIGs were flown by
Russian Air Force pilots, not Chinese or North Koreans.

Ike was delighted to meet the three pilots and put them so much at ease that before they left they had given him a blow by blow account of their battle, complete with hand gestures and body English.

Time went swiftly for Ike in Korea and the final day of his stay came and he still had not returned the call of President Rhee, which was a must. Ike had half promised to return the call when he saw Rhee the day before he departed. That day Ike had asked Rhee to go with him on a tour of Korean infantry training areas. While the three of us were walking from one demonstration to another Ike said to Rhee that he hoped to visit him sometime the next day. He added, "I'll have General Clark get in touch with you tomorrow and make the arrangements."

Next day around noon I telephoned Rhee and told him General Eisenhower was involved in many conferences and asked if I could call him back later in the afternoon when I had more information. Rhee was agreeable.

Late in the afternoon I telephoned President Rhee again and asked him if I could see him immediately at his residence. He said yes and I drove to his home on a hill behind the capitol. As usual I was ushered into the drawing room, but something was different. Except for the man who opened the door for me, the house seemed empty. It was dark by the time I arrived.

Rhee entered the drawing room and I handed him a letter from Ike. I could tell by his expression that this was a great disappointment for even before he opened the envelope he felt that the letter meant Ike would not visit him. A visit from Eisenhower was important to Rhee politically for it would be a demonstration to his people that he stood well with the Americans who had contributed so much to the defense of their country.

Then I told Rhee confidentially that Ike would be there at exactly 5:45 p.m. for just a few minutes to return his call and say good-by. Rhee's face lit up. Then he excused himself and left the room briefly. I made my usual inquiry about Madame Rhee and the President replied that because he had expected the President she was not there. He said he felt that only men should be present when he met Eisenhower. I volunteered that I knew Ike would be sorry for I knew he would be pleased to meet Madame Rhee. The President excused himself hurriedly again and apparently got in touch with Madame Rhee right away, for when Ike arrived she was on hand to greet him.

The President-elect arrived at the appointed minute and entered the presidential residence with some of his official party. The meeting was very short, as Ike was preparing to take off for home. As Ike said good-by President Rhee said, "I would like you to meet my cabinet," and for the third time that afternoon he disappeared from the reception room.

Doors were flung open and there in the halls was a multitude. The people were crowded to overflowing and obviously had been summoned there by Rhee. They were dressed in their best and were waiting the chance to meet our President-elect. Newspaper people were there, including still and movie photographers. Rhee was certain he was going to have a fine record of the Eisenhower visit.

After many introductions, many handshakes and many photographs, Ike left the house.

But he didn't get away from ceremony that easily.

Outside, in the spacious driveway that fronts the Korean presidential mansion, were huge floodlights, an ROK Army, Navy and Air Force Honor Guard, bands and photographers. It looked like a Hollywood opening night. Rhee had really laid it on.

The President-elect took off that night with as little fuss as possible. Despite the huge outpouring of people at the presidential mansion, we still were trying to achieve secrecy.

Therefore all the military commanders said farewell to him at Eighth Army Headquarters and watched him drive off with his party to the airfield. We wondered what his decision would be.

We had not long to wait for it was only a few weeks before it became certain.

Our government had decided to seek an armistice.

17

"Little Switch"

The President-elect and his party left Korea December 5, 1952. There was no change in the tempo of the war for months after his visit, nor was there any move by either side to resume negotiations for an armistice. If anything, indications were that the Reds had dug their heels in deeper and were prepared for a long, long wait.

We didn't know it at the time, but the first move toward eventual agreement had been taken just a few days after Eisenhower left Korea. On December 13, 1952, the Executive Committee of the League of Red Cross Societies, meeting in Geneva, adopted a resolution proposed by the Indian delegate that recommended the sick and wounded prisoners be exchanged in advance of a truce. The resolution passed fifteen to two. Russia and Communist China opposed. It was hardly an auspicious omen for an armistice, yet it was the action which set in motion a chain of events which finally resulted in cease-fire.

Two months later, on February 19, 1953, the Joint Chiefs of Staff advised me that a similar resolution might soon be introduced in the United Nations General Assembly. They added that the State Department suggested that I pick up the ball in advance and put the proposition of exchanging sick and wounded POW's directly to the Communist commanders.

I followed the suggestion and three days later, on February 22, I wrote directly to Kim Il Sung and Peng Teh-huai through the liaison officers who continued to make contact at Panmunjom even during the period that truce talks were suspended. In the letter I said:

240

The Executive Committee of the League of Red Cross Societies, in a resolution adopted in Geneva, Switzerland, on 13 December 1952, called on both sides in the Korean conflict as a gesture of good will to take immediate action in implementing the humanitarian provisions of the Geneva Convention by repatriating sick and wounded prisoners of war in accordance with appropriate Articles of the Geneva Convention.

As has been repeatedly stated to you in the course of negotiations at Panmunjom, the United Nations Command has from the very beginning adhered scrupulously to the humanitarian provisions of the Geneva Convention and in particular has been prepared to carry out the provisions of the Geneva Convention in regard to the sick and wounded prisoners in its custody. The United Nations Command remains ready immediately to repatriate those seriously sick and seriously wounded captured personnel who are fit to travel in accordance with provisions of Article 109 of the Geneva Convention.

I wish to be informed whether you are prepared for your part to proceed immediately with the repatriation of seriously sick and wounded captured personnel of the United Nations Command who are in your hands. The United Nations Command liaison officers will be prepared to meet your liaison officers to make necessary arrangements for impartial verification of the condition and for the mutual exchange of such seriously sick and wounded in accordance with the provisions of Article 109 of the Geneva Convention.

There was dead silence from the Communists for over a month, a month that was of supreme importance to Communists all over the world. For on March 5, 1953, Joseph Stalin died and Communists in every country had to reorient themselves to the new conditions and new leadership.

The silence was broken, finally, on March 28. The Communists sent me a letter which reached Tokyo in the middle of the night. I was called out of bed to read the letter. One passage made me prick up my ears. Kim and Peng not only agreed to exchange sick and wounded prisoners, but proposed a resumption of full-dress truce negotiations, in suspension for almost six months.

I don't pretend to know what, if anything, the death of Soviet dictator Stalin had to do with the Communist about-face—except that it signaled a general change in Red tactics all over the world. The peace offensive was in full swing and the Korean Armistice appeared to be the main showpiece in the Communist propaganda display. I could not help but think, as I read the proposal to resume armistice talks, that perhaps it was the anesthetic before the operation.

The Communist letter of agreement to the exchange of sick and wounded was worded cleverly to shift the blame for delay to us, despite the fact that since December of 1951 we had suggested repeatedly that sick and wounded prisoners be exchanged during hostilities, in conformity with the Geneva Convention.

Marshal Kim and General Peng wrote to me:

Concerning the question of repatriating with priority seriously sick and seriously injured prisoners of war of both sides, the Delegates for armistice negotiations of both sides had, as a matter of fact, reached agreement, in accordance with humanitarian principles, on Paragraph 53 of the Draft Korean Armistice Agreement. It was solely because the Korean armistice negotiations were suspended that there was no way to implement this agreed provision. In consequence, it has not been possible up to the present to repatriate seriously sick and seriously injured prisoners of war of both sides.

It had been possible, and I was ready to do it, but I was not going to haggle over that point when the really important business at hand was to get back our sick and wounded and achieve an armistice.

Kim and Peng continued:

Since your side now expresses readiness to apply the provisions of the Geneva Convention to sick and injured prisoners of war in the custody of both sides, our side, as an expression of the similar intent, fully agrees to your side's proposal to exchange sick and injured prisoners of war of both sides during the period of hostilities. This proposal should be dealt with in accordance with the provisions of Article 109 of the Geneva Convention.

At the same time, we consider that the reasonable settlement of the question of exchanging sick and injured prisoners of war of both sides during the period of hostilities should be made to lead to the smooth settlement of the entire question of prisoners of war, thereby achieving an armistice in Korea for which people throughout the world are longing. Therefore our side proposes that the Delegates for armistice negotiations of both sides immediately resume the negotiations at Panmunjom.

This proposal to resume armistice talks was interesting, but I was worried about the true Communist intent. Kim and Peng made no reference in their letter to our condition that talks could be resumed only if the Communists agreed to a formula which would insure anti-Communist prisoners the right of political asylum in the free world. I was most wary of agreeing to anything that would force us to return to Panmunjom just to listen to a flood of abuse and propaganda, as we had in the past. It had been difficult enough to break off the talks the first time to shut off this propaganda barrage and I did not want to go through the tedious process again.

Therefore I was most careful in wording my reply to the Communist commanders. I proposed to them that high-ranking liaison officers meet at Panmunjom "to make necessary detailed arrangements for the exchange of these captured personnel," expressed agreement with their statement that they hoped the exchange of sick and wounded would "make more likely a smooth settlement of the entire prisoner of war question," and added:

> Accordingly, I will be prepared to instruct my Liaison Group *as a second order of business* to meet with your Liaison Group to arrange for a resumption of Armistice Negotiations by our respective delegations. We take it as implicit in your suggestion in this respect that you would be prepared to accept United Nations Command proposals or make some comparable constructive proposal of your own which would constitute a valid basis for resumption of delegation meetings.

Another break in the preliminary negotiations came two days later on March 30, 1953, when Premier and Foreign Minister Chou En-lai of Red China issued a long statement in which he declared the governments of Red China and North Korea had agreed that in order to attain an armistice they would accept a plan in which all prisoners opposed to repatriation would be turned over to a neutral agency so that their right to return home could be explained to them. My government had long before indicated it would accept such a settlement as long as there was clear understanding that the period of explanation would have a time limit and that the agreement provided a clear path to political asylum for any prisoner who

persisted in his refusal to return to his homeland. The nub of the
Chou proposal was contained in the following sentence:

> To this end, the Government of the People's Republic of China and the
> Government of the Democratic People's Republic of Korea propose that
> both parties to the negotiations should undertake to repatriate immedi-
> ately after the cessation of hostilities all those prisoners of war in their
> custody who insist upon repatriation and to hand over the remaining
> prisoners of war to a neutral state so as to ensure a just solution to the
> question of their repatriation.

Then followed the claim that the UN Command had coerced
and intimidated captured Communist soldiers into renouncing their
homelands, a face-saving claim that was disproved completely later
in the year when Communist explainers failed miserably in their
efforts to persuade prisoners to come home.

Next day Kim Il Sung issued a formal statement supporting the
Chou En-lai plan to the hilt.

Out of long experience with the Communists I had learned to be
most cautious. A radio broadcast of a purported statement by Chou
En-lai was a good indication of what the Communists wanted to
do, but it had no binding force on the Communist negotiators at
Panmunjom. It sounded good to me, though, and I wanted to encourage the Communists to make the proposal official by letting
them know we were interested.

Immediately after hearing the Chou statement, therefore, I made
public the following comment:

> I have read with great interest the statement attributed to Chou En-lai
> which was broadcast by the Peiping radio a few hours ago. When and if
> the proposal outlined in the broadcast is received officially from the Com-
> munist Armistice Delegation at Panmunjom, it will receive immediate and
> careful consideration. Until that time, it would be inapproprate for me to
> comment further except to emphasize the fact that the United Nations
> Command will welcome any constructive proposal which will achieve a
> just and honorable armistice in Korea.

The Communists backed their words with deeds. On April 2,
1953, they proposed that liaison officers meet in Panmunjom on

April 6 "to arrange preliminarily the matter of exchange by both sides of injured and sick prisoners of war and to discuss and decide on the date for resuming the armistice negotiations." The Communists also made the Chou En-lai proposal official by enclosing a full copy of the statements made by Chou and Kim on the full exchange of prisoners.

Other deeds by the Communists sent hopes for armistice sky-high despite all previous setbacks. During the last ten days of March there were several harmless and inadvertent flights of UN warplanes over the neutralized zone of Panmunjom. Always in the past such overflights had been followed by vitriolic charges from the Communists and demands for joint investigations. But for the first time since the security agreements made Panmunjom a neutral island on the battlefront the Communists were silent about the overflights.

The Communists made a good show of their peaceful intentions in other ways. On March 27 UN security officers stationed at Panmunjom reported that all civilians were evacuated from Palson-ni, a village just south of the neutral zone perimeter. After the evacuation of the civilians, who farmed the Panmunjom area, the Communists began building a six-foot, ten-strand barbed-wire fence around the village, in apparent preparation for the reception of sick and wounded prisoners.

The Reds knew we were alert to all these surface indications of intent, and frequently through the negotiations built or tore down physical facilities, such as meeting halls and reception barracks, to make it appear that they were either hopeful or pessimistic about the chances of armistice.

At the end of March, 1953, the Communists did everything they could to make it appear that they thought an armistice was but a matter of days away. It was obvious they wanted to make us so anxious for a truce that we might be in a mood to give away something extra just to get the thing done.

The truce fever spread all the way from Panmunjom to Washington, where President Eisenhower said publicly that the United States should take every Communist offer at face value "until it was proved unworthy of our confidence." Newsmen of all media began flocking to Korea as they hadn't since the first summer of the war, eager to be on the scene for the wind-up.

On April 5 I wrote to the Communist High Command that our liaison officers would meet with theirs the following day to arrange the exchange of sick and wounded, and also to keep the door wide open for discussions on the whole prisoner exchange issue.

At as early a date as possible, [I wrote] I request that your Liaison Group furnish our Liaison Group with a detailed statement of suggestions on the implementation of the proposal for settling the entire question of repatriating prisoners of war as set forth in the statement of Foreign Minister Chou En-lai, and endorsed by Marshal Kim Il Sung, in order that it may be studied while reasonable settlement of the repatriation of sick and wounded is being effected.

Progress toward the Armistice never was so fast. Liaison officers, headed by Rear Admiral John C. Daniel, USN, and Major General Lee Sang Cho, North Korean People's Army, met on April 6 and next day Lee accepted the UNC draft agreement for repatriation of sick and wounded as the basis for discussion. One day later the liaison groups exchanged estimates of the number of sick and wounded to be exchanged. The UNC said it had 5,100 Koreans and 700 Chinese sick and wounded ready to go home. The Communists offered a disappointing estimate of 450 Koreans and 150 non-Koreans.

On April 10 we received an answer to my request for suggestions from the Communists on how their proposal for exchange of all prisoners who wanted to go home would be effected. The answer was vague, merely repeating the main points of the proposal Chou En-lai made on March 30, copies of which were delivered to us officially on April 2. The two points of the Chou statement which were repeated were agreement to the concept of no forced repatriation and agreement to the plan for a neutral state to take custody of those prisoners who did not want to go home. The core of the letters from Kim and Peng was:

The Korean and Chinese side does not acknowledge that there are prisoners of war who are allegedly unwilling to be repatriated. Therefore, the question of the so-called "forced repatriation" or "repatriation by force" does not exist at all, and we have always opposed this assertion. Based on this stand of ours, our side maintains that those captured personnel of our side who are filled with apprehensions and are afraid to return home as a result of having been subjected to intimidation and oppression, should be handed over to a neutral state, and, through explanations given by our side, gradually freed from apprehensions, thereby attaining a just solution to the question of repatriation.

As a beginning it sounded pretty good. Many questions remained unanswered. And as time went on the word "gradually" as used by the Communists took on an ever greater importance. In fact, Red negotiators tried to make the term "gradually" mean "indefinitely" as they fought at the conference table for agreement on a plan which would force anti-Communist prisoners to remain imprisoned as long as it took the Communists to force them to change their minds about going home.

Next day, on April 11, 1953, the liaison groups agreed on the terms for the exchange of sick and wounded. Agreement had been achieved in just five days, an all-time record for the Panmunjom negotiations. Staff officers then went to work on all the many details of the physical work of the exchange, set to begin on April 20.

Far to our rear, meanwhile, the Communists permitted no relaxation of pressure from their POWs in our hands, men who now constituted a "Sixth Column." The Communist prisoners continued their demonstrations, agitation and even attacks on UN Guards. On Koje, at Chogu-ri, chanting, shouting Communist POWs had to be brought under control with tear gas and other non-toxic irritants. At Camp No. 1 on Koje two POWs on work detail were overheard plotting an attack in which they would try to seize the weapon of a guard. Separated from the work detail, one of the prisoners attacked the guard with a rock and the guard was forced to fire in self-defense. Six other prisoners at the camp attacked a guard with a pick and a club and the whole compound was unruly and rebellious until tear gas forced the prisoners into their barracks buildings.

On April 17 General Harrison told the Communists in a letter that I had authorized him to agree to a liaison group meeting to discuss the possibility of reopening armistice talks. Harrison pointed out that the full explanation of the Chou En-lai statement, which I had requested, was not satisfactory, so he listed the basic suggestions of the UNC. He suggested that Switzerland or some other nation "traditionally recognized as appropriate in matters of this kind" be named the neutral custodian of the prisoners refusing repatriation. That was necessary because we remembered the difficulty we had once before when the Communists tried to palm off Russia on us as a neutral. He suggested a sixty-day period of explanations to the prisoners, after which the neutral custodial power would handle the relocation of POWs still refusing to go home.

We had learned to know the Communists well. These two issues, the nomination of neutral nations and the time limit on explanations, proved to be the most difficult barriers we had to hurdle to achieve the Armistice. Harrison also told the Communists in no uncertain terms that he would not again submit to their continuous propaganda barrage. "The United Nations Command," Harrison wrote, "is of the opinion that unless meetings of full delegations indicate that an acceptable agreement will be reached in a reasonable time, it will be advisable to recess meetings again."

While on the one hand my headquarters was up to its ears in work planning for a resumption of full armistice talks, on the other it was deeply involved in planning for the exchange of sick and wounded.

The problem of the exchange of sick and wounded was twofold. We had to plan the movement of the Communists north and the reception and handling of the UN POWs released by the Reds.

There was no precedent by which we could be guided in the handling of our people returning from Red prison camps. Never before had our men been subjected to the indoctrination and brainwashing tactics of the Communist jailers. We knew that the brainwashing had had at least some effect. Some Americans had broadcast for the Communists, or signed messages which were broadcast to the United States for them. We had no way of knowing for certain just what would be in the minds of the men the Communists turned back to us, although we had every confidence that once they were back adjustment would be rapid.

A State-Defense message directed that my headquarters should handle the task of gathering intelligence information from returning POWs. That meant my headquarters would have to question each prisoner in a search for the names of men who had turned pro-Communist or who had ratted on their fellows in the prison camps in order to win small favors from the Reds. The closer we came to the starting date of Little Switch, the more anxious were the messages I received from Washington. The main concern was that some Americans would come home spouting the Communist line. The Joint Chiefs wanted me to spot these people and put them under wraps. I opposed this plan. I felt it would be preferable to talk to the returning POWs either after they got home or while they were aboard ships en route to the United States. Otherwise, I pointed out to the Joint Chiefs, I would have to hold each returned prisoner in the Far East until the Communists had released the last of our men. Only in that way could I give every prisoner the opportuniity to point an accusing finger at the men who had misbehaved, ratted or turned pro-Communist.

Washington came up with another plan which I did not like. This was to segregate suspected pro-Communists and ship them back in isolated groups. To me this was pure character assassination. Any man sent home in a pro-Communist group would be branded for life, no matter what later evidence was brought forth to show he was not a prison camp "progressive."

The Communists used Little Switch for all the propaganda value they could wring from it. In addition to withholding the most seriously sick and wounded prisoners so that they could try to make the world believe they had treated POWs well, the Communists stacked the list of the first returnees with some men they *thought* had been more or less won over to communism—the so-called progressives. Not all the men returned in Little Switch were in this category, by any means, but some were. They had been selected carefully on a geographic basis with home towns scattered in many of our industrial centers. The Communists obviously hoped they would become troublemakers among American industrial workers.

Apparently, only an insignificant percentage of the men were deeply and lastingly affected by the months and even years of intense brainwashing to which they had been subjected. Many underwent physical and psychological torture to force them to sign germ warfare "confessions" or "peace appeals." Some pretended to swallow the Communist arguments as a matter of survival or, at worst, as the line of least resistance. As one returnee told newsmen, "There's nothing the matter with our minds that can't be cured by a beer, a blonde and a home-town newspaper."

I believe firmly it was a mistake to order special treatment and partial segregation for the so-called progressives in Little Switch. Someone in Washington apparently was paralyzed with fright at the possibility of our American boys spouting the Communist line. On my recommendation, there was no such segregation or special treatment for suspects who came home in Big Switch after the Armistice was signed.

I hold no brief for the Americans who did rat in the prison camps. I feel that we should continue to investigate very carefully any questionable conduct of Americans in the Communist prison camps. Where there is substantiating evidence I feel there should be trial and punishment of men found guilty of giving military information to the enemy, of making false confessions that were against the interests of the United States or of injuring fellow POWs by turning stool pigeon for the Communists.

Certainly some of the men who succumbed to certain kinds of pressure the Communists applied showed definite weaknesses of character. Many men, we know, were heroes. They withstood the worst the Communists could give them and did not crack. Others stood out long against the mind-annihilating tactics of the Reds and cracked only when faced with certain death. Some even died for their country rather than submit to the Communist pressure, applied with everything from the worst of tortures to sugared blandishments.

Militarily, of course, if we now condone the weakness of some of these POWs we would find in any future war that Americans captured by the enemy would feel justified in giving any kind of information in order to curry favor with their captors. The spirit of loyalty which has supported Americans taken prisoner in our wars down through history would be destroyed and in its place would be the feeling in every American that if he is captured he will not be blamed by his fellow Americans for any act of disloyalty that will bring some extra comfort to his imprisonment.

Official Washington was so leery of possible pro-Communist expressions from the returning POWs that it was suggested to me that I keep any such expression a tight secret. I dug up the old plans for press coverage of returning prisoners, plans written before I arrived in the Far East. These plans did not envisage any opportunity for the press to see pro-Communists, and severely restricted the press access to any of the returning prisoners. The plans said that no prisoner would be permitted to talk with newsmen anywhere in Korea and that only a carefully selected handful would be made available for interviews in the reception hospitals scattered all over Japan.

I felt strongly that any good that could come to us from prisoner interviews would have to come early. A delay of as much as a day, or even a few hours, would leave us open to Communist propaganda charges that we had instructed the prisoners what to say. I was convinced the great majority of prisoners would return to us damning their Communist captors, and that was the story I wanted out—quick.

In Tokyo I met frequently with the bureau chiefs of the three American press associations to keep them advised of progress of the negotiations and to get their ideas of how the returning prisoners should be permitted to tell their stories. These meetings were of particular value during the time that the negotiations at Panmunjom were held in secret. We played honest poker and kept the talks secret, but the Communists cheated by leaking information over the Peiping radio and directly to our newsmen through agents Winnington and Burchett at Panmunjom. Off the record I let the three wire service bureau chiefs know blow by blow what was happening in the conference hut at Panmunjom. That way they at least had a yardstick by which to judge the information that was being spoon-fed their correspondents by Winnington and Burchett. They never violated this confidence.

Finally I asked Don Nugent, our P.I.O., to call in a group of newsmen to work with us in formulating plans for press coverage of the sick and wounded coming home through Little Switch. Out of this conference came the procedures that were adopted, procedures that went as far as possible toward meeting the requirements of the newsmen. Naturally we could not go all the way. There even were conflicts within the military, in addition to the conflicting interests between the military and the press. The medical men, for instance, opposed any plan to interrogate the returning men exhaustively as soon as they came into our hands. The doctors pointed out such interrogation might jeopardize the physical or mental health of the men.

We mulled over every imaginable possibility in many conferences. Basically, I realized that the emotional reaction of men released by the Communists would be extreme, sometimes perhaps violent. The emotion was liable to be highest among men who returned with guilty consciences about their conduct in the prison camps.

I wanted to safeguard these men during the emotional period of their return from behind the Iron Curtain. The three things we had to guard against most were:

1. Statements that would disclose real security information or would damage the UN cause, such as an admission of germ warfare which never took place. I realized that the Communists might have convinced some POWs that there had been germ warfare.

2. Statements that disclosed information which would jeopardize men still prisoners in enemy camps.

3. Statements that, in the height of emotional excitement, might tend to incriminate the prisoner himself and haunt him for the rest of his life.

We found little trouble in keeping the men from disclosing facts that would endanger the buddies they left behind. The returning POWs were far more acutely aware of that danger than we. There were great stories they could have told, too, about an anti-Communist organization that spread from camp to camp, about escapes, about defiances in the face of threat of torture.

The first two rules were that no returning prisoner had to see the newsmen unless he wanted to and that no returning prisoner could see newsmen if examining physicians decided he was too sick physically or mentally to take the ordeal of questioning in the hot, crowded tents that were used for the press interviews.

Procedures finally adopted for Little Switch enabled us to move the sick and wounded prisoners through the processing and press interviews with a minimum of delay. At Panmunjom the Communist ambulances drove the sick and wounded prisoners to a chalk line fronting a series of our reception tents. There, at the chalk line, our officers counted the prisoners and signed a receipt for their delivery, a necessary procedure even though it may seem humiliating to sign receipts for human beings. We had to protect ourselves against possible false Communist claims that they had returned more men than they did.

Each POW was helped or conducted to a reception tent where the first cursory medical check was made to see whether he could stand the forty-five-minute ambulance ride to Freedom Village at Munsan-ni or whether it was necessary to fly him there in a helicopter. The POWs were moved quickly through the processing tents, out the back and into the waiting ambulances or helicopters.

The two Freedom Villages, one for ROKs and the other for American and UN POWs, were huge compounds with processing and hospital tents.

I went to both villages to greet the first men who returned, and others who came back during the days that followed.

The cheerful soldiers who opened the ambulance doors at the UN village impressed me. As he opened each ambulance he called jovially to the POWs: "Welcome to Freedom Village. You're home now, unlax and take it easy."

It was a warm welcome which the POWs thoroughly appreciated. Each man grinned from ear to ear with happiness. Then the soldier would tell each ambulance load of POWs: "General Mark Clark, the

Commander in Chief of the United Nations Command, is here to welcome you home."

I shook hands with each POW, told him how glad we were to welcome him home and how proud of him we were. It pleased me that in nearly every ambulance at least one man told me he had served with me in Italy.

In the processing tents the returning POWs were given more thorough physical examinations, were issued new uniforms and prepared for the next step in their journey home. They also were briefed quickly on the press interview situation, asked whether they wanted to talk to reporters, told that was the fastest way for them to get a message home, and warned against saying anything that would hurt them, the buddies they left behind or their country.

Those who wanted to talk with reporters were escorted through a wooden door into the interview tent where four separate interview tables were set up, some with facilities for radio and television microphones and cameras. One Air Force captain, Zach Dean, even talked to his wife, a Red Cross worker in Tokyo, on a radio-telephone hookup arranged by the American radio network men on the scene.

The interviews were monitored carefully by military public information officers but for the most part the POWs were careful to avoid the proscribed subjects and a frequent answer to newsmen's questions was "I'd rather talk with my government about that." Every man interviewed was most wary of anything that might hurt anyone still imprisoned by the Communists.

I was most pleased that although the POWs had a minimum of briefing before they faced the press, most came through in good shape. Their frank, honest answers to questions, their detailed accounts of their harrowing life in Red hands, achieved the objective of spreading the story on the record with great dramatic impact and with the unquestioned ring of truth.

We learned early that the Communists had cheated again in their selection of men to come home in Little Switch. They were not the worst of the sick and wounded from the camps. Many returning POWs said they were puzzled about why they had been picked when the Communists passed over so many others who were sicker than they.

The answer was simple, of course. The Communists knew the first exchange would have the big emotional impact on people at home and would make the lasting impression. Part of Communist propaganda always had been the claim that they treated prisoners well and we treated prisoners badly. The men we got back in Little Switch included amputees and some seriously ill with chest ailments. But more of them were healthy-looking men who looked even better in photographs. What the Communists wanted to create was an impression of good treatment.

At the same time they worked hard to create the corollary impression that the United Nations Command mistreated its prisoners. The Sixth Column did everything possible to embarrass the UN Command right to the point of exchange and beyond. They started fights aboard the train that each night carried them north to a siding near Panmunjom. They discarded soap, toothbrushes and other comfort items. They ripped and tore clean, new clothing and threw it away. Chinese prisoners staged a sitdown strike and refused to leave LSTs which had taken them from Cheju-do to Pusan. Firehoses had to be used to induce them to debark. At the end the prisoners rejected food and medical attention. They wanted to look as mistreated as possible when they returned to their Communist masters.

One thing the prisoners could not hide. That was their physical condition which had improved during the long months that they received good food and medical attention in the prison camps. They were heavier than when they were captured. Their wounds had been well tended over long periods. The last minute effort to achieve the appearance of abuse failed miserably, but that did not stop their masquerade. Chinese and North Korean POWs who started to walk from our ambulances across the chalk line at the Communist reception center were shouted at by Communist officials and soldiers who instructed them to go into an act. They did. Men perfectly able to walk alone collapsed and called for Chinese and North Korean girl soldiers to help them. Others who missed the shouted cues and began walking alone to the processing tents were grabbed by

Chinese and North Koreans and helped over the line whether they liked it or not. There was singing and shouting and sobbing. Returning Chinese and North Korean POWs stripped off the clothing that the UNC had given them, flung it on the ground and trampled on it.

Hordes of Communist still and movie photographers caught all these scenes, of course.

But so did representatives of most of the United Nations countries involved in the Korean War, and they were able to report home the truth of the phony demonstration the Communists staged.

Despite these annoyances, so commonplace throughout our dealings with the Communists that we had become inured to them, progress toward armistice appeared to be rapid. None of the disagreements that still existed appeared to be too difficult to overcome. Certainly the Communists had sent at least some of our sick and wounded home to us, as agreed, even though they cheated again and failed to send home all the sick and wounded. The only note of caution came from the realization that things had looked rosy many times in the past, but always armistice had been blocked by new Communist demands that were completely unacceptable to us.

This time, however, the issues had been narrowed so fine that it appeared there was a smooth road to cease-fire.

Yet it was close to four months before the shooting stopped—a period that saw some of the bloodiest fighting and trickiest bargaining of the Korean war. I found myself engaged in a two-front diplomatic battle—with the Communists at Panmunjom and with President Syngman Rhee in Seoul.

The biggest trouble came from Rhee. His violent opposition to an armistice was dormant while there was no real chance that the Communists would agree to a cease-fire. But once armistice appeared imminent Rhee threatened to blow negotiations sky-high with a gun "made in the USA."

18

The Rocky Road to the Armistice

During the hectic final four months before the cease-fire in Korea the UN Command was confronted almost literally with a crisis a day. Never, it seemed to me, was it more thoroughly demonstrated that winning a satisfactory peace, even a temporary one, is more difficult than winning a war.

The truce barometer fluctuated wildly. In April we were reasonably sure an armistice would be signed. In May the Communists gave such indications of bad faith and evasiveness that for the first time I was granted authority from Washington to *terminate*, not recess, the Panmunjom truce talks if the Reds refused our final order.

If it came to the point of terminating the armistice talks then I was to prosecute the war along lines we had not yet taken to make the Communists wish they had accepted our terms. That sounded more like the American way of doing business.

In June and July, when we seemed to be making progress at the conference table, the Chinese launched their most violent offensives in two years. They threw so much artillery at our lines that there was strong suspicion they deliberately were using up all the shells they had stockpiled near the front during the two years of the talking war.

And throughout this entire period, like a lighted fuse sputtering toward the powder barrel, President Syngman Rhee threatened to wreck any armistice we signed. My relations with South Korea's venerable, patriotic and wily chief of state had been excellent right up to the moment the United States indicated clearly it intended to go through with an armistice that might leave his country divided and the northern portion in the hands of Chinese Communist troops.

257

Then I became the whipping boy for his bitterness and frustration.

As I have said, the long view may one day prove Rhee was right in his one-track determination to keep us fighting until all Korea was won. But to achieve this would have required an extension of the war beyond Korea, something my government, and to a greater extent its UN allies, were not prepared to do. In fact the major objective seemed to be to prevent an extension of the war.

President Eisenhower had promised the American people to end the Korean War. He had been elected by a landslide. As UN Commander under two administrations, I found that with such a mandate the Republicans were ready to go further than the Democrats to achieve a truce.

Little Switch, the exchange of sick and wounded prisoners, gave us the first concrete proof that the Communists had altered their truce tactics radically. For all their sound and fury over our alleged "massacre" and "torture" of Communist POWs, the Reds never had shown the slightest interest in getting back these disabled men until March, 1953. Our first proposal to exchange the sick and wounded was made to the Communists way back in December, 1951, but the Reds had rejected it and all our subsequent pleas for this humanitarian exchange.

But in March and April of 1953, to our surprise, the Communists gave in on almost every disputed issue in the talks that led to Little Switch. On April 20 the actual exchange began. The Communists took six days to return 684 ailing UN POWs, of whom 149 were American. We took one day longer to give them 6,670 North Koreans and Chinese.

Heartened by the success of Little Switch, although still disturbed by the now solid evidence that the most seriously ailing UN POWs still were held in Red prison camps, we went into full negotiations for an armistice on April 26. The talks had been in recess for more than six months, since October 8, 1952.

The one issue blocking an armistice remained the question of whether captured Communists would be given the right to ask for and accept political asylum in the free world. The Communists still

clung to their principle that all prisoners eventually must be repatriated. They called their principle by the high-sounding name of "no
forcible retention," a name nicely calculated to serve propaganda
purposes by raising a question about the UN Command motives in
demanding the right of political asylum for the prisoners.

April 26 was a Sunday and the Communists made it a holiday at
Panmunjom. Never had so many Communists crowded into the
little roadside hamlet for a negotiating meeting. They even sent a
Russian correspondent of *Pravda* to Panmunjom, the first Russian
we knew who had visited the conference site in any capacity.

Nam Il was ready with a package six-point proposal and presented it right away. He hoped to strike while the iron was hot and
the momentum toward an armistice was great. We had generated a
good deal of momentum in the swift negotiations for Little Switch
and the even swifter completion of the exchange. The Communists
tried to ride that momentum through to a sneak diplomatic victory
that would have denied the right of political asylum to the prisoners.

The Nam Il proposal briefly was that within three months after
the Armistice was signed all prisoners who refused repatriation and
demanded political asylum should be moved to a neutral state.
There they would be held prisoner for another six months while
agents from their governments tried to persuade them to come
home. Any prisoners who withstood the blandishments of the per-
suading agents then would be held prisoner indefinitely in the neutral state while the Political Conference recommended by the
armistice negotiators would try to settle their fate.

Boiled down to its essentials, this meant that to win political
asylum a prisoner would have to submit to a minimum of nine
months' imprisonment after the Armistice and then would have to sit
indefinitely in a prison camp while UN and Communist politicians
sat down as equals and tried to agree on what to do with him. The
prisoner didn't even have assurance that there would be a political
conference as recommended by the armistice negotiators. Personally, I had my doubts if such a conference ever would be held.
Beyond that, the prisoner knew from the record that there was little
chance of UN and Communist negotiators agreeing on such a con-

troversial issue, an issue which had prolonged the war by a full year already.

The prisoner would have been forced to accept repatriation just to escape the prison camp.

That was the proposal Nam Il handed us on the day of great optimism, the proposal that killed optimism and halted the momentum toward the cease-fire.

General Harrison objected immediately. He objected about the failure of the Communists to nominate a neutral nation, the provision which would force indefinite detention upon prisoners refusing repatriation, and the provision which would require the movement of prisoners from Korea to a neutral state.

Nam Il said six months of explanations were necessary and declared the UNC nominee for neutral custodian, Switzerland, was unsuitable.

The delegates then settled down to the kind of haggling which had become the rule in these negotiations—acrimonious, angry and stubborn.

As though there were not enough points of friction in the talks about the Armistice itself, the UN Command was shocked to learn from the men who returned in Little Switch of the large number of sick and wounded who had been left behind. On May 1 we protested to the Communists that we knew of 234 non-Koreans and 141 Koreans who were sick or wounded, but able to travel, who had not been repatriated in Little Switch. The Communists, of course, did nothing about it and under the circumstances I had neither the authority nor power to force them to act.

Haggling on the nomination of a neutral nation continued until May 7 when the Communists, who had steadfastly refused to name their choice and had just as steadfastly demanded that all POWs refusing repatriation be moved to a neutral nation, came up with an eight-point written proposal that eventually became the basis for the Armistice. The Communists proposed that India, Poland, Czechoslovakia, Switzerland and Sweden be members of a five-nation neutral Repatriation Commission that would take custody of the prisoners inside Korea. The plan still failed, however, to provide a

clear path to political asylum for men who persisted in their refusal
to return home. The Communists continued to insist that the Political Conference make the final decision on what to do with these
people. Harrison said bluntly, "There is no guarantee whatsoever
that the political conference will be able to settle the problem."

While the Armistice talks bumbled along angrily, real trouble was
developing in the rear. With the first indication that the truce talks
might get under way again with a fair chance of success, there
came an ominous rumbling from the South Korean Government. As
early as April 3, 1953, the ROK Foreign Minister, Pyun Yung Tai,
talked to American Ambassador Ellis O. Briggs in terms that indicated the ROKs might demand a price for co-operating with the
Armistice. Immediately I informed the Joint Chiefs of Staff that
another South Korean antitruce campaign was threatened.

On April 24, two days before the full armistice talks resumed,
the Korean Ambassador to Washington made it official. He advised
President Eisenhower that President Rhee was preparing to withdraw ROK military forces from the UN Command if any armistice
was signed that permitted Chinese Communist troops to remain
south of the Yalu River.

This threat was serious enough to warrant a special flight for me
to Seoul three days later to see Rhee. We conferred alone, as we
had so often before and would many times again, in the small,
rather cheerless sitting room of the palace-like presidential residence. This room was poorly heated and I always wore long johns
and an extra sweater or two under my uniform, depending on how
long—or "hot"—I thought the conference would be. Luckily on this
cold spring day I was well prepared. It was a long conference.

I tried to convince Rhee of the futility of our demanding unilateral withdrawal of Chinese forces from Korea after we had spent
two and a half years in a fruitless effort to force them out at gunpoint. I emphasized that there was neither victor nor vanquished
in this war and that we were in no position to make demands that
could be enforced only by victory on the battlefield. I suggested
that the truce document might contain a provision for the simultane-

ous withdrawal of *all* non-Korean forces from Korea after the Armistice became effective.

Then I got to the point. How serious was his threat to withdraw ROK forces from the UN Command? That, said Rhee, was an eventuality for the future. He was not thinking of doing anything like that just then, he said. Before he took any such action, he solemnly promised me, he would discuss the matter personally with me. I was to remember this promise with considerable bitterness some six weeks later.

We also touched on other aspects of the negotiations. I became convinced that Rhee did not care what we did with the Chinese POWs who said they didn't want to go back to Red China, but was sensitive to any tampering with Korean POWs who refused to return to North Korea.

As far back as September of 1952 I had explored ways by which we might free these 83,000 Korean and Chinese anti-Communists. Aside from the expense involved, guarding them tied up many battalions of military manpower sorely needed at the front. However, the political implications put the problem outside my jurisdiction and release of the anti-Communists might have led to retaliatory action against UN prisoners in Communist hands. But as the suspension of negotiations continued well into 1953 and there was no apparent change in the Communist attitude, I made specific recommendations for the immediate release of the prisoners and forwarded them to Washington through an officer from my headquarters, Lieutenant Colonel Arthur Kogstad, an expert on the POW situation.

Kogstad presented my recommendations on March 6. I was later notified that my views were under favorable consideration, and there the matter ended. I am convinced that if we had released these prisoners then, in an orderly fashion, we would not have faced the embarrassment and bloodshed which resulted when Rhee let Korean nonrepatriates go on the eve of the truce, and when the remainder were turned over to Indian troops after the Armistice. I am also convinced that the Communists would have signed an armistice even if we had released them.

Three days after our meeting Rhee sent me a letter. He apparently had had second thoughts about the idea of simultaneous withdrawal of Chinese and UN forces after an armistice. He would never agree to this, he wrote, unless he was given several ironclad U.S. guarantees. The most remarkable of these was that a buffer strip on the *north* side of the Korean border be established, supervised and maintained by the UN Command until permanent peace was established in the Far East. The *north* side of the boundary line was in Chinese and Russian territory. Rhee, in effect, proposed that the United Nations occupy the territory of Russia and China, neither of which was in the Korean War officially, as though we had defeated the Soviet and Chinese armies.

Rhee was a very sharp politician. He knew full well how outlandish was this demand. But he also knew outlandish demands made good bargaining weapons. If he hadn't known it long before he certainly had seen the technique demonstrated well by the Communists at Panmunjom.

Next day Rhee opened the troublesome public agitation against the truce. He came out with a flat public statement that there would be no armistice while Chinese Communists remained on Korean soil.

Rhee also declared he would never permit Korean anti-Communists to be transported out of Korea to a neutral nation to be forced to listen to North Korean Communists coax them to return to Communist hands. I was sure that this statement was not a bargaining lever, but that Rhee meant exactly what he said. That was one reason I was so opposed to the Communist plan to ship all the nonrepatriates to a neutral country.

The eight-point Communist proposal of May 7 was unacceptable to us as it was presented, but it had many similarities to the Indian Resolution which had been passed in the UN General Assembly in December, 1952, with American support after American amendments had been accepted. I was directed by Washington to accept the Nam Il plan as the starting point for discussion.

The most important Red concession in the eight-point plan was the agreement that the prisoners would remain inside Korea and not be transported to a neutral nation. In addition, the Reds finally broke their long silence with regard to the neutrals acceptable to them for the custodial job. And the Red proposal of a five-nation agency instead of a single neutral was a fresh concept that opened possibilities for agreement.

But the Red plan had some formidable gimmicks. One was the requirement that Communist Czech and Polish members of the five-nation neutral Repatriation Commission as well as Chinese and North Korean Communist persuader teams be given freedom to travel into South Korea to persuade the nonrepatriates to come home. Since it had been agreed that press coverage would be permitted, this also meant that we would have to play host to an unknown number of Communist newspapermen. We knew from experience at Panmunjom, if nowhere else, that a Red newspaperman was a Red agent. The ROKs quickly pointed out, too, that the proposal as made would permit the Red agents to travel freely over the main supply and communication routes of South Korea and would give them much freedom in the five major cities and ports of the country.

On May 12 I called on President Rhee again and explained my government's position. I found him angrier and more anti-Armistice than ever. He declared he would never let this crowd of potential spies, saboteurs and agitators into his rear areas, and I couldn't blame him. As UN Commander, they were my rear areas, too.

Then he brought up another objection which was to be most troublesome in the hectic weeks to follow. He said he would not permit any Indian troops on ROK soil as neutrals or anything else. He said that rather than countenance the presence of Indian troops in his country he might, on his own, release the nonrepatriates "without involving the UN Command." This was the first positive storm warning of what was to come. I reminded Rhee that the ROK security troops guarding the POWs were under my command and that for him to take such unilateral action would be contrary to his pledge, even though I previously had recommended the release of the nonrepatriates.

In some respects Rhee had my complete sympathy. I knew what

it was to have a Communist repatriation mission operating in my rear areas. I had had bitter experience with the Russian Repatriation Mission which operated in the American Occupation Zone of Austria in 1945 and early 1946. This mission, as I have said, was authorized to pick up Red Army deserters and suspected war criminals among the 750,000 refugees who were under our protection. Instead of sticking to the job, the agents in the mission spent most of their time in espionage and in trying to browbeat unwilling DPs into returning to the land of the hammer and sickle. Their activities culminated in an armed attempt to kidnap one of our Austrian counterintelligence agents. Several members of the mission were caught in this attempt, red handed, so to speak. Next day I repatriated the Repatriation Mission.

I had experienced what Rhee feared would happen to his country if the United Nations Command signed an agreement to let Red agents from Czechoslovakia, Poland, China and North Korea roam about South Korea, an agreement that would carry with it the tacit pledge that the United Nations Command would guarantee safety and freedom of movement for the Red agents.

Therefore after I left Rhee that day I sent a lengthy report to the Joint Chiefs. I recommended that the UN Command stick by its decision to release the Korean nonrepatriates as civilians at the exact time of armistice, without further screening or explanations by the Communists. I cited two reasons. First, the Communists already had set the precedent by "releasing" fifty thousand captured South Koreans "at the front" during hostilities in the early days of the war —and forcing them to fight against the ROK and UN troops. Second, while Rhee might be bluffing about a lot of other things, he was in dead earnest in his desire to release the Korean nonrepatriates and his determination to use arms if necessary to resist the entry of Communist observers and Indian troops into his rear areas.

I don't think this was sufficiently appreciated in Washington. A few days later the Joint Chiefs replied that I might use as my *initial* position the demand that these Korean nonrepatriates be released as civilians at the signing of the Armistice. This was a useless authority. The Communists probably never would agree to it. But they might, and as I have already pointed out, I was certain they would, accept it as a *fait accompli* and go ahead and sign an armistice, regardless.

In the end that was just what they did after Rhee released 27,000 prisoners.

The day after I talked with Rhee, on May 13, Harrison gave the Communists a twenty-sixth-paragraph UNC counterproposal to their eight-point plan of May 7. Our counterproposal accepted much of what the Communists had proposed, with three important differences. The Communists wanted all nonrepatriates turned over to the Neutral Nations Repatriation Commission. We proposed that the Commission take custody of the Chinese nonrepatriates but that the Koreans be turned loose as civilians on the day of armistice with freedom to settle where they desired in North or South Korea. Secondly, the Communists wanted each of the five nations of the Repatriation Commission—India, Poland, Czechoslovakia, Switzerland and Sweden—to provide an equal number of soldiers to guard the nonrepatriates. We proposed that only Indian troops be used. Finally, the Communist plan remained vague on final disposition of the nonrepatriates. We proposed concrete, foolproof procedures by which a prisoner could obtain political asylum.

General Nam Il blew up. He declared the proposal to release the Korean anti-Communists was "a step backward" in the negotiations. Instead of bargaining he resorted to wearisome and familiar propaganda tirades to try to force us to make concessions. Three days later he was still at it, so I told General Harrison to recess for four days, until May 20, when our final position would be crystallized.

I pointed out to Washington that the time was ripe for positive action on our part. I said we must either secure Communist agreement or show up the Reds in the eyes of the world as men seeking a truce only on their own unreasonable terms. To do this we had to present our final position and convince the Reds that it *was* our final position. Giving in bit by bit only encouraged them to demand more.

The Communist "Sixth Column," meanwhile, remained active. In Camp No. 1 on Koje hard-core Communists disobeyed orders, threw notes between compounds and assaulted UN guards. Another factor gained new importance, however. The internal struggle among the prisoners was intensified as the Communists worked harder to gain full control over the compounds. In one compound two prisoners were killed by their fellow POWs. Another prisoner was drowned.

Syngman Rhee seemed somewhat mollified. He liked the plan to release all Korean anti-Communists as civilians on the day of the Armistice.

The day before we were scheduled to meet the Communists again a message came from Washington with instructions that any action designed to bring matters to a head must be co-ordinated at the highest governmental level and with our Allies. I was told to ask for a five-day extension of the recess. This I did gladly.

On May 23 the answer came from Washington. I was to follow generally the terms of the Indian Resolution, insist on the principle of no forced repatriation and insure that no intimidation be used to make the anti-Communist prisoners go home.

Then came the rub. I was instructed to agree to turn over to the Neutral Repatriation Commission all Korean as well as Chinese nonrepatriates—a point that made many in the ROK Government feel that we had betrayed them. In addition, I was instructed to agree to the Communist demand that all disputes within the Repatriation Commission would be decided by a majority vote rather than by unanimous vote. This gave the Communists an edge since India, although avowedly neutral, recognized and was sympathetic to Red China.

Beyond these points I was given fairly wide latitude in negotiating the Terms of Reference for the prisoner exchange.

If, however, the Communists rejected this final offer and made no constructive proposal of their own, I was authorized to *break off* the truce talks rather than to recess them, and to carry on the war in new ways never yet tried in Korea. At this writing the plans still cannot be disclosed, for there still is only a truce or cease-fire in Korea, not a peace.

I was not in complete agreement with the set of instructions

Washington sent me. I felt we were only postponing big trouble in failing to recognize Rhee's implacable stand against turning over Korean nonrepatriates to the Repatriation Commission and his equal determination to prevent Communist members of the Commission, and Indians, from roaming about South Korea. But I felt sure this first "take it or leave it" offer would bring about a truce or at least end the bickering at Panmunjom.

It was decided to hold the Panmunjom meetings in secret executive sessions—the Communists willing—because we had found we made more progress when the enemy stopped talking for the propaganda effect, which he always did at open meetings. In this way we would be able to make it clear that this was our final proposal without running the risk of adverse public opinion—either because we were too soft or because we were too tough in the manner in which we handed the ultimatum to the Reds.

On the day that General Harrison was to put our final plan on the conference table, May 25, I was directed by Washington to inform Rhee personally of what we were proposing. Ambassador Briggs and I were instructed to explain to Rhee our final position and to deliver to him a personal message from President Eisenhower in which was outlined the details of American military and economic aid that would be forthcoming if South Korea went along with the Armistice.

Briggs and I arrived at the presidential residence at 10:00 A.M.—an hour before General Harrison was to hand our proposal to Nam Il at Panmunjom. The timing of our call was fixed by Washington. With President Rhee was his foreign minister, Pyun Yung Tai. Whether from personal conviction or from a desire to please Rhee, Pyun habitually was more caustic and difficult to deal with than his chief. On occasion he became downright insulting to my government. Pyun was well schooled in the tricks of philosophic logic and his English, spoken with a clipped Oxford intonation, was masterful.

Briggs and I worked from the same document—Briggs dealing with the economic and political aspects and I with the military. After I outlined our new position for a truce, Pyun remarked that it was inconceivable to him how we could notify the ROK Government of our new and different stand at the very moment we were negotiating it with the Communists, which I had to admit to myself was a fairly valid objection for him to make.

What we offered Rhee was this: early announcement by the sixteen United Nations that had fought against Communism in Korea of a joint policy which guaranteed that all sixteen nations would band together against the Reds should the Communists violate the truce in Korea. Included in this proposed policy statement was the most important proviso that if the Communists broke the truce the sixteen nations might not confine their retaliatory efforts to Korea.

Unilaterally the United States promised to build up the ROK Army to twenty divisions, with appropriate air and naval strength. This was quite a promise, for it costs between 150 and 200 million dollars to equip a ROK division and supply it in combat for one year. The United States also promised Rhee economic rehabilitation of his country, a billion-dollar project at least, and further assured him that American troops would be kept on the alert in and near Korea until peace was established firmly.

In return for this we asked Rhee to co-operate with the armistice negotiations, refrain from agitation against the talks and go along with the agreement once it was signed.

Above all, Rhee was asked to leave his armed forces in my UN Command.

The emotional effect of this on Rhee was profound. I had never seen him so disturbed. He sat bolt upright in his chair, the muscles of his face twitched occasionally and he kept rubbing the ends of his fingers, which, I had heard, had been burned by Japanese secret police in the early days of his fight for Korean independence. Once he broke in to our recital of our plans and promises and said:

"I am deeply disappointed. Your government changes its position often. You pay no attention to the view of the ROK Government."

As it became increasingly clear that an armistice was a distinct probability and that Rhee's lifelong goal of an independent and undivided Korea had to be pushed into a future he might not live to see, the President became overwrought.

"One thing we must insist upon is the withdrawal of Chinese Communists from our territory," he said. "There can be no peaceful settlement without that. Your threats have no effect upon me. We want to live. We want to survive. We will decide our own fate. Sorry, I cannot assure President Eisenhower of my co-operation under the circumstances."

At another point he said, "Please tell my dear friend, President Eisenhower, that I am not agitating against an armistice, but it is the popular will of the people. The people will not accept these new terms even if I tell them to."

I was inclined to doubt this. The average South Korean, to this date, probably knows little of the actual terms of the Armistice, but is mighty glad the shooting has stopped.

Minister Pyun warned Briggs and me that to permit the Communists to have access to the anti-Communist POWs in Korea for a long period was tantamount to forceful repatriation. "Many of the prisoners will commit suicide," he warned, and, as a matter of fact, some did.

Rhee asked me to send a personal message to President Eisenhower to tell him that no Indian soldier would be permitted to set foot in South Korea.

"We are at a point where we cannot drag on any longer," Rhee said. "If the United States wants to save democracy for the world, it had better do it now. Please do not destroy the anti-Communist and democratic people all over the world.

"The world requires great leadership. The Kremlin will think twice before it starts another World War. Do not be weak. Do not turn back. Democracy must not go backwards. Some day the United States will have to fight alone. Do not wait for that day."

As he sometimes did when he wanted to illustrate a point, Rhee quoted an old Korean proverb. Two fish were dying of thirst at the bottom of the Yellow Sea, which for the purposes of the proverb apparently had dried up. "Never mind," said one fish, "the world is turning and soon we will have water from the East Sea." "By that time," said the other fish who was obviously a spokesman for the ROK Government, "we will both be dead and in the dried fish market."

Another Korean proverb was applicable to the situation. It would have described the ROK Government and the United Nations at that juncture. It says "same bed, different dreams."

Briggs and I could do little but weather this storm of oratory and try to point out the benefits to be derived from a policy of cooperation. Each of us argued our best; I, despite the fact that I agreed with much of what Rhee said and believed personally that the wisest long-range course for our country would be military victory over the Communists in Korea. And I was wholehearted in my conviction that since my government was determined to end the fighting by an armistice, then the best possible course for Rhee was cooperation. I firmly believed he would hurt both his country and mine if he took any lone action against the Reds.

After a full two hours of trying discussion, Rhee said solemnly and with great emotion:

"We cannot accept. It is entirely contrary to the view of my people. Please say to your President, please let the Koreans fight alone if need be. It is the only way we can survive."

As ringing as this declaration sounded, and perhaps it was meant in all sincerity, the most certain way for the Korean Republic to commit suicide was to try to fight alone. Suicide, some ROKs said, would be better than the fate of Czechoslovakia, which had succumbed to the Reds without a fight. Through suicide, they argued, Korea at least would go down in history as a nation of great honor and the sacrifice of Korea might be a lesson to the rest of the free world.

While Briggs and I were talking with Rhee and Pyun the ROKs boycotted the armistice talks. They maintained their boycott right to the end. There was great commotion at Munsan, the UN Command Advance Base which was home for the armistice negotiators. Major General Choi Duk Shin, the ROK delegate to the talks, was all ready to board a helicopter for Panmunjom when he was called to a telephone. Apparently someone got the word to him, for Choi never made the helicopter and never returned to Panmunjom.

At our request the meetings at Panmunjom again were held in secret. This time the ROKs, not the Communists, saw fit to reveal large portions of the record, which still was available to them for even though Choi continued his boycott of the Panmunjom meetings, he and his associates knew what was transpiring. Stories quoting ROK sources began to break out of Seoul during the secret talks. The stories outlined the main provisions of the final offer we had made, and accurately stated that the Communists very early accepted all but minor provisions.

The Communists asked for two recesses to consider our proposal. My hopes began to rise—but there was the constant threat that Rhee might upset the applecart in any one of eight ways. These, as I outlined them to Washington, were:

Prior to the truce signing he could unilaterally release the Korean anti-Communist POWs (he did); he could offer a separate ROK proposal to the Communists (he did not); he might announce ROK refusal to comply with the provisions of an armistice if signed (he did); he might withdraw ROK forces from the UN Command (he did not); he could sanction riots and demonstrations against the truce (he did); after the truce he might refuse to withdraw ROK troops from the Demilitarized Zone (he did not); he might refuse to permit Indian troops into Korea to implement the Armistice (he did); and he might initiate an attack upon the enemy in violation of the truce (which at this writing he has not done but which he still has the capability of doing).

Behind all of Rhee's spoken and unspoken threats was the psychological whammy he had on us. He knew that no matter what happened we could not, after three years of war, after all the blood and treasure we lost, let Korea go to the Reds by default because of a quarrel "in the family."

By this time, with an armistice apparently within our grasp, Washington was thoroughly alarmed about what Rhee might do. He was another big question mark that prompted the State Department to appoint Bob Murphy, outgoing American Ambassador to Japan, as my political adviser. One of my closest friends, Bob and I spoke the same language, worked together daily and saw eye to eye on the problems in Korea. In fact, Murphy accused me of instigating his appointment, which upset his plans to go home.

"I didn't do it," I told him, "but if I'd thought of it, I would have."

More reserved than Murphy was the American Ambassador to Korea, Ellis O. Briggs, whose last previous post was Ambassador to Communist Czechoslovakia. Briggs never had worked closely with the military before, and his job was all the tougher because in Korea the war was the main show. A series of visits, in which he and his wife came to Tokyo to see us and I went to Pusan to stay with them, formed a firm basis for friendship. We found it to our advantage to call on President Rhee together when the political and military aspects of the armistice question overlapped.

At the end of May, and before the Communists had answered our last proposal, Briggs and I were instructed to inform Rhee that the United States was ready to start negotiating a mutual defense treaty with South Korea along the lines of the Philippine and ANZUS treaties. I pointed out to Washington that Rhee would want such a pact in existence before the Armistice was signed, and that while it would not guarantee his wholehearted co-operation, it would lessen his opposition. Briggs and I decided not to broach the defense pact proposal to him until the Communist answer showed how close to a truce we really were.

Meanwhile, the Joint Chiefs of Staff had authorized me, as the theater commander, to take whatever action I felt necessary to insure the integrity of my forces should Rhee knock the bottom out. Since South Korean troops, backed by American specialized units, manned two-thirds of the front, a sudden decision by Rhee to remove them from my command presented all sorts of nightmare possibilities, chief of which was the frightening chance that an order by Rhee could take the major part of the war right out from under my command. Therefore we had an emergency plan ready for immediate execution.

Quite a different kettle of fish was the question of what I would or could do if Rhee decided to throw open the prison camp gates and release the Korean nonrepatriates. This was something he not only threatened to do but something that I felt he was most *likely* to do, as soon as the Armistice appeared to be in the bag. And yet it was the course of action I was least prepared to prevent.

I talked over the facts of this nettlesome problem with the com-

manders of the Eighth Army, Korean Communications Zone and
the POW Command. Fact one—all anti-Communist POW enclosures were guarded by South Korean troops with a small headquarters of U.S. administrative personnel in charge. Fact two—
General Taylor could not spare more U.S. combat units from the
battle to watch these POWs. Fact three—even if we had the troops
to spare, I was reluctant to use them for fear they might come into
conflict with the ROK guards should a mass breakdown be ordered by Rhee. Fact four—I felt strongly, and Washington agreed,
that firearms should not be used against professed anti-Communists
who were basically on our side. I was not going to be a party to the
mass slaughter with machine guns of these people.

In the last analysis all we could do was to keep our fingers
crossed and assure the nonrepatriates over and over that the UN
Command would never sell them down the river to the Communists. ROK agents, on instructions from the ROK Government, were
telling them just the opposite and the prisoners showed increasing
fears that they would be forced back into Communist hands.

On June 4 the Communists came in with their long-awaited reply
to our final offer. In all major respects they accepted it.

The news of the Communist reaction was revealed almost immediately by ROK sources. After that, news leaks became so frequent
that the suspicion was raised that the ROKs had decided these
revelations might help win public opinion in Allied nations to their
side.

The day after the Communists gave us their favorable reply,
Briggs and I hurried over to see Rhee to tell him that the Armistice
was only a matter of time. We felt him out to learn whether a mutual defense pact would assure his co-operation. He declined to answer, and after we had left issued a public statement setting forth
four conditions for ROK support of a truce. They were: the mutual
defense pact, U.S. military and economic support, retention of
American air and naval forces outside of but near Korea, and simultaneous withdrawal of UN and Chinese troops.

This was a milder set of demands than we had anticipated and
since Rhee assured me again that he would take no action to en-

danger the security of UN forces without prior consultation with me, I thought things might smooth over a bit.

I was never so wrong—as I found out two days later when I called on Rhee again, this time alone.

One sure barometer of the Korean President's relations with me was the presence, or absence, of his wife just before our business discussions. Madame Rhee is a petite but strong-willed Austrian lady, born Francesca Donner, whom Rhee met in Geneva and married in 1934. I found her gracious and amiable, and discovered we had mutual Austrian friends. I also discovered that she wielded tremendous influence with the President. She speaks perfect English, a little Korean, handled all of Rhee's personal correspondence and a good deal of his behind-the-scenes relations with ROK and U.S. military officials. When all was well between the President and me, Madame Rhee usually joined us before or after our conference. Almost invariably she wore flowing Korean national dress and served tea and cakes. As the armistice controversy came to a boil, I saw her less and less.

On this day there was no Madame Rhee. The President and his little dog greeted me in the sitting room. Only the pup seemed glad to see me, perhaps as a fellow-tenant of his dog house.

I found Rhee alternating between despair and defiance. We went over the same ground again. He would never accept the armistice terms as they stood, he told me.

"The Republic of Korea Army will fight on, if it means a suicide, and I will lead them," he told me, adding that the United States was making a great mistake in appeasing communism.

For my part, I tried to impress him with the fact that my country would always support Korea's legitimate aims, but was determined to have an armistice on the present terms. I suggested the possibility of moving the nonrepatriates to an island, like Cheju or Koje, where Communist interrogators would have less chance of causing disturbances and no excuse for setting foot on the mainland of South Korea.

His only answer was to announce that hereafter he would feel free to take any action he deemed appropriate. Did this mean the withdrawal of ROK troops from my command? "Not today, not tomorrow," he replied, "but if it comes to that I will discuss it with you in advance."

At Panmunjom rapid progress was made in cleaning up the last remaining disagreements. The Terms of Reference on prisoner exchange were signed on June 8. The Terms of Reference were detailed and specific in setting forth the responsibility of each side in the disposition of the prisoners of war. I reported to the Joint Chiefs that an armistice could be signed as early as June 18. That was an ironic guess. I was to remember that date for quite another reason. June 18 was the day Rhee released the first of 27,000 anti-Communist Koreans from our prison camps and threw the whole armistice situation into a tailspin.

At the time the agreement on prisoner exchange was signed, Rhee's overwhelming concern was that the Communists would inject technical loopholes into the document so that they could achieve their objective of prolonging the imprisonment of the anti-Reds indefinitely. I was equally concerned about this possibility.

I knew the Indian Army fairly well. In Italy three Indian divisions were under my command. I was friends with many of their officers. In Italy they fought well and I knew that in Korea they would do a good job of guarding the prisoners. My fear was not that the military might fail in its assigned duties, but that political influence from India would guide the Indian custodians to a pro-Communist course.

Therefore I was most careful of the wording of the Terms of Reference we signed to regulate the handling of the anti-Communist prisoners. Our government also was most concerned that we make certain that a clear avenue was left open to political asylum for these men. That was what we had been fighting for during the past year.

We anticipated strongly the possibility that there never would be a political conference as recommended by the military men who negotiated the Armistice. The Communists we felt might well refuse to agree to such a conference because unsettled political conditions in Korea would suit their purposes well.

Therefore I personally directed that there be written into the agreement a proviso which would permit the anti-Communist prisoners to go free at a specified time if there was no political conference. We were most careful to make certain that the agreement would give the Reds no legal grounds for a claim that if a political conference was not held the anti-Communists would have to remain in prison camps indefinitely. That, of course, was the Communist objective. The only way they could avert the terrible propaganda defeat that would come if thousands of former Communist soldiers demanded and got asylum in the free world would be to rig the agreement so that the only way these men could possibly get out of prison camps would be to return to communism.

Every proposal the Communists made was designed to make it as difficult as possible for an anti-Communist to gain political asylum. First the Communists wanted to interview the prisoners for six months and then turn them over to the political conference at which Communists would have an equal voice with men of the free world. As I saw it there wasn't a chance that Communists at the political conference would vote to permit the prisoners to attain their freedom.

Basically the Communists wanted an agreement by which they could delay and frustrate the prisoners so long that finally each prisoner would give up hope and ask for repatriation to his Communist homeland just to get out of prison.

Rhee emphasized this point many times in conversations with me and later with Assistant Secretary of State Walter Robertson, sent out as President Eisenhower's personal envoy to try to win Rhee's promise of co-operation with the Armistice. Time and again Rhee asked us what guarantee we and these unfortunate prisoners had that ultimately, *at a certain fixed time*, they would be released from prison as free men.

We did two things. First I insisted that in the Terms of Reference on the prisoner exchange we include the following sentence:

The Neutral Nations Repatriation Commission shall declare the relief from the prisoner of war status to civilian status of any prisoners of war who have not exercised their right to be repatriated and for whom no other disposition has been agreed to by the political conference within one hundred and twenty (120) days after the Neutral Nations Repatriation Commission has assumed their custody.

This avenue to political asylum was safeguarded further by the following provisions which said:

Thereafter, according to the application of each individual, those who choose to go to neutral nations shall be assisted by the Neutral Nations Repatriation Commission and the Red Cross Society of India. This operation shall be completed within thirty (30) days, and upon its completion, the Neutral Nations Repatriation Commission shall immediately cease its functions and declare its dissolution.

Nothing could be clearer. If there was a political conference it could consider the disposition of the prisoners but it could not block their way to freedom. If there was not a political conference, no power had a legal right to hold the prisoners to wait for one. The path to freedom was clearly outlined. The prisoners who desired political asylum would get it exactly 120 days after the Indian troops took them into custody for the Neutral Nations Repatriation Commission.

After the Communists agreed to and signed these safeguards I wrote to President Rhee, with the full concurrence of our government, that it was the position of the UN and the U.S. Government that the provisions of the Armistice were perfectly clear and that at the end of 120 days these POWs would be released. I signed that letter to Rhee with wholehearted sincerity, firm in the conviction that the written words of the Armistice Agreement could not be distorted. And that's the way it finally worked out.

I was deeply disturbed, therefore, to read in the press the questioning statements from the Communists and others on this point, statements indicating that the POWs should be held until a political conference, in its own sweet time, decided what to do with them. Such questions violated the letter and spirit of the agreement. I was happy to see the firm stand my government took on the issue with its insistence that every prisoner who wanted asylum would be set free on January 23, 1954.

The letter of assurance I sent to Syngman Rhee helped a good deal to make the Armistice more palatable to the ROK Government, but still Rhee kept up a barrage of public statements and press interviews along the familiar line: Never, never, never!

In a supreme effort to bring Rhee around before he did something drastic, President Eisenhower formally, but secretly, invited him to the White House to talk things over. Rhee declined. He said he could not leave Korea at that critical time. But he suggested that Secretary of State John Foster Dulles come to Seoul. Such a visit at that time, of course, would have added immeasurably to Rhee's prestige at home and throughout Asia. Dulles replied that inasmuch as President Eisenhower desired him to remain in Washington until Congress adjourned he would like to send Walter Robertson, Assistant Secretary of State for Far Eastern Affairs, to confer with Rhee. On June 17 Rhee agreed to Robertson's coming.

The following day all hell broke loose, by Rhee's order. It was June 18. At six o'clock in the morning I was awakened with the news that what we had feared was happening. During the night, on orders from Rhee, ROK guards at anti-Communist prison camps all over South Korea had opened the gates and some 25,000 prisoners walked out and lost themselves among the civilian population. During the following few nights another 2,000 were released, boosting the total to 27,000 Korean POWs freed in a dramatic, well-planned operation.

Everyone concerned in the mass release was well briefed. The prisoners knew when they would go, what to take, where to shed and burn their prison garb, where to get civilian clothing and where to hide. South Korean police were instructed on what they were to do to help the fugitives. As the break was under way high ROK officials broadcast the news to the country. The people were told to take care of the men from the prison camps. The people did. They took them into their homes. South Korean police stood watch to warn of the approach of American soldiers on a manhunt for the prisoners.

There were many stories of the reception the South Korean people gave the prisoners, stories that supported the idea that although the ROKs ordered demonstrations, the demonstrators more often than not believed in the slogans they were instructed to chant. The South Koreans welcomed the prisoners as heroes, brought out the best in food, drink and tobacco. Even South Koreans who disagreed with Rhee and were fearful of the consequences expressed great pride in the daring of the release. All signs indicated Rhee reached a new high of popularity among his people the day of the big release.

American and other foreign newspapermen went hunting for the prisoners for stories. A newsreelman searched all morning in the Inchon area for just one prisoner, any prisoner. He knew several hundred were in the area, but he was unable to locate a single one, or any Korean who would admit having seen one. Finally, the newsreelman went to a Korean police station and told his story to the chief. From then on there was no trouble. The chief and one other policeman took the photographer directly to the house where one of the escaped prisoners had taken refuge. The chief went into the house with the cameraman. The other policeman stood guard outside to watch for American MPs. The photographer got his pictures and a story.

Similar incidents were legion. Every United Nations newsman who wanted to talk to a prisoner could. But the South Korean civilian population acted as partisans to guard the POWs from our military dragnet.

The first step I took was to order Major General Herren, Korean Communications Zone Commander, to replace the South Korean prison camp guards with U.S. troops. Some of the ROK guards had disappeared with the prisoners and all the ROK guards were suspect. At one camp the South Korean troops had held a lone American GI at gunpoint until the inmates were safely away. At others ROK officers and enlisted men simply disobeyed or ignored their American detachment commanders.

The exodus continued sporadically for four days while we tried to scrape up enough troops from our meagre battlefront reserves to hold the remaining POWs. In some instances a few prisoners were killed and others wounded. A few Chinese also escaped from their enclosures but, as I suspected, Rhee was not interested in them.

Not so the Koreans. All but nine thousand escaped clean. The Korean National Police and the civilian population were too well organized to absorb the prisoners to permit effective roundups by our troops. And the ROK Provost Marshal announced that his men would resist all efforts by our troops to recapture the POWs. It soon became apparent our efforts were getting nowhere, and might lead to armed clashes between U.S. and ROK troops, so after a while the manhunt just petered out.

The fat was in the fire and the truce that had appeared so tantalizingly close had, for all we knew, gone glimmering again. Ironically, all the articles of the Armistice had been signed by June 18. All that remained was detail work to determine the date and arrangements for the signing ceremony. Since we could not now live up to our signed agreement to turn over so many thousand POWs to the Repatriation Commission, the Communists would have an awfully good case, in the eyes of the world, to delay the signing or stop negotiating altogether.

Criticism of Rhee came from all over the world. Washington reacted by postponing Robertson's visit to Seoul, pending a "clarification" of Rhee's actions.

I dispatched two letters, one to Rhee and one to the Communist commanders. I reminded Rhee that in 1950 he had assigned authority over all his forces to the UN Commander. Therefore, I stated, ". . . I am profoundly shocked by this unilateral abrogation of your personal commitment. On several occasions in recent weeks you have personally assured both Ambassador Briggs and me that you would not take unilateral action with reference to ROK forces under my control until after full and frank discussion with me. Your actions today have clearly abrogated these assurances."

It was the strongest official criticism of Rhee made by an American official. I had not meant to make the letter public but it was suggested I do so by Washington. Somebody had to put it on the line. The Communists were accusing us of complicity in the release of the POWs.

To the Communists I gave a factual account of what had happened and told them we were trying to recapture the escapees—which we were at the time. They came back with some searching questions which plagued us until the day the Armistice was signed. Mainly the Communists wanted to know: Was the UN Command able to control the ROK Government and Army? Did the Armistice in Korea include the "Rhee clique"? If the ROK was not included, what assurance was there that South Korea would live up to the truce terms? Would the UN recover the escaped POWs?

I could not reply just then for the good reason that I didn't know the answers myself. Washington told me to use my discretion in replying. I did and sent Washington a copy. The Panmunjom sessions were recessed until further notice. We could not negotiate until we had some assurance from Rhee he would not disrupt the Armistice. Robertson had the main burden of that task.

Meanwhile, fearful of more trouble, I dispatched the 187th Airborne Regimental Combat Team from Japan to Korea and later moved the 24th U.S. Infantry Division to Korea as well.

The impact of world criticism must have had its effect on Rhee. When I visited him four days after the breakout he appeared nervous and under considerable strain. He was more formal than usual, and mentioned not a word of my strong letter to him.

I asked Rhee point blank, "Why did you remove the South Korean troops from my command and release the prisoners without the notification that you promised me?"

Poker-faced, he replied: "It must be obvious why I could not notify you in advance," meaning, of course, that I could have taken appropriate measures to prevent the breakout.

But he asked me to assure President Eisenhower that he was still trying to work things out with the United States. I told him he must reconcile himself to accepting this truce, and emphasized the rather obvious point that we were not prepared to eject the Chinese from Korea by force. I said a political conference following the Armistice would deal with that—and hoped I sounded more convinced than I felt.

Rhee's Provost Marshal, Lieutenant General Won Yong Duk, was at that time threatening to release the remaining Korean nonrepatriates who were by then under guard of U.S. troops. "I am particularly concerned," I told Rhee, "with the possibility of clashes between U.S. and ROK troops at Korean nonrepatriate POW camps. There must never be physical violence between them."

Rhee assured me that henceforth "I will exert every influence to avoid such incidents." He kept his word.

I agreed with Rhee that there should be a time limit on the political conference, but he wanted a further commitment which it certainly was beyond my authority to make. He wanted America to agree that if after ninety days of haggling in a political conference there still was no concrete step toward agreement that would settle the political problems of Korea, then the Armistice would end and the war would recommence. It was up to us, Rhee said, to decide whether we should fight alongside the ROKs or pull our troops out of his country and let him go it alone against the Communists.

In the next breath Rhee expressed great interest in the proposed US-ROK Mutual Security Treaty and said he understood that, of course, the United States could not come to the aid of his nation if it were the aggressor. The unspoken implication here was that it would take a lot of evidence to induce America to call an ally an aggressor against the Communists, who were the primary aggressors in the Korean War. And if the ROK Army got into serious trouble Rhee could bank on our having to bail him out, no matter what.

I pointed out the impotence of the ROK Army as it then existed for independent action. In my judgment the ROK Army at that date could not have withstood alone a Chinese offensive, let alone attempt to mount a campaign to drive the Chinese out of the truly formidable underground defenses of North Korea. I also pointed out to Rhee that he could benefit from an armistice by gaining the time to train and beef up his forces with American aid. Thus, I said, he would be better prepared to meet any future Communist aggression.

Rhee's most important statement, I thought, was this: Although South Korea could not *sign* an armistice which agreed to a division of the country, it could *support* such an armistice. Since the ROK Government was not to be a party to the agreement, which was a purely military pact between opposing commanders, such support was all we required.

Just before leaving, I suggested a possible solution to Rhee's objection to Indian troops and Communist explanation teams in his back yard. "I don't know yet how my government will react to this," I told him, "but if the Communists agree, we can move the Chinese anti-Communist POWs to a neutral state and the Korean anti-Communist prisoners to the Demilitarized Zone, and there will be no need for Indians or 'persuaders' to set foot in South Korea." Rhee was keenly interested but made no commitment. As it turned out, I later decided we might just as well move all the nonrepatriates, Chinese as well as Korean, to the Demilitarized Zone, the buffer strip that separated the area controlled by the Eighth Army and the Communists.

I realized full well the administrative and logistical problem involved in the movement of these nonrepatriates and the Indian Custodial Forces to the Demilitarized Zone. I knew it would cost millions of dollars to build new camps for the prisoners and their guardians inside the zone, and that we already had camps ready for the prisoners south of the line. As a matter of fact, the materials, labor and equipment for the new camp facilities did cost us $7,756,460.

During this whole period the Communist propagandists were blasting us with false charges that we connived in the release of the 27,000 Korean anti-Communists.

But by the time Robertson and his party arrived in Tokyo on June 24 the Communist propaganda broadcasts from Peiping had undergone a subtle change in tone. The Reds no longer denounced the UN Command for complicity in allowing the nonrepatriates to escape, but concentrated their attacks almost solely on Rhee and the ROK Government. This was an apparent effort to sow discord among the Allies, but more important to the business at hand was that it indicated the Communists still wanted a truce, almost at any price.

After a huddle that included Robertson, Bob Murphy and Ambassador Briggs, we informed Washington that it was our opinion we should go full steam ahead to sign an armistice. We recommended that I should reply as quickly as possible to the questions the Communists had put to me on June 20 and said it was our opinion that the Communists probably would accept the Armistice even if we were unable to vouch for Rhee's conduct. We also said we believed the Reds would agree to the removal of the POWs to the Demilitarized Zone. Some understanding would have to be made with Rhee to move them there, or else they would be permitted to escape en route through action by Won Yong Duk's Provost Marshal force. But I believed that the Communists would accept an armistice even if the remaining anti-Communist prisoners did escape. Such an escape would relieve the Communists from the full force of the propaganda defeat that came with renunciation of communism by so many captured Red troops. They could claim that Rhee "kidnaped" the prisoners and denied them the right to come home, a claim they made about the 27,000 who did escape. The Communists were interested in their face, not the prisoners' lives.

I had had my doubts about the wisdom of sending a special emissary to Rhee because I felt that those who knew the problem intimately and had had personal contact with him could make better use of a blank-check authority in dealing with him. At the same time I realized that the South Korean President might be favorably impressed by my government's sincerity in sending some one from Washington to confer with him. So I gave my complete support to the Robertson mission.

I wished Walt Robertson luck when he took off for Seoul. I was convinced of his great ability, but I knew he was unfamiliar with many facets of the problem that confronted him.

Robertson arrived in Seoul on the third anniversary of the Communist invasion of South Korea. Antiarmistice streamers were stretched across the main thoroughfares and on the Capitol Building, mostly English language streamers. Demonstrators surged through the streets, as they would again during the latter part of the Robertson visit. The main slogan on the lips of the demonstrators was "puk chin, puk chin," which meant "go north, go north." They chanted "puk chin" continuously as they marched or ran through the streets, chanted it so much and in so many places that it became the main background sound of the city.

These well-disciplined "spontaneous" outbursts even included hysterical school girls who threw themselves, chanting slogans, against the barbed wire on the gates of the UN war correspondents' compound. One afternoon the school girls put on as strange a demonstration as was ever held anywhere. They marched past the Capitol Building to the correspondents' compound, several blocks away singing, laughing and chattering. They stopped in the middle of the dusty intersection before the compound and at a whistled signal every girl sat down in the dirt and began to cry. This weeping went on for half an hour or more, growing in volume in an amazing display of mass psychology. In the beginning there were few tears, but it wasn't long before great tears ran down the cheeks of most of the girls. The slogan that day was "Don't sell Korea," a near-English version of the expression, "Don't sell out Korea."

The propaganda techniques were obvious. Almost every demonstration wound up in front of the UN correspondents' billet. In that way the Koreans knew that pictures and stories of the demonstrations would be certain to be sent back to the free-world nations. The newsmen had to cover stories that broke on their doorstep. Obviously the ROKs were out to prove that "the people" would stand for nothing less than the immediate unification of Korea.

Robertson met with Rhee almost daily during the eighteen days he was in Korea. The record of the talks showed the U.S. leaned over backwards to meet nearly all of Rhee's demands, only to have him throw in a few new ones. One of the press associations called the Rhee-Robertson conversations with the Little Truce talks.

It was on June 27, only two days after the Rhee-Robertson talks started, that Rhee admitted President Eisenhower had acceded to all his conditions. Rhee asked Robertson to put the results of the talks in writing as the basis for a firm agreement. Robertson did and was surprised when Rhee added new conditions that hadn't even been mentioned before.

I attended some of these meetings but soon left for Tokyo. At one conference I was explaining how the United States Government would not be a party to duress or intimidation by Communist interrogators trying to persuade the unwilling POWs to go home. Foreign Minister Pyun challenged this statement. I replied, "I guarantee you, Mr. Minister, that this is a pledge from my government."

"The pledges of your government," retorted Pyun, "I have found in the past sometimes cannot be counted upon."

This was the most openly insulting remark Pyun had yet made and this time I didn't let it go by. I told him I could not sit there and listen to statements of that kind directed against my country. He made no reply, but Rhee interjected, "Now, gentlemen, let's not have any arguments. I'm sure Mr. Pyun does not intend to question the good faith of the United States."

When Robertson left for Tokyo on July 12 he carried from Rhee a letter to President Eisenhower which stated that since Eisenhower had requested it, Rhee would not obstruct the implementation of the Armistice. That is what we needed.

In return Rhee obtained from Robertson:

A. The promise of a US-ROK Mutual Security Pact after, not before, the Armistice on the assurance that Secretary Dulles had met with Senate leaders and got a favorable reaction to the treaty. (Such a pact must have Senate ratification.)

B. Long-term economic aid and a first installment of two hundred million dollars. Over and above that, I, as UN Commander, was told to distribute ten million pounds of food—valued at nine and a half million dollars—to the Korean people as soon as the Armistice was signed.

C. An agreement that both South Korea and the United States would withdraw from the postarmistice political conference after ninety days, should no concrete achievements result, both governments to discuss future acts toward the unification of the country.

D. Agreement—as already planned—to expand the ROK Army

to cover twenty divisions, with appropriate increases of the navy and air force.

E. Agreement to hold high-level American-ROK conferences on all aspects of our joint objectives before the political conference opened. (Secretary Dulles and party flew to Seoul in August to fulfill this bargain.)

There was an extra dividend for Rhee. His stature in Asia increased a great deal through the mere fact that the envoy of the President of the United States came to him day after day from June 26 to July 12 to ask for co-operation. Rhee thus pushed himself into the role of a man with influence over the question of whether the free and Communist worlds would continue to war in his country, or could sign an armistice. This position of power he relished to the fullest extent.

Rhee gave up one demand that was not in our power to grant him anyway. This was the demand for the withdrawal of the Chinese from Korea and the immediate unification of the country. He agreed that the nine thousand Korean nonrepatriates still remaining in prison camps be turned over to the Repatriation Commission inside the Demilitarized Zone. He also raised no objection to Indian troops entering the Zone, provided they did not set foot in South Korea on their way.

I don't think there is much point in totting up who got the best of the bargain. The most that can be said is that the talks proved to the world that South Korea was no puppet state. No doubt we saved Rhee much face in handling him the way we did. But, as I pointed out to Washington, there comes a time when it is necessary to save our own face.

We lost more than face. We lost lives. The war at that time was costing us an average of nine hundred UN casualties a day and the maddening part of it was that we had been virtually in complete agreement with the Communists on the truce terms and were down to talk about the signing ceremony when the prisoners were released. I pointed out in a message to R. M. Kyes, the Deputy Secretary of Defense, that Rhee would continue to obstruct an armistice by every means until he became convinced that we had made our last concession. It was my opinion that we had made it and that Rhee should have been so informed.

During the Rhee-Robertson talks, while everything on that front was still in flux, I decided I no longer could put off answering the Communist letter of June 20, no matter what was happening in the "Little Truce talks" in Seoul. One June 29 I sent my answer. I was armed with a Washington directive giving me the "widest latitude" in resuming negotiations with the Communists, as long as I honored the principle of no forced repatriation and used no force against the ROKs to ensure their compliance.

I notified Rhee that negotiations would be resumed and then sent the letter to the Communist commanders through the Panmunjom liaison officers. I pointed out that my command had no authority over the ROK *Government*, an independent sovereign state, but that the ROK had violated its commitments which put the ROK Army under my command by "issuing orders unknown to me through other than recognized military channels to certain Korean Army Units which permitted the POWs to escape." I said that the UNC and interested governments would make every effort to secure ROK co-operation, but that it was not feasible to recapture the 27,000 escapees. That would be as impossible for us, I told the Reds, "as it would be for your side to recover the 50,000 South Korean prisoners 'released' by your side during the course of hostilities."

In effect my letter asked the Communists to sign an armistice despite the release of the 27,000 anti-Communist Koreans. It was a sincere estimate of the situation, if not too reassuring to the Communists, but the feeling was prevalent now that the Reds needed and wanted a truce.

After my letter was made public I heard one combat officer growl, "If they go along with that they must be hurting so much we should never have offered them an armistice in the first place."

To make it crystal clear that we were preparing for any eventuality, I ordered my senior U.S. commanders to a Tokyo powwow. Shortly afterwards in Korea, General Taylor and his commanders, including ROK generals, met to discuss plans to give the whole front over to the ROKs should that become necessary because of Rhee's actions.

Of one thing I was determined. That was that under no circumstances would we permit a situation to develop in which American and ROK troops had to fight each other. If the ROK Government decided despite everything to go it alone in Korea, we were going to get out of the way.

At the same time I wanted to impress all levels of the ROK command with what it would mean if we took up Rhee's dare that he would "go it alone." Many of the South Korean officers knew their army's limited capabilities and had no desire to commit suicide in a doomed "puk chin" attack. But it was worth their careers to say so publicly. These officers were torn between their first loyalty to their country and leader, and their faith in the UN Command under which they had fought and gained strength for three years. One South Korean major in charge of a POW camp had refused on June 18 to free his prisoners on the clandestine "orders" given him by the ROK Government. He was later relieved and we had good evidence that he was charged with treason.

As it developed we and the ROKs suffered directly and grievously from the prolongation of the war by Rhee. It was the Communists' turn to stall. On July 8 they replied to my letter that while my answers to their questions failed to satisfy them, they were ready to resume meetings on the tenth.

Twenty-four hours before the meeting took place, on schedule, the Chinese launched their last big push against our lines.

Their first impulse was a two-division punch against the ROK 5th Division, spreading to the ROK 8th Division on the east flank of the central front. They penetrated our main lines for a distance of four miles on a nine-mile sector, forcing us to establish a new line of defense on the Pukhan River.

The second impulse was a six-division smash against the entire central front in the Kumsong-Kumhwa area. The brunt of this push was borne by the ROK Capitol, 3rd, 5th, 6th, 8th Divisions, one regiment of the ROK 11th Division and the American 3rd Division which was thrown hastily into the battle. This final effort rolled through our main battle positions to a depth of seven miles on a twenty-three-mile front. A UN advance which met little or no resistance reduced the penetration to approximately seventeen miles wide and five and a half miles deep.

There is no doubt in my mind that one of the principal reasons, if not the only reason, for the Communist offensive was to give the ROKs a "bloody nose" and show them and the world that "puk chin"—"go north"—was easier said than done.

Heavy fighting raged while the Communists at Panmunjom methodically questioned our ability to carry through the armistice terms in view of the daily and often contradictory statements made by Rhee and others in the ROK Government.

I informed the Joint Chiefs that I believed the Communists had a right to know that UN military support would be withdrawn from the ROKs should they violate the Armistice. Washington, however, did not give me that authority until later. On July 11, at the close of their talks, Rhee handed Robertson his letter to President Eisenhower promising not to obstruct implementation of the Armistice.

With this to back him up, General Harrison informed the Communists the next day at Panmunjom that: ". . . in consequence of negotiations just completed . . . you are assured that the UNC, which includes the ROK forces, is prepared to carry out the terms of the armistice."

The Communists, however, were in no hurry. They countered with specific questions which I, as a military commander, would have felt justified in asking in their place. Meantime, they battered away at the ROKs who fought valiantly in some sectors and had to give ground in others.

On July 16 I flew to Korea to get firsthand information on the battle situation. I visited IX Corps Commander Lieutenant General Reuben Jenkins, and from there flew by helicopter to the ROK II Corps where I spoke not only with South Korean officers but to the American KMAG (Korean Military Advisory Group) advisers with each of the ROK divisions. I was discouraged by what they told me concerning the performance of some South Korean commanders.

I flew back to Seoul and saw Rhee before supper. I gave him the military situation frankly and told him how some ROK commanders had not come up to expectations. Rhee took the position that the Chinese offensive had met success only because the Eighth Army by remaining on the defensive so long had let the Communists build up their strength.

By July 19 the Reds decided they had gained as much as they could from their final offensive and that day announced they were "prepared to conclude" discussions on the Armistice. In their ten-day push the Reds undoubtedly suffered extremely heavy casualties. Just how many would be merely an estimate on our part. I *know* we suffered fourteen thousand killed, wounded and missing, mostly South Koreans.

The Communists made public the list of "guarantee" questions they had asked, along with our answers. Two of the questions were of lasting importance. They were:

"If the South Korean forces undertake aggressive action after the armistice, and if we take necessary action to resist their aggression in order to safeguard the armistice, will the UNC maintain the state of armistice?" Our answer was yes.

"If the South Korean forces undertake aggressive action after the armistice, will the UNC *not* give support to South Korea, including support in equipment and supplies?" Again our answer was what the Communists wanted. We said we would *not* support aggression by the Republic of Korea.

The next day we presented our amendment to turn over the non-repatriates to the Neutral Nations Repatriation Commission in the Demilitarized Zone. Agreement was reached on this on July 23. Staff officers went to work to redraw the Demarcation Line so as to include changes wrought in the battle line by the final-hour Chinese offensive.

Then came the agreement we had been waiting for since early in July, 1951, more than two years before.

We agreed that the armistice-signing ceremony would be held on July 27.

But it would have been out of the character of these negotiations if everything had worked out smoothly, even then. We hit another last minute snag. Originally it had been planned that the opposing commanders, I for the UNC and Marshal Kim and General Peng for the Communists, would face each other across a table at Panmunjom and sign the armistice documents. The Communists even built a hall behind the conference hut to house the ceremonies.

But at the last minute the Communists inexplicably asked that the agreement be signed by the respective commanders at their own headquarters, following which the copies would be returned to Panmunjom to be signed by the senior truce delegates and exchanged.

There were all sorts of suppositions why the Communist commanders were shy about coming to Panmunjom. The guesses ranged from possible fear of air attack en route south to a rumor that Kim Il Sung had been killed or liquidated months before. After kicking it back and forth for a few days, the Reds agreed to our way, with Kim, Peng and me gathering under a single roof to sign the documents. But they threw in a gimmick I could not accept. They said Kim and Peng would come to Panmunjom only on condition that no South Korean would attend in any capacity and no Chinese Nationalist newsmen would be permitted in the neutralized zone on the day of Armistice. The actual ceremony, said the Communists, could not be recorded by only ten official photographers from each side.

These terms were unacceptable. I particularly wanted a ROK representative present. I would not be a party to any arrangement which was an insulting exclusion of the representatives of these people who had fought so valiantly and sacrificed so much to withstand Communist aggression. Another reason for my objection was that I knew the extraordinary lengths to which the world press had gone to cover the historic event and felt that full coverage was necessary.

Therefore I agreed to a third plan: The documents would be signed first at Panmunjom by General Harrison for the UN and General Nam for the Communists, twelve hours after which the guns would stop firing. A few hours later the documents would be signed by the supreme commanders at their respective headquarters.

Immediately after the agreement was made I sent a message to President Rhee to inform him that the final arrangements had been made. I did not want him to get the first news about the agreement from the newspapers. I also invited Rhee to send military representatives to my advance headquarters at Munsan for the signing ceremony. Immediately afterward I flew to Seoul and visited Rhee. Again I extended the invitation and explained that inasmuch as it was a military affair it would be appropriate for him to have military representation. I told him the names and ranks of the men of other nations who would be there and specified that the invitation to him included generals of his army and air force and an admiral from his navy. As happened so often, Rhee did not react immediately to the invitation.

But shortly before I left Eighth Army Headquarters for Munsan to sign the documents, I received a message which said that Rhee had accepted my invitation and had designated my old friend and associate, Major General Choi Duk Shin. I was delighted, for I wanted our staunch ROK Allies represented on this historic occasion.

At precisely 10:00 A.M. Harrison and Nam sat down in the large wooden building the Communists had thrown up at Panmunjom as the Armistice Hall.

That building itself had been a cause of friction between us and the Communists. The Reds originally adorned the building with two copies of Picasso's "Dove," a painting the Communists everywhere had adopted as their own special symbol of peace. When I heard of this in Tokyo I telephoned Harrison at Munsan and told him we would not meet in that building under any conditions unless the Red symbols were removed. I used a direct radio-telephone link that I knew the Communists monitored. This was one message I wanted the Communists to hear, for I wanted them to know we meant business. Frequently I used that telephone to talk with Harrison. Sometimes we used a little informal code but on occasion we talked straight out so that the Communists couldn't miss what we were saying.

This was an old trick. I had used it in Moscow during the Coun-

cil of Foreign Ministers meeting in 1947, when our experts found
a microphone hidden in my hotel room by the Russian secret police.
Instead of removing it, which would have been a useless gesture,
we made use of it. Often we carried on long and ridiculous conversations purely for the benefit of the microphone listeners, and
occasionally we made remarks hinting that some good, faithful
Communist official in Austria had been working for us as a spy or
a saboteur. Whenever we really wanted to talk about anything important, we went to the American Embassy or strolled up and down
the streets. I eventually developed a regular routine for conferences—a stroll around the Kremlin walls.

The Picasso "Doves" were painted over and could not be seen on
the day that the Armistice was signed.

It took Harrison and Nam twelve minutes to sign the eighteen
documents prepared by their own side and the eighteen prepared
by the other side.

Then they left the building without speaking.

That's the way it had been throughout the negotiations. Never
during the talks did the delegates of either side nod or speak a
greeting or farewell during the daily meetings. Each day's session
opened with a statement by one chief delegate or the other along
the lines of "I have a question to ask", or "I have a statement to
make."

The ceremony at Panmunjom was witnessed by three hundred
persons. There were no restrictions on the nationality of the press.
Fifty-seven UN-accredited newsmen were actually seated in the
signing room, along with twenty photographers and five radio and
television men.

President Eisenhower had requested that I sign the Armistice
on Korean soil. I flew to Munsan-ni, my UN advance headquarters
where the UN armistice delegation had been located in an apple
orchard for two years. Exactly three hours after the Panmunjom
ceremony I entered the camp theater which was packed with
officers and men. I was glad to see that General Choi was on hand,
for he had boycotted the armistice talks from May 25 on. I sat
down at a long table just in front of the stage, where the orchestra

pit would have been in an ordinary theater. The lights which flooded the scene for the benefit of newsreel and TV cameras made the heat unbearable.

Only after I'd written "Mark W. Clark, Commander-in-Chief, United Nations Command," eighteen times with the pens the Parker Company had sent me for the occasion did I get that "It's over" sensation. In a statement I read afterwards I said:

I cannot find it in me to exult in this hour. Rather, it is a time for prayer, that we may succeed in our difficult endeavor to turn this armistice to the advantage of mankind. If we extract hope from this occasion, it must be diluted with recognition that our salvation requires unrelaxing vigilance and effort.

One little incident illustrates better, perhaps, my feeling on the outcome of the Armistice. During the final weeks before the Armistice was signed, it was announced that my son, Major Bill Clark, would be married in New Orleans on August 3. I sent him a message: "You are liable to be asked if I am coming home for your wedding. If you are, tell them I am coming if the situation here permits." I wanted his answer to be the same as mine.

Bill was asked and he followed instructions to the letter. "I hope that the Armistice will be signed in time for Dad to attend," he said.

Returning to Toyko from Korea a few days later I was met by a newsman who referred to Bill's statement and then asked, "Suppose it isn't signed, will you go home?"

I said, "I can't leave now, I have to stay with these negotiations."

Then the newsman said, "Which would you rather do, attend your son's wedding or sign the Armistice?"

"Go to my son's wedding," I said. "I know the results of that affair are going to be successful."

I was thankful the Armistice had ended the killing. But when I signed the Armistice I knew, of course, that it was not over—that the struggle against communism would not be over in my lifetime. The Korean War was a skirmish, a bloody, costly skirmish, fought on the perimeter of the free world.

We won this skirmish in that, for the first time, communism failed in direct armed aggression against another country.

We lost in that the enemy remained undefeated and even more powerful and threatening than before. By more powerful I mean that communism's Asian armies have learned how to fight modern ground warfare. They learned from us, by fighting us. What they didn't know earlier in the game we taught them, and it only cost them lives, cheap on their scale of values.

19

Inside the Communists' Prison Camps

Little Switch gave us a clear picture of just how awful were the conditions in Communist prison camps in Korea, despite the fact that the Communists rigged the operation for propaganda by making a careful selection of the men we got back in the exchange of sick and wounded, a selection of men who did not appear too badly mistreated.

But it took Big Switch after the Armistice was signed to fill in the full details of Communist prison camp villainy, to give us the complete picture of the atrocities, the murders and the perfidy. In Big Switch we got back the worst of our sick and wounded, the men in really bad shape. Through Big Switch we learned that the Chinese and North Koreans, like the Communists in Russia, had refused to return all the prisoners they captured. Why the Reds refused to return all our captured personnel we could only guess. I think one reason was that they wanted to hold the prisoners as hostages for future bargaining with us, possibly for some concession such as a seat for Red China in the United Nations.

As I have said, we had solid evidence after all the returns were in from Big Switch that the Communists still held 3,404 men prisoner, including 944 Americans.

I was in a quandary. The question to me was, "How do you get these people back without pointing a gun at the Communists?" When you have no gun threatening the Reds there is no way to demand and enforce compliance from them.

Preparations for Big Switch were necessarily elaborate. At Munsan we had a huge warehouse stocked high with clothing, blankets, medical equipment and other supplies for the returning POWs. At Freedom Village nearby we had a complete hospital unit ready. It was one of the Mobile Army Surgical Hospitals (MASH) which had done such magnificent work close to the front through most of the war.

The Indians were a particular problem. We had to go to great lengths to live up to our pledge to Syngman Rhee that no Indian troops would set foot on South Korean soil. Therefore we set up an airlift operation which carried more than six thousand Indians from the decks of our carriers off Inchon by helicopter to the Demilitarized Zone. It was a major undertaking which just about wore out our helicopter fleet in Korea.

Immediately after Little Switch I had recommended to the Department of the Army that all interrogation of POWs returning in Big Switch should be done either in America or aboard ships en route home. This was done. Interrogators were on the ships that carried the POWs back to America and they had their work finished by the time the ships docked at San Francisco.

This system permitted smooth handling of the POWs on our end. We rushed them to Inchon where they boarded the ships. There was little or no delay for questioning in Korea. Much of the physical rehabilitation of the POWs was accomplished aboard ship so that when the POWs were met by loved ones in San Francisco they were in much better physical condition than they had been when we first received them at Panmunjom. In addition, the two weeks or more of medical treatment and good food and rest aboard the ships permitted many POWs to avoid the necessity of reporting to Army hospitals in America on their arrival.

As the full story of conditions in the prison camps became clear through the interrogations aboard ship our Army began thinking about ways to reveal the shocking account to the people of the world, ways that would do the most good in exposing the Communists for the barbarians that they were.

The Defense Department radioed Tokyo that it was considering the possibility that I might go before the United Nations in New York and tell the full, tragic story. It was thought that would be a fitting report from the UN Commander in Chief who had signed the Armistice.

I worked on a speech in Tokyo and officials of the Department of the Army worked on a draft in Washington, from information unavailable to me because of the fact that the prisoner interrogations were not conducted by my command. After my return to the United States the speech was completed through co-ordination of my draft and the one written in Washington. Then I conferred with our representatives to the UN, Henry Cabot Lodge and Governor James Byrnes, and agreed with them that I was not the one to make the revelations at the UN. The logic was simple. If I, as the UN Commander in Chief, made such a speech at United Nations Headquarters, then the Russians and the other Communists at UN would demand that their commanders, Kim, Peng or both be given the opportunity to appear before the General Assembly and tell their side of the story, a side that we knew would be a fabric of lies, distortions and propaganda. Lodge and I agreed it would be best to avoid even as much as a debate on whether or not to hear the Communist commanders.

But the speech that was prepared carries the full, shocking story of atrocities which the civilized world had once thought were things of the ancient past. It was carefully documented and worded so that every phrase could be supported and proved by evidence and witnesses. It carried the horrible truth of the enemy that stands in the way of peace and liberty. It was the valid, considered judgment of our government regarding the truth of the atrocities of the Communists in Korea. For that reason the prepared speech, although never made as planned, remains worthy of a hearing.

The draft I had ready to read to the United Nations said on this subject:

I speak of the atrocities committed by the communists in Korea. I speak of the 10,032 individuals whose murdered bodies stand as mute witness to the savagery of communist aggression. We have evidence that not just 10,032 but 29,815 murders were actually committed by the communists, of which 11,622 were your soldiers.

The United Nations Command has been most meticulous and objective insofar as such is humanly possible, in its investigation of the background upon which I base my report. I assure you that the UNC is prepared to furnish documentary evidence of the communist atrocity record upon your call.

Stunning as it is, this total of 29,815 murders is by no means all inclusive; it does not include hidden atrocities as yet uncovered; it does not include those thousands of reported murders which currently lack sufficient evidence to establish a probable total of victims.

Communist atrocities in Korea have been under investigation since 1950 and are substantiated by the voluntary statements of survivors and witnesses. In many cases, we hold actual confessions of the perpetrators of such war crimes. More than 1,700 open cases—some documented with such statements and confessions, some with actual photographs of victims —are on file in the UN Command in Korea. Investigation is continuing, as many new leads are being developed; however, it is improbable that the whole story of communist brutality will ever be known. In some cases, *all victims and witnesses perished.*

As the former commander of the UN forces in Korea, I will *first* limit myself to the 11,622 members of the United Nations Command who were slaughtered while defenseless prisoners of war. This is a grim figure. It is based upon terrible facts. (I am duty-bound to bring this grave account of bestiality to you.)

A review of these cases clearly reveals that these atrocities were premediated. Furthermore, we find the identical criminal pattern in Korea that was evidenced in the communist massacre of Free Poland's Officer Corps in Katyn Forest. The cold-blooded design manifested throughout 1950–53 suggests that the contemporary Chinese and North Korean Communists received able tutelage from their Eurasian compatriots. In Korea, these calculated killings targeted upon our military personnel were often committed while the individual prisoner's hands were bound behind his back. True to Red design, however, many variations were introduced which would have paled torturers and inquisitors of past centuries. In some instances, gasoline was poured over the wounded and ignited by either grenades or matches. In other cases, helpless men were tortured by bamboo spears until God granted merciful death to terminate such continuing agony. Normally, and in the pattern of Katyn, it was a Russian-made bullet in the back of the head that ended the victim's dedication to the Free World cause. Let me cite some specific cases. Bear in mind that such are documented; further, that many witnesses or survivors of these atrocities are now in their respective UN homelands. These individuals are ready to recount the stark terror engendered by a communist scheme of brutality which recognized no limit.

Case No. 218:

On 10 April 1951, on a mountain 26 kilometers northwest of Yonchon, 32 soldiers of the Turkish Army were captured by elements of the 65th Chinese Communist Army. Twenty-five of the uninjured captives immediately were dispatched to the rear; the remaining seven Turks, on order of the company commander, were murdered. Korean villagers were forced to bury the victims at the place of execution.

Case No. 16:

At dawn on the morning of 15 August 1950 on Hill 303, a platoon of the 5th US Cavalry Regiment, while awaiting reinforcements, was overrun by the communists. The captives were then escorted to a nearby orchard where their boots and identification tags were removed and all their personal property stolen. The prisoners' hands were tied behind their backs with either wire or their own boot-laces.

For two days, they were kept hidden in ravines during the day and forced to march at night. Suddenly, on the afternoon of 17 August 1950, and without warning, communist guards opened fire upon these bound victims and then left the scene.

Thirty four US soldiers were slaughtered in this massacre—only four men survived. Later the same day, these men were rescued by a United Nations patrol; photographs were taken and two of the communist perpetrators of this crime were captured near the scene. Since this time, communist prisoners have admitted participation in the heinous act.

Case No. 76:

When the fall of the North Korean capital of Pyongyang to the United Nations forces seemed imminent, the communists entrained all prisoners of war for movement northward. Men were herded into open gondolas, packed to overflowing, and forced to ride unprotected in the raw October weather. Pneumonia and exposure exacted its daily toll among the weakened survivors. Their comrades conducted burial parties whenever an adequate halt was made. After such inhumane treatment, which extended over a period of nine days, the train arrived at a railroad tunnel approximately four and a half miles northwest of Sunchon, where it remained inside the mountain all day.

During the early afternoon of 20 October 1950, the starving men were promised their first meal in several days. Communist tormentors took an American major, together with a group of selected prisoners, purportedly as a detail to go to a nearby village to prepare food. None of these prisoners were seen or heard from again. Hours later, the men remaining in the tunnel were informed that food had been prepared for them, and that they were to be conducted in small groups to a Korean house to eat.

Accordingly, the first group of 30 men was removed from the tunnel, escorted down the tracks and told to hide in an erosion ditch until food was brought. As soon as they had relaxed on the ground, their guards opened point-blank fire upon them with Russian-made burp guns and rifles. Those who survived the initial burst of fire were then either shot or bludgeoned individually. Thank God, at least some survived by feigning death, though seriously wounded.

Remaining groups were then brought out and treated in a like manner. In each case, the helpless men were slaughtered either while sitting on the ground or standing *with empty rice bowls in their hands.*

When the United Nations forces overran the Sunchon area on the following day, the bodies of 68 murdered soldiers were recovered. In addition, seven more bodies were discovered inside the tunnel; the corpses of men who had apparently died of malnutrition.

At least 137 UN soldiers lost their lives in this atrocity. The evidence is convincing and confirmed. An actual perpetrator was in custody; we hold his testimony. Of overriding concern, however, is the fact that this entire happening *should be scored* against Red leaders who condone and, at least tacitly, encourage such brutality.

Case No. 693:

On 23 April 1951, the UN Belgian Battalion requested aid from the Royal Ulster Rifles. A Battle Patrol was immediately dispatched but was attacked by enemy forces after advancing for approximately 100 yards across the Imjin River. The group attempted to withdraw, leaving ten men to cover the retreat. The men found themselves surrounded and decided to surrender.

They were assembled on a hillside, together with three or four previously captured Belgians, near the junction of the Hant-Gang and Imjin Rivers, one kilometer northwest of Wachon—a point where they were slated to be murdered. Three British and one Belgian soldiers escaped. On 31 May 1951, Belgian UNC forces discovered the bodies of three British soldiers and five Belgian soldiers. Although these corpses were partly decomposed, it was possible to recognize their features. In a death pattern, so symbolic of communist brutality, all of the bodies were so grouped as to reveal the grim truth—all had suddenly been shot down without warning. Two of the British had been shot in the back of the head, one Belgian had been shot or bayonetted in the back.

Case No. 10:

No respecters of either the Red Cross or any symbol of belief in the Almighty, the communists overran a group of 18 to 20 wounded UN soldiers being ministered to by a regimental surgeon, prominently identifiable through display of his Red Cross brassard, and an Army chaplain. None of these individuals was armed. The communists immediately opened fire, wantonly executing the group with Russian-made rifles and burp-guns. The surgeon, although wounded, managed to escape.

Thus far I have presented solely examples of communist atrocities against military personnel. The rape of South Korea is an even more sordid story. From the results of the UNC investigation, it is estimated that the communists, in an effort to erase all dissident political elements in this wartorn country, murdered 14,000 defenseless South Korean civilians. In Korea, the pattern of brutality parallels that which the communists devised and perpetrated in other parts of the world. This extermination of anti-communist civilians, religious people and governmental officials was manifested in the premeditated annihilaton of those South Koreans whose allegiance was to *any* cause other than that of communism.

As in the case of atrocities against military personnel, the UN Command, in coordination with the Republic of Korea, has developed documented case files from which my facts were obtained. The following is just one of the many Korean war crimes cases involving civilian victims which reveals Red methodology underlying the slaughter of innocent men, women and children without cause.

Case No. 28:

Within the annals of barbarism, the city of Taejon long will be recorded as a monstrous mass extermination site. Countless civilians—some estimates reach as high as the 5,000 mark—as well as 42 American and 17 Republic of Korea Army prisoners, were slaughtered at Taejon in deference to the communist watchword—political expediency.

During the summer of 1950, following the capture of this city by the enemy, a North Korean "Home Affairs" Department was established with the express purpose of apprehending all persons unsympathetic to the communist cause, to include those who believed in Christian faiths. This totalitarian-type of "security" force then proceeded summarily to arrest prominent business and professional men, together with all persons in the area who had been employees of the Republic of Korea. Each such unfortunate, subsequently was brought to a confession-extraction headquarters, paradoxically located in a Catholic mission. The next link in this chain of wanton savagery was the Taejon city prison. Some 150 cells, each of which was packed with from 40 to 70 hapless victims, constituted this North Korean counterpart of Moscow's infamous Lubiyanka Prison. When it became impossible to squeeze additional persons into these cell blocks, the overflow was jammed within the mission confines. Military prisoners were not segregated from those of civil life.

Repeatedly, throughout incarceration, communist soldiers were granted ready access to these defenseless captives.

When the recapture of Taejon by United Nations forces appeared imminent, the communists determined that, prior to withdrawal, mass liquidation would be the fate of this prisoner group.

Commencing 23 September 1950, several groups—numbering from 100 to 200 each—were efficiently removed from their cells at night; hands were tied behind backs, and each individual, in turn, was bound to his fellow prisoner. They were then transported to previously selected sites, dumped into open trenches or ditches dug expressly for this purpose, and summarily shot. A check was made to locate survivors, and where found, their skulls were crushed. A light coating of earth was hastily applied to mark the death site.

By 26 September 1950, the Communist police evidently decided that execution tempo must be accelerated if the fiendish purpose was to be consummated prior to departure. Additional trenches were dug in the police station courtyard and a North Korean Army unit was summoned to assist in completing the bloody task. The ambulatory military prisoners were led out in small groups and promptly killed. Several wounded American soldiers were carried out on litters, dumped into the trenches and either shot or beaten to death. As time ran out on the executioners, the remaining South Koreans were dragged from the prison into the already filled trenches and killed. At the same time, those who had been retained in the Catholic Mission interrogation center were executed as rapidly as possible. When these trenches were filled with bodies, others were slain in the churchyard and basement; many corpses thrown down a well. The perpetrators then fled.

Examination of these bodies revealed that most had been beaten and mutilated prior to execution. Of these thousands of unfortunates, *only six* survived; three civilians, one Republic of Korea Army soldier and two Americans. Thousands of bodies ultimately were exhumed.

Allow me now to lay before you briefly what befell the free men whom the communists captured. Purposely I shall keep to general terms. Many of the individual experiences are too sickening to bear detailed recount before an assemblage where moderation and dignity should prevail. I assure you, however, that I am understating, not overstating, what has been reported by repatriated prisoners of war.

From the first days of the conflict, it appeared that the enemy was bent upon reversing all provisions of the international conventions on the treatment of war prisoners. The North Koreans argued to the effect that, since they had not adhered formally to such conventions, they possessed the right and meant to dispense with all humane regard for their captives. What mankind had agreed was right and proper, the communists maintained was invalid. As individuals, human beings became stark ciphers.

Statements of our personnel returned during prisoner exchange operations provide data for the development of an over-all pattern of communists' mistreatment of UN prisoners. This picture is grim. It is a chronicle of patent communist refusal to abide by provisions of the Geneva Convention. It stands as an indictment against the communist commission of atrocities which stagger the imagination of all civilized peoples.

Throughout these affidavits of returning prisoners run the threads of a diabolic pattern of treatment. Many prisoners who participated in the same death marches to internment and were detained at the same prison compounds point out—in eyewitness accounts—identical incident patterns. On the other hand, isolated incidents reported by ex-prisoners, separated insofar as time and place of incarceration are concerned, show considerable similarity in mode of treatment. A summary of the over-all pattern of communist mal-practices follows:

Upon capture by communist forces, the unwounded and walking wounded were herded into marching groups. The seriously wounded were left on the field and often killed either by concentrated small arms fire, bayonetting or a combination of both. In many cases, UN personnel carried their wounded buddies. Many marches were made under severe climatic conditions. Communist guards took shoes and other articles of clothing from some of the prisoners. The freezing of feet and hands was commonplace. Prisoners report marching in bare feet until the flesh was ripped from their toes. Little medical treatment, other than occasional and haphazard bandaging, was provided to the wounded. Marches were long, grueling and set at a pace that could not be maintained by the majority of the wounded. Savagely, the guards kept men moving. Stragglers were clubbed or kicked when they fell. Many who could not continue were left along the way to die. In countless instances, communist guards dropped out to shoot prisoners who lagged behind. Repeated eyewitness accounts testify that prisoners were pushed off cliffs. Out of 700 men beginning one such three-week march, approximately 250 arrived alive at the first camp. A large percentage disappeared on the line of march; so far as is known, these men never were subsequently accounted for by their inhuman captors.

Along another march route, the intermediate disposition post was known as "Bean Camp"; on still another it was grimly called "Death Valley." Here prisoners were herded into squalid huts. The daily death rate soared. Causes of deaths, as reported by prisoners and accompanying medical officers, included: lack of medical attention, malnutrition, dysentery, pneumonia. What little food the communists provided was substandard; all too often, there was no food at all. To supplement such a meager ration, starving prisoners were desperate to the point of hunting down dogs and other stray animals along the route north.

Once the men arrived at permanent prison installations, conditions were not bettered. At such camps, throughout the winter of 1950, there were no medical facilities, no heat, no blankets. Estimates of prisoners, some of whom were on burial squads, report that approximately 1,600 men died in a ninety-day period at one camp alone. Similar conditions and a comparable death rate characterized "life" within other camps. Many of these soldiers, of course, died from malnutrition due to insufficient diet. The inescapable fact, however, is that while these prisoners were being starved to death, communist jailers were supplied with ample rations.

In the detention of war prisoners, most of our nations have adhered to both the letter and the spirit of pertinent international agreements. We have sought to sustain them in an orderly and reasonably daily existence. Our aim has been to restore them as soon as possible to normal peaceful pursuits.

Not so the communists. Evidence points to the fact that the Reds want to detain some prisoners indefinitely, either to serve some future dark purpose or, perhaps, to prevent them from exposing what has been done to them. Further, those they release, preferably, must be so altered in personality structure as to preclude their return to normal life with any degree of facility. It is intended that as many of them as possible become focal points of discontent in their homes and communities. Thus they will serve to breed situations which will further the communist objective of total world domination. Fighting on the battle front may end, but the war must continue in another guise.

This, I assure you, is not nonsense born of a bad dream. There can be no other explanation of what transpired in the prisoner of war camps of the Chinese and North Korean communists. Moreover, it bears out what we have been told befell the Germans, the Japanese and other nationalities taken prisoners during World War II; thousands of whom remain unaccounted for and must be presumed either to be hostages in secret captivity or to have been killed under the rigors of transformation into communist automatoms.

The grim process in the camps, call it what you will, begins with the formation of a suitable psychological atmosphere. This is done by a special staff trained in psychological cause and effect. The men are segregated from their officers, commissioned and non-commissioned, and any within this group who reveal traits of leadership are weeded out. The individual must stand alone, unable to turn to any source of authority except his captors. The word is disseminated that there are informers in the compound, and the individual begins to distrust his companions. Close friendships are prohibited. Family ties are broken, for at this stage of the process letters cannot be written.

The individual, thus isolated, experiences the sensation of great danger. Other men have disappeared. They may have been killed. He may share this fate. The threat of brutal punishment is ever present.

Meanwhile, the prisoner has nothing to do. This inactivity is calculated to enhance his personal fears and sensitize his reception to the next phase. Then indoctrination starts. Participation in a "discussion group" seems harmless; further, it will dispel the ominous portent of inactivity. The discussion leader, who may be an English-speaking Chinese or North Korean or even a fellow-prisoner who has bought privileges by prostituting his soul through collaboration, seems benign and even reasonable. He lectures about the evils of capitalism, the virtues of communism and the "correct" way of viewing society. The group then parrots his sloganized guidance in "discussion."

As the pace accelerates, this process is sustained to the exclusion of everything else. Repetition follows repetition; the Pavlovian "conditioned response" pattern is building to a climax. Soon prisoners cannot advance concepts differing from those of the discussion leader. It soon becomes obvious to the prisoner group that receipt of such meager favors as cigarettes, food, clothing and reading matter—the last of which is always communist—hinges upon supplying the "correct" answer. If stubborn, they are punished. Many were hung on ropes by their hands; were crammed into small cages; were forced to stand naked in freezing temperatures and submit to cold water dousings; were beaten and thrown into solitary, unheated dark holes partly filled with water for long periods of time. When punishment does not serve the Red end, "recalcitrant" captives are removed from the compound and summarily dispatched to some unknown destination.

With the passage of time, what at first was parroted in order to avoid trouble and obtain favors becomes fixed in the minds of the men. They now believe what they say. They are terrified at the possibility of becoming confused and saying the "wrong" thing. It becomes increasingly easy to inform on one another. A sense of guilt attaches itself to any failure to inform; with this manifestation, the individual personality change is complete. Some of the men now are ready to inflict the process on others.

We tell ourselves comfortingly that a few weeks in normal surroundings will cleanse the minds of returned prisoners of all that was thus inscribed on them. I want to believe that such is so, but I am convinced that the communists were confident it would not be so.

I have reported to you on those UN prisoners of war who were murdered and upon those who have returned from the unrelenting horror of the communist prison camps; mention now must be made of those missing members of the UN fighting forces whom the UNC believes the communists still hold.

Within the last month the Soviet Union has released, *eight years after World War II*, hundreds of German troops who had been held in the living purgatories of Soviet Siberia. While in Japan, I saw the return of Japanese soldiers and citizens who had been released by the Chinese Communists *eight years after the surrender of Japan*.

The UNC has asked the Chinese and North Koreans to account for over 3,000 *UN* personnel that we have reason to believe they still may hold. The communists replied that the bulk of these men never had been captured at all; the remainder, they claimed, either had been released, were refusing repatriation or had died in captivity. Yet, on September 11th, one of their own communist correspondents, Wilfred Burchett, acknowledged that the communists *are* holding an unspecified number of UN airmen who they claim were shot down in "Neutral" territory.

How many more UN POWs may we expect the communists to yield, possibly seven or eight years from now? And how many may we never see again who will die in the wastes of Korea—Manchuria—Siberia?

Although I did not make this report to United Nations, Ambassador Lodge did deliver a full report which encompassed much of the material that was used in my draft speech.

To me a crucial section of the report was the analysis of the brain-washing techniques of the Communists. This analysis was an important warning, for the techniques the Communists used to distort facts in the minds of the POWs are identical with those the Communists use in their mass-psychology campaigns to mold the thoughts of men and women everywhere, behind the Iron Curtain and in the free world. The prison camps in Korea were the mirror through which we could see these techniques reflected baldly. The Communist strives to make his victim believe slogans through repetition. He strives to make his victim feel that any doubt about the Communist line means the victim, not the line, is weak and unable to comprehend the true meaning of the life around him. More than anything else, perhaps, the Communist tries to cut off each individual from the rest of mankind with a mental wall so that in his isolation the individual will believe that any doubts he has about communism are his alone, unshared by any other living human being.

It was my conviction, after studying the reports of the men who came back from Communist imprisonment, that everything possible must be done to make these facts of Communist tactics known to everyone in the free world. Only thus can we arm our people to resist the Red pressure if they ever again are forced into Communist prison camps in another war.

The experience of our troops in Communist imprisonment revealed the need for a revision of our military education program to prepare our men for any possible future war with communism. Under old concepts of war we instructed our troops simply that if they were captured they were protected by laws of the civilized world which said they did not have to reveal anything beyond their name, rank and serial number.

That does not apply with the Communists. The war in Korea taught us that our soldiers now must be given a thorough education to prepare them for the rigors and pressures they can expect if they are captured by the Reds.

This education must be designed to strengthen men psychologically so they can better combat the Communist brainwashing. We can be proud of the record of the great majority of the Americans who were captured.

One aspect that was touched on but briefly in the prepared talk was that of medical care of prisoners in the Communist camps, or, rather, the lack of it.

The full story was unfolded by the careful interrogation of the men who returned from the camps and by consultation with medical officers who treated them after they returned.

As a general statement the evidence proved that medical care given the POWs was deplorable. During the first nine months of the conflict, captured UN troops got virtually no medical care at all. The Communists grossly maltreated the sick and injured. Every returned POW who was captured in the fall and winter of 1950 and early 1951 reported that the sick were abused by beatings, forced marches, crowded, unsanitary housing conditions and lack of food and clothing.

When the Communists finally were prevailed upon to do something to help the desperately sick and wounded, they administered hot water as the sole medication.

Conditions improved very slightly after the first year. By that time hundreds and probably thousands of sick and wounded POWs had died. The most common causes of death in the prison camps were freezing, starvation and dysentery. The improvements after the first year consisted largely of crude surgical procedures which were tortures in themselves. Operations were performed without ordinary aseptic precautions. Usually there was no anesthesia, even for amputations. The food supply improved slightly and the POWs began to improvise better shelters and clothing.

Right up to the day the Armistice was signed there was no regular medical service for the prisoners. Many POWs returned and reported that all the medication they received for various kinds of serious illness were pills, apparently opium in some cases, aspirin in others. The POWs said the pills had little or no effect on their illness.

There was nothing but a token effort to maintain the most rudimentary kind of public health facilities for the POWs. Latrines were open and untended ditches and were used sometimes as punishment holes in which the prisoners had to stand for long periods.

The first effort to control lice, ticks and rats came in 1953. Before that nothing was done in any of the camps to protect the prisoners from these disease-bearing pests. Only in a few isolated places was any effort made to boil or disinfect water.

Inoculations for typhus and typhoid were given to some favored groups of prisoners or for propaganda purposes. In several places the prisoners were told on camp loudspeakers that a "germ bomb" had been dropped near the camp. A great show was made of an immunization campaign in each instance. The prisoners were rushed into lines and inoculated. One needle and syringe were used for hundreds of men. On one occasion a severe outbreak of jaundice spread through a camp because two men in the inoculation line had an infectious form of the disease, which was spread by the inoculation needle the Communists used on many men after they had used it on the two sick POWs.

Few of the POWs ever saw a hospital, no matter how badly they needed hospitalization. Others were in camps close to hospitals but made every effort to stay out of them. The nicknames used by the POWs to describe these "hospitals" tell the reason why they tried to stay out of them. One was called "The Morgue" and another "The Death House."

In one of these hospitals an injection was given to each of a large number of seriously ill POWs. All were dead within a few hours.

Neither were captured UN medical officers permitted to treat sick and wounded POW's, although there were many stories of great work done by officers and enlisted men alike in doing the best they could to help their fellows. One Turkish medical corpsman, for instance, was heralded by returning POWs, as a hero who saved many lives by constant care and untiring efforts.

There was evidence that the Communists used POWs as human guinea pigs for medical experiments. One returned doctor said he was forced to use inadequate quantities of drugs or take measures of which he disapproved. Some prisoners said chicken livers and other parts of animals were implanted beneath the skin of sick prisoners as experiments in healing techniques.

Everywhere in the camps the promise of medical care was used as a propaganda device against the prisoners. They were told time and again that they could have medicine and treatment only if they co-operated with their Communist jailers.

The so-called progressives who parroted the Communist line either from conviction or for favors were given treatment. So were informers. But medicine and medical attention were denied the reactionaries.

To me this use of medicine and the denial of medicine as a weapon against the POWs is perhaps the greatest of all the atrocities committed by the Communists in Korea, a device of torture which must rank high among the instances of man's inhumanity to man. No rack, no whip was necessary to torture the UN troops held prisoner by the Communists, although physical torture was used. But the worst torture was that month after month, year after year, the captured men had to live with the agonizing temptation that comfort, favors and perhaps life itself was theirs if only they would play up to the Communists. It was the awful tyranny of choice, a tyranny that tried to turn a man's mind away from all he believed was honorable and good.

I have no doubt that the worst of those who succumbed were the twenty-one Americans who at the end chose communism. They were the men who shouted blasphemies from their prison compound at the Americans who were there to try to tell them that they could come home if they wished.

On September 17, 1953, before I knew the identity or number of Americans who might refuse to come home, I issued a press statement which was transmitted so as to reach any Americans who might be among the 320 or more UN captives the Reds said would not return.

The statement was most carefully worded, and stressed the American concept of due process of law.

If I could communicate with these men at this time [I said] I would remind them of the American tradition of freedom—the freedom for which they fought before their capture. I would assure them of our sympathy for the hardships they have suffered, our understanding of the pressures to which they have been subjected, and our determination that the legal rights and protection which are theirs under the laws of our country will not only be respected, but will be jealously guarded for them.

As time went on, however, and the Americans remained adamant in their refusal to come home, whatever sympathy I had for them in the beginning vanished. My sympathy was for their loved ones.

And at the end, when they made their refusal final, my only thought was that America was better off without them.

But let me emphasize: To the eternal credit of the strength of the spirit of freedom in our country, by far the majority of the prisoners spurned treachery and refused to toady to the Communists.

There were heroes in those prison camps, great heroes.

There were but few rats.

20

The Over-all Picture in Asia

The time for decision in Korea was the day the Chinese Communist Government threw its legions into the fighting. The North Korean People's Army was in rout, no longer an effective fighting force. The brilliant amphibious attack on Inchon had sealed the fate of the North Koreans. Fingers of the United Nations Army reached the Yalu itself in the East and were within a dozen miles of it on the West. MacArthur and other officials issued statements designed to assure the Chinese that the UN would stop at the Yalu, would not attack Chinese territory.

But the Communist hierarchy decided the Peiping Government must intervene. A clumsy attempt was made to camouflage this intervention through the claim that all the hundreds of thousands of Chinese who plunged into the war in Korea were volunteers. The Communist propaganda line was that each individual Chinese soldier hated the Americans so much that he was forced by inner compulsion to leave his home and spring to arms in a foreign land. The hollow character of this ridiculous sham was exposed completely when so many of the Chinese captured in Korea declared they would rather die than go back to the Communists. But with straight face the Chinese maintained the fiction right to the end, and when General Peng Teh-huai signed the Armistice it was as Commander of the Chinese People's Volunteers, not as a general of the Red Chinese Army nor as Vice-Chairman of the People's Revolutionary Military Council, which he was at the time.

The big decision by America and the free world had to be made the day the Chinese plunged full force into the fighting in Korea in November of 1950. It had to be made while our American, UN and ROK troops were being overrun, cut off, slaughtered, while the shrill cry of the little Chinese battle horn was just becoming a familiar sound in the crisp wintry air of Korea.

The question that had to be answered by the free world, but particularly by America, was this:

Would we accept the Peiping Government's disclaimer of responsibility and permit the Army of China to battle our troops in Korea without considering ourselves at war with their government or country?

On the answer to that question rested our chances of winning military victory over the Communists in Korea.

I realized the decision could not be made from a strictly military viewpoint. Political considerations of highest consequence were involved, as were the views of our allies.

Naturally, however, any commander whose forces are threatened wants to use every means to protect them and to destroy the attackers. Had I been the commander on the scene, looking at it through the sights of a rifle, I would have screamed to the high heavens for authority to bomb the bases, airfields and other installations in Manchuria and China from which these aggressors derived their source of strength and power.

Even though there was a danger of spreading the conflagration to world war proportions, an eventuality I personally considered improbable at that time, it was inconceivable to me, as I am sure it was to General MacArthur, that we did not announce to the world that if these Chinese troops were not withdrawn immediately we would consider ourselves officially at war with Red China and would hurl our air might at their most vital installations, wherever they were located, in any part of China. It was beyond my comprehension that we would countenance a situation in which Chinese soldiers killed American youths in organized, formal warfare and yet we would fail to use all the power at our command to protect those Americans.

I still was unable to understand this situation after I succeeded to the command of United Nations Forces in Korea. I appreciated that Allied opinion and the danger of World War III had to be taken into account. But I also was convinced personally that World War III would be more likely to result eventually from a weaker policy than a stronger one in Korea. I was convinced that in the long run we would save American lives by making sacrifices for victory in Korea.

To me, our tacit acceptance of the Chinese Communist fiction that Red China was not in the war officially could only encourage the enemy to build up militarily and to become more arrogant and demanding in dealing with us. As time went on each of these fears was proven to be valid. Red China went into the war a mass ground army, with little air or artillery support. Her main strength was in her ability to force thousands upon thousands of foot soldiers to sacrifice their lives in human-sea assaults that overwhelmed their enemies by sheer numbers of men. Red China came out of the shooting phase of the war less than three years later with a ground army that had become much smarter and more effective through experience against a first-class modern military power. Her artillery was first rate by the end of the shooting phase, both in numbers of batteries and in marksmanship. Her air force had been built up to a fleet of more than two thousand warplanes in the Yalu area alone, more than half of the planes being fast, maneuverable, high-flying Russian MIG-15 jet fighters.

We accepted the Chinese fiction of nonintervention in Korea by self-imposed ground rules that forbade us to bomb the bases which spawned the killers who attacked our American and allied men in Korea.

As the military commander on the spot, still looking through a gun sight, I felt we not only could have won victory if we had so decided, but that the mere threat of an attack on the Chinese homeland would have produced a happier situation than the one we had in the Far East at the time the Armistice was signed. That threat, of course, would have been most effective if we had amassed the power in the Far East to carry it out—and let the enemy know that we had the force on hand and ready to be unleashed.

As I have said, I felt that if there was to have been a change in our government policy the logical time for it would have been when the new administration took office in Washington and re-examined the whole world situation. I felt then, when I was over there, and came to know later when I returned to the United States, that the American people were thoroughly disgusted with the manner in which the war was being conducted, with the blood that was being spilled in such an inconclusive war. There were questions in the minds of the people as to whether this war would result in more safeguards and security for America.

I knew the new President-elect well. We had been associated closely since cadet days at West Point from 1913 to 1915 and we were intimately associated during and after World War II. It was fine for Eisenhower to come to Korea after he was elected President and before he assumed office. It permitted him to see the situation on the ground and then to fit in what he found there with the other parts of the puzzle that constituted the critical world situation as he knew it. I realized fully that mine was an on-the-scene perspective where men under my command were being killed every day in a war we were not trying to win militarily. I realized, too, that the President-elect had to look at Korea as only one part of his problem, and that high on the list of his concerns was the danger of the outbreak of World War III as a result of one of his decisions.

Therefore despite my personal disappointment that my government did not find it expedient to whip the Communists thoroughly in our first shooting war with them, I was aware of the worldwide factors which led Eisenhower to make his decision to seek an armistice.

The decision having been made, I accepted it fully. There was no use continuing the frustrated stalemate where we were going no place, and suffering thirty thousand American casualties a year. Therefore, I devoted all the energy I possessed to the task of consummating the Armistice that my government sought.

The Armistice was obtained and I signed it. But I would be less than truthful if I failed to record that I put my signature on that document with a heavy heart. I was grateful that the killing was ended for a time at least. But I had grave misgivings that some day my countrymen would be forced to pay a far higher price in blood than it would have cost if the decision had been made to defeat the Communists in Korea.

After the Armistice was signed I received a message from President Eisenhower in which I particularly noted his reference to "this onerous duty" which I was then completing.

Dear Wayne [the president wrote], Once again you have successfully handled difficult negotiation with an enemy of our country. I assure you that during these long and trying months your problems have been much on my mind, as have also your patience, your stamina and your devotion to this onerous duty. I should like also for you to inform General Harrison of my deep personal and official appreciation of his tireless efforts under your direction to bring about an honorable armistice. Both of you have performed in a manner to deserve the thanks of your country. So far as I am permitted to speak for the country, it is the purpose of this telegram to convey those thanks. With the hope that Renie is improving, and with warm personal regards to yourself. Dwight D. Eisenhower.

There was no note of victory in the President's message as there was in the message Prime Minister Sir Winston Churchill sent me later as I was leaving the Far East. Sir Winston said:

Allow me to express to you, before you leave the United Nations Command, our admiration for the courage and tenacity you have displayed as Supreme Commander. You have held the aggressors at bay and brought them to a truce. The armistice marks the first victory of collective resistance over aggression. There could be no finer culmination to a soldier's career.

I thank you for the ready understanding you have shown over our problems. The British troops who have served under you in Korea count it an honour to have done so.

This is not the first time we have worked together.

Winston S. Churchill.

Korea was but one corner of the picture of Asia. During the late winter of 1953, while the war and armistice talks remained stalemated in Korea, I was able to get away long enough to visit some of the other key spots in Asia and get ideas about their relation to the whole.

The visit developed from continuing correspondence with my

close friend, Marshal Alphonse Juin of France. At my invitation he came to Japan and Korea in February of 1953. In Korea we went together to the U.S. 2nd Infantry Division with which the splendid French battalion was serving, visited Eighth Army and Fifth Air Force Headquarters and other installations. Juin also talked with President Rhee.

Next day we got down to cases. I took Juin to Kwangju to inspect the ROK Army school center, then to Cheju-do to visit the ROK replacement training division. I wanted him to see all he could of the ROK training program, to learn how we were helping the ROKs and how they were helping themselves. It was our thought that the French, fighting the common enemy in Indo-China, might be able to learn something that would make their Vietnamese allies more effective fighters.

Juin was impressed. He was outspoken in his praise of the development of the ROK Army. We decided that it would be helpful for French and Vietnamese officers from Indo-China to visit in Korea and for a group of American and ROK officers to go to Indo-China. It seemed to me an exchange of ideas might be beneficial.

Next month, in March of 1953, I visited Indo-China at the invitation of the French High Commissioner, M. Jean Letourneau. The purpose of the trip was to discuss the situation and determine whether there was any assistance we in the Far East Command could give the French in their war with communism in Indo-China.

Mrs. Clark and ground, air and naval representatives of my staff accompanied me. En route to Indo-China we stopped at Clark Field in the Philippines to visit the Air Force units there that were under my command. Then we flew to Manila where I talked with Ambassador Raymond A. Spruance, the admiral who had such a great record in the Pacific during the war as commander of the U.S. Fifth Fleet. It was our first meeting and he impressed me as a splendid American, worthy of our finest tradition. It was heartening to me that we were represented so well diplomatically in the Philippines which are a showpiece of American success in the foreign field and a vital link in our free world Pacific defenses. I also conferred with Philippine political and military leaders.

From the Philippines we flew to Hanoi where we were joined by my good friend Maurice DeJean, then French Ambassador to Tokyo who later succeeded M. Letourneau as High Commissioner in Indo-China. At Hanoi General Raoul Salan and General François Gonzales de Linares, old friends and comrades-in-arms from the North African and Italian campaigns, briefed me and I called on Prime Minister Nguyen Van Tam. Later I conferred with the Vietnam Army, Navy and Air Force Chiefs of Staff and then went to Dalat for a conference with Bao Dai, the former emperor who was Chief of State of Vietnam.

The military situation in Vietnam was entirely different from the situation in Korea. Although the same unscrupulous enemy faced the free world on both battlegrounds, the tactics and strategy were different. In Korea we had trench warfare along a stabilized battle-front that crossed the peninsula. In Indo-China the enemy was everywhere, in front, in the rear and both flanks. There was no front line, as we had in Korea, but rather a series of isolated strong points.

The enemy had no trouble infiltrating through the wide gaps between the strong points, particularly in view of the fact that Ho Chi-minh's Communist soldiers violated the rules of land warfare and wore native garb to camouflage their movements. The Reds also cached arms and ammunition behind the French so their disguised soldiers did not have to carry anything that would mark them as infiltrating enemy.

It was apparent at once that the Vietnamese forces had to be strengthened and developed. My judgment was that the only way the French could extricate themselves from the war of position in which large numbers of French troops were pinned down to static defensive positions was to develop rapidly new light infantry battalions in the Vietnamese Army. These battalions could take over the strong points and permit the French to mobilize their own troops into a strategic striking force that could punish the Red rebels effectively.

My chief interest was in the training of the Vietnamese. If the French had some new tricks in the process of turning out fighting men, I wanted to learn them so we could use them in Korea. The equipment requirements of the Vietnam Army were entirely different from those in Korea. The heavy weapons, artillery, and tanks we used to such good advantage in Korea were not the big need in Indo-China. What the French required were light armored vehicles and airplanes that could carry them quickly to threatened sectors. They needed small draft power boats to travel the many navigable streams. They needed light arms for fast-moving infantry units.

But more than any of this they needed a well-organized system of basic training for their infantrymen. Their Vietnamese riflemen were inadequately trained. The training system was decentralized, each local commander having control of his own training program. The result was an uneven product. Some local commanders trained their men adequately, some didn't. But no local commander had the resources or ability to train infantrymen as well as a centralized organization, with well-calculated training standards, could do. We had learned that in our own Army at home and the ROKs had learned it from us.

The French were well aware of this fault but were having difficulty correcting it. The French did not have the same affectionate association with Vietnamese troops as we had with the ROK soldiers in Korea. For one thing, of course, the Koreans never had been under American colonial rule, as the Vietnamese had been under the French.

Development of the Vietnamese army was directly dependent upon supplies that we could furnish from America. Because of the difference in the nature of the wars in Korea and Indo-China, there was little conflict between the needs of one front and the other. The Vietnamese needed rifles, automatic rifles, machine guns, light mortars and transportation facilities that could carry them over the water-soaked rice paddies in the Delta sector. They also needed our Flying Boxcar-type transport planes that could carry men and equipment quickly to threatened, isolated garrisons.

As a result of my trip to Indo-China we were able to arrange some helpful exchanges. Some of our KMAG people experienced in helping the ROKs develop their army were sent to Indo-China, along with some ROK officers. In many conferences they gave the benefit of their experience to the Vietnamese and the French. Later I invited the Vietnamese Army Chief of Staff, General Hinh, to come to Korea with a group of French and Vietnamese officers to see how the ROK Army was being trained into such a fine fighting force. The exchange of views paid big dividends.

After I returned to Tokyo I was able to recommend to my government that certain types of sorely needed equipment be sent to Indo-China to help the French and Vietnamese with their part of the war with communism. And from my own resources in the Far East Command I was able to send some aircraft, including some Flying Boxcars, and other equipment. This movement of equipment from other parts of the Far East was of particular benefit during the trouble in the state of Laos where the situation became precarious. The Boxcars immediately raised the question of whether my government was willing to have American military pilots engaged, as they would be, in the Indo-China war. I questioned Washington and the answer was no. To comply with the decision our transport pilots gave French airmen a quick checkout in the transport planes, and the French flew them.

En route back to Tokyo I stopped at Hongkong and visited Lieutenant General Terrance Airey, the British commander, who had been with me all through the Italian campaign. Airey made it possible for me to inspect British defenses on the island of Hongkong and to cover the front-line areas on the Kowloon Peninsula, the section of the Crown Colony which has a land border with Red China below Canton.

My visit to Hongkong impressed me more than ever of the strategic importance of this communications hub of southeast Asia, a hub at which the rivers, the seas and the airlanes join.

We flew on to Formosa at the invitation of Generalissimo Chiang Kai-shek. Madame Chiang arrived from the United States the same day we landed.

On Formosa I had the opportunity of being briefed by all the Chinese air, sea and ground commanders and by Major General

William C. Chase and key staff members of his Military Assistance Advisory Group. I visited Chinese infantry units to get a firsthand picture of their training, combat readiness and morale. I was impressed with the fighting spirit of the men I saw, with the thoroughness of their basic training and their splendid physical condition.

It was true that the average age of the Chinese Nationalist soldier, about twenty-nine, was above the ideal age we desire in the United States Army. At the time of my visit in the spring of 1953, however, the Chinese Nationalist soldier still had several good years of fight left in him. I always felt that there on Formosa was a tremendous pool of trained military manpower that should be used in the conflicts in the Far East. To me we had but a single enemy and there should be a rational use of our resources to meet this foe.

The Generalissimo and Madame Chiang entertained us and I conferred with him several times. We discussed the entire political and military situation in the Far East and I found that we agreed on our understanding of the objectives, intentions and tactics of the Communist enemy. We also were in complete agreement that it was dangerous to try to placate the Reds.

Our discussions finally led to the subject of the employment of Chiang's forces. As I said earlier, I long before had recommended that two Nationalist divisions be sent to Korea. The recommendation was not accepted. On Formosa during our talks Chiang volunteered the offer to send up to three of his best divisions to Korea to serve as part of the United Nations Command if my government requested the troops from him. I informed Washington of his offer but the request was not forthcoming. By that time, of course, every day seemed to bring an armistice closer and since a cease-fire was the objective it would have been contradictory for our government to have made such a provocative move.

A major question mark in Asia was India where Jawaharlal Nehru, leader of 350 million people, aspired to the role of peacemaker between East and West. I had no contact with Indian politicians but I had known Indian troops well in Italy and I found that they could be depended upon, were good soldiers and well trained.

Shortly after their arrival in the Demilitarized Zone I flew north to talk with the Indians. I was pleased to find that many of their officers had served with me in Italy.

During that visit I said publicly that I was confident that the Indian troops would conduct themselves in a highly satisfactory manner. But I soon was concerned over a nonmilitary issue. General K. S. Thimayya, Commander of the Indian Custodial Forces and Chairman of the Neutral Nations Repatriation Commission, seemed to doubt that the Chinese and Korean nonrepatriates really had renounced communism.

I felt compelled to record my objections to this attitude. Thimayya seemed to think that most of the nonrepatriated Chinese and North Korean POWs really wanted to go home behind the Iron Curtain. That was what the Communists claimed, of course, and during the first three weeks of the operation of the NNRC it appeared that Thimayya and some of the other commission members believed it.

On October 6, 1953, the day before I departed for home, I sat down and composed one of the longest letters I ever wrote in my life. It said in part:

In summary, it appears that the decisions and activities of the Commission to date have been predicated upon the assumption that the prisoners in your custody actually desire repatriation. This is especially difficult to understand in view of the strong opposition Korean and Chinese anticommunist prisoners have demonstrated, individually and collectively, even to the physical presence of communist representatives. It would seem that the Commission has not taken full cognizance of the fact that the Korean and Chinese prisoners made their choice many months ago and that, in the absence of force or coercion, the vast majority will adhere to their decision.

After I left the Far East I noticed a gradual change in the attitude of the Indians at Panmunjom, although press reports indicated there was no change in the viewpoint of the Indian Government regarding the prisoner release. Thimayya and his staff officers had been given a visible demonstration of Communist duplicity and trickery at Panmunjom and had learned by eyewitness experience that virtually none of the Chinese and Korean prisoners in their custody wanted to return to the Communists. They had learned the hard way, just as we had learned before them, the nature of the Communist aggressor.

While we were learning the character of the enemy, the Communists got a long head start in organizing the military power of their people in Asia. After the Pacific War, while we disarmed Japan and limited South Korea to a constabulary force with antiriot weapons, the Russians supported a gigantic military build-up of Chinese and North Koreans, as well as their own in Siberia. In three years of war in Korea the Communists demonstrated that they were mobilized and ready to fight a co-ordinated war on several fronts with organized armies in Korea, guerrilla-type armies in Indo-China and guerrilla raider bands in Malaya.

The Communists had harnessed their power for aggression. It behooved us in the free world to harness our power for defense. That was being done in Europe, which to many minds was the fulcrum of the power balance between communism and the democracies. But I learned in Asia that if Europe was the fulcrum, Asia was the weight that might well tip the scales one way or the other.

How could we harness the defensive might of the free peoples of Asia?

To my mind one step was essential.

We had to organize a defensive confederation along the lines of NATO in Europe. Call it PATO—Pacific Treaty Organization.

The first steps toward PATO had been taken. The United States had mutual security treaties with four Pacific nations—Japan, the Philippines, Australia and New Zealand. A fifth treaty was being concluded with the Republic of Korea. Without a treaty, but by Presidential declaration, the territorial integrity of Chiang Kai-shek's Formosa had been made part of our national policy. In addition Chiang's army, navy and air force were being supplied by the United States and a large American military advisory group worked constantly with the Chinese Nationalists.

The only centralizing force in this defense system, however, was one country, the United States. There was no mutual security agreement which required one Asian country to come to the aid of another threatened by Red aggression. Each treaty nation had made its bargain directly with the United States, which alone was pledged to help ward off aggressors.

There was some effort toward collective security but it never matured. In 1949, as the Communist military victory in China was becoming final, Chiang Kai-shek and President Elpidio Quirino of the Philippines talked about collective security. Chiang flew to Baguio to talk with Quirino and then to Korea to confer with Rhee. Nothing came of the talks, but four years later, after the Korean Armistice was signed, Rhee flew to Formosa to talk with Chiang about the same general subject.

To my mind it was inconceivable that the free world would long continue to permit the force of Free Asia, potentially great, to be dissipated through failure to harness it into a single organization.

I felt that there should be an over-all headquarters for PATO, at Okinawa or nearby, and that PATO should be open to all countries desirous of maintaining their independence against Communist encroachment.

The formation of PATO would tend to wrest the initiative from the Reds and, for a change, force them to worry about *our* next move.

Where India, with her 350 million people, would stand on such an organization is a question. But there are important populations in Asia whose leaders are more likely to welcome formation of a collective security organization. They have a population of between 300 and 400 million. Some of these Asian nations already have cast their lot with the Free World and fought against communism in Korea. Included among the nations of Asia which might favor a collective security alliance are Japan with 87 million people, Indonesia with 76 million, Pakistan with 75 million, Indo-China with 27 million, and South Korea, the Philippines, Burma and Thailand with populations of about 20 million each.

As in Europe the problems of organization would be difficult. We have seen how much trouble there was in relations between Japan and Rhee's Korea. To a lesser extent there are other national frictions that would have to be smoothed out. The Filipinos, the Australians and the New Zealanders still are wary of Japan. The Filipinos also are resentful of the "White Australia" policy of their neighbors to the south. But also as in Europe these frictions would have to be eliminated or smoothed over for the common security of all.

To be willing to resist the pressure of two Goliaths like Red China and Soviet Russia, the free countries of Asia would have to have something to fight for—genuine independence. It is to our vital interest, therefore, to encourage friendly nationalism, not resist it. Colonialism is dead in Asia and any Western power that fails to help bury it is digging its own grave.

The immediate problem of Korea was the most difficult one my government faced after the Armistice. The objective was a solution that would strengthen, not weaken, the fabric of freedom in the Far East, whether the Communists agreed or not.

There was no clause in the Armistice that said the belligerents were required to hold a political conference to settle the Korean question. All the Armistice said was that the military commanders of both sides recommended such a conference. But granting that one was held, there was no guarantee that it would solve anything. Having participated in political conferences designed to produce peace treaties for Germany and Austria and having witnessed Communist diplomatic knavery at first hand, I was and am doubtful that any Korean conference would achieve satisfactory results.

In my opinion the Communists have reversed Clausewitz' old adage that war is a continuation of politics by other means. To them, politics—and in this case the Armistice—is a continuation of war by other means. The outcome of a conference in Korea would be dependent upon the objectives the Communists have set for themselves, rather than on the persuasion of logic of the democratic countries. The only effective persuasion is the big stick—and the announced willingness to use it.

Whether or not there is a political conference, and whether or not it appears to accomplish anything, the cornerstone of our own American future military policy regarding Korea, in my opinion, should be this:

Never, never again should we be mousetrapped into fighting another defensive ground war on that peninsula. Never should we commit numerically inferior American troops—the first team at that —against numerically superior forces of the enemy's second team unless we are prepared to win.

Let us get out of Korea, preferably with the Chinese Reds, but let us get our troops out. Let us announce in unmistakable terms that should Korean sovereignty again be violated as a result of Communist aggression, the full might of American technical superiority will be brought to bear on the aggressor wherever he may be.

To me the best American military policy in the Far East would be:

Withdrawal of ground forces from Korea and the movement of a few American infantry divisions to Okinawa and Japan, coupled with the continued American buildup of the ROK Army.

Maintenance of American infantry forces in Japan during the time necessary for the Japanese to develop their own defenses.

Rapid build-up of the Vietnamese Army so it could man the defenses in Indo-China and permit the French to concentrate their own forces in swift-striking mobile units.

Maintenance of a strong American air and naval force ready to strike any aggressor from bases that form the front door to Asia.

Encouragement of the formation of a Treaty Organization of the Pacific.

In the poker game we have been playing with the Communists during the nine postwar years they have cheated and bluffed. Let's not have our full house bluffed by a pair of deuces. The mere threat of the use of all our American power, in my opinion, would have brought us a quicker and more favorable conclusion of the Korean fighting, and would have saved us many lives.

At any Korean Political Conference or elsewhere, let us first seek agreement on the simultaneous withdrawal of Chinese and UN troops from Korea in a reasonably short time. The Communists tried hard in 1951 to make such an agreement a basic condition for an armistice. Their motive at that time was transparent enough. South Korean forces still were weaker than North Korean forces. Such is not the case now. The United States has undertaken to equip and maintain a ROK ground force of the equivalent of twenty-one divisions, including Marine elements, with appropriate air and naval forces. This military establishment, with proper logistic support and its fighting heart, could, in my opinion, withstand any attack by purely North Korean troops.

Under these conditions President Rhee or the ROK Government might feel encouraged to "go for broke" in a lone march to the Yalu. I doubt that they would if we made it unmistakably clear that any such attempt would brand them as aggressors before the world and Korea would get not a cartridge for its military nor a penny for its rehabilitation.

My concern is that South Korea might try to drag us back into another stalemated ground war in Korea. The ROKs have the capability of creating a small incident that would involve us without warning in another shooting police action. With the impatience of the very old, Rhee could try to precipitate a borderline action that might light up the battlefield once more. This we must avoid at all costs.

If I have seemed critical of this doughty, single-minded patriarch who has been called the George Washington of his country, it is not for lack of admiration of his virtues or those of his countrymen. I consider the South Koreans one of our great allies, a people who know communism and hate it and are not afraid to die fighting it. I consider Rhee a great leader *within the limits of his national aspirations.*

But these aspirations must not be permitted to hobble America's freedom of action, our right to choose the time and place to fight, if fight we must.

As one who spent forty years in the Army, it is only natural for me to emphasize the military safeguards I think my country must take to avoid disaster.

I know that while bullets may kill Communists, they alone won't kill communism. This is a malignancy that grows on misery and dissatisfaction—two enemies we must fight and defeat.

I believe the only hope—however slim—for a peaceful solution of the Korean problem is for all foreign forces to pull out. In the vacuum thus created, North and South Koreans *may* settle their differences.

The Communists, of course, would try to achieve through infiltration, sabotage and propaganda against the ROK Government what they failed to win by direct aggression.

They tried that before the Korean War and failed. Their chances are even less after the war. But our job is to strengthen the South Korean spirit of resistance to communism, or at least to provide the economic climate in which this anticommunism could remain strong. Through our economic support the living standard of the South Korean must be raised to a point where he not only can resist the blandishments of communism but give him such a good life that he would be an attractive example to the starved, demoralized people of North Korea. High living standards are the weapon we in the free world have to use against Communist intrigue, propaganda and agitation. In Korea there is a chance high living standards could lure the North Koreans south and away from communism. In fact more than two million North Koreans fled to the south during the war.

This new kind of war, this contest between the benefits of two ways of life, may foreshadow the nature of the final world struggle between the democracies and communism. Perhaps both sides, with the frightening instruments of total destruction in their hands, may decide that these terrible weapons must never be used.

I pray fervently that this be true, not only because of the lives that would be saved, but also because I know America can reap a richer harvest from peace than can her enemies.

But peace will be granted us only if we are strong, if the Russians and their followers know we are strong and if they are convinced we have the *determination* and *courage* to use that strength to achieve a military victory the next time we are called to war against communism.

Appendix

Armistice activity during April was confined to Staff Officers' meetings concerning final arrangements for the exchange of sick and injured prisoners of war. Climaxing this series of discussions was the actual commencement of Operation Little Switch on 20 April and all meetings were discontinued for this operation until 26 April when the exchange terminated.

At the 123d Plenary Session on 26 April, first to be convened since the indefinite recess called by General Harrison on 6 October 1952, General Nam Il presented a proposed pattern for discussions of POW repatriation problem. Pertinent extracts from Nam's statement follow:

". . . our side now presents the following concrete proposal for implementation with regard to the settlement of the entire question of the repatriation of prisoners of war:

(1) Within two (2) months after the Armistice Agreement becomes effective, both sides shall, without offering any hindrance, repatriate and hand over in groups all those prisoners of war who insist upon repatriation to the side to which the prisoners of war belong in accordance with the related provisions of Paragraph 51, Article III, of the Armistice Agreement and in conformity with the final name-lists exchanged and checked by both sides.

(2) Within the time limit of one (1) month after the completion of the direct repatriation of all those prisoners of war who insist upon repatriation, the detaining side shall be responsible for sending to a neutral state, agreed upon through consultation by both sides, the remaining prisoners of war who are not directly repatriated, and then release them from its military control; Such prisoners of war shall be received and taken into custody by the authorities of the neutral state concerned in an area designated by such authorities. The authorities of the neutral state concerned shall have the authority to exercise their legitimate functions and responsibilities for the control of the prisoners of war under their temporary jurisdiction.

(3) Within six (6) months after the date of arrival of such prisoners of war in the neutral state, the nations to which they belong shall have the freedom and facilities to send personnel to that neutral state to explain to all the prisoners of war depending upon these nations, so as to eliminate their apprehensions, and to inform them of all matters related to their return to their homelands, particularly of their full right to return home to lead a peaceful life.

(4) Within six (6) months after the arrival of the prisoners of war in the neutral state, and after the explanations made by the nations to which they belong, the speedy return to their fatherlands of all those prisoners of war who

request repatriation shall be facilitated by the authorities of the neutral state concerned, and there should be no obstruction. The administrative details of the repatriation of such prisoners of war shall be settled through consultation between the authorities of the neutral state concerned and the authorities of the nations to which the prisoners of war belong.

(5(If, at the expiration of the time limit of six (6) months, stipulated in paragraphs three and four of the present proposal, there are still prisoners of war in the custody of the neutral state, their disposition shall be submitted for settlement through consultation, to the Political Conference provided in Paragraph 60, Article IV of the Armistice Agreement.

(6) All the expenditures of the prisoners of war during their stay in the neutral state, including their traveling expenses in returning to their fatherlands, shall be borne by the nations to which they belong."

In reply, General Harrison reviewed Communist proposals of 9 April in which physical delivery of non-repatriate POWs to a neutral nation for disposition and a six-month period for "explanations" were recommended, and a UNC counter-proposal of 16 April suggesting Switzerland as a neutral nation to take custody of the non-repatriate POWs in Korea, and suggesting 60 days as a logical period of explanations. He reiterated and re-emphasized the qualifications of Switzerland and pointed out the unfeasibility of removing prisoners physically to whatever neutral is selected.

The remainder of the session was devoted to an exchange of views on the suitability of Switzerland as a neutral and a restatement of the stands previously taken by both sides.

With the exception of a Communist-inserted proposal to name an "Asian nation" (none specifically mentioned) as the neutral custodial agency on 29 April (126th Plenary Session), discussions in the Armistice sessions were devoted entirely to exchanges of views on the physical removal of non-repatriate POWs from Korea for further disposition and the length of the explanation period, with no new proposals presented until 7 May at which time the Communists presented the following "compromise" proposal:

(1) Within two months after the Armistice Agreement becomes effective, both sides shall, without offering any hindrance, repatriate and hand over in groups all those prisoners of war who insist upon repatriation to the side to which the prisoners of war belong, in accordance with the related provisions of Paragraph 51, Article 3 of the Armistice Agreement and in conformity with the final name lists exchanged and checked by both sides.

(2) In order to facilitate the return to their homelands of the remaining prisoners of war who are not directly repatriated, both sides agree that a Neutral Nations Repatriation Commission shall be established, to be composed of an equal number of representatives appointed respectively by five nations, namely, Poland, Czechoslovakia, Switzerland and Sweden, the four nations provided for in Paragraph 37, Article 2 of the Armistice Agreement, and India as agreed upon by both sides.

(3) All prisoners of war of both sides, with the exception of those prisoners of war who shall be directly repatriated as provided for in Paragraph 1 of this proposal, shall be released from the military control and custody of the detaining side at the original places of detention and to be handed over to the Neutral Nations Repatriation Commission, provided for in Paragraph 2 of this proposal, which shall receive them and take them into custody. The Neutral Nations Repatriation Commission shall have the authority to exercise its legitimate functions and responsibilities for the control of the prisoners of war under its tem-

porary jurisdiction. In order to ensure the effective execution of this authority, the member nations of the Neutral Nations Repatriation Commission shall each provide an equal number of armed forces.

(4) The Neutral Nations Repatriation Commission, after having received and taken into custody those prisoners of war who are not directly repatriated, shall immediately make arrangements so that within the time limit of four months after the Neutral Nations Repatriation Commission takes over the custody, the nations to which the prisoners of war belong shall have freedom and facilities to send personnel to the original places of detention of these prisoners of war to explain to all the prisoners of war depending upon these nations so as to eliminate their apprehensions and to inform them of all matters relating to their return to their homelands, particularly of their full right to return home to lead a peaceful life.

(5) Within four months after the Neutral Nations Repatriation Commission receives and takes into custody the prisoners of war, and after the explanations made by the nations to which they belong, the speedy return to their fatherlands of all those prisoners of war who request repatriation shall be facilitated by the Neutral Nations Repatriation Commission, and the detaining side shall not offer any obstruction. The administrative details for the repatriation of such prisoners of war shall be settled through consultation between the Neutral Nations Repatriation Commission and the two sides.

(6) If, at the expiration of the time limit of four months as provided in Paragraphs 4 and 5 of this proposal, there are still prisoners of war in the custody of the Neutral Nations Repatriation Commission, their disposition shall be submitted for settlement through consultation to the Political Conference as provided in Paragraph 60, Article 4 of the Armistice Agreement.

(7) All the expenditures of the prisoners of war during the period in the custody of the Neutral Nations Repatriation Commission, including their traveling expenses in returning to their fatherlands, shall be borne by the nations to which they belong.

(8) The terms of this proposal and the arrangements arising therefrom shall be made known to all prisoners of war.

Meetings on 8, 9, 10, 11 and 12 May were confined to discussions of details of the 7 May Communist proposal, centering mainly around the question of whether the final decision concerning the non-repatriate POWs should rest exclusively with a political conference. During this time, also, the Communists revised their demands for a six-month explanation period to four months. On 13 May, after reviewing UNC objections to the Communist proposal and pointing out which portions thereof were acceptable, General Harrison presented the following UNC proposal for a Terms of Reference for the Neutral Nations Repatriation Commission:

Within two (2) months after the Armistice Agreement becomes effective, both sides shall, without offering any hindrance, repatriate and hand over in groups all those prisoners of war in its custody who insist on repatriation to the side to which they belonged at the time of capture. Repatriation shall be accomplished in accordance with the related provisions of Article III of the Draft Armistice Agreement. In order to expedite the processing of such personnel, each side shall, prior to the signing of the Armistice Agreement, exchange the total numbers, by nationalities, of personnel to be repatriated direct. Each group delivered to the other side shall be accompanied by rosters, prepared by nationality, to include name, rank (if any) and internment or military serial number.

On the date the armistice becomes effective, all prisoners of war of Korean nationality who, while in the custody of the detaining powers have elected not to avail themselves of their right to be repatriated, shall be released to civilian status. Those who may subsequently desire to return to the area under the military control of the side to which they formerly belonged shall be permitted and assisted to do so under the provisions of Article 59 of the Draft Armistice Agreement.

TERMS OF REFERENCE
FOR PRISONER OF WAR CUSTODIAL COMMISSION

I. *General*

1. In order to insure that all prisoners of war have the opportunity to exercise their right to be repatriated following an armistice, Sweden, Switzerland, Poland, Czechoslovakia and India shall each be requested by both sides to appoint a member to a Prisoner of War Custodial Commission which shall be established to take custody in Korea of those prisoners of war who, while in the custody of the detaining powers, have elected not to avail themselves of their right to be repatriated, and who are not released to civilian status on the date the armistice becomes effective. The Prisoner of War Custodial Commission shall establish its headquarters within the Demilitarized Zone in the vicinity of Panmunjom. Subordinate bodies of the same composition as the Prisoner of War Custodial Commission shall be stationed at those locations at which the Custodial Commission assumes custody of prisoners of war.

2. The armed forces and any other operating personnel required to assist the Custodial Commission in carrying out its functions and responsibilities shall be provided exclusively by India, whose representative shall also be chairman and executive agent of the Custodial Commission. Representatives from each of the other four (4) powers shall be allowed staff assistants in equal number not to exceed ten (10) each. The arms of all personnel provided for in this paragraph shall be limited to military police type small arms.

3. No force or threat of force shall be used against the prisoners of war specified in Paragraph 1 above to prevent or effect their repatriation, and no violence to their persons or affront to their dignity or self-respect shall be permitted in any manner for any purpose whatsoever (but see Paragraph 7 below). This duty is enjoined on and entrusted to the Prisoner of War Custodial Commission and each of its representatives. Both sides shall have representatives with appropriate representatives of the Prisoner of War Custodial Commission to determine that any personnel who request return to the other side have not been coerced into making this decision. Prisoners of war shall at all times be treated humanely in accordance with the specific provisions of the Geneva Convention, and with the general spirit of that Convention.

II. *Custody of Prisoners of War*

4. All prisoners of war who do not avail themselves of the right of repatriation following the effective date of the Armistice Agreement, or who are not released to civilian status on that date, shall be released from the military control and from the custody of the detaining side as soon as practicable, and, in all cases, within sixty (60) days subsequent to the effective date of the Armistice

Agreement to the Custodial Commission at locations in Korea to be designated by the detaining side,

5. The locations specified in the preceding paragraph shall be demilitarized by the withdrawal of the military forces of the detaining side to a distance of at least two (2) kilometers from the perimeter of the prisoner of war installation at the time the Custodial Commission assumes control thereof.

6. Notwithstanding the provisions of Paragraph 5 above, the Indian representative is entitled to call upon the detaining side in the area under whose military control prisoner of war installations are physically located, to provide such administrative and security forces as may be needed to augment the forces provided by India. Forces so provided shall be under the operational control of the senior officer of the Indian security forces.

7. Notwithstanding the provisions of paragraph 3 above, nothing in this agreement shall be construed as derogating from the authority of the Custodial Commission to exercise its legitimate functions and responsibilities for the control of the prisoners under its temporary jurisdicton.

III. *Verification*

8. Each side shall be afforded an opportunity to verify or ascertain the attitude towards repatriation of its captured personnel while they are in the custody of the Custodial Commission. To this end, its representatives shall be afforded access to its captured personnel to explain to them their rights, and to inform them on any matters relating to their return to their homelands, under the following provisions:

a. The number of such verifying representatives shall not exceed one (1) per thousand (1000) prisoners of war held in custody by the Custodial Commission, but the minimum shall not be less than five (5);

b. The hours during which the verifying representatives shall have access to the prisoners shall be as determined by the Custodial Commission, and generally in accord with Article 53 of the Geneva Convention Relative to the Treatment of Prisoners of War;

c. All verifications and interviews shall be conducted in the presence of a representative of each member nation of the Custodial Commission;

d. Additional provisions governing verification shall be prescribed by the Custodial Commission, and will be designed to employ the principles outlined in paragraph 3 above.

9. Prisoners of war in its custody shall have freedom and facilities to make representations and communications to the Custodial Commission and to representatives and agencies of the Custodial Commission and to inform them of their desires on any matter concerning themselves, in accordance with arrangements made for the purpose by the Custodial Commission.

IV. *Disposition of Prisoners of War*

10. Any prisoner of war who, while in the custody of the Custodial Commission, decides to avail himself of the right of repatriation, shall so certify to a body consisting of a representative of each member nation of the Custodial Commission. Upon execution of such certificate, he shall, while still in the custody of the Custodial Commission, be delivered forthwith to the prisoner of war exchange point at Panmunjom for repatriation under the procedure prescribed in the Armistice Agreement.

11. Sixty (60) days after transfer of custody of the prisoners of war to the Custodial Commission is completed, prisoners of war who have not availed

themselves of the right to be repatriated shall be released to civilian status, the Custodial Commission ceasing its functions and being dissolved.

V. *Red Cross Visitation*

12. Essential Red Cross service for prisoners of war in custody of the Custodial Commission shall be provided by India in accordance with regulations issued by the Custodial Commission.

VI. *Press Coverage*

13. The Custodial Commission shall insure freedom of the press by:

a. Providing for observance of the entire operation in South Korea by representatives of the press accredited to the United Nations Command.

b. Providing for observance of the entire operation in North Korea by representatives of the press accredited to the Korean People's Army or the Chinese People's Volunteers.

VII. *Logistical Support for Prisoners of War*

14. Each side shall provide logistical support for the prisoners of war in the area under its military control, delivering required support to the Custodial Commission at an agreed delivery point in the vicinity of each prisoner of war installation.

15. The cost of repatriating prisoners of war from the exchange point at Panmunjom shall be borne by the side on which said prisoners depend in accordance with Article 118 of the Geneva Convention.

16. The Custodial Commission is entitled to call upon the detaining side to provide specified unarmed personnel for the operation of facilities or the provision of services within the prisoner of war installations within the area under its military control.

17. The Custodial Commission shall provide medical support for the prisoners of war as may be practicable. The detaining side shall provide medical support as practicable upon the request of the Custodial Commission and specifically for those cases requiring extensive treatment or hospitalization. The Custodial Commission shall maintain custody of prisoners of war during such hospitalization. The detaining side shall facilitate such custody. Upon completion of treatment, prisoners of war shall be returned to a prisoner of war installation as specified in paragraph 4 above.

18. The Custodial Commission is entitled to obtain from both sides such legitimate assistance as it may require in carrying out its duties and tasks.

VIII. *Logistical Support for the Custodial Commission*

19. Each side shall be responsible for providing logistical support for the personnel of the Custodial Commission stationed in the area under its military control, and both sides shall contribute on an equal basis to such support within the Demilitarized Zone. The precise arrangements shall be subject to determination between the Custodial Commission and the detaining side in each case.

20. Each of the detaining sides shall be responsible for protecting the verifying representatives from the other side while in transit over lines of communication within its area, as set forth in Paragraph 23 for the Prisoner of War Custodial Commission, to a place of residence and while in residence in the vicinity of but not within each prisoner of war installation. The Custodial Commission shall be responsible for the security of such representatives within the actual limits of prisoner of war installations.

21. Each of the detaining sides shall provide transportation, housing, communication, and other agreed logistical support to the verifying representatives of the other side while they are in the area under its military control. Such services shall be provided on a reimbursable basis.

IX. *Publication*

22. The terms of this agreement shall be made known to all prisoners of war, who, while in the custody of the detaining power, have failed to avail themselves of their right of repatriation.

X. *Movement*

23. The movement of the Custodial Commission, its personnel, and repatriated prisoners of war shall be over lines of communication as determined by the command(s) of the opposing side and the Custodial Commission. A map showing these lines of communication shall be furnished the command of the opposing side and the Custodial Commission. Movement of such personnel, except in the demilitarized areas established in Paragraph 5 above, around locations as designated in Paragraph 4 above, shall be under the control of, and escorted by, personnel of the side in whose area the travel is being undertaken.

XI. *Procedural Matters*

24. The interpretation of this agreement shall rest with the Custodial Commission. The Custodial Commission, and/or any subordinate bodies to which functions are delegated or assigned by the Custodial Commission, shall operate on the basis of unanimity, except with respect to procedural matters; on procedural matters decision shall be by majority vote.

25. The Custodial Commission shall make reports to the opposing Commanders once each week concerning the status of prisoners of war in its custody and any other important matters relating to its functions and responsibilities.

26. When this agreement has been acceded to by both sides and by the five (5) powers named herein, it shall become effective upon the date the Armistice becomes effective.

Done at Panmunjon, Korea, at (———) hours on the (———) day of (———) 1953, in English, Korean, Chinese, all texts being equally authentic.

This proposal was summarily rejected by the Communists on the day it was presented, and, at the following three meetings, similarly denounced as "unacceptable." There were no Plenary Sessions held between 16 May and 25 May. On the latter date the delegates went into executive session and General Harrison presented a revised UNC proposal, a mimeographed copy of which is appended hereto. Minor revisions were effected in this draft during executive sessions from 25 May to 7 June, and final agreement was reached and the Terms of Reference signed on 8 June.

HEADQUARTERS
UNITED NATIONS COMMAND
PUBLIC INFORMATION OFFICE

For Immediate Release

United Nations Command Armistice Proposal of 25 May 1953

A. INTRODUCTION

Within two (2) months after the Armistice Agreement becomes effective, both sides shall, without offering any hindrance, repatriate and hand over in groups all those prisoners of war in its custody who insist on repatriation to the side to which they belonged at the time of capture. Repatriation shall be accomplished in accordance with the related provisions of Article III of the Draft Armistice Agreement. In order to expedite the processing of such personnel, each side shall, prior to the signing of the Armistice Agreement, exchange the total numbers, by nationalities, of personnel to be repatriated direct. Each group delivered to the other side shall be accompanied by rosters, prepared by nationality, to include name, rank (if any) and internment or military serial number.

B. TERMS OF REFERENCE FOR PRISONER OF WAR CUSTODIAL COMMISSION

I. *General*

1. In order to insure that all prisoners of war have the opportunity to exercise their right to be repatriated following an armistice, Sweden, Switzerland, Poland, Czechoslovakia and India shall each be requested by both sides to appoint a member to a Prisoner of War Custodial Commission which shall be established to take custody in Korea of those prisoners of war who, while in the custody of the detaining powers, have elected not to avail themselves of their right to be repatriated. The Prisoner of War Custodial Commission shall establish its headquarters within the Demilitarized Zone in the vicinity of Panmunjom. Subordinate bodies of the same composition as the Prisoner of War Custodial Commission shall be stationed at those locations at which the Custodial Commission assumes custody of prisoners of war. Representatives of both sides shall be permitted to observe the operations of the Custodial Commission and its subordinate bodies to include verifications and interviews.

2. The armed forces and any other operating personnel required to assist the Custodial Commission in carrying out its functions and responsibilities shall be provided exclusively by India, whose representative shall also be chairman and executive agent of the Custodial Commission. Representatives from each of the other four (4) powers shall be allowed staff assistants in equal number not to exceed fifty (50) each. The arms of all personnel provided for in this paragraph shall be limited to military police type small arms.

3. No force or threat of force shall be used against the prisoners of war specified in paragraph 1 above to prevent or effect their repatriation, and no violence to their persons or affront to their dignity or self-respect shall be permitted in any manner for any purpose whatsoever (but see Paragraph 7 below). This duty is enjoined on and entrusted to the Prisoner of War Custodial Commission and each of its representatives. Both sides shall have representatives with appropriate representatives of the Prisoner of War Custodial Commission to determine that any personnel who request return to the other side have not been coerced into

making this decision. Prisoners of war shall at all times be treated humanely in accordance with the specific provisions of the Geneva Convention, and with the general spirit of that Convention.

II. *Custody of Prisoners of War*

4. All prisoners of war who do not avail themselves of the right of repatriation following the effective date of the Armistice Agreement shall be released from the military control and from the custody of the detaining side as soon as practicable, and, in all cases, within sixty (60) days subsequent to the effective date of the Armistice Agreement to the Custodial Commission at locations in Korea to be designated by the detaining side.

5. The locations specified in the preceding paragraph shall be demilitarized by the withdrawal of the military forces of the detaining side to a distance of at least two (2) kilometers from the perimeter of the prisoner of war installation at the time the Custodial Commission assumes control thereof.

6. Notwithstanding the provisions of Paragraph 5 above, the Custodial Commission is entitled to call upon the detaining side in the area under whose military control prisoner of war installations are physically located, to provide such administrative and security forces as may be needed to augment the forces provided by India. Forces so provided shall be under the operational control of the senior officer of the Indian security forces

7. Notwithstanding the provisions of Paragraph 3 above, nothing in this agreement shall be construed as derogating from the authority of the Custodial Commission to exercise its legitimate functions and responsibilities for the control of the prisoners under its temporary jurisdiction.

III. *Verification*

8. Each side shall be afforded an opportunity to verify or ascertain the attitude towards repatriation of its captured personnel while they are in the custody of the Custodial Commission. To this end, its representatives shall be afforded access to its captured personnel to explain to them their rights, and to inform them on any matters relating to their return to their homelands, under the following provisions:

a. The number of such verifying representatives shall not exceed one (1) per thousand (1000) prisoners of war held in custody by the Custodial Commission, but the minimum shall not be less than a total of five (5);

b. The hours during which the verifying representatives shall have access to the prisoners shall be as determined by the Custodial Commission, and generally in accord with Article 53 of the Geneva Convention Relative to the Treatment of Prisoners of War;

c. All verifications and interviews shall be conducted in the presence of a representative of each member nation of the Custodial Commission and a representative from the detaining power.

d. Additional provisions governing verification shall be prescribed by the Custodial Commission, and will be designed to employ the principles outlined in Paragraph 3 above.

9. Prisoners of war in its custody shall have freedom and facilities to make representations and communications to the Custodial Commission and to representatives and agencies of the Custodial Commission and to inform them of their desires on any matter concerning themselves, in accordance with arrangements made for the purpose by the Custodial Commission.

IV. *Disposition of Prisoners of War*

10. Any prisoner of war who, while in the custody of the Custodial Commission, decides to avail himself of the right of repatriation, shall so certify to a body consisting of a representative of each member nation of the Custodial Commission. Upon execution of such certificate, which is validated by majority vote of the Custodial Commission or one of its subordinate organizations, he shall, while still in the custody of the Custodial Commission, be delivered forthwith to the prisoner of war exchange point at Panmunjom for repatriation under the procedure prescribed in the Armistice Agreement.

11. Ninety (90) days after the transfer of custody of the prisoners of war to the Custodial Commission is completed, access of representatives to captured personnel as provided for in Paragraph 8, above, shall terminate, and question of disposition of the prisoners of war who have not availed themselves of their right to be repatriated shall be submitted for settlement to the political conference recommended to be convened in Paragraph 60, Draft Armistice Agreement. Any prisoners of war who have not availed themselves of their right to be repatriated and for whom no other disposition has been agreed to within 120 days after the Custodial Commission has assumed their custody shall be released to civilian status, the Custodial Commission ceasing its functions and being dissolved; (or, as an alternate solution: "Any prisoners of war who have not availed themselves of their right to be repatriated and for whom no other disposition has been agreed to within 120 days after the Custodial Commission has assumed their custody shall be promptly referred to the United Nations General Assembly. The Custodial Commission shall retain custody of these prisoners of war until decision is reached on their disposition by the United Nations General Assembly.")

V. *Red Cross Visitation*

12. Essential Red Cross service for prisoners of war in custody of the Custodial Commission shall be provided by India in accordance with regulations issued by the Custodial Commission.

VI. *Press Coverage*

13. The Custodial Commission shall insure freedom of the press and other news media in observing the entire operation as outlined herein, in accordance with procedures to be established by the Custodial Commission.

VII. *Logistical Support for Prisoners of War*

14. Each side shall provide logistical support for the prisoners of war in the area under its military control, delivering required support to the Custodial Commission at an agreed delivery point in the vicinity of each prisoner of war installation.

15. The cost of repatriating prisoners of war to the exchange point at Panmunjom shall be borne by the detaining power and the cost from the exchange point by the side on which said prisoners depend in accordance with Article 118 of the Geneva Convention.

16. The Custodial Commission is entitled to call upon the detaining side to provide specified unarmed personnel for the operation of facilities or the provision of services within the prisoner of war installations within the area under its military control.

17. The Custodial Commission shall provide medical support for the prisoners of war as may be practicable. The detaining side shall provide medical support

as practicable upon the request of the Custodial Commission and specifically for those cases requiring extensive treatment or hospitalization. The Custodial Commission shall maintain custody of prisoners of war during such hospitalization. The detaining side shall facilitate such custody. Upon completion of treatment, prisoners of war shall be returned to a prisoner of war installation as specified in Paragraph 4 above.

18. The Custodial Commission is entitled to obtain from both sides such legitimate assistance as it may require in carrying out its duties and tasks.

VIII. *Logistical Support for the Custodial Commission*

19. Each side shall be responsible for providing logistical support for the personnel of the Custodial Commission stationed in the area under its military control, and both sides shall contribute on an equal basis to such support within the Demilitarized Zone. The precise arrangements shall be subject to determination between the Custodial Commission and the detaining side in each case.

20. Each of the detaining sides shall be responsible for protecting the verifying representatives from the other side while in transit over lines of communication within its area, as set forth in Paragraph 23 for the Prisoner of War Custodial Commission, to a place of residence and while in residence in the vicinity of but not within each prisoner of war installation. The Custodial Commission shall be responsible for the security of such representatives within the actual limits of prisoner of war installations.

21. Each of the detaining sides shall provide transportation, housing, communication, and other agreed logistical support to the verifying representatives of the other side while they are in the area under its military control. Such services shall be provided on a reimbursable basis.

IX. *Publication*

22. The terms of this agreement shall be made known to all prisoners of war, who, while in the custody of the detaining power, have failed to avail themselves of their right of repatriation.

X. *Movement*

23. The movement of the Custodial Commission, its personnel, and repatriated prisoners of war shall be over lines of communication as determined by the command(s) of the opposing side and the Custodial Commission. A map showing these lines of communication shall be furnished the command of the opposing side and the Custodial Commission. Movement of such personnel, except in the demilitarized areas established in Paragraph 5 above, around locations as designated in Paragraph 4 above, shall be under the control of, and escorted by, personnel of the side in whose area the travel is being undertaken.

XI. *Procedural Matters*

24. The interpretation of this agreement shall rest with the Custodial Commission. The Custodial Commission, and/or any subordinate bodies to which functions are delegated or assigned by the Custodial Commission, shall operate on the basis of majority vote.

25. The Custodial Commission shall submit a weekly report to the opposing Commanders on the status of prisoners of war in its custody, indicating the numbers repatriated and remaining at the end of each week.

26. When this agreement has been acceded to by both sides and by the five

(5) powers named herein, it shall become effective upon the date the Armistice becomes effective.

ARMISTICE AGREEMENT Volume I

TEXT OF AGREEMENT

Agreement between the Commander-in-Chief, United Nations Command, on the one hand, and the Supreme Commander of the Korean People's Army and the Commander of the Chinese People's Volunteers, on the other hand, concerning a military armistice in Korea

Preamble

The undersigned, the Commander-in-Chief, United Nations Command, on the one hand, and the Supreme Commander of the Korean People's Army and the Commander of the Chinese People's Volunteers, on the other hand, in the interest of stopping the Korean conflict, with its great toll of suffering and bloodshed on both sides, and with the objective of establishing an armistice which will insure a complete cessation of hostilities and of all acts of armed force in Korea until a final peaceful settlement is achieved, do individually, collectively, and mutually agree to accept and to be bound and governed by the conditions and terms of armistice set forth in the following Articles and Paragraphs, which said conditions and terms are intended to be purely military in character and to pertain solely to the belligerents in Korea.

ARTICLE I. MILITARY DEMARCATION LINE AND DEMILITARIZED ZONE

1. A Military Demarcation Line shall be fixed and both sides shall withdraw two (2) kilometers from this line so as to establish a Demilitarized Zone between the opposing forces. A Demilitarized Zone shall be established as a buffer zone to prevent the occurrence of incidents which might lead to a resumption of hostilities.

2. The Military Demarcation Line is located as indicated on the attached map (Map 1).

3. The Demilitarized Zone is defined by a northern and a southern boundary as indicated on the attached map (Map 1).

4. The Military Demarcation Line shall be plainly marked as directed by the Military Armistice Commission hereinafter established. The Commanders of the opposing sides shall have suitable markers erected along the boundary between the Demilitarized Zone and their respective areas. The Military Armistice Commission shall supervise the erection of all markers placed along the Military Demarcation Line and along the boundaries of the Demilitarized Zone.

5. The waters of the Han River Estuary shall be open to civil shipping of both sides wherever one bank is controlled by one side and the other bank is controlled by the other side. The Military Armistice Commission shall prescribe rules for the shipping in that part of the Han River Estuary indicated on the attached may (Map 2). Civil shipping of each side shall have unrestricted access to the land under the military control of that side.

6. Neither side shall execute any hostile act within, from, or against the Demilitarized Zone.

7. No person, military or civilian, shall be permitted to cross the Military

Demarcation Line unless specifically authorized to do so by the Military Armistice Commission.

8. No person, military or civilian, in the Demilitarized Zone shall be permitted to enter the territory under the military control of either side unless specifically authorized to do so by the Commander into whose territory entry is sought.

9. No person, military or civilian, shall be permitted to enter the Demilitarized Zone except persons concerned with the conduct of civil administration and relief and persons specifically authorized to enter by the Military Armistice Commission.

10. Civil administration and relief in that part of the Demilitarized Zone which is south of the Military Demarcation Line shall be the responsibility of the Commander-in-Chief, United Nations Command; and civil administration and relief in that part of the Demilitarized Zone which is north of the Military Demarcation Line shall be the joint responsibility of the Supreme Commander of the Korean People's Army and the Commander of the Chinese People's Volunteers. The number of persons, military or civilian, from each side who are permitted to enter the Demilitarized Zone for the conduct of civil administration and relief shall be as determined by the respective Commanders, but in no case shall the total number authorized by either side exceed one thousand (1,000) persons at any one time. The number of civil police and the arms to be carried by them shall be as prescribed by the Military Armistice Commission. Other personnel shall not carry arms unless specifically authorized to do so by the Military Armistice Commission.

11. Nothing contained in this Article shall be construed to prevent the complete freedom of movement to, from, and within the Demilitarized Zone by the Military Armistice Commission, its assistants, its Joint Observer Teams with their assistants, the Neutral Nations Supervisory Commission hereinafter established, its assistants, its Neutral Nations Inspection Teams with their assistants, and of any other persons, materials, and equipment specifically authorized to enter the Demilitarized Zone by the Military Armistice Commission. Convenience of movement shall be permitted through the territory under the military control of either side over any route necessary to move between points within the Demilitarized Zone where such points are not connected by roads lying completely within the Demilitarized Zone.

ARTICLE II. CONCRETE ARRANGEMENTS FOR CEASE-FIRE AND ARMISTICE

A. *General*

12. The Commanders of the opposing sides shall order and enforce a complete cessation of all hostilities in Korea by all armed forces under their control, including all units and personnel of the ground, naval, and air forces, effective twelve (12) hours after this Armistice Agreement is signed. (See Paragraph 63 hereof for effective date and hour of the remaining provisions of this Armistice Agreement.)

13. In order to insure the stability of the Military Armistice so as to facilitate the attainment of a peaceful settlement through the holding by both sides of a political conference of a higher level, the Commanders of the opposing sides shall:

a. Within seventy-two (72) hours after this Armistice Agreement becomes effective, withdraw all of their military forces, supplies, and equipment from the Demilitarized Zone except as otherwise provided herein. All demolitions, minefields, wire entanglements, and other hazards to the safe movement of personnel of the Military Armistice Commission or its Joint Observer Teams, known to exist within the Demilitarized Zone after the withdrawal of military forces therefrom, together with lanes known to be free of all such hazards, shall be reported to the Military Armistice Commission by the Commander of the side whose forces emplaced such hazards. Subsequently, additional safe lanes shall be cleared; and eventually, within forty-five (45) days after the termination of the seventy-two (72) hour period, all such hazards shall be removed from the Demilitarized Zone as directed by and under the supervision of the Military Armistice Commission. At the termination of the seventy-two (72) hour period, except for unarmed troops authorized a forty-five (45) day period to complete salvage operations under Military Armistice Commission supervision, such units of a police nature as may be specifically requested by the Military Armistice Commission and agreed to by the Commanders of the opposing sides, and personnel authorized under Paragraphs 10 and 11 hereof, no personnel of either side shall be permitted to enter the Demilitarized Zone.

b. Within ten (10) days after this Armistice Agreement becomes effective, withdraw all of their military forces, supplies, and equipment from the rear and the coastal islands and waters of Korea of the other side. If such military forces are not withdrawn within the stated time limit, and there is no mutually agreed and valid reason for the delay, the other side shall have the right to take any action which it deems necessary for the maintenance of security and order. The term "coastal islands," as used above, refers to those islands which, though occupied by one side at the time when this Armistice Agreement becomes effective, were controlled by the other side on 24 June 1950; provided, however, that all the islands lying to the north and west of the provincial boundary line between HWANGHAE-DO and KYONGGI-DO shall be under the military control of the Supreme Commander of the Korean People's Army and the Commander of the Chinese People's Volunteers, except the island groups of PAENGYONG-DO (37°58′N, 124°40′E), TAECHONG-DO (37°50′N, 124° 42′E), SOCHONG-DO (37°46′N, 124°46′E), YONPYONG-DO (37°38′N, 125°40′E), and U-DO (37°36′N, 125°58′E), which shall remain under the military control of the Commander-in-Chief, United Nations Command. All the islands on the west coast of Korea lying south of the above-mentioned boundary line shall remain under the military control of the Commander-in-Chief, United Nations Command. (See Map 3.)

c. Cease the introduction into Korea of reinforcing military personnel; provided, however, that the rotation of units and personnel, the arrival in Korea of personnel on a temporary duty basis, and the return to Korea of personnel after short periods of leave or temporary duty outside of Korea shall be permitted within the scope prescribed below. "Rotation" is defined as the replacement of units or personnel by other units or personnel who are commencing a tour of duty in Korea. Rotation personnel shall be introduced into and evacuated from Korea only through the ports of entry enumerated in Paragraph 43 hereof. Rotation shall be conducted on a man-for-man basis; provided, however, that no more than thirty-five thousand (35,000) persons in the military service shall be admitted into Korea by either side in any calendar month under the rotation policy. No military personnel of either side shall be introduced into Korea if the introduction of such personnel will cause the aggregate of the military personnel of that side admitted into Korea since the effective date of this Armistice Agreement to exceed the cumulative total of the military personnel of that side who have departed from Korea since that date. Reports concerning arrivals in and departures from Korea of military personnel shall be made daily to the Military Armistice Commission and the Neutral Nations Supervisory Commission; such reports shall include places of arrival and departure and the number of persons arriving at or departing from each such place. The Neutral Nations Supervisory Commission, through its Neutral Nations Inspection Teams shall conduct supervision and inspection of the rotation of units and personnel authorized above, at the ports of entry enumerated in Paragraph 43 hereof.

d. Cease the introduction into Korea of reinforcing combat aircraft, armored vehicles, weapons, and ammunition; provided, however, that combat aircraft, armored vehicles, weapons, and ammunition which are destroyed, damaged, worn out, or used up during the period of the armistice may be replaced on the basis of piece-for-piece of the same effectiveness and the same type. Such combat aircraft, armored vehicles, weapons, and ammunition shall be introduced into Korea only through the ports of entry enumerated in Paragraph 43 hereof. In order to justify the requirement for combat aircraft, armored vehicles, weapons, and ammunition to be introduced into Korea for replacement purposes, reports concerning every incoming shipment of these items shall be made to the Military Armistice Commission and the Neutral Nations Supervisory Commission; such reports shall include statements regarding the disposition of the items being replaced. Items to be replaced which are removed from Korea shall be removed only through the ports of entry enumerated in Paragraph 43 hereof. The Neutral Nations Supervisory Commission, through its Neutral Nations Inspection Teams, shall conduct supervision and inspection of the replacement of combat aircraft, armored vehicles, weapons and ammunition authorized above, at the ports of entry enumerated in Paragraph 43 hereof.

e. Insure that personnel of their respective commands who violate any of the provisions of this Armistice Agreement are adequately punished.

f. In those cases where places of burial are a matter of record and graves are actually found to exist, permit graves registration personnel of the other side to enter, within a definite time limit after this Armistice Agreement becomes effective, the territory of Korea under their military control, for the purpose of proceeding to such graves to recover and evacuate the bodies of the deceased military personnel of that side, including deceased prisoners of war. The specific procedures and the time limit for the performance of the above task shall be determined by the Military Armistice Commission. The Commanders of the opposing sides shall furnish to the other side all available information pertaining to the places of burial of the deceased military personnel of the other side.

g. Afford full protection and all possible assistance and cooperation to the Military Armistice Commission, its Joint Observer Teams, the Neutral Nations Supervisory Commission, and its Neutral Nations Inspection Teams, in the carrying out of their functions and responsibilities hereinafter assigned; and accord to the Neutral Nations Supervisory Commission, and to its Neutral Nations Inspection Teams, full convenience of movement between the headquarters of the Neutral Nations Supervisory Commission and the ports of entry enumerated in Paragraph 43 hereof over main lines of communication agreed upon by both sides (See Map 4), and between the headquarters of the Neutral Nations Supervisory Commission and the places where violations of this Armistice Agreement have been reported to have occurred. In order to prevent unnecessary delays, the use of alternate routes and means of transportation will be permitted whenever the main lines of communication are closed or impassable.

h. Provide such logistic support, including communications and transportation facilities, as may be required by the Military Armistice Commission and the Neutral Nations Supervisory Commission and their Teams.

i. Each construct, operate, and maintain a suitable airfield in their respective parts of the Demilitarized Zone in the vicinity of the headquarters of the Military Armistice Commission, for such uses as the Commission may determine.

j. Insure that all members and other personnel of the Neutral Nations Supervisory Commission and of the Neutral Nations Repatriation Commission hereinafter established shall enjoy the freedom and facilities necessary for the proper exercise of their functions, including privileges, treatment, and immunities equivalent to those ordinarily enjoyed by accredited diplomatic personnel under international usage.

14. This Armistice Agreement shall apply to all opposing ground forces under the military control of either side, which ground forces shall respect the Demilitarized Zone and the area of Korea under the military control of the opposing side.

15. This Armistice Agreement shall apply to all opposing naval forces, which naval forces shall respect the waters contiguous to the Demilitarized Zone and to the land area of Korea under the military control of the opposing side, and shall not engage in blockade of any kind of Korea.

16. This Armistice Agreement shall apply to all opposing air forces, which air forces shall respect the air space over the Demilitarized Zone and over the area of Korea under the military control of the opposing side, and over the waters contiguous to both.

17. Responsibility for compliance with and enforcement of the terms and provisions of this Armistice Agreement is that of the signatories hereto and their successors in command. The Commanders of the opposing sides shall establish within their respective commands all measures and procedures necessary to insure complete compliance with all of the provisions hereof by all elements of their commands. They shall actively cooperate with one another and with the Military Armistice Commission and the Neutral Nations Supervisory Commission in requiring observance of both the letter and the spirit of all of the provisions of this Armistice Agreement.

18. The costs of the operations of the Military Armistice Commission and of the Neutral Nations Supervisory Commission and of their Teams shall be shared equally by the two opposing sides.

B. *Military Armistice Commission*

1. COMPOSITION

19. A Military Armistice Commission is hereby established.

20. The Military Armistice Commission shall be composed of ten (10) senior officers, five (5) of whom shall be appointed by the Commander-in-Chief, United Nations Command, and five (5) of whom shall be appointed jointly by the Supreme Commander of the Korean People's Army and the Commander of the Chinese People's Volunteers. Of the ten members, three (3) from each side shall be of general or flag rank. The two (2) remaining members on each side may be major generals, brigadier generals, colonels, or their equivalents.

21. Members of the Military Armistice Commission shall be permitted to use staff assistants as required.

22. The Military Armistice Commission shall be provided with the necessary administrative personnel to establish a Secretariat charged with assisting the Commission by performing record-keeping, secretarial, interpreting, and such other functions as the Commission may assign to it. Each side shall appoint to the Secretariat a Secretary and an Assistant Secretary and such clerical and specialized personnel as required by the Secretariat. Records shall be kept in English, Korean, and Chinese, all of which shall be equally authentic.

23. a. The Military Armistice Commission shall be initially provided with and assisted by ten (10) Joint Observer Teams, which number may be reduced by agreement of the senior members of both sides on the Military Armistice Commission.

b. Each Joint Observer Team shall be composed of not less than four (4) nor more than six (6) officers of field grade, half of whom shall be appointed by the Commander-in-Chief, United Nations Command, and half of whom shall be appointed jointly by the Supreme Commander of the Korean People's Army and the Commander of the Chinese People's Volunteers. Additional personnel such as drivers, clerks, and interpreters shall be furnished by each side as required for the functioning of the Joint Observer Teams.

2. FUNCTIONS AND AUTHORITY

24. The general mission of the Military Armistice Commission shall be to supervise the implementation of this Armistice Agreement and to settle through negotiations any violations of this Armistice Agreement.

25. The Military Armistice Commission shall:

a. Locate its headquarters in the vicinity of PANMUNJOM (37°57′29″N, 126°40′00″E). The Military Armistice Commission may re-locate its headquarters at another point within the Demilitarized Zone by agreement of the senior members of both sides on the Commission.

b. Operate as a joint organization without a chairman.

c. Adopt such rules of procedure as it may, from time to time, deem necessary.

d. Supervise the carrying out of the provisions of this Armistice Agreement pertaining to the Demilitarized Zone and to the Han River Estuary.

e. Direct the operations of the Joint Observer Teams.

f. Settle through negotiations any violations of this Armistice Agreement.

g. Transmit immediately to the Commanders of the opposing sides all reports of investigations of violations of this Armistice Agreement and all other reports and records of proceedings received from the Neutral Nations Supervisory Commission.

h. Give general supervision and direction to the activities of the Committee for Repatriation of Prisoners of War and the Committee for Assisting the Return of Displaced Civilians, hereinafter established.

i. Act as an intermediary in transmitting communications between the Commanders of the opposing sides; provided, however, that the foregoing shall not be construed to preclude the Commanders of both sides from communicating with each other by any other means which they may desire to employ.

j. Provide credentials and distinctive insignia for its staff and its Joint Observer Teams, and a distinctive marking for all vehicles, aircraft, and vessels, used in the performance of its mission.

26. The mission of the Joint Observer Teams shall be to assist the Military Armistice Commission in supervising the carrying out of the provisions of this Armistice Agreement pertaining to the Demilitarized Zone and to the Han River Estuary.

27. The Military Armistice Commission, or the senior member of either side thereof, is authorized to dispatch Joint Observer Teams to investigate violations of this Armistice Agreement reported to have occurred in the Demilitarized Zone or in the Han River Estuary; provided, however, that not more than one half of the Joint Observer Teams which have not been dispatched by the Military Armistice Commission may be dispatched at any one time by the senior member of either side on the Commission.

28. The Military Armistice Commission, or the senior member of either side thereof, is authorized to request the Neutral Nations Supervisory Commission to conduct special observations and inspections at places outside the Demilitarized Zone where violations of this Armistice Agreement have been reported to have occurred.

29. When the Military Armistice Commission determines that a violation of this Armistice Agreement has occurred, it shall immediately report such violation to the Commanders of the opposing sides.

30. When the Military Armistice Commission determines that a violation of this Armistice Agreement has been corrected to its satisfaction, it shall so report to the Commanders of the opposing sides.

3. GENERAL

31. The Military Armistice Commission shall meet daily. Recesses of not to exceed seven (7) days may be agreed upon by the senior members of both sides; provided, that such recesses may be terminated on twenty-four (24) hour notice by the senior member of either side.

32. Copies of the record of the proceedings of all meetings of the Military Armistice Commission shall be forwarded to the Commanders of the opposing sides as soon as possible after each meeting.

33. The Joint Observer Teams shall make periodic reports to the Military Armistice Commission as required by the Commission and, in addition, shall make such special reports as may be deemed necessary by them, or as may be required by the Commission.

34. The Military Armistice Commission shall maintain duplicate files of the reports and records of proceedings required by this Armistice Agreement. The Commission is authorized to maintain duplicate files of such other reports, records, etc., as may be necessary in the conduct of its business. Upon eventual dissolution of the Commission, one set of the above files shall be turned over to each side.

35. The Military Armistice Commission may make recommendations to the Commanders of the opposing sides with respect to amendments or additions to this Armistice Agreement. Such recommended changes should generally be those designed to insure a more effective armistice.

C. *Neutral Nations Supervisory Commission*

1. COMPOSITION

36. A Neutral Nations Supervisory Commission is hereby established.

37. The Neutral Nations Supervisory Commission shall be composed of four

(4) senior officers, two (2) of whom shall be appointed by neutral nations nominated by the Commander-in-Chief, United Nations Command, namely, SWEDEN and SWITZERLAND, and two (2) of whom shall be appointed by neutral nations nominated jointly by the Supreme Commander of the Korean People's Army and the Commander of the Chinese People's Volunteers, namely, POLAND and CZECHOSLOVAKIA. The term "neutral nations" as herein used is defined as those nations whose combatant forces have not participated in the hostilities in Korea. Members appointed to the Commission may be from the armed forces of the appointing nations. Each member shall designate an alternate member to attend those meetings which for any reason the principal member is unable to attend. Such alternate members shall be of the same nationality as their principals. The Neutral Nations Supervisory Commission may take action whenever the number of members present from the neutral nations nominated by one side is equal to the number of members present from the neutral nations nominated by the other side.

38. Members of the Neutral Nations Supervisory Commission shall be permitted to use staff assistants furnished by the neutral nations as required. These staff assistants may be appointed as alternate members of the Commission.

39. The neutral nations shall be requested to furnish the Neutral Nations Supervisory Commission with the necessary administrative personnel to establish a Secretariat charged with assisting the Commission by performing necessary record-keeping, secretarial, interpreting, and such other functions as the Commission may assign to it.

40. a. The Neutral Nations Supervisory Commission shall be initially provided with, and assisted by, twenty (20) Neutral Nations Inspection Teams, which number may be reduced by agreement of the senior members of both sides on the Military Armistice Commission. The Neutral Nations Inspection Teams shall be responsible to, shall report to, and shall be subject to the direction of, the Neutral Nations Supervisory Commission only.

b. Each Neutral Nations Inspection Team shall be composed of not less than four (4) officers, preferably of field grade, half of whom shall be from the neutral nations nominated by the Commander-in-Chief, United Nations Command, and half of whom shall be from the neutral nations nominated jointly by the Supreme Commander of the Korean People's Army and the Commander of the Chinese People's Volunteers. Members appointed to the Neutral Nations Inspection Teams may be from the armed forces of the appointing nations. In order to facilitate the functioning of the Teams, sub-teams composed of not less than two (2) members, one of whom shall be from a neutral nation nominated by the Commander-in-Chief, United Nations Command, and one of whom shall be from a neutral nation nominated jointly by the Supreme Commander of the Korean People's Army and the Commander of the Chinese People's Volunteers, may be formed as circumstances require. Additional personnel such as drivers, clerks, interpreters, and communications personnel, and such equipment as may be required by the Teams to perform their missions, shall be furnished by the Commander of each side, as required, in the Demilitarized Zone and in the territory under his military control. The Neutral Nations Supervisory Commission may provide itself and the Neutral Nations Inspection Teams with such of the above personnel and equipment of its own as it may desire; provided, however, that such personnel shall be personnel of the same neutral nations of which the Neutral Nations Supervisory Commission is composed.

2. Functions and Authority

41. The mission of the Neutral Nations Supervisory Commission shall be to carry out the functions of supervision, observation, inspection, and investigation, as stipulated in Sub-paragraphs 13c and 13d and Paragraph 28 hereof, and to report the results of such supervision, observation, inspection, and investigation to the Military Armistice Commission.

42. The Neutral Nations Supervisory Commission shall:

a. Locate its headquarters in proximity to the headquarters of the Military Armistice Commission.

b. Adopt such rules of procedure as it may, from time to time, deem necessary.

c. Conduct, through its members and its Neutral Nations Inspection Teams, the supervision and inspection provided for in Sub-paragraphs 13c and 13d of this Armistice Agreement at the ports of entry enumerated in Paragraph 43 hereof, and the special observations and inspections provided for in Paragraph 28 hereof at those places where violations of this Armistice Agreement have been reported to have occurred. The inspection of combat aircraft, armored vehicles, weapons, and ammunition by the Neutral Nations Inspection Teams shall be such as to enable them to properly insure that reinforcing combat aircraft, armored vehicles, weapons, and ammunition are not being introduced into Korea; but this shall not be construed as authorizing inspections or examinations of any secret designs or characteristics of any combat aircraft, armored vehicle, weapon, or ammunition.

d. Direct and supervise the operations of the Neutral Nations Inspection Teams.

e. Station five (5) Neutral Nations Inspection Teams at the ports of entry enumerated in Paragraph 43 hereof located in the territory under the military control of the Commander-in-Chief, United Nations Command; and five (5) Neutral Nations Inspection Teams at the ports of entry enumerated in Paragraph 43 hereof located in the territory under the military control of the Supreme Commander of the Korean People's Army and the Commander of the Chinese People's Volunteers; and establish initially ten (10) mobile Neutral Nations Inspection Teams in reserve, stationed in the general vicinity of the headquarters of the Neutral Nations Supervisory Commission, which number may be reduced by agreement of the senior members of both sides on the Military Armistice Commission. Not more than half of the mobile Neutral Nations Inspection Teams shall be dispatched at any one time in accordance with requests of the senior member of either side on the Military Armistice Commission.

f. Subject to the provisions of the preceding Sub-paragraph, conduct without delay investigations of reported violations of this Armistice Agreement, including such investigations of reported violations of this Armistice Agreement as may be requested by the Military Armistice Commission or by the senior member of either side on the Commission.

g. Provide credentials and distinctive insignia for its staff and its Neutral Nations Inspection Teams, and a distinctive marking for all vehicles, aircraft, and vessels, used in the performance of its mission.

43. Neutral Nations Inspection Teams shall be stationed at the following ports of entry:

Territory under the military control of the United Nations Command		Territory under the military control of the Korean People's Army and the Chinese People's Volunteers	
INCHON	(37°28'N, 126°38'E)	SINUIJU	(40°06'N, 124°24'E)
TAEGU	(35°52'N, 128°36'E)	CHONGJIN	(41°46'N, 129°49'E)
PUSAN	(35°06'N, 129°02'E)	HUNGNAM	(39°50'N, 127°37'E)
KANGNUNG	(37°45'N, 128°54'E)	MANPO	(41°09'N, 126°18'E)
KUNSAN	(35°59'N, 126°43'E)	SINANJU	(39°36'N, 125°36'E)

These Neutral Nations Inspection Teams shall be accorded full convenience of movement within the areas and over the routes of communication set forth on the attached map (Map 5).

3. GENERAL

44. The Neutral Nations Supervisory Commission shall meet daily. Recesses of not to exceed seven (7) days may be agreed upon by the members of the Neutral Nations Supervisory Commission; provided, that such recesses may be terminated on twenty-four (24) hour notice by any member.

45. Copies of the record of the proceedings of all meetings of the Neutral Nations Supervisory Commission shall be forwarded to the Military Armistice Commission as soon as possible after each meeting. Records shall be kept in English, Korean, and Chinese.

46. The Neutral Nations Inspection Teams shall make periodic reports concerning the results of their supervision, observations, inspections, and investigations to the Neutral Nations Supervisory Commission as required by the Commission and, in addition, shall make such special reports as may be deemed necessary by them, or as may be required by the Commission. Reports shall be transmitted by a Team as a whole, but may also be submitted by one or more individual members thereof; provided, that the reports submitted by one or more individual members thereof shall be considered as informational only.

47. Copies of the reports made by the Neutral Nations Inspection Teams shall be forwarded to the Military Armistice Commission by the Neutral Nations Supervisory Commission without delay and in the language in which received. They shall not be delayed by the process of translation or evaluation. The Neutral Nations Supervisory Commission shall evaluate such reports at the earliest practicable time and shall forward their findings to the Military Armistice Commission as a matter of priority. The Military Armistice Commission shall not take final action with regard to any such report until the evaluation thereof has been received from the Neutral Nations Supervisory Commission. Members of the Neutral Nations Supervisory Commission and of its Teams shall be subject to appearance before the Military Armistice Commission, at the request of the senior member of either side on the Military Armistice Commission, for clarification of any report submitted.

48. The Neutral Nations Supervisory Commission shall maintain duplicate files of the reports and records of proceedings required by this Armistice Agreement. The Commission is authorized to maintain duplicate files of such other reports, records, etc., as may be necessary in the conduct of its business. Upon eventual dissolution of the Commission, one set of the above files shall be turned over to each side.

49. The Neutral Nations Supervisory Commission may make recommenda-

tions to the Military Armistice Commission with respect to amendments or additions to this Armistice Agreement. Such recommended changes should generally be those designed to insure a more effective armistice.

50. The Neutral Nations Supervisory Commission, or any member thereof, shall be authorized to communicate with any member of the Military Armistice Commission.

Article III. Arrangements Relating to Prisoners of War

51. The release and repatriation of all prisoners of war held in the custody of each side at the time this Armistice Agreement becomes effective shall be effected in conformity with the following provisions agreed upon by both sides prior to the signing of this Armistice Agreement.

a. Within sixty (60) days after this Armistice Agreement becomes effective, each side shall, without offering any hindrance, directly repatriate and hand over in groups all those prisoners of war in its custody who insist on repatriation to the side to which they belonged at the time of capture. Repatriation shall be accomplished in accordance with the related provisions of this Article. In order to expedite the repatriation process of such personnel, each side shall, prior to the signing of the Armistice Agreement, exchange the total numbers, by nationalities, of personnel to be directly repatriated. Each group of prisoners of war delivered to the other side shall be accompanied by rosters, prepared by nationality, to include name, rank (if any) and internment or military serial number.

b. Each side shall release all those remaining prisoners of war, who are not directly repatriated, from its military control and from its custody and hand them over to the Neutral Nations Repatriation Commission for disposition in accordance with the provisions in the Annex hereto: "Terms of Reference for Neutral Nations Repatriation Commission."

c. So that there may be no misunderstanding owing to the equal use of three languages, the act of delivery of a prisoner of war by one side to the other side shall, for the purposes of this Armistice Agreement, be called "repatriation" in English, " 송환 " (SONG HWAN) in Korean, and " 遣返 " (CH'IEN FAN) in Chinese, notwithstanding the nationality or place of residence of such prisoner of war.

52. Each side insures that it will not employ in acts of war in the Korean conflict any prisoner of war released and repatriated incident to the coming into effect of this Armistice Agreement.

53. All the sick and injured prisoners of war who insist upon repatriation shall be repatriated with priority. Insofar as possible, there shall be captured medical personnel repatriated concurrently with the sick and injured prisoners of war, so as to provide medical care and attendance en route.

54. The repatriation of all of the prisoners of war required by Sub-paragraph 51a hereof shall be completed within a time limit of sixty (60) days after this Armistice Agreement becomes effective. Within this time limit each side undertakes to complete the repatriation of the above-mentioned prisoners of war in its custody at the earliest practicable time.

55. Panmunjom is designated as the place where prisoners of war will be delivered and received by both sides. Additional place(s) of delivery and reception of prisoners of war in the Demilitarized Zone may be designated, if necessary, by the Committee for Repatriation of Prisoners of War.

56. a. A Committee for Repatriation of Prisoners of War is hereby established. It shall be composed of six (6) officers of field grade, three (3) of

whom shall be appointed by the Commander-in-Chief, United Nations Command, and three (3) of whom shall be appointed jointly by the Supreme Commander of the Korean People's Army and the Commander of the Chinese People's Volunteers. This Committee shall, under the general supervision and direction of the Military Armistice Commission, be responsible for coordinating the specific plans of both sides for the repatriation of prisoners of war and for supervising the execution by both side of all of the provisions of this Armistice Agreement relating to the repatriation of prisoners of war. It shall be the duty of this Committee to coordinate the timing of the arrival of prisoners of war at the place(s) of delivery and reception of prisoners of war from the prisoner of war camps of both sides; to make, when necessary, such special arrangements as may be required with regard to the transportation and welfare of sick and injured prisoners of war; to coordinate the work of the joint Red Cross teams, established in Paragraph 57 hereof in assisting in the repatriation of prisoners of war; to supervise the implementation of the arrangements for the actual repatriation of prisoners of war stipulated in Paragraphs 53 and 54 hereof; to select, when necessary, additional place(s) of delivery and reception of prisoners of war; to arrange for security at the place(s) of delivery and reception of prisoners of war; and to carry out such other related functions as are required for the repatriation of prisoners of war.

b. When unable to reach agreement on any matter relating to its responsibilities, the Committee for Repatriation of Prisoners of War shall immediately refer such matter to the Military Armistice Commission for decision. The Committee for Repatriation of Prisoners of War shall maintain its headquarters in proximity to the headquarters of the Military Armistice Commission.

c. The Committee for Repatriation of Prisoners of War shall be dissolved by the Military Armistice Commission upon completion of the program of repatriation of prisoners of war.

57. a. Immediately after this Armistice Agreement becomes effective, joint Red Cross teams composed of representatives of the national Red Cross Societies of the countries contributing forces to the United Nations Command on the one hand, and representatives of the Red Cross Society of the Democratic People's Republic of Korea and representatives of the Red Cross Society of the People's Republic of China on the other hand, shall be established. The joint Red Cross teams shall assist in the execution by both sides of those provisions of this Armistice Agreement relating to the repatriation of all the prisoners of war specified in Sub-paragraph 51a hereof, who insist upon repatriation, by the performance of such humanitarian services as are necessary and desirable for the welfare of the prisoners of war. To accomplish this task, the joint Red Cross teams shall provide assistance in the delivering and receiving of prisoners of war by both sides at the place(s) of delivery and reception of prisoners of war, and shall visit the prisoner of war camps of both sides to comfort the prisoners of war and to bring in and distribute gift articles for the comfort and welfare of the prisoners of war. The joint Red Cross teams may provide services to prisoners of war while en route from prisoner of war camps to the place(s) of delivery and reception of prisoners of war.

b. The joint Red Cross teams shall be organized as set forth below:

(1) One team shall be composed of twenty (20) members, namely, ten (10) representatives from the national Red Cross Societies of each side, to assist in the delivering and receiving of prisoners of war by both sides at the place(s) of delivery and reception of prisoners of war. The chairmanship of this team shall alternate daily between representatives from the Red Cross

Societies of the two sides. The work and services of this team shall be co-ordinated by the Committee for Repatriation of Prisoners of War.

(2) One team shall be composed of sixty (60) members, namely, thirty (30) representatives from the national Red Cross Societies of each side, to visit the prisoner of war camps under the administration of the Korean People's Army and the Chinese People's Volunteers. This team may provide services to prisoners of war while en route from the prisoner of war camps to the place(s) of delivery and reception of prisoners of war. A representative of the Red Cross Society of the Democratic People's Republic of Korea or of the Red Cross Society of the People's Republic of China shall serve as chairman of this team.

(3) One team shall be composed of sixty (60) members, namely, thirty (30) representatives from the national Red Cross Societies of each side, to visit the prisoner of war camps under the administration of the United Nations Command. This team may provide services to prisoners of war while en route from the prisoner of war camps to the place(s) of delivery and reception of prisoners of war. A representative of a Red Cross Society of a nation contributing forces to the United Nations Command shall serve as chairman of this team.

(4) In order to facilitate the functioning of each joint Red Cross team, sub-teams composed of not less than two (2) members from the team, with an equal number of representatives from each side, may be formed as circumstances require.

(5) Additional personnel such as drivers, clerks, and interpreters, and such equipment as may be required by the joint Red Cross teams to perform their missions, shall be furnished by the Commander of each side to the team operating in the territory under his military control.

(6) Whenever jointly agreed upon by the representatives of both sides on any joint Red Cross team, the size of such team may be increased or decreased, subject to the confirmation by the Committee for Repatriation of Prisoners of War.

c. The Commander of each side shall cooperate fully with the joint Red Cross teams in the performance of their functions, and undertakes to insure the security of the personnel of the joint Red Cross team in the area under his military control. The Commander of each side shall provide such logistic, administrative, and communications facilities as may be required by the team operating in the territory under his military control.

d. The joint Red Cross teams shall be dissolved upon completion of the program of repatriation of all the prisoners of war specified in Sub-paragraph 51a hereof, who insist upon repatriation.

58. a. The Commander of each side shall furnish to the Commander of the other side as soon as practicable, but not later than ten (10) days after this Armistice Agreement becomes effective, the following information concerning prisoners of war:

(1) Complete data pertaining to the prisoners of war who escaped since the effective date of the data last exchanged.

(2) Insofar as practicable, information regarding name, nationality, rank, and other identification data, date and cause of death, and place of burial, of those prisoners of war who died while in his custody.

b. If any prisoners of war escape or die after the effective date of the supplementary information specified above, the detaining side shall furnish to the other side, through the Committee for Repatriation of Prisoners of War, the data pertaining thereto in accordance with the provisions of Sub-paragraph 58a hereof. Such data shall be furnished at ten-day intervals until the completion of the program of delivery and reception of prisoners of war.

c. Any escaped prisoner of war who returns to the custody of the detaining side after the completion of the program of delivery and reception of prisoners of war shall be delivered to the Military Armistice Commission for disposition.

59. a. All civilians who, at the time this Armistice Agreement becomes effective, are in territory under the military control of the Commander-in-Chief, United Nations Command, and who, on 24 June 1950, resided north of the Military Demarcation Line established in this Armistice Agreement shall, if they desire to return home, be permitted and assisted by the Commander-in-Chief, United Nations Command, to return to the area north of the Military Demarcation Line; and all civilians who, at the time this Armistice Agreement becomes effective, are in territory under the military control of the Supreme Commander of the Korean People's Army and the Commander of the Chinese People's Volunteers, and who, on 24 June 1950, resided south of the Military Demarcation Line established in this Armistice Agreement shall, if they desire to return home, be permitted and assisted by the Supreme Commander of the Korean People's Army and the Commander of the Chinese People's Volunteers to return to the area south of the Military Demarcation Line. The Commander of each side shall be responsible for publicizing widely throughout territory under his military control the contents of the provisions of this Sub-paragraph, and for calling upon the appropriate civil authorities to give necessary guidance and assistance to all such civilians who desire to return home.

b. All civilians of foreign nationality who, at the time this Armistice Agreement becomes effective, are in territory under the military control of the Supreme Commander of the Korean People's Army and the Commander of the Chinese People's Volunteers shall, if they desire to proceed to territory under the military control of the Commander-in-Chief, United Nations Command, be permitted and assisted to do so; all civilians of foreign nationality who, at the time this Armistice Agreement becomes effective, are in territory under the military control of the Commander-in-Chief, United Nations Command, shall, if they desire to proceed to territory under the military control of the Supreme Commander of the Korean People's Army and the Commander of the Chinese People's Volunteers, be permitted and assisted to do so. The Commander of each side shall be responsible for publicizing widely throughout the territory under his military control the contents of the provisions of this Sub-paragraph, and for calling upon the appropriate civil authorities to give necessary guidance and assistance to all such civilians of foreign nationality who desire to proceed to territory under the military control of the Commander of the other side.

c. Measures to assist in the return of civilians provided for in Sub-paragraph 59a hereof and the movement of civilians provided for in Sub-paragraph 59b hereof shall be commenced by both sides as soon as possible after this Armistice Agreement becomes effective.

d. (1) A Committee for Assisting the Return of Displaced Civilians is hereby established. It shall be composed of four (4) officers of field grade, two (2) of whom shall be appointed by the Commander-in-Chief, United Nations Command, and two (2) of whom shall be appointed jointly by the Supreme Commander of the Korean People's Army and the Commander of the Chinese People's Volunteers. This Committee shall, under the general supervision and direction of the Military Armistice Commission, be responsible for coordinating the specific plans of both sides for assistance to the return of the above-mentioned civilians, and for supervising the execution by both sides of all of the provisions of this Armistice Agreement relating to the return of the above-mentioned civilians. It shall be the duty of this Committee to make necessary arrangements, including those of transportation, for expediting and coordinating the movement of the above-mentioned civilians; to select the crossing point(s) through which the above-mentioned civilians will cross the Military Demarcation Line; to arrange for security at the crossing point(s); and to carry out such other functions as are required to accomplish the return of the above-mentioned civilians.

(2) When unable to reach agreement on any matter relating to its responsibilities, the Committee for Assisting the Return of Displaced Civilians shall immediately refer such matter to the Military Armistice Commission for decision. The Committee for Assisting the Return of Displaced Civilians shall maintain its headquarters in proximity to the headquarters of the Military Armistice Commission.

(3) The Committee for Assisting the Return of Displaced Civilians shall be dissolved by the Military Armistice Commission upon fulfillment of its mission.

ARTICLE IV. RECOMMENDATION TO THE GOVERNMENTS CONCERNED ON BOTH SIDES

60. In order to insure the peaceful settlement of the Korean question, the military Commanders of both sides hereby recommend to the governments of the countries concerned on both sides that, within three (3) months after the Armistice Agreement is signed and becomes effective, a political conference of a higher level of both sides be held by representatives appointed respectively to settle through negotiation the questions of the withdrawal of all foreign forces from Korea, the peaceful settlement of the Korean question, etc.

ARTICLE V. MISCELLANEOUS

61. Amendments and additions to this Armistice Agreement must be mutually agreed to by the Commanders of the opposing sides.

62. The Articles and Paragraphs of this Armistice Agreement shall remain in effect until expressly superseded either by mutually acceptable amendments and additions or by provision in an appropriate agreement for a peaceful settlement at a political level between both sides.

63. All of the provisions of this Armistice Agreement, other than Paragraph 12, shall become effective at 2200 hours on 27 July 1953.

Done at Panmunjon, Korea, at 1000 hours on the 27th day of July, 1953, in English, Korean, and Chinese, all texts being equally authentic.

KIM IL SUNG
Marshal, Democratic
  People's Republic
  of Korea
Supreme Commander,
Korean People's Army

PENG TEH-HUAI
Commander
Chinese People's
  Volunteers

MARK W. CLARK
General, United States
  Army
Commander-in-Chief,
United Nations
  Command

PRESENT

handwritten signature   W . K . Harrison

NAM IL
General, Korean People's Army
Senior Delegate,
Delegation of the Korean People's
  Army and the Chinese People's
  Volunteers

WILLIAM K. HARRISON, JR.
Lieutenant General, United States
  Army
Senior Delegate,
United Nations Command
  Delegation

ANNEX
TERMS OF REFERENCE
FOR
NEUTRAL NATIONS REPATRIATION COMMISSION
(See Sub-paragraph 51b)

I. *General*

1. In order to ensure that all prisoners of war have the opportunity to exercise their right to be repatriated following an armistice, Sweden, Switzerland, Poland, Czechoslovakia and India shall each be requested by both sides to appoint a member to a Neutral Nations Repatriation Commission which shall be established to take custody in Korea of those prisoners of war who, while in the custody of the detaining powers, have not exercised their right to be repatriated. The Neutral Nations Repatriation Commission shall establish its headquarters within the Demilitarized Zone in the vicinity of Panmunjom, and shall station subordinate bodies of the same composition as the Neutral Nations Repatriation Commission at those locations at which the Repatriation Commission assumes custody of prisoners of war. Representatives of both sides shall be permitted to observe the operations of the Repatriation Commission and its subordinate bodies to include explanations and interviews.

2. Sufficient armed forces and any other operating personnel required to assist the Neutral Nations Repatriation Commission in carrying out its functions and responsibilities shall be provided exclusively by India, whose representative shall be the umpire in accordance with the provisions of Article 132 of the Geneva Convention, and shall also be chairman and executive agent of the Neutral Nations Repatriation Commission. Representatives from each of the other four powers shall be allowed staff assistants in equal number not to exceed fifty (50) each. When any of the representatives of the neutral nations is absent for some reason, that representative shall designate an alternate representative of his own nationality to exercise his functions and authority. The arms of all personnel provided for in this Paragraph shall be limited to military police type small arms.

3. No force or threat of force shall be used against the prisoners of war specified in Paragraph 1 above to prevent or effect their repatriation, and no violence to their persons or affront to their dignity or self-respect shall be permitted in any manner whatsoever (but see Paragraph 7 below). This duty is enjoined on and entrusted to the Neutral Nations Repatriation Commission. This Commission shall ensure that prisoners of war shall at all

times be treated humanely in accordance with the specific provisions of the Geneva Convention, and with the general spirit of that Convention.

II. *Custody of Prisoners of War*

4. All prisoners of war who have not exercised their right of repatriation following the effective date of the Armistice Agreement shall be released from the military control and from the custody of the detaining side as soon as practicable, and, in all cases, within sixty (60) days subsequent to the effective date of the Armistice Agreement to the Neutral Nations Repatriation Commission at locations in Korea to be designated by the detaining side.

5. At the time the Neutral Nations Repatriation Commission assumes control of the prisoner of war installations, the military forces of the detaining side shall be withdrawn therefrom, so that the locations specified in the preceding Paragraph shall be taken over completely by the armed forces of India.

6. Notwithstanding the provisions of Paragraph 5 above, the detaining side shall have the responsibility for maintaining and ensuring security and order in the areas around the locations where the prisoners of war are in custody and for preventing and restraining any armed forces (including irregular armed forces) in the area under its control from any acts of disturbance and intrusion against the locations where the prisoners of war are in custody.

7. Notwithstanding the provisions of Paragraph 3 above, nothing in this agreement shall be construed as derogating from the authority of the Neutral Nations Repatriation Commission to exercise its legitimate functions and responsibilities for the control of the prisoners of war under its temporary jurisdiction.

III. *Explanation*

8. The Neutral Nations Repatriation Commission, after having received and taken into custody all those prisoners of war who have not exercised their right to be repatriated, shall immediately make arrangements so that within ninety (90) days after the Neutral Nations Repatriation Commission takes over the custody, the nations to which the prisoners of war belong shall have freedom and facilities to send representatives to the locations where such prisoners of war are in custody to explain to all the prisoners of war depending upon these nations their rights and to inform them of any matters relating to their return to their homelands, particularly of their full freedom to return home to lead a peaceful life, under the following provisions:

a. The number of such explaining representatives shall not exceed seven (7) per thousand prisoners of war held in custody by the Neutral Nations Repatriation Commission; and the minimum authorized shall not be less than a total of five (5);

b. The hours during which the explaining representatives shall have access to the prisoners shall be as determined by the Neutral Nations Repatriation Commission, and generally in accord with Article 53 of the Geneva Convention Relative to the Treatment of Prisoners of War;

c. All explanations and interviews shall be conducted in the presence of a representative of each member nation of the Neutral Nations Repatriation Commission and a representative from the detaining side;

d. Additional provisions governing the explanation work shall be prescribed by the Neutral Nations Repatriation Commission, and will be designed to employ the principles enumerated in Paragraph 3 above and in this Paragraph;

e. The explaining representatives, while engaging in their work, shall be allowed to bring with them necessary facilities and personnel for wireless communications. The number of communications personnel shall be limited to one team per location at which explaining representatives are in residence, except in the event all prisoners of war are concentrated in one location, in which case, two (2) teams shall be permitted. Each team shall consist of not more than six (6) communications personnel.

9. Prisoners of war in its custody shall have freedom and facilities to make representations and communications to the Neutral Nations Repatriation Commission and to representatives and subordinate bodies of the Neutral Nations Repatriation Commission and to inform them of their desires on any matter concerning the prisoners of war themselves, in accordance with arrangements made for the purpose by the Neutral Nations Repatriation Commission.

IV. *Disposition of Prisoners of War*

10. Any prisoner of war who, while in the custody of the Neutral Nations Repatriation Commission, decides to exercise the right of repatriation, shall make an application requesting repatriation to a body consisting of a representative of each member nation of the Neutral Nations Repatriation Commission. Once such an application is made, it shall be considered immediately by the Neutral Nations Repatriation Commission or one of its subordinate bodies so as to determine immediately by majority vote the validity of such application. Once such an application is made to and validated by the Commission or one of its subordinate bodies, the prisoner of war concerned shall immediately be transferred to and accommodated in the tents set up for those who are ready to be repatriated. Thereafter, he shall, while still in the custody of the Neutral Nations Repatriation Commission, be delivered forthwith to the prisoner of war exchange point at Panmunjom for repatriation under the procedure prescribed in the Armistice Agreement.

11. At the expiration of ninety (90) days after the transfer of custody of the prisoners of war to the Neutral Nations Repatriation Commission, access of representatives to captured personnel as provided for in Paragraph 8 above, shall terminate, and the question of disposition of the prisoners of war who have not exercised their right to be repatriated shall be submitted to the Political Conference recommended to be convened in Paragraph 60, Draft Armistice Agreement, which shall endeavor to settle this question within thirty (30) days, during which period the Neutral Nations Repatriation Commission shall continue to retain custody of those prisoners of war. The Neutral Nations Repatriation Commission shall declare the relief from the prisoner of war status to civilian status of any prisoners of war who have not exercised their right to be repatriated and for whom no other disposition has been agreed to by the Political Conference within one hundred and twenty (120) days after the Neutral Nations Repatriation Commission has assumed their custody. Thereafter, according to the application of each individual, those who choose to go to neutral nations shall be assisted by the Neutral Nations Repatriation Commission and the Red Cross Society of India. This operation shall be completed within thirty (30) days, and upon its completion, the Neutral Nations Repatriation Commission shall immediately cease its functions and declare its dissolution. After the dissolution of the Neutral Nations Repatriation Commission, whenever and wherever any of those above-mentioned civilians who have been relieved from the prisoner of war status desire to return to their fatherlands,

the authorities of the localities where they are shall be responsible for assisting them in returning to their fatherlands.

V. *Red Cross Visitation*

12. Essential Red Cross service for prisoners of war in custody of the Neutral Nations Repatriation Commission shall be provided by India in accordance with regulations issued by the Neutral Nations Repatriation Commission.

VI. *Press Coverage*

13. The Neutral Nations Repatriation Commission shall insure freedom of the press and other news media in observing the entire operation as enumerated herein, in accordance with procedures to be established by the Neutral Nations Repatriation Commission.

VII. *Logistical Support for Prisoners of War*

14. Each side shall provide logistical support for the prisoners of war in the area under its military control, delivering required support to the Neutral Nations Repatriation Commission at an agreed delivery point in the vicinity of each prisoner of war installation.

15. The cost of repatriating prisoners of war to the exchange point at Panmunjom shall be borne by the detaining side and the cost from the exchange point by the side on which said prisoners depend, in accordance with Article 118 of the Geneva Convention.

16. The Red Cross Society of India shall be responsible for providing such general service personnel in the prisoner of war installations as required by the Neutral Nations Repatriation Commission.

17. The Neutral Nations Repatriation Commission shall provide medical support for the prisoners of war as may be practicable. The detaining side shall provide medical support as practicable upon the request of the Neutral Nations Repatriation Commission and specifically for those cases requiring extensive treatment or hospitalization. The Neutral Nations Repatriation Commission shall maintain custody of prisoners of war during such hospitalization. The detaining side shall facilitate such custody. Upon completion of treatment, prisoners of war shall be returned to a prisoner of war installation as specified in Paragraph 4 above.

18. The Neutral Nations Repatriation Commission is entitled to obtain from both sides such legitimate assistance as it may require in carrying out its duties and tasks, but both sides shall not under any name and in any form interfere or exert influence.

VIII. *Logistical Support for the Neutral Nations Repatriation Commission*

19. Each side shall be responsible for providing logistical support for the personnel of the Neutral Nations Repatriation Commission stationed in the area under its military control, and both sides shall contribute on an equal basis to such support within the Demilitarized Zone. The precise arrangements shall be subject to determination between the Neutral Nations Repatriation Commission and the detaining side in each case.

20. Each of the detaining sides shall be responsible for protecting the explaining representatives from the other side while in transit over lines of communication within its area, as set forth in Paragraph 23 for the Neutral Nations Repatriation Commission, to a place of residence and while in residence in the

vicinity of but not within each of the locations where the prisoners of war are in custody. The Neutral Nations Repatriation Commission shall be responsible for the security of such representatives within the actual limits of the locations where the prisoners of war are in custody.

21. Each of the detaining sides shall provide transportation, housing, communication, and other agreed logistical support to the explaining representatives of the other side while they are in the area under its military control. Such services shall be provided on a reimbursable basis.

IX. *Publication*

22. After the Armistice Agreement becomes effective, the terms of this agreement shall be made known to all prisoners of war who, while in the custody of the detaining side, have not exercised their right to be repatriated.

X. *Movement*

23. The movement of the personnel of the Neutral Nations Repatriation Commission and repatriated prisoners of war shall be over lines of communication as determined by the command(s) of the opposing side and the Neutral Nations Repatriation Commission. A map showing these lines of communication shall be furnished the command of the opposing side and the Neutral Nations Repatriation Commission. Movement of such personnel, except within locations as designated in Paragraph 4 above, shall be under the control of, and escorted by, personnel of the side in whose area the travel is being undertaken; however, such movement shall not be subject to any obstruction and coercion.

XI. *Procedural Matters*

24. The interpretation of this agreement shall rest with the Neutral Nations Repatriation Commission. The Neutral Nations Repatriation Commission, and/or any subordinate bodies to which functions are delegated or assigned by the Neutral Nations Repatriation Commission, shall operate on the basis of majority vote.

25. The Neutral Nations Repatriation Commission shall submit a weekly report to the opposing Commanders on the status of prisoners of war in its custody, indicating the numbers repatriated and remaining at the end of each week.

26. When this agreement has been acceded to by both sides and by the five powers named herein, it shall become effective upon the date the Armistice becomes effective.

Done at Panmunjum, Korea, at 1400 hours on the 8th day of June 1953, in English, Korean, and Chinese, all texts being equally authentic.

NAM IL	WILLIAM K. HARRISON, JR.
General, Korean People's Army	Lieutenant General, United States
Senior Delegate,	Army
Delegation of the Korean People's	Senior Delegate,
Army and the Chinese People's	United Nations Command
Volunteers	Delegation

TEMPORARY AGREEMENT SUPPLEMENTARY TO THE
ARMISTICE AGREEMENT

In order to meet the requirements of the disposition of the prisoners of war not for direct repatriation in accordance with the provisions of the Terms of Reference for Neutral Nations Repatriation Commission, the Commander-in-Chief, United Nations Command, on the one hand, and the Supreme Commander of the Korean People's Army and the Commander of the Chinese People's Volunteers, on the other hand, in pursuance of the provisions in Paragraph 61, Article V of the Agreement concerning a military armistice in Korea, agree to conclude the following Temporary Agreement supplementary to the Armistice Agreement:

1. Under the provisions of Paragraphs 4 and 5, Article II of the Terms of Reference for Neutral Nations Repatriation Commission, the United Nations Command has the right to designate the area between the Military Demarcation Line and the eastern and southern boundaries of the Demilitarized Zone between the Imjin River on the south and the road leading south from Okum-ni on the northeast (the main road leading southeast from Panmunjom not included), as the area within which the United Nations Command will turn over the prisoners of war, who are not directly repatriated and whom the United Nations Command has the responsibility for keeping under its custody, to the Neutral Nations Repatriation Commission and the armed forces of India for custody. The United Nations Command shall, prior to the signing of the Armistice Agreement, inform the side of the Korean People's Army and the Chinese People's Volunteers of the approximate figures by nationality of such prisoners of war held in its custody.

2. If there are prisoners of war under their custody who request not to be directly repatriated, the Korean People's Army and the Chinese People's Volunteers have the right to designate the area in the vicinity of Panmunjom between the Military Demarcation Line and the western and northern boundaries of the Demilitarized Zone, as the area within which such prisoners of war will be turned over to the Neutral Nations Repatriation Commission and the armed forces of India for custody. After knowing that there are prisoners of war under their custody who request not to be directly repatriated, the Korean People's Army and the Chinese People's Volunteers shall inform the United Nations Command side of the approximate figures by nationality of such prisoners of war.

3. In accordance with Paragraphs 8, 9 and 10, Article I of the Armistice Agreement, the following paragraphs are hereby provided:

a. After the cease-fire comes into effect, unarmed personnel of each side shall be specifically authorized by the Military Armistice Commission to enter the above-mentioned area designated by their own side to perform necessary construction operations. None of such personnel shall remain in the above-mentioned areas upon the completion of the construction operations.

b. A definite number of prisoners of war as decided upon by both sides, who are in the respective custody of both sides and who are not directly repatriated, shall be specifically authorized by the Military Armistice Commission to be escorted respectively by a certain number of armed forces of the detaining sides to the above-mentioned areas of custody designated respectively by both sides to be turned over to the Neutral Nations Repatriation Commission and the armed forces of India for custody. After the prisoners of war have been taken over, the armed forces of the detaining sides shall be withdrawn